THE
HUDSON RIVER
BASIN

Environmental Problems and Institutional Response

VOLUME 2

1979

ACADEMIC PRESS

A Subsidiary of Harcourt Brace Jovanovich, Publishers

New York   London   Toronto   Sydney   San Francisco

ACADEMIC PRESS, INC.
111 Fifth Avenue, New York, New York 10003

United Kingdom Edition published by
ACADEMIC PRESS, INC. (LONDON) LTD.
24/28 Oval Road, London NW1 7DX

Library of Congress Cataloging in Publication Data
Main entry under title:

The Hudson River Basin.

    Includes index.
    1. Regional planning––New York metropolitan area.
2. Regional planning––Hudson River Valley. 3. Environ–
mental policy––New York metropolitan area. 4. Environ–
mental policy––Hudson River Valley. I. Richardson,
Ralph W. II. Tauber, Gilbert.
HT394.N5H83   309.2'5'097473   78–19999
ISBN 0–12–588402–8 (v. 2)

PRINTED IN THE UNITED STATES OF AMERICA

79 80 81 82   9 8 7 6 5 4 3 2 1

THE
HUDSON RIVER
BASIN

Environmental Problems and Institutional Response

VOLUME 2

Edited by

RALPH W. RICHARDSON, Jr.

GILBERT TAUBER

Natural and Environmental Sciences Division
The Rockefeller Foundation
New York, New York

Contents

Foreword

The Hudson Basin displays a wide array of environmental problems that are sufficiently serious or complex to have become public issues. That so many of these problems have escalated to the level of issues is not so much an indication of the poor state of the environment itself as it is a reflection of the inadequacy of existing institutions.

Most of the environmental problems in the Hudson Basin today are the result, direct or indirect, of the tremendous population and economic growth in the 25 years following World War II. The physical development required to accommodate that growth was often poorly planned and placed tremendous stress on environmental resources. During the same 25-year period, there were also major movements in population and shifts in industrial location. These eroded the fiscal base of the region's older cities and placed a great strain on the governmental and social institutions of both the central cities and the developing suburban areas. In the 1970s there has been increasing recognition of the environmental problems generated in the two previous decades. But because the region's economy has also slackened in this decade, the money needed to repair existing environmental damage is not currently available. Therefore, present efforts must focus on preventing further damage.

Natural systems in the Hudson Basin have been heavily impacted by man, not only since World War II but also over several generations. When, however, one considers the region's huge concentrations of population and economic activity, its natural systems are still quite productive. Nevertheless, we have no grounds for complacency. Relatively little is known about the underlying dynamics, and therefore the carrying capacity of the basin's natural systems, including their ability to assimilate pollutants and to recover from other types of stress caused by human activity.

The Project's ten task groups presented numerous case studies of environmental controversies or "problem situations" in the Hudson Basin. Most of these problem situations illustrate one or more of the following:

- Multiple effects of siting large-scale energy-producing facilities
- The lack of land use control above the local level
- The lack of local capacity to control the effects of large-scale initiatives that induce development or otherwise influence land use
- Inadequate legislation leading to court battles in which diffuse environmental interests are pitted against highly focused economic interests
- The "taking issue," i.e., the lack of clarity and consensus on how far the public can assert an interest in private land before it becomes a "taking" which must be compensated
- The neglect of existing rail freight facilities while public investment encourages increased reliance on truck transportation
- The inadequacy of scientific and institutional capacity to allocate water resources among competing uses in the Hudson Basin
- The difficulty of controlling pressures that are accelerating the withdrawal of land from agricultural use
- The distorting effects of the property-tax system on land use
- The inadequacy of existing procedures for assessing the costs and benefits of environmental decisions

The environment management needs of the Hudson Basin are manifold. Based on the work of the Project's task groups, the following appear to need the most attention:

- The rehabilitation of the inner-city environment and the control of the urban sprawl
- The reduction of health hazards in the work and home environments
- The improvement of institutional capacity for regional water management
- The filling of the gaps in land use planning and regulation
- The moderation of solid-waste generation and the improvement of disposal techniques
- The protection of ecologically significant land and water resources
- The integrated planning of transportation modes and land use
- The moderation of energy demand and the augmentation of supply
- The improvement of the management of interstate air quality

- The optimization of public and private investment policies affecting the environment

States and many of their constituent units of local government have assigned most of their functions to single-purpose agencies and departments. The most fundamental weakness of the single-purpose unit is the limited scope of its mandate, mission, authority, expertise, and funding, which results in the inability to manage the consequence of its actions. The need to strengthen environmental management institutions has been identified by the Hudson Basin Project as the most important underlying problem in the study area. The measures needed to correct present deficiencies can be summed up as follows: Improve information management, Broaden assessment processes, Increase and strengthen arenas for conflict resolution, Improve the substance and explicitness of policy, Strengthen institutional capacity to formulate and execute policy.

The above steps, if pursued over time by all affected interests, would strengthen the public's perception and its will to act on the primary need to improve institutional capacity for environmental decision-making. As a next step, it is proposed that a new organization be created to involve environmental research producers, funders, and users in the pursuit of the recommendations outlined in Volumes 1 and 2. The organization's primary task would be to develop and execute projects and programs that lead to more effective decisions about specific environmental problems in the basin. Concurrent tasks would include basic research, the development of a regional research agenda, and information transfer.

Chapter 1, originally published as the Project's final report, is the product of a collaborative effort of a staff and consultant team consisting of Leonard B. Dworsky, Chadborne Gilpatric, Caroline F. Raymond, Gilbert Tauber, Anthony Wolff, and the undersigned. A complete list of Project participants and a brief history of the Project are included in the appendixes to Volume 2. Although the analysis, conclusions, and recommendations presented here represent the sense of what can be fairly drawn from the Project's work, it does not necessarily reflect a consensus of all participants. Therefore, responsibility for the final form, substance, and emphasis of this report must rest with the undersigned.

For the contributions and assistance so unstintingly tendered by all—The Rockefeller Foundation, the Advisory Panel, task group members, consultants, and Project staff—deepest appreciation is extended.

C. David Loeks

Preface

These two volumes are drawn from the work of the Hudson Basin Project, a three-year study of environmental problems and issues and of the institutions that are attempting to manage them. The Project, initiated in 1973, was funded by The Rockefeller Foundation and carried out by Mid-Hudson Pattern, Inc., a nonprofit regional planning organization, under the direction of C. David Loeks.

Some of the environmental issues analyzed in the Project have been resolved; others are still being debated. However, the Project's contribution to environmental policy analysis goes beyond specific issues or the boundaries of a specific region.

The Project's innovative approach begins with the delineation of its study area, which comprises the New York Metropolitan region plus that portion of its hinterland within the Hudson River watershed. It is an area large enough to reveal the interrelationships of environmental problems, yet small enough to be comprehended in concrete terms. Within this area, the Project was able to examine the very broad range of issues resulting from long-term interaction between human settlement and its surrounding natural resource base.

Another distinctive feature of the Project was the division of "the environment" into ten "policy sectors." An interdisciplinary task group was asked to view the basin's environment from the standpoint of a given policy sector and to examine the interactions between its sector and each of the other nine. At the outset, the participants were asked to suspend temporarily their preconceptions about what constitutes "the environment." As the reader will soon note, the definition that emerged was very broad indeed.

Approximately 125 people contributed to the Hudson Basin Project. They produced over 4000 pages of memoranda, working documents, and reports. The Project's final report and the ten task group reports were published in "working paper" format by the Rockefeller Foundation in 1976 and 1977.

Early in 1978, Academic Press proposed that the report series be edited for publication in book form, thereby making the material available to a larger audience and in a more permanent form. Chapter 1 of the present work is a summation of the entire Project as presented in the final report. Chapters 2 through 11 are drawn from the work of the individual task groups concerned with the ten policy sectors.

In editing the earlier report series for publication in these two volumes, it was necessary to condense some of the reports and to omit several detailed background papers prepared by individual task group members.

We hope we have succeeded in retaining essentially all of the material of long-term interest to students of environmental management and policy analysis, and hope also that we have done justice to the many people who gave so generously of their time and talents. If any errors of commission or omission have been made in editing the present volumes, the responsibility lies with the undersigned, rather than with the task group members or with the Project's director.

Ralph W. Richardson, Jr.
Gilbert Tauber

Contents of Volume 1

THE
HUDSON RIVER
BASIN

Environmental Problems and Institutional Response

VOLUME 2

Chapter 7

WATER RESOURCES

7.1 The Current Picture

The Hudson Basin Project study area covers more than 26,000 square miles in the states of New York, New Jersey, and Connecticut. It includes the entire drainage area of the Hudson River and portions of the drainage areas of Lake Champlain, the Delaware River, the coastal areas of northern New Jersey, Long Island, and small parts of the Great Lakes area. [It should be noted that the study area boundaries follow political (county) boundaries and not drainage or physiographic ones.] Although this area is one of the most populated regions of the United States, only 11.6% of it is developed. About 53% of the area is woodland, 10.8% is used for agriculture, and 24.6% is open land, recreation land, wetland, and water area.

The Hudson River Basin

The Hudson below Albany is unique in the northeastern United States. Nowhere else does a large navigable river at sea level connect the ocean to

Members of the Water Resources Task Group: James J. Ferris, Richard J. Kalish, Harry E. Schwarz, Edward I. Selig, Robert V. Thomann, and Erwin H. Zube.

points miles inland, winding its way through terrestrial systems of differing altitudes and a wide variety of natural and man-made landscape elements.

The Hudson River drainage area above the New York metropolitan area covers about 13,400 square miles. The amiable climate and fertile soil types of the Hudson Valley stimulated early settlement and the development of dairy farming, livestock, and fruit farming. Today, agricultural usage of the water resources in the Hudson Basin is confined to stock watering and to a small amount of irrigation on fruit farms and nurseries. Light manufacturing has become increasingly important and is responsible for heavy population concentrations around Utica, Rome, Albany, Schenectady, and Troy, the larger towns of the area. The population of the area in 1970 was greater than 20 million. Population densities in 1970 ranged from fewer than three people per square mile in Hamilton County to 545 per square mile in Albany County.

The Hudson River is now regulated by over two million acre-feet of storage. Several large reservoirs in the upper basin, such as Sacandaga Reservoir and Indian Lake, are multiple purpose. Uses include flood control, navigation, municipal supply, recreation, and power. Most storage in the remainder of the basin is used for municipal water supply.

The Hudson is navigable for ocean-going vessels to Troy, and existing navigation projects provide a system for shallow-draft vessels extending from New York Harbor to the Great Lakes, Lake Champlain, and the St. Lawrence River. In 1973, the Port of Albany handled approximately 1.1 million tons of general cargo, while the Port of New York handled more than ten times that amount. Water transport is an important factor in economic activity throughout the Hudson Basin, and an important consideration in long-term water resources planning for the region.

The upper Hudson drainage basin has an area of 4650 square miles, with the Hudson branch of it having an average flow of 6780 cubic feet per second (cfs). As part of the Champlain Canal it is canalized from Fort Edward to Cohoes (Martin, 1973). The Mohawk River basin (3450 square miles) is bisected by the Mohawk River, which enters the Hudson slightly north of the Troy Dam and has an average flow of 5820 cfs. The New York State Barge Canal follows or combines with the Mohawk in this area.

The lower Hudson River (Albany to New York City) is 150 miles long and consists of a mixed estuary, in part because of marine infusion and tidal influences. The salt-front limit can extend up the river 70 miles depending on the freshwater flow (Van Tassell, 1973). The basin is 5300 square miles and its estimated tributary flow is 7100 cfs. More than 25 major streams enter the lower Hudson, some of which carry excessive nutrient loadings from nearby population centers.

Average annual runoff in the basin is approximately 13,190 million gallons per day (mgd). The existing minimum monthly flow is 2400 mgd and the corresponding 7-day minimum is about 55% of this total, or 1325 mgd. The addition of 96 mgd as an allowance for consumptive losses and 840 mgd developed for export to New York City results in an existing firm resource available for use within this area of about 2261 mgd, or 17% of the average runoff.

The practical limit of development within the area, based on potential yield of new surface storage and additional groundwater, would provide a maximum available resource of 7838 mgd, or 59% of the average runoff. Potential sources which would develop the increase of 5577 mgd include major storage, accounting for 61% of the increase; upstream storage, 28%; and groundwater development, 11%.

New York Metropolitan Area

The southeastern New York metropolitan area covers 1901 square miles and includes the five boroughs of New York City, parts of Westchester County, and Long Island's Nassau and Suffolk counties. The land form in this urbanized area is undulating. Twenty-one percent of the area consists of a farm–forest pattern and the remainder is city. The population of the area in 1970 was more than 10.7 million. The overall density was 5644 people per square mile in 1970, but densities ranged from 1213 per square mile in Suffolk County to 66,923 per square mile in New York County (Manhattan).

Water is generally not available in this area, except for the groundwater sources that supply Long Island. Supplies for all of New York City and Westchester County must be imported. Municipal and industrial pollution seriously degrade the quality of the area's water, particularly in the New York City–Westchester area.

Average annual runoff, including subsurface outflow of groundwater, is approximately 1900 mgd. About 910 mgd of this represents surface outflow, most of which is derived from groundwater. The existing minimum monthly streamflow (shortage index, 0.01) is 220 mgd, and the corresponding 7-day minimum is about 85% of this total, or 185 mgd. Owing to the unique hydrologic and geological nature of Long Island, the developed groundwater resource is not generally reflected in surface-outflow measurements. Accordingly, the assumed existing available resource includes an allowance for this, which is based on estimated 1965 groundwater use, including consumption. This results in an existing firm resource available for use of 623 mgd, not including about 1380 mgd that can be imported into the area from New York City. The practical limit of development within the area, based on potential yield of additional groundwater, including 300 mgd of anticipated artificial recharge, would provide a maximum available resource of 1212 mgd, or 64% of the average runoff.

Northern New Jersey Metropolitan Area

The northern New Jersey area consists of 2376 square miles of drainages into Newark Bay and the west side of Arthur Kill and Raritan Bay. This area includes 157 square miles in New York State's Orange and Rockland counties, as well as 2219 square miles in nine northeastern New Jersey counties. The Passaic and the Raritan are the area's two major river basins. Nearly two-thirds of the area consists of rolling hills, with the balance in undulating hills. Over one-half of the area consists of city landscape, and the remainder consists mostly of town–farm and some forest–town landscape. The 1970 population of the area exceeded 4.2 million. The population is concentrated in and around the area's three SMSAs: Newark, Jersey City, and Paterson–Clifton–Passaic. Population density varied from 110 people per square mile in Hunterdon County to more than 13,000 per square mile in Hudson County. Water supplies will be insufficient to meet the area's needs, and significant quantities will have to be imported. The existing water resources are severely degraded in the vicinity of the many population and industrial centers.

Average annual runoff is approximately 2580 mgd. The existing minimum monthly flow (shortage index, 0.01) is 855 mgd, and the corresponding 7-day minimum is about 85% of this total, or 735 mgd. The addition of 117 mgd, an allowance for the portion of the consumptive losses reflected in streamflow records, results in an existing firm resource available for use of about 852 mgd, or 33% of the average runoff. This does not include any imports. Under the Supreme Court decree of 1954, the State of New Jersey is authorized to divert up to 100 mgd out of the Delaware. In 1965, the maximum monthly diversion was 71 mgd and the annual average was 61 mgd.

The practical limit of development within the area, based on potential yield of new surface storage and additional groundwater, would provide a maximum available resource of 1496 mgd, or 58% of the average runoff. Potential sources which would develop the increase of 644 mgd include major storage, accounting for 46% of the increase; upstream storage, 39%; and groundwater development, 15%.

Water Quality

This section describes water quality and related problems in a few locations that can be considered typical of the Hudson Basin Project area.

The Hudson and Mohawk Rivers

The process of eutrophication continues to receive the attention of the technical community in its assessment of water resources within the basin. Studies of this phenomenon, and particularly of the roles of nitrogen (N) and phosphorus (P), have been widespread. Estimates of the N and P contributions have been made relative to modified average values for untreated sewage: Biological oxygen demand (BOD) is 200 mg/liter; total nitrogen is 44 mg/liter; phosphates are 30 mg/liter; the nitrogen/BOD ratio is 0.22, and the phosphates/BOD ratio is 0.15. Total BOD discharges to the upper Hudson River exceed 250,000 pounds per day, principally from paper plant effluents. These effluents are low in nitrogen and phosphorus but contain undesirable toxic elements, such as heavy metals.

Total BOD discharges to the Mohawk exceed 120,000 pounds per day. The ratio of municipal to industrial BOD ranges from 0.7 to 1.1. Relatively high nitrogen and phosphorus loadings enter the Mohawk from tanneries and glue factories.

The lower Hudson receives more than 300,000 pounds per day of total BOD. Effluents from industries on this stretch of the river are typically low in nitrogen and phosphorus. Since the section below New York City receives mainly municipal wastewater, however, relatively high concentrations of nitrogen and phosphorus are seen in that region. Calculated nutrient loadings from wastewater and runoff, with total nutrient loadings also noted, are shown in Tables 7-1, 7-2, and 7-3 (Tofflemire and Hetling, 1969).

On the basis of dissolved oxygen profiles, the Hudson River has two particularly critical sites. These are slightly south of the Albany pool, at mile 125, where DO is about 1.0 to 3.0 mg/liter, and in the New York City region. Coliform counts in excess of 5000 coliforms/100 ml of Hudson water sampled have been detected immediately south of Albany, and range up to 10,000/100 ml at a point 40 miles south of Albany. In the middle portion of the river concentrations of these microbes range from 200 to 5000/100 ml. South of the New York City line, counts rise again, ranging from 10,000 to 50,000/100 ml.

The scarcity of time-series nutrient data and the virtual absence of biological data throughout the Hudson and Mohawk rivers depress serious discussion of the physical–chemical–biological relationships so relevant in assessing water quality today. Additional research is needed to explain the full breadth of these ecological relationships.

In general, the quality of the Hudson River begins to decline from about Tarrytown south, as a result of waste discharges from the New York–New Jersey metropolitan area. This reach, including New York Harbor, now receives over 1600 mgd of waste flows, representing a total discharge BOD

TABLE 7-1. Hudson River Nutrient Loadings from Wastewater[a]

Drainage basin	Total BOD (lb/day)	Municipal BOD/ industrial BOD	NH$_3$+organic N as N (lb)/BOD (lb)	PO$_4$ (lb)/ BOD (lb)	NH$_3$+Org N as N (lb/day)	PO$_4$ (lb/day)
Upper Hudson (Subbasin I)	250,600[b]	0.1[c]	0.05	0.03	12,500	7,500
Mohawk River (Subbasin II)	111,000[d]	0.7[e]	0.20	0.14	22,000	15,400
Total (Subbasins I and II)	360,600	—	—	—	34,500	22,900
Lower Hudson to New York City line	293,000	1.1[f]	0.15	0.10	44,000	29,300
Total Hudson less New York City and New Jersey	653,600	—	—	—	78,500	52,200
New York City and New Jersey	1,340,000	15.0	0.22	0.15	295,000	201,000
Total Hudson (Subbasins I, II, and III)	1,993,600	—	—	—	373,500	253,200

[a] From Tofflemire and Hetling (1969), reproduced by permission.
[b] Quirk Lawler and Matusky Engineers (1968).
[c] Industries include many paper mills; wastewater low in P and N.
[d] Hydroscience, Inc. (1968).
[e] Industries include several tanneries; wastewater high in P and N.
[f] Industries include paper mills; aggregate washing companies, oil companies, and chemical companies; wastewater low in P and N.

TABLE 7-2. Hudson River Nutrient Loadings from Runoff[a]

Drainage basin	Area[b]	Land[c]	NO₂ + NO₃ as N		NH₃ + Org N as N		PO₄	
			(lb/day/mi²)	(lb/day)	(lb/day/mi²)	(lb/day)	(lb/day/mi²)	(lb/day)
Upper Hudson (Subbasin I)	4,650	F=85% A=15%	2.5	11,600	0.45	2,090	0.60	2,790
Mohawk River (Subbasin II)	3,450	F=55% A=40% U= 5%	3.0	10,350	0.50	1,720	0.70	2,410
Total (Subbasins I and II)	8,100	—	—	21,950	—	3,810	—	5,200
Lower Hudson to New York City line	5,300	F=50% A=40% U=10%	3.5	18,500	5.3	2,810	0.85	4,500
Total Hudson less New York City and New Jersey	13,400	—	—	40,450	—	6,620	—	9,700
New York City and New Jersey	100	U=100%	2.7	270	6.7	67	1.10	100

[a] From Tofflemire and Hetling (1969), reproduced by permission.
[b] U.S. Geological Survey (1968).
[c] Factors in pounds/day/square mile calculated from relative percentages of forested (F), agricultural (A), and urban (U) land, utilizing measured land runoff values from the Potomac River basin:

Land use	PO₄	NO₂ – NO₃ as N	NH₃ + Org N as N
F	0.5	2.02	0.4
A	1.25	5.3	0.65
U	1.1	2.7	0.67

7

TABLE 7-3. Hudson River Total Nutrient Loadings[a]

Drainage basin	Flow (cfs)	Wastewater Total N (lb/day)	Wastewater Total PO$_4$ (lb/day)	Runoff Total N (lb/day)	Runoff Total PO$_4$ (lb/day)	Calculated total N and PO$_4$ — N (lb/day)	N (mg/liter)	PO$_4$ (lb/day)	PO$_4$ (mg/liter)	Observed values (mg/liter) N	PO$_4$
Upper Hudson (Subbasin I)	6,780	12,500	7,500	13,690	2,790	26,190	0.719	10,290	0.282	1.3	0.2
Mohawk River (Subbasin II)	5,820	22,000	15,400	12,070	2,410	34,070	1.085	17,810	0.568	1.7	0.4
Total (Subbasins I and II)	12,600	34,500	22,900	25,760	5,200	60,260	0.890	28,100	0.415	—	—
Lower Hudson to New York City	7,100	44,000	29,300	21,310	4,500	63,310	—	33,800	—	—	—
Total Hudson less New York City and New Jersey	19,700	78,500	52,200	47,070	9,700	125,570	1.18	61,900	0.582	1.6 1.3	0.6 0.3
New York City and New Jersey	19,700	295,000	201,000	337	100	295,340	—	201,000	—	—	—

[a] From Tofflemire and Hetling (1969), reproduced by permission.

load of about 1.35 million pounds per day. This load represents an overall removal of about 50%. In addition to this organic waste load, considerable quantities of nitrogen and phosphorus, trace metals, and other organic and inorganic residues are discharged in this region. The trace-metal residuals are from a variety of sources, including plant effluents, urban runoff, untreated sewage, and metals in the sludges barged to the New York Bight area.

Dissolved oxygen levels are relatively good in the mid-Hudson region but begin to decline at about mile 30 (Tarrytown). At the Battery, average values of dissolved oxygen are about 2 to 3 mg/liter, with individual values significantly less than this. Average saturation of DO is therefore between 25 and 40%. The classification for this area is Special Class I, for which the dissolved oxygen must be greater than 50% at all times. Conditions are more depressed elsewhere in the Harbor area. For example, values of about 10% DO saturation have been observed in the East River. In the sludge discharge area of the New York Bight, DO values of less than 3 mg/liter have been observed in the water overlying the sediments.

Trace-metal and nutrient concentrations vary considerably over the region. For example, cadmium levels range from less than 1 g/liter to over 8 g/liter. (Mean cadmium concentrations for open ocean water are about 0.1 g/liter.) The causal relationship between these levels and controllable discharges has, however, not yet been established.

Over its 315-mile length, the Hudson River in New York has many regions, each characteristic of its surrounding geomorphology. The upper Hudson is a typical fast-flowing mountain stream. There is practically no habitation in this region, designated Region 1 in Table 7-4. Farther south, at Luzerne and Corinth, the river widens, decreases in velocity, and flows through a region where human influence is present in the form of a few industrial and municipal discharges. This is designated as Region 2 in Table 7-4. Below the Troy Dam, the Hudson is tidal, with a mean tidal range of 5.5 feet. It also receives a large quantity of both treated and untreated industrial and municipal waste, along with wastes brought in by the Mohawk River. The oxygen concentration is often near zero for about 30 miles south of Troy (Region 3 in Table 7-4). Table 7-4 lists the typical dissolved and suspended metal concentrations in these three regions of the Hudson along with other pertinent parameters. Typical concentrations are also listed for the river at Poughkeepsie, about 80 miles south of Troy (Region 4). The upper Hudson shows higher dissolved iron (Fe) and manganese (Mn) than farther downstream, where the river flows through glacial till and sedimentary rocks.

Little change in the chemical nature of the water is evident, but there is probably significant dilution from incoming streams. The incoming streams in Region 1 are high in manganese, probably from the forest litter, since

TABLE 7-4. Metal Concentrations (μg/liter) in the Hudson River[a,b]

	Fe		Cr		Mn		Ni		Cu		Zn		Alkalinity (mg/liter)	Hardness (mg/liter)	pH
	Dis.	Sus.	Dis.	Sus.	Dis.	Sus.	Dis.	Sus.	Dis.	Sus.	Dis.	Sus.			
Hudson River															
Region 1	89.5	82.3	<0.3	<2.5	2.5	3.4	2.4	2.2	3.2	1.7	4.3	<0.5	13.0	18	6.6
Region 2	6.2	31.2	<0.6	<2.5	<.3	5.0	3.4	5.0	7.1	1.2	9.3	1.2	14.0	12	6.7
Region 3	57.2	178.0	3.6	<2.5	13.3	22.4	21.4	2.7	10.0	3.1	15.8	3.7	55.5	72	7.1
Region 4	58.0	—	6.0	—	2.1	—	<1.0	—	11.0	—	57.0	—	50.0	80	7.4
Streams influent to the Hudson															
Region 1	15.5	6.2	<0.3	<2.5	1.8	0.6	3.7	2.2	3.4	<0.5	0.9	<0.5	10.0	14	6.4
Region 2	34.2	16.7	<0.3	<2.5	1.2	2.0	6.3	1.3	3.6	<0.5	0.6	<0.5	18.0	24	7.0
Region 3	16.7	68.8	9.6	<2.5	17.4	22.5	86.8	1.9	13.6	1.9	5.8	1.1	214.0	493	7.7

[a] From Williams et al. (1974), reproduced by permission.
[b] Abbreviations used: Dis, dissolved; Sus, suspended.

these measurements were made in the fall. The copper (Cu) and zinc (Zn) are higher in Region 2, probably as a result of municipal and industrial discharges, since the unpolluted incoming streams show low levels of Cu and Zn. In Regions 3 and 4, where there are large municipal and industrial discharges, there is an increase in hardness and alkalinity as well as in the concentrations of the dissolved metals. Soluble chromium is found in the river and influent streams in this region. Copper and zinc are also much higher (Williams et al., 1974).

In addition to the increase in dissolved metals in the polluted portions of the Hudson River, Table 7-4 shows a large increase in suspended Fe and Mn. This increase is due partly to the increase in pH, alkalinity, and hardness of the river water, which causes some of the dissolved iron and manganese to precipitate. It is also due to the discharge of particulate matter to the river and the transport of suspended iron and manganese in the influent streams, as shown at the bottom of Table 7-4. The metal concentrations found in the various regions of the Hudson are typical of those found in similar streams and rivers (S. L. Williams, personal communication, 1974; Williams et al., 1974).

Considerable recreational use (i.e., boating, water skiing, swimming, sport fishing, sightseeing, and camping) is made of the Hudson Basin's water resources, including the Hudson River estuary, although these uses are often limited by poor water quality. Large numbers of lakes in the basin are of fine water quality and offer exceptional and sometimes unique locations for all types of water-based recreation.

There are about 40 public beaches and waterfront parks on the lower Hudson River. Most of these parks are located below Croton-on-Hudson, where population pressures are greatest. Swimming is not authorized in the Hudson downstream from Kingsland Point Park in North Tarrytown. Authorized swimming areas include Croton Point Beach and Nyack Beach State Park. However, people do swim at many private docks and piers along the Hudson River despite polluted conditions. Swimming and sightseeing uses in populated areas along the Hudson would probably increase if the pollution were lessened (Tofflemire and Hetling, 1969).

There are about 98 private marinas and yacht clubs on the Hudson between Ellis Island and Troy. About 125,000 to 150,000 pleasure boats use the Hudson and Mohawk rivers annually; their numbers may reach 250,000 to 300,000 by 1985 (Tofflemire and Hetling, 1969).

To control pollution, zoning of riverfront areas into commercial, industrial, and recreational areas was suggested by the Hudson River Valley Commission. The Commission also recommended that the state consider promoting more public access to the river through launching sites, marinas, and parks. Pollution control, zoning, and controlled access should be promoted not only for the Hudson River but also for other water resources (e.g., lakes, ponds, marine systems) of the basin, to widen its recreational and scenic values.

In the past, commercial fishing was a major industry on the Hudson River. Shellfish, striped bass, and shad were abundant. Shellfishing can no longer be practiced because of excessive pollution. Annual commercial catches of striped bass and shad declined from 770,000 to 250,000 pounds over the years 1959–1963. The average total catch from 1941 to 1950 was 35 million pounds. This apparent reduction since 1950 may be exaggerated, since this was a period of increased fishing effort (Tofflemire and Hetling, 1969). It should be recognized that many factors (climate, market conditions, fishing effort) influence the catches.

Angling or recreational fishing is carried out in the lower brackish waters of the river for striped bass, flounder, snapper, bluefish, white perch, and croakers. In the freshwater portion of the river and throughout the numerous lakes and other freshwater streams in the basin, bullheads, catfish, sunfish, largemouth and smallmouth bass, various types of lake and brook trout, yellow perch, and carp are caught regularly.

At present, fishing in the Hudson River is somewhat limited by waste discharges that cause objectionable tastes and aesthetic objections. Fishing on the tributaries is less limited by pollution. Trout are taken from Popolopen Creek, Saw Kill Creek, Rondout Creek, Esopus Creek, Kinderhook Creek, and Catskill Creek, among others (Tofflemire and Hetling, 1969).

Freshwater Lakes

Saratoga Lake   The Hudson Basin contains several thousand lakes and reservoirs. Two that exemplify the spectrum of lacustrine water quality within the Hudson Basin are Saratoga Lake and Lake George.

Saratoga Lake is a stratified lake with a total volume of about 3.75×10^9 cubic feet and a total surface area of 1.44×10^8 square feet (Roetzer, 1973). In recent years, the lake's chemical quality has been considered in terms of factors influencing the overall eutrophication process. The general decline in the lake's water quality can be observed in increased biological growth, especially nuisance algae and aquatic weeds.

Saratoga Lake receives substantial amounts of nutrient input and associated metals from nearby towns and lakeside cottages. Typical values of total organic carbon for the lake are relatively constant, i.e., 4 to 5 mg/liter. Saratoga is a well-buffered lake system—alkalinity as $CaCO_3$ is 85 mg/liter—with a stable and slightly alkaline pH range of 7.3 to 8.0. Mean concentrations of the heavy metals—iron, manganese, copper, and zinc—show expected seasonal changes with striking increases in fall concentrations of suspended, yet not particulate, iron and manganese in the region of the lake below the thermocline (Table 7-5). This is typical of such a lake, although these increases usually occur in suspended as well as particulate fractions (Williams et al., 1974).

The nutrients measured in Saratoga Lake show significant seasonal and depth-of-water variation. Nitrogen and phosphorus (and their fraction forms) and dissolved silica have been measured in this water body. Although the objective of this discussion is not a treatise on the delineation of lake processes relative to nutrient loading, a concise evaluation is warranted.

Silicon appears to play a major role in the seasonal succession of algal species. The major source of nutrients entering Saratoga Lake is its major inflow, Kayaderosseras Creek. This stream receives effluent, directly and indirectly, from two wastewater treatment facilities, both of which are in-

TABLE 7-5. Mean Metal Concentrations and Hardness in Saratoga Lake[a]

	Winter	Spring	Summer	Fall
Epilimnion				
Fe (μg/liter)				
Dissolved	28.4	12.5	23.7	34.0
Particulate	34.2	14.2	28.2	35
Mn (μg/liter)				
Dissolved	4.5	2.9	3.4	4.9
Particulate	9.1	1.8	2.2	5.6
Cu (μg/liter)				
Dissolved	10.8	2.9	2.2	3.5
Particulate	0.57	2.9	2.1	1.8
Zn (μg/liter)				
Dissolved	29.6	<0.4	<0.8	<0.8
Particulate	0.57	15.0	<0.5	3.5
Hardness (mg/liter as $CaCO_3$)	84	82	82	86
Hypolimnion				
Fe (μg/liter)				
Dissolved	22.4	11.6	15.1	36.0
Particulate	20	15.6	39.1	148
Mn (μg/liter)				
Dissolved	2.0	1.8	2.8	4.8
Particulate	8.5	2.2	11.7	711
Cu (μg/liter)				
Dissolved	7.0	3.5	3.7	2.6
Particulate	1.5	2.8	0.4	0.4
Zn (μg/liter)				
Dissolved	11.5	<0.4	<0.4	<0.8
Particulate	<0.5	10.6	<0.4	0.4
Hardness (mg/liter as $CaCO_3$)	80	80	77	72

[a] From Williams et al. (1974), reproduced by permission.

adequate or inoperative. If we look at water quality relating trophic level to nutrient loading, Saratoga Lake receives approximately 5.5 g/m² annually of inorganic nitrogen and 0.5 g/m² annually of phosphorus (Roetzer, 1973).

Maximum total nutrient content in the lake is expected in early spring, during mixing. Therefore, the standing-mass values of nutrients are most relevant at that time. The orthophosphate concentrate is about 0.033 mg/liter of phosphorus throughout the lake, and the sum of the inorganic nitrogen components (i.e., nitrate and ammonia) is approximately 0.7 mg/liter of nitrogen. This corresponds to standing-mass values of 3.3×10^6 g of orthophosphate phosphorus and 7×10^7 g of inorganic nitrogen. By late autumn the hypolimnion orthophosphate concentration is about 0.067 mg/liter of phosphorus and the inorganic nitrogen level is 0.95 mg/liter of nitrogen. Since one-sixth of the lake volume is below the thermocline, the standing mass in the portion of the lake is about 1.1×10^7 g of orthophosphate phosphorus and 1.4×10^7 g of inorganic nitrogen.

Some might classify Saratoga Lake as late mesotrophic to very early eutrophic on the basis of lake morphology; but in terms of nutrient loading (Vollenweider, 1968), this lake is in the advanced eutrophic state.

Lake George   Lake George is a stratified glacial lake at the eastern edge of the Adirondack Mountains. Precipitation is the major water input to the lake. Annual precipitation is about 93 cm, or 31 inches. The drainage basin of the lake covers an area of 606 km², with 19% of the area (114 km²) covered by the lake. Extensive research, both basic and applied, has been conducted at Lake George since 1968 (Ferris and Clesceri, 1974).

The two major nutrients assessed relative to their role in biological productivity in Lake George have been nitrogen and phosphorus. In many lakes, these elements have been shown to limit algal growth under various conditions. The best information suggests that 300 µg/liter of phosphorus represented a critical level for control of algae blooms in a lake (Vollenweider, 1968). Saratoga Lake, discussed previously, shows nitrogen and phosphorus levels in the lake water consistently much greater than these critical values. It has been stated that both nitrogen and phosphorus can be limiting at certain times in Lake George. The nitrogen and phosphorus added to Lake George originate from precipitation, runoff, and wastewater effluents (Aulenbach and Clesceri, 1973). The total amounts are approximately 175,000 kg of nitrogen (61% to the south basin, 39% to the north basin) and 20,000 kg of phosphorus (82% to the south basin and 18% to the north basin). Levels of phosphorus and nitrogen in Lake George itself are consistently below those critical levels of 300 µg/liter of nitrogen and 10 µg/liter of phosphorus. Indeed, average values range from 6 to 8 µg/liter of phosphorus (orthophosphate) and are estimated to be 100 of 110 µg/liter of nitrogen (Aulenbach and Clesceri, 1973).

Periodic measurements of iron, manganese, copper, and zinc have been made in lake water, in precipitation falling on the lake, and in the influent streams (Tables 7-6 and 7-7). The amounts of iron, manganese, and zinc in the suspended material in this lake were too low to be measured (less than 5 g/liter for iron, and less than 0.25 μg/liter for manganese and zinc). Copper was occasionally as high as 1 μg/liter in the suspended material, but usually less than 0.25 μg/liter. The levels of dissolved iron, manganese, and copper in the lake are consistently lower than the concentrations in the entering streams and precipitation, indicating that these elements are being lost to the bottom sediments (Williams et al., 1974).

Lake George, in contrast to Saratoga Lake and many lakes in the Hudson Basin Project region, continues to be maintained as late oligotrophic to early mesotrophic in quality. However, it is rapidly being impacted by phosphorus loading to an early eutrophic state, especially in certain high-population-density areas in the south basin (Ferris and Clesceri, 1974). Its characteristic delineation from Saratoga Lake can be observed visually and is easily noted when various ecologic profiles (e.g., dissolved oxygen) are compared.

The information presented in this section is merely a brief review of selected data for some of the water resources of the Hudson Basin. Many additional factors—physical, chemical, and biological—some of which are

TABLE 7-6.   Mean Seasonal Concentrations of Fe, Mn, Cu, and Zn in the North and South Lakes of Lake George[a]

	Depth (m)	South Lake (μg/liter)				North Lake (μg/liter)			
		Fe	Mn	Cu	Zn	Fe	Mn	Cu	Zn
Winter	3	27.2	2.0	5.2	43.4	35.2	1.9	2.7	51.1
(Jan. 1–Mar. 31)	9	42.1	2.1	3.5	49.3	34.8	1.3	2.0	79.6
	15	30.6	1.6	3.7	44.4	50.7	2.3	2.2	76.6
Spring	3	25.1	3.2	3.9	32.7	41.5	2.9	2.6	33.5
(Apr. 1–June 21)	9	17.3	2.5	4.2	28.0	26.2	2.5	3.5	53.2
	15	16.9	4.0	3.8	30.4	35.4	3.2	3.2	38.6
Summer	3	29.0	2.6	3.4	46.4	29.8	2.0	3.0	74.9
(June 21–Sept. 21)	9	23.5	2.2	3.1	31.8	23.8	3.3	3.2	40.4
	15	28.8	4.1	2.9	34.2	23.6	1.9	2.9	23.9
Fall	3	46.1	1.8	3.1	25.1	13.8	1.4	1.6	71.1
(Sept. 21–Dec. 7)	9	39.9	1.7	2.5	23.3	20.5	1.2	1.7	88.3
	15	30.3	2.5	2.6	43.5	14.5	1.1	2.0	74.5

[a] From Williams et al. (1974), reproduced by permission.

TABLE 7-7.   Mean Concentrations of Fe, Mn, Cu, and Zn in Influent Streams and Precipitation
for Lake George, 1970[a]

	Streams[b]				Precipitation[b]			
	Fe	Mn	Cu	Zn	Fe	Mn	Cu	Zn
Winter	48.8	7.1	3.6	27.7	43.1	3.8	6.4	31.3
Spring	38.5	2.1	3.9	8.9	75.0	8.1	11.2	48.5
Summer	39.7	7.5	3.7	7.3	45.1	3.2	7.6	32.1
Fall	42.5	7.2	6.8	10.0	36.0	7.5	21.4	84.9
Snowpack on lake					6.2	5.6	23.8	23.0

[a] From Williams et al. (1974), reproduced by permission.
[b] All values are expressed as micrograms per liter.

not available, would enter into a more definitive description of the current status of the basin's water resources. The relevance of these parameters to water quality can be examined via mathematical techniques (see Section 7.3). Correlations of the physical and chemical factors with the individual and overall biological systems within the waters of the basin, and in regions throughout the nation, may eventually be used to determine factor rankings relative to water quality and to establish water quality guidelines.

7.2   The Interdependence of Policy Areas

Every policy area is related to every other one and, similarly, every sub-division of a policy area can be shown to be influenced by every other one. But this maze of interdependencies sheds little light on the problem of priorities in environmental management. Therefore, this analysis is limited to water uses and deals with only those interrelationships that are direct and of major significance. The subdivisions of the water-resources policy area were restricted to water uses, such as municipal water supply or aesthetics, only because the management problems, such as flood damage management or erosion and sedimentation, are products of the interactions between water uses and the concerns of each of the other nine policy areas. Different relationships exist between two policy areas, depending on which is taken to be the causative agent. Therefore, each set of interactions was viewed with each item in the pair as the causative agent.

The interactions noted in Fig. 1-6 represent the combined judgments of the task group members. The major, or most direct, interactions of water resources are those with land use human settlement, biological com-munities, and leisure time and recreation. Intermediate-level interactions are those with transportation, environmental service systems, energy, land use/natural resource management, and human health. There is a low level of interaction between water resources and air resources. Examples of some of the interactions with other policy areas that formed the base for the group's judgment include the following.

Land Use/Human Settlement

Large-lot grid zoning must be supported by costly and extensive road building, shopping centers, sewers, and other public utilities. Paving increases the ratio of impermeable to permeable land surfaces, thereby increasing polluted runoff, which degrades water quality apart from the collection and treatment systems built to control the point sources. If cluster zoning were used instead, the cost of public utilities to service developments would be reduced, pollution from nonpoint sources would be minimized, and there could be more open public spaces afforded recreational access to waterways.

Pollution of ground or surface waters results from too many septic tanks in a particular area in which intensive residential or second-home development has occurred. The area ought to be sewered, but the concerned municipality resists sewering because of the cost, which the EPA will not subsidize, and because of the further uncontrollable development that will be stimulated by sewer lines. If the area is sewered, and the effluent brought to a downstream site for treatment, the upstream area will lose the groundwater recharge on which it has traditionally depended for water quantity to support instream recreational uses.

Biological Communities

The discharge of excessive pollutants (municipal and/or industrial) into the waters of the basin may affect the structure and function of the biological communities of the total aquatic ecosystem and the responses of its specific components. Of special significance are stimulatory or inhibitory effects on biological productivity from point and nonpoint sources of pollution, as well as the introduction of unwanted organism types and their effects on the ecosystem's stability and diversity. Attention should be directed to the evaluation of the effects from cultural and natural discharges on the components and biological composition of the aquatic system and on cost-benefit ratios of effluent limitations for different water usages.

Leisure Time and Recreation and Human Health

The setting aside of certain water bodies as Class A public water supplies precludes their use for fishing, swimming, and boating. It would be possible instead to permit such uses and to subject the water to treatment upon intake, but public health agencies favor minimal treatment of drinking water supplies, in part because of the remote risk that such works might fail. There is also a public mystique favoring natural water fresh from the tap. No mechanism exists for compensating upstream communities (in which the Class A reservoir is located) for the recreational opportunities they forego to preserve the water's natural purity for the benefit of downstream communities that incur little or no cost for treating it before use.

Transportation

The usage of fishing and other water-related recreation areas is a function both of the quality of the water and recreational facilities, and of the access to these facilities. Thus, transportation affects water recreational facilities while these facilities also place demands on the transportation system.

Environmental Service Systems

Stricter wastewater-treatment standards require removal of increasing quantities of pollutants from waterborne effluents. The residues thereby removed must be disposed of in some way. Landfill sites may not be available; ocean dumping may be prohibited; incineration will be costly and may jeopardize air quality. Theoretically, recycling would be the best strategy, but federal tax and rate-setting policies favor further depletion of natural resources over recycling of resources already in use, with the result that recycling is often not a viable alternative. If recycling were a viable alternative, then revenue-producing facilities for recapturing and recycling residues—possibly from both wastewater and solid-waste sources—could prevent pollution, benefit the economy of the region, and avoid shutdowns of industries that might not otherwise be able to afford the costs of controlling their process wastes.

Energy

A hydroelectric power plant in the basin would spur its economy without befouling its air or heating its water, but could harm biological communities and scenic values.

Land Use/Natural Resources and Human Health

Pursuant to a policy of encouraging continuation of agricultural land uses, it is proposed that secondarily treated effluents be sprayed onto crops at no expense to the farmer. Such a practice would also recharge groundwaters. But public health agencies at local and state levels object to spray irrigation because they fear it might jeopardize drinking water supplies or render crops unfit for human consumption. Although data are lacking that would support these fears, they prevail in a climate of bureaucratic inertia and aversion to risk. Thus, proposals for spray irrigation are often vetoed by the public health establishment.

7.3 Applicable Technology for Water Resources

Various methodologies have been used independently of each other and for conflicting reasons to establish water resource priorities throughout the nation. No comprehensive system of these technologies has, however, been employed to develop alternative water resource planning schemes relative to ecosystem stability, water quality, and water quantity. Success in reestablishing water quality has often occurred solely by independent technical decision-making. For example, the diversion of Seattle's sewage effluents away from Lake Washington fostered a return to acceptable water quality in that lake system. The same measure, however, was ineffective in the Madison (Wisconsin) lakes, since there were enough nonpoint nutrient sources to cause continued eutrophication of those lakes at the prediverted rate. In both cases, the technology was not at fault. Indeed, technical efficacy was employed within a framework of economic feasibility. But in neither case were the available data fully relevant to anticipate success or failure.

Two technologies can be distinguished in any water resource problem setting: assessment or analysis technology and the technology of implementation (structural and nonstructural). Ideally, an assessment framework should precede the establishment of specific structural control techniques, largely on the grounds of cost effectiveness. In general, this has been the case for water supply problems. A more or less classical engineering economic analysis is applied, say, to a water supply and demand problem. Such an analysis provides the basis for the design of certain controls (e.g., dams, conduits) to achieve a demand objective. This analysis is normal and to be expected. In the case of water quality problems, however, application of the analysis framework prior to construction is more often the exception rather than the rule. Finally, for both water quality and water supply problems, the system is rarely viewed comprehensively and the analyses often tend to be rather narrowly focused. There is no intention here to provide a detailed review of all of the available technological approaches, but rather to provide an overview of the many ways that environmental control can be exercised.

Assessment or Analysis Technology

An assessment technology that attempts to view the system comprehensively should include sociopolitical, economic, and biological–chemical–physical analyses. Currently, a comprehensive and integrated analysis incorporating such a framework has not been made in the Hudson Basin or, in fact, any basin in the country. Attempts, however, have been made to synthesize most of these components. One of the earlier attempts was the Delaware Estuary Study, which incorporated water quality modeling, optimization analysis, and cost and benefit estimation, together with a crude attempt at policy analysis through interactions between water-using interest groups.

More recently, the North Atlantic Regional (NAR) Water Resources Study (NAR, 1972) has incorporated such components as input–output models and water supply and demand models. Planning goals for the study were analyzed in the overall programming model by "sensitizing" various key points in the analysis framework (e.g., stream flow as an indicator of ecological considerations).

An ongoing program at the University of Texas to develop operational guidelines for Texas coastal zone management has integrated a number of assessment and implementation components, including input–output models, demographic models, spatial allocation models, waste-residual generation, preliminary water quality models, and resource capacity analysis.

Water Quality Modeling

Water resource analysis, like all resource allocation problems, is carried out on several time and space scales of interest. The ability to estimate environmental directions or consequences, using mathematical models of water quality, is closely tied to the determination of relevant time and space scales; e.g., for the Hudson Basin Project, there are the following scales: (a) basinwide space (approximately 50 to 150 miles) and long-term (approximately 1 to 10 years or greater) time scales; (b) subbasin space scale (25 to 50 miles), long-term and seasonal time scales; (c) regional and subregional scales (5 to 25 miles), long-term and seasonal time scales; and (d) local space scales (approximately 1 to 5 miles), and seasonal and short-term (hour-to-hour) time scales. There are many other variations on this general structure, including, for example, very short-term (hours) transient effects on a basinwide scale (hundreds of miles) caused by a large storm or hurricane.

From a water quality viewpoint, large time and space scales are usually associated with large-scale capital works (e.g., dams and reservoirs, large treatment plants, flow diversions). The short-term time scales and local space scales are usually associated with transient operational problems such as the effect of a stormwater overflow of combined sewage and rainfall on a local level, or the effect of accidental waste spill on water quality. Some transient effects may undoubtedly have long-term biological effects that transcend local space scales.

Water quality can be represented by a set of variables reflecting the uses to which a given water resource may be put. An exhaustive list might include several hundred variables. A more manageable look at what constitutes water quality can, however, be obtained by a listing representative of the more critical indicator variables, as follows: *physical variables,* e.g., temperature, salinity (chlorides), turbidity, and water flow and currents; *chemical/biochemical variables,* e.g., biochemical oxygen demand, dissolved and particulate organic matter, dissolved oxygen, phosphorus and its fraction forms, nitrogen and its fraction forms, acidity, alkalinity, pH, hazardous pollutants; *heavy metals,* e.g., lead, zinc, mercury, cadmium, chromium; *microbiological variables,* e.g., total coliform bacteria, fecal coliform bacteria, viruses, other pathogenic microorganisms; and *biological variables,* e.g., phytoplankton, rooted aquatic plants (macrophytes). One might consider higher-order biological variables, such as the benthic flora and fauna, zooplankton, small fish, and then the top carnivores of the food chain, as belonging to a general class of ecological variables.

Class I Variables   There is a class of water-quality variables in which the state-of-the-art of modeling water responses due to external environmental inputs is well advanced. For this class, the results of the model output can be incorporated into the decision-making process and can provide valuable insight into the consequences of proposed actions. These Class I variables are (a) salinity (chlorides), (b) water temperature, (c) coliform bacteria, (d) dissolved oxygen, (e) total phosphorus and nitrogen, and (f) miscellaneous chemical elements.

For this class of variables, both long- and short-term analyses are possible. For example, the day-to-day and week-to-week intrusion of salinity from the ocean into an estuary has been predicted with a reasonable degree of success. Similarly, the movement of coliform bacteria in a body of water on account of combined sewer overflows after a rainstorm can be analyzed in sufficient detail for use in the decision-making process.

The dissolved-oxygen variable has a long history of application in the water resource field. It is one indication of the general health of a body for certain biological parameters (e.g., fish). Waste-treatment requirements are often related to the dissolved oxygen. Thus, modeling the DO response of a water body to waste-load additions or removals is well advanced, and can also provide significant input into rational decision-making.

Class II Variables   In this class of variables, attempts at modeling are relatively recent (within 5 years), which is not long enough to judge fully the usefulness of the predictive framework. These variables represent an intermediate class of knowledge and predictive utility. They include (a) phytoplankton; (b) some naturally occurring elements and compounds (e.g., calcium, magnesium); (c) acidity, alkalinity, pH; (d) fecal coliform bacteria; and (e) available phosphorus, nitrogen.* Generally, modeling efforts for these variables are proceeding rapidly in various areas around the country. In some instances, the results of even preliminary modeling efforts have been eagerly sought to aid in decisions regarding environmental control actions.

Class III Variables   This class essentially includes "everything else." It comprises those variables that have just begun to be modeled or key variables that essentially have not been modeled at all. For some of these variables, significant policy decisions have already been made without the benefit of a rigorous cause–effect analysis. Some of these decisions (e.g., pesticide control) are obviously based upon significant environmental evidence of detrimental biological impact; nevertheless, the effect of the policy is presumed to be beneficial. In other cases, policy decisions have been based on scanty evidence. Such policies generally promise much more than they are likely to deliver. In this regard, refer to the analysis of policies on removals of metals in the New York metropolitan area in Klein *et al.* (1974). Some of the more important Class III variables are (a) turbidity (light extinction), (b) heavy metals (e.g., cadmium, zinc, lead, mercury, chromium), (c) chlorinated hydrocarbons (e.g., DDT), (d) integrated aquatic ecosystem models (e.g., phytoplankton, zooplankton, benthos, decomposers, fish), and (e) viruses. Water quality and aquatic ecosystem variables in this class demand a considerable level of additional input before utility in decision-making is ensured.

Water Quantity Analysis

Three parameters and their interrelationships form the framework within which quantative analysis of water systems is carried out. These are water quantity (expressed either as a volume or rate), time, and spatial location. The techniques of hydrology and hydraulics describe these relationships and serve as the basis for analyses. Neither of these scientific disciplines is new and, as new and improved techniques are steadily forthcoming, they have served to explain the phenomena associated with the spatial and time distribution of water flow. Similarly, the understanding of the stochastic processes of hydrology is not new. What has, however, developed over the last one or

---

*Available phosphorus or nitrogen is the amount of the nutrient that can be utilized by phytoplankton for growth (i.e., not all of the *total* phosphorus and/or nitrogen can be utilized by phytoplankton).

two decades is the synthesis of hydrologic and hydraulic concepts with those of modern mathematical statistics and the field of systems analysis.

This marriage of techniques and the availability of the electronic computer have opened up a wide range of capabilities heretofore closed to the water resources planner. Rainfall–runoff relationships, surface water systems, groundwater systems, combined surface and groundwater systems, large basins, and man's intervention in the natural regimen can be analyzed using these techniques. Two basic types of analyses, mathematical programming and simulation, are most useful in water resources.

Mathematical programming involves the analysis of a mathematical model to obtain a result that maximizes (or minimizes) a specific objective function. The word *programming* here does not refer to computer programming; rather, it is a synonym for planning. There is a wide range of mathematical techniques in programming such as linear, nonlinear, integer, or dynamic. Generally, however, mathematical programming models are characterized by the use of simplifying assumptions and clear-cut objectives. Typically, allocation of resources and optimal timing of projects are problems susceptible to this method of analysis.

Simulation involves the mathematical reproduction of the physical system. Such models can be made extremely complex, reproducing in great detail any function of a system that can be quantified and for which functional relationships are known. The power of this approach lies in the ability of the operator to change the system or to change the input and observe the consequences of these changes at any point in the system. Typically, physical, economic, and social systems, and combinations thereof, are subjects for simulation. Sensitivity analysis—the observation of the effect in the variation of one or more variables—commonly uses this technique, as well as large planning models and real-time operation models.

In the Hudson Basin Project area, both types of models would be useful and should be developed. Portions of the basin have been modeled as part of New York City water supply studies, the Corps of Engineers NEWS Study, and other water resources studies. A large model of the interactions among the physical, socioeconomic, and biological systems is feasible but has not been attempted.

Economic Assessment Technology

The methodology of economic assessment has evolved rapidly in the last few years. In the 1930s and 1940s the general emphasis was on market models: estimating future prices, supplies, demands, and costs for private goods, or what were then considered as private goods. The newer techniques of economic analysis have included the problems associated with nonmarket goods, such as public education, and quasi-market goods such as water, land, recreation, and fisheries. The essential distinction here is the reasonableness of using market prices and costs as fully representing the total prices and costs in economic assessment models.

Market prices and costs may not be fully representative of total prices and costs for a variety of reasons. For each of the "wedges" between true costs and benefits and market prices and costs, there is a method (often more than one method) of assessment available to estimate the size of the "wedge" and thus provide a more accurate picture of the actual costs and benefits. A divergence between private benefits or costs and social benefits or costs leads to an allocation of resources that is less than optimum. To achieve a higher level of efficiency in resource allocation, it is necessary to assess and evaluate the impacts of proposed changes in resource availability upon the regional or national economy.

A proposal to construct a waste treatment plant, to prohibit discharges into a water course, or to change the availability of water to present users is implicitly a proposal to reallocate resources. The general approach for assessing the economic impacts of public allocation decisions in water resources is the cost–benefit framework, which in itself is an attempt to replicate the market mechanism where the market does not function efficiently in making allocation decisions. In its broadest form, cost–benefit merely attempts to compare the benefits derived by society against the costs incurred in carrying out a particular project or decision. If the discounted net benefit exceeds expected costs, then a project is economically feasible. The decision whether or not a particular project should be undertaken depends not on whether it has a positive net benefit, but whether it returns greater benefits relative to costs than alternative projects.

Although cost–benefit analysis has been used in federal water resource planning since the mid-1930s, and is widely used and referred to in project evaluation, there are still some conceptual difficulties with the analysis which must be taken into account. The first is the question of what rate of discount is appropriate for public projects; the second is the difficulty encountered in establishing dollar measures for project-related benefits. The discount rate problem is often handled by relying on the market rate or by using some "accepted" public rate. The measurement of benefits is often done by imputation, employing a variety of available techniques.

Gravity models and cost-of-travel are widely used techniques for establishing demand, or consumer preferences, for recreation. Once determined, demand serves as a basis for measuring project benefits. To estimate regional benefits or impacts of proposed changes in existing water resource availability, techniques such as input–output and multiplier analysis are employed. Both methods of analysis attempt to establish the economic impact of a change in resource availability by tracing the interaction between major sectors of the regional economy and by predicting the cumulative economic effect of the potential change. Both techniques are static, and entail a set of somewhat severe limiting assumptions. To add dynamism to the analysis, econometric modeling is used. There are additional techniques for estimating economic impacts of potential changes in water resources availability, such as location analysis and social accounts. Each of these techniques provides better information to the resource manager and contributes to efficiency and equity in the formulation of plans.

To assess the optimality of a single or multipurpose project, a series of modeling techniques has evolved, including linear and dynamic programming, queuing theory, and simulation. Each attempts to assess a plan or program for water resource management on the basis of maximum efficiency in the allocation of resources within given constraints. The constraints in these models can be specified in greater detail and with more characteristics than in cost–benefit analysis.

Elements of Institutional Analysis

Institutions can be analyzed in either of two major ways. The first employs rigorous techniques familiar to behavioral scientists, e.g., systems models, hypothesis formulation and testing, and quantitative measurement. The aim here is to describe and explain phenomena, not to criticize or to prescribe. The second employs "softer" empirical knowledge and critical skills: reflection upon working experience, direct observation, practical knowledge of causes and effects, perception of goals and constraints, historical awareness, and educated common sense.

The first of these modes cannot be explored adequately within the scope of the present report, beyond noting that there is a substantial body of literature in the science of institutional analysis, but that it generally has no practical impact, either because it does not appear in useful form for decision-makers or because decision-making itself is not receptive to scientific inputs. What, if anything, can be done to remove these obstacles is an interesting question that definitely warrants further research.

The second mode, which combines descriptive and evaluative approaches, may also shed considerable light on both formal and operating characteristics of institutions. At the same time, it results in formulation of issues for public debate. It is policy-oriented analysis, the type with which we are primarily concerned here. Policy-oriented analysis of institutional arrangements for managing natural resources may be divided into two parts, critique of institutional design and critique of institutional performance. The two are not mutually exclusive, since performance is to some extent a function of design. But since factors other than design also influence performance, the distinction is useful for purposes of analysis.

Components of Institutional Design   In exploring the range of institutional alternatives, one would have to consider the following major sets of variables: (a) program areas (e.g., water pollution control or water supply services); (b) functions (e.g., planning or regulating); (c) levels and jurisdictions of government (e.g., federal administrative agency, county planning board); and (d) constitutions of government agencies (e.g., appointed or elected officials).

PROGRAM AREAS   Different sets of institutions (with considerable overlapping) can be identified for four major program areas affecting water resources in the Hudson River basin:

1. Wastewater management: the collection, transmission, and treatment of waterborne wastes
2. Water supply services: both wholesale and retail, including intake treatment, transmission, and delivery to ultimate residential, industrial, or commercial users
3. Water resources management: measures to protect or manipulate the resource for a variety of instream and withdrawal needs, including navigation, recreation, flood control, power generation, and water supply. Such measures would include water intake, storage and return facilities, channel dredging or alteration, instream treatment or aeration, and stream zoning
4. Water-related land use control: regulation of existing and future land development to protect water quality and to avoid excessive demands on water supply

The first task is to identify the legislative authorities, agencies, programs, and procedures that characterize activity in the particular area under consideration. What is needed is no mere inventory of institutional components, but an overview of how they operate in relation to one another, to promote—or frustrate—a defined set of management objectives.

FUNCTIONS   It is useful to analyze institutional arrangements and activities within each program area in terms of the following functions: planning, financing, designing and constructing facilities, operating and maintaining facilities, monitoring, regulating, and enforcing.

Planning, simply stated, is the function of deciding what will be and often connotes a merely advisory function; many plans can safely be ignored. But the interesting question is where planning *power* resides and how it is exercised. The power to prescribe for the future, as by adopting authoritative plans, is a fundamental policy-making power. It can be exercised openly or covertly. Perhaps too frequently, it is not exercised at all or only ad hoc, without really ordering the sequence of events in accordance with coherent, predetermined strategy. Such ordering is the essence of the planning function.

Financing includes all the fiscal dimensions of natural resource management. The power to supply the necessary funding for a project or activity is a formidable power, especially because its exercise can be conditioned on any number of planning or regulatory prerequisites. Methods of raising the necessary funds—whether through taxes, current appropriations, debt, user charges, or some combination of these—are also prime subjects for analysis under this heading, not so much for their economic as for their legal and administrative implications.

In environmental management, engineering, including designing and constructing facilities, plays a critical role too often overlooked from the institutional point of view. The character of the engineering profession itself, the politics of engineering in the context of various professional–client relationships, and quality control in the design and construction of facilities are subjects where much research is still desirable.

The importance of operating and maintaining facilities has been recognized increasingly. There is no point in building facilities that will not be operated and maintained correctly. Yet the level of performance, particularly in wastewater management facilities, has generally been so poor as to suggest the need for institutional change.

Monitoring includes a set of information-gathering functions that serves several partially conflicting purposes: to provide a data base for planning, to indicate the need for technical assistance or other resources in the management of facilities, and to disclose evidence of violations. Sampling, recording, and reporting are the principal subfunctions. Stream modeling, research and development, and technical assistance to facility operators are closely related functions that may also be considered under this heading.

Regulating is the most general of all the functions. It is the power of one agency to prescribe rules or standards that another agency or person must observe. Any function or activity may be made subject to regulation in greater or lesser detail. The discretionary power of the regulatee varies inversely with the degree to which he is regulated.

Enforcement is not synonymous with regulation or implementation. Rather, it denotes the entire range of remedial actions that can be taken against behavior that departs from established legal norms. Enforcement action can be administrative or judicial, and it may involve such widely varying techniques as issuing orders to do or to refrain from doing something, assessing penalties, and taking over malfunctioning facilities.

One might well proceed by asking which of the foregoing functions are, or should be, vested in which agencies of government, and with what provisions for interfunctional coordination. Some combinations will be found to work better than others; each has its peculiar strengths and pitfalls. One should also note whether a particular function is a duty laid upon a particular agency or a power that the agency is free to exercise or not, at its discretion. In institutional analysis, much can hinge on the difference between "shall" and "may." Alternative ways of exercising a function, and conditions precedent or subsequent to its exercise, should also be explored.

LEVEL AND JURISDICTION OF GOVERNMENT   Another critical dimension of analysis concerns the levels of government at which particular functions are lodged. Setting aside international possibilities, there are five major levels: federal, interstate–regional, state, substate–regional, and local. Within each level, functions may be combined in a single agency or dispersed among several. For each program area, there is a set of intergovernmental relationships running from the federal down to the municipal level, and there are sets of interagency relationships at each level. The entire web of vertical and horizontal relationships can be articulated largely in terms of the distribution of functions, powers, and duties. For example, under A-95 review procedures, substate regional agencies will test proposed federal construction grants to states or municipalities for consistency with regional plans. A state agency may allocate available water supplies among competing municipal and industrial users, but it may be a different agency that undertakes or approves measures for regulating stream flow. Thus, the dynamics of institutional processes can begin to be explained by using the recommended categories of analysis.

An adequate description of existing institutional processes will reveal weaknesses that ought to be corrected and will teach valuable lessons to those who would design new institutions instead of tinkering with the old. For example, a function is best lodged in a federal agency if there is need for consistent national policy or a set of standards with respect to it, and in municipal governments if considerable variation can be tolerated from one locality to another.

The federal government and the states share primary constitutional status under our federal system. Radical departures from this political tradition are not likely to succeed. States have, however, delegated many of their powers (e.g., zoning) down to the municipal level, and extensive fragmentation of functions can be observed at all three major levels of government—federal, state, and local. Such fragmentation may safeguard against tyrannical or ill-advised decision-making, but it may also obstruct the development and execution of coherent policy. The points where these obstructions are likely to occur are prime targets for analysis.

Regional governments, whether of interstate or substate jurisdiction, are theoretically attractive alternatives, especially for internalizing externalities and achieving efficiency in environmental management, but they have never fared well within our federal system. The bias against them may need to be reexamined and, if possible, corrected.

For the conduct of a capital investment program, quasi-autonomous authorities with revenue-bonding powers have been found efficient at several levels of government, yet they are criticized for narrow-mindedness, mercantilist behavior, and unresponsiveness to the public. And so the analysis would proceed by reviewing actual or alternative combinations and distributions of functions in the several program areas.

CONSTITUTIONS OF GOVERNMENT AGENCIES   Some major variables under this topic are whether officials entrusted with particular functions are elected or appointed; what qualifications, terms of service, and emoluments are attached to their offices; whether decisions are made by single executives, boards, or bicameral processes, with or without review or participation by any other agency or interest group; and what fiscal, manpower, and other resources are available to the agency for performance of its mission. The functions of an agency may also be viewed, of course, as part of its constitution, but here the focus will be on how an agency's organizational structure affects the ways in which it approaches its mission.

Constitutional analysis, in the sense here employed, may also yield guidelines for testing and evaluating institutional alternatives. The closer an agency comes to deciding questions of fundamental social choice, the stronger the argument for having its members directly elected by the people rather than appointed by elected officials. Conversely, appointment is appropriate to offices charged with implementing policies already established by some legislature. The powers and emoluments attached to an electoral office should be generous enough both to induce candidates to stand for election at their own expense and to facilitate the trade-offs by which majorities are fashioned from various interests and constituencies represented in the legislative body.

Voluntary boards, serving by appointment without pay, cannot be expected to exercise much independent judgment, but will tend to lean heavily—for better or worse—upon their full-time staffs. Appointments to a board for fixed staggered terms can insulate its operations to some extent from the vagaries of politics and promote continuity in the pursuit of programs; appointees serving at the pleasure of their appointing officials, on the other hand, will be more responsive to immediate political pressures. Since councils of local governments are congeries of fragmentary local interests, they will resist the development and application of regional perspectives, except where generous federal subsidies are conditioned on interlocal cooperation.

Examples of these dimensions of analysis could be multiplied indefinitely. Inquiry into the structure and modus operandi of government agencies is essential to understanding their successes, failures, and limitations.

COORDINATING THE COMPONENTS OF INSTITUTIONAL ANALYSIS   By combining analyses of program areas, functions, interagency relationships, and agency constitutions, it is possible to build toward a critical taxonomy of institutions, which need not be biased in favor of particular political ideologies and which will be of service both in examining problems of environmental management and in fashioning institutional reforms for resolving them more effectively. At the same time, the limits of government itself, in any form, as a tool for accomplishing social objectives, will have to be acknowledged. Institutional reform also cannot make up for deficits in political or bureaucratic motivation. These limits become apparent in the critique of actual institutional performance, to which we now turn.

Institutional Performance   This branch of analysis furnishes indispensable inputs to the task of analyzing, evaluating, and designing institutional arrangements. It is axiomatic that the way an institution looks on paper is not the way it performs in fact. Performance analysis will generally reveal how an agency interprets its mission, regardless of whether it performs well or poorly. Surprises may be encountered in the course of such analysis. For example, an overt function may prove to be the vehicle for exercising a latent one. Generally, although not always, the performance is less impressive than the promise. For any number of reasons, which need to be documented, powers may be abused or may go unexercised, or duties may be disregarded.

A PATHOLOGY OF CURRENT INSTITUTIONAL PERFORMANCES   There are many reasons why institutions fail. We indicate here only some of the more common elements of diagnosis, by way of illustrating this set of analytic tasks. Legislatures are fond of creating agencies with high-sounding missions, only to starve them for lack of appropriations and other resources. The expressive function of law is morally satisfying and light on the pocketbook; its regulatory and substantive functions are quite another matter. Bureaucracies, moreover, operate by rules of their own, regardless of the law. Civil-service restrictions, professional jealousies, psychological inertia, and public employment as a form of public welfare are among the bureaucratic phenomena that need to be examined, along with the contempt of society for those who manage its wastes. At the top, officials may be appointed with no other qualifications than political loyalty, and it is common practice for regulators to be drawn from and returned to the ranks of the regulatees. Legislators are more interested in public works for their districts than in whether facilities, once constructed, will be operated correctly. Polluters with political clout can successfully resist the pressures of the law by a variety of means, ranging from interference by their legislative representatives in the administrative process, to litigation that ties up legal and judicial resources for years at a stretch. On the one hand, legislatures fail to make policy but delegate broad discretionary powers to administrative agencies, as if the latter were better equipped both to make policy and to implement it responsibly in the absence of legislative direction. On the other hand, legislation too often diffuses or splits powers among various agencies, or establishes conflicting policies and programs without clarifying their functional relationships—another prescription for failure.

TECHNIQUES FOR IMPROVING INSTITUTIONAL PERFORMANCE   After diagnosing the causes of failure, the analysis would proceed to the range of possible remedies. Foremost among these may well be opening up the decision-making process to public scrutiny and public participation at critical junctures, as the trend of current legislation increasingly requires. Citizen suits can also play a critical role in checking abuses of official discretion. New agencies can be made expressly exempt from civil-service requirements; qualifications for office can be established along with other provisions tending to mitigate the worst effects of the spoils system; canons of professional ethics can be extended to separate regulators more effectively from the interest they regulate; laws can require better monitoring of agency performance and better lines of interagency communication. Funding for programs can be made more generously—or at least more predictably—available from year to year. Some improvements, however, may have to await the results of long-range pressures to reform legislative and bureaucratic processes. Thus the critique of institutions leads inevitably to considerations of practical politics, unless one is content to confine it to an academic exercise.

Technology of Implementation (Structural and Nonstructural)

Structural

A variety of environmental controls are available to achieve water resource objectives. Some controls, such as dams, reservoirs, and aqueducts, are obviously directed toward direct fulfillment of water uses for man: water supply, flood protection, power, and recreational facilities. Other environmental controls, such as wastewater treatment plants, are directed to a fulfillment of various water uses for man, but are also aimed at improving or maintaining the general biological diversity of a water body on more general philosophical grounds. In either case, decisions are often made on the basis of the ability of an environmental control device to perform technologically, and the cost of achieving that specified level of performance. To place applicable technology for water resources in a manageable framework, therefore, two elements are necessary: engineering and scientific effectiveness, and economic efficiency. Indeed, water resource management, like it or not, eventually revolves about the notions of effectiveness and efficiency.

This rubric does not exclude social or political considerations, or unquantifiable aesthetic factors; it merely faces the reality of the decision-making process.

Some measure of the trade-off between effectiveness and economic efficiency can be obtained by examining the cost of successive reductions in municipal wastewater residues. A general overview is provided in Table 7-8. As indicated, costs increase substantially as higher and higher removals are demanded. Note also that even at Level III, 100% removal is not indicated, largely on technological engineering grounds. First, 100% removal of wastewater residues is not technologically feasible now and is not likely to be feasible in the reasonably near future (10 years). Second, costs increase almost exponentially for each percentage of removal demanded above a nominal 75 to 85%. Thus, the concept of zero discharge of pollutants may not represent the best use of the societal resources available for water resource management.

The technology of increasing the available quantity of water for its various uses is generally well developed. Storage, withdrawal and return facilities, conveyance facilities, and pumped-storage facilities are in this category.

Surface storage is a multiple-purpose device that may serve up to five possible withdrawal needs (publicly supplied water, industrial self-supplied water, rural water, irrigation, and power plant cooling), and may serve up to eight instream needs (navigation, hydroelectric power generation, water recreation, fish and wildlife, visual and cultural values, health, flood damage reduction, and water quality maintenance). Technology for storing water is

TABLE 7-8. Efficiency and Costs at Various Levels of Municipal Wastewater Treatment

Treatment level	Overall percentage removal			Approximate marginal cost ($) lb/day organic matter removed[a]
	Organic matter	Dissolved salts	Phosphorus	
I—Conventional treatment	60–85	5	10	400
II—Advanced[b] treatment	95	15	95	2200
III—Advanced[c] treatment	99	50	99	5800

[a] Present value dollars = 7% − 25 years + 25% at each level for contingencies.
[b] Level II—conventional plant and coagulation and absorption.
[c] Level III—Level II and electrodialysis.

well established. Reservoir and dam designs can be varied to meet a variety of needs at once while minimizing adverse impacts. But such structures are large in relation to their surroundings and may have significant esthetic, ecological, or cultural impacts.

There appear to be no significant technologic advances that are likely to change major storage facilities. Storage facilities are most beneficial under an economic-development objective, because they most easily aid economic activities. Under an environmental-quality objective the costs of these facilities are high, since they disrupt environmental resources, and they are generally limited in this use.

Water intake and return facilities are required for any withdrawal need. The primary sources of withdrawals are rivers, lakes, estuaries, the ocean, or groundwater. River and lake intakes will be the primary device to fulfill freshwater needs.

Wells tapping groundwater resources are likely to increase in use in some parts of the basin. This source of water is very site dependent. A complete management approach is needed, since there is a direct relationship between surface and groundwater, and because there is a serious saltwater intrusion danger in Long Island, where groundwater is the major water supply source. Groundwater recharge is used there now and should see increasing use in the future.

The weirs, intakes, pumping stations, and wells that remove surface or groundwater from its natural conveyance are quite efficient, and future technology would provide only marginal efficiency gains. In the field of site-specific design, however, greater improvements are possible. Devices to return water to surface-water bodies are similarly a part of a fully developed technology. Effects here are also localized and site specific. Quality control of the returned waters is a major problem. Devices to return water to the ground (recharge facilities) are part of a developing technology. The problem here is more of applying known technology than developing a new one. Significant improvements in water-return technology appear feasible and their application is practical. The environmental impacts of such devices are significant, visually because of their size and extent, and ecologically because of their changing the groundwater level and water quality. Withdrawal and return facilities are compatible with most all objectives.

Every time water withdrawal occurs, conveyance facilities (e.g., tunnels, pumped-storage devices, pipelines) are required to transport the water to the point of use. Water conveyance technology is used within localized systems and over long distances connecting basins and distant regions. Techological advances in tunneling methods are likely in the near future, making tunnel construction faster and cheaper. These changes would reduce the local environmental impacts of large conveyance devices. Also, pumped-storage devices may emerge as a future mechanism for water supply (in addition to meeting power needs) if proper environmental impact considerations are part of the plan.

Three basic methods of flood damage reduction are applicable within the Hudson Basin region. They are reducing flood peaks by reservoirs and watershed management, keeping streams away from damageable property by local engineering works, and managing the use of floodplains. The last one should be considered first, but each has a place in the development of flood control plans. Reservoirs for flood control are likely to be multipurpose and to serve other water needs as well. Thus, the discussion of dam and reservoir technology is equally applicable under this rubric.

Watershed management is used to help meet the needs of fish and wildlife, visual and cultural values, upstream flood-damage reduction, and drainage control. It also aids in decreasing sedimentation in streams and rivers and in managing wildlife. Watershed management is directed toward reducing overland water flow and runoff, and increasing water interception, infiltration, and soil-moisture storage. The specific devices include small floodwater-detention facilities and various land management practices. These management practices include crop rotation, terracing, contour-strip cropping, selective planting of cover crops, wildlife habitat development, selective timber harvest and logging, reforestation, and control of grazing, fire, and insects. This device is used for all drainage control needs as a complement to drainage practices. Although the technology for this type of management is rather new, it is well established and rather stable.

Channeling, levees, small holding reservoirs, bypass channels, and drainage systems are several of the devices included in local flood protection projects. These devices are used alone or in combination with reservoirs and floodplain management to fulfill upstream and mainstream flood-damage reduction needs. These devices are also used to fulfill tidal and hurricane flood-damage reduction needs. The technology used to protect flood hazard areas by local works is an old one. There is little likelihood of improvements other than the use of new materials or construction techniques. Local flood protection structures are site specific, and improvements can be made by designs appropriate to the location and its specific problems.

Nonstructural

Floodplain management tools include mapping, zoning, land purchases, insurance, taxes, landscaping, leasing, floodproofing, emergency warning systems, and other measures. These tools are under local, state, and federal jurisdiction. They can be applied in various combinations to assist in meeting upstream and downstream flood-damage reduction needs, as well as visual and cultural, water recreation, and fish and wildlife needs. The technology of flood-proofing measures is well developed, and changes are apt to be only incremental. The land-use-control side of floodplain management is a problem of institutional change. Here, the techniques for effecting change are rudimentary at best. Floodplain management appears to be the only technology capable of reducing flood damage beyond the limits imposed (for many reasons) on flood control structures.

Although most of the Hudson Basin has sufficient water available, the practical limits of resource development are being approached. The time has come to initiate demand management as a real alternative. Changes in demand are the ultimate and, in the very long range, the only permanent solutions to some water demand problems. On the basis of past experience, however, the prospects for large advances in demand reduction or reallocation in the near future are not reassuring. Reduction of water use through changes in technological processes in heavy water-using industries has already had some impact on demands, and can be expected to produce significant improvements in the future. Tandem use of water—the use of high-grade water for some activity and the reuse of its degraded effluents for another activity that can accept lower grade water—is beginning to be of importance. Planning for the reuse of wastewaters after treatment is also progressing, and a few such plants are in operation for municipal and industrial supplies throughout the world.

There are still significant risks involved in reuse of water. Full-scale prototype plants are needed to develop design and operational criteria. The near and mid-range future will see improvements and increased application of water reuse technology.

Pricing and rationing have so far met with little, and usually only temporary, success in changing demand. Techniques to induce change in people's views on water use and to induce change in institutional arrangements controlling water demand are generally lacking, and the near future, at least, does not appear bright. Restriction of demand growth through population and economic development limits are techniques of uncertain acceptability. Metering, however, is a basic necessity for all demand-control technologies. Although it probably has little influence on demand in itself, simple equity requires its use.

The impacts of demand reduction on the natural environment would generally be zero. But the cultural impacts would be significant, and in the long run would force basic changes in life style and resource consumption. In the short run, demand constraints are likely to conflict with regional development objectives while significantly complementing the environmental quality objective. In the long run, they are likely to be the most important steps toward the solution of water resources problems, and compatible with all objectives.

Tools of Implementation

A wide variety of means can be used by public authorities to implement water resource goals. Generally, these means are categorized as prohibition, regulation, taxes, subsidies, and direct government provision of services.

Prohibition   Government (federal, state, or local) can prohibit the discharge of any residual into water bodies. Any individual or group disregarding the prohibition would be subject to payment of some penalty (possibly including imprisonment). Whereas this is apparently a most simple solution, there are numerous questions that must be confronted. What will be the impact on the total environment? Will prohibited discharges find their way into the environment through increased air pollution or solid waste? Is this the most efficient, or least expensive solution to water pollution, or are there better alternatives? The usual difficulty with "blanket" prohibition is that it is all-inclusive and general, and thus may be more costly than society needs or is willing to bear.

Regulation   Perhaps the most widely used technique of policy implementation in the United States is the system of regulation and enforcement. Control agencies directly regulate discharges and withdrawals from water bodies, using the police power of the state to enforce their regulations. Tools of enforcement include injunctions, fines, permits, licenses, seizure, and zoning. Regulation and enforcement are carried out through administrative agencies, where the actual enforcement process usually involves a bargaining situation.

Taxes and Charges   One of the traditional means by which public authority attempts to influence private economic behavior is through taxes. Taxes might be used to discourage activities considered harmful to public goods. In the area of water pollution, a tax may be imposed on the polluter to discourage the production of the undesirable discharge. A user charge may be viewed as a more specific type of direct tax, a tax whose payment is related directly to the amount of service utilized. For an effluent charge, the size of payment is based on the amount of discharge into the receiving media. For water charges, the payment is based on the amount of water withdrawn from the system. It is possible to devise a whole set of user charges based on additions to, or withdrawals from, the environment.

User charges have gained great support among economists as a policy tool. Effluent charges become another cost of production, and producers will take steps necessary to reduce this cost and pass it on to the consumer. Increases in the product price may affect the ultimate demand for the finished product, and in this manner the final price of the product more accurately reflects both the private and social costs (pollution costs) of production. Hence the supply and the demand for the product are affected. For the individual, in the case of water-use charges, the process is similar. Faced with a payment more accurately reflecting the costs of the production and distribution of water, the consumer will alter his consumption patterns to reflect actual costs and satisfactions more accurately.

Another feature of the user charge that makes it appear advantageous to economists is that once the bargaining process has established the base and the rate for charges, the imposition of the charge and the amount of the payment no longer rest on political bargaining, as with regulation, but operate in an impersonal manner. This automatic mechanism precludes tax avoidance, or relaxing of penalties, because of the unequal political or economic bargaining strength of the polluter. Examples of user charges include effluent charges, water charges, sewage treatment charges, and user charges for public recreation.

Subsidies   Subsidies are another traditional form of public intervention to influence private activities. They have been widely used to encourage individuals and firms to refrain from various undesirable actions. To prevent water pollution, the state may pay potential polluters not to produce offending discharges. In the more common case, subsidies are used to help defray the costs of pollution abatement as an inducement for action. Public subsidies may take numerous forms, including grants, loans, tax reductions, leases, and research.

7.4   Issues Affecting Water Resources Management

Defining Water Resources Issues

The term *issue*, as used in this chapter, refers to unresolved decisions, i.e., to an area of decision-making in which the choices have been identified but not acted upon. Nine broad categories of issues have been identified. They are not necessarily unique to the Hudson Basin, nor are they intended as a taxonomy of water resources issues. They are, however, considered to be of particular significance to the basin.

These issue categories provide a basis for defining research priorities in reference to water resources management. Each issue is discussed in detail in the following paragraphs and is ranked to determine its relative research priority (Table 7-9) using the following criteria:

1. The issue represents an area of general public concern; there is a significant level of public interest.

TABLE 7-9.   Research Priorities in Water Resources Management[a]

Issue categories	Public concern	Chance of success	Implications of wrong decision	Insufficient present progress
1. Demographic and economic growth versus protection of water resources and related environmental values	H	M	H	M
2. Definition of water quality objectives	L	M	M	L
3. Efficiency in implementation of water quality objectives	L	L	H	L
4. Allocation of water resources among competing users	M	L	M	L
5. Coordination of water-related land uses with water resource objectives	M	M	H	H
6. Institutional structure for regulating overall basin development	L	L	M	H
7. Equity in the distribution of water-related benefits	M	L	H	H
8. Data base for water resource planning	L	H	M	M
9. Water-oriented recreation	H	M	L	M

[a] Abbreviations used: H, high; M, moderate; and L, low or none.

   2. The problems resulting from the issue are amenable to present and anticipated analysis frameworks, and there is a reasonable chance of success in arriving at "solutions."
   3. The implications of a "wrong" decision in resolving the issue are significant as measured in quantitative (dollar) and/or qualitative (amenity) terms.

A review of the interactions indicated in Table 7-9 suggests the following priorities for research. It should be pointed out, however, that low priority in this list is simply the lowest of a set of nine high-priority categories.

The highest priority categories are demographic and economic growth versus protection of water resources and environmental values; coordination of water-related land use with water resource objectives; and equity in the distribution of water-related benefits. Somewhat less important (moderate) priorities include institutional structures for regulating overall basin development; a data base for water resources planning; and water-oriented recreation. Definition of water quality objectives, efficiency in implementation of water quality objectives, and allocation of water resources among competing users are considered low-priority categories.

Issue Categories

Demographic and Economic Growth versus Protection of Water Resources and Related Environmental Values

The Hudson River basin may well become a test case for attempts to resolve the clash between the growth ethic and the newer environmental ethic. The former is still deeply embedded in our society and is, in fact, promoted by the constitutionally recognized rights of people to travel and settle wherever they please. In the absence of any new national policy on the subject, no region or locality in this country is entitled to set limits on the degree of growth it will tolerate. But unrestricted development will sooner or later deplete water supplies, degrade water quality, and destroy water-related scenic and recreational amenities, along with other environmental values.

Advanced technologies for water resource management can postpone and mitigate these conflicts, but only within limits of ingenuity and acceptable cost. The question, therefore, becomes whether the two competing ethics can be reconciled. There has been much talk of "striking a balance" between them, but this is neutral phraseology that merely restates the question. The objective must be to move beyond generalities to substantive commitments.

It may be possible to devise regulatory institutions and processes that will preserve environmental values by channeling, rather than throttling, development. The Adirondack Park Agency, for example, is currently attempting to fulfill this role for the entire Park area. The price of such a strategy, however, may well be substantial loss of local autonomy and individual freedom with respect to land use—a third major value that must also be taken into account. It is really a tripolar conflict. How to resolve it in a legally and politically acceptable fashion will be a question worthy of sustained future inquiry.

Definition of Water Quality Objectives

Under the Federal Water Pollution Control Act (FWPCA), as amended by the Federal Water Quality Act of 1965, states were largely free to designate different uses and corresponding target levels of water quality for different stretches of water, and to allocate accordingly the burdens of waste reduction among dischargers, consistent with certain minimum standards of treatment. Within limits, the carriage and assimilation of wastes were recognized as legitimate uses of receiving waters. However, the limits received little, if any, definition by sources other than the discharger. The task of the water quality planner is to define and implement those limits consistently with other uses for which a stretch might be designated. Theoretically, at least, the water quality standard represented a point of equilibrium between the marginal cost of further waste reduction and the marginal benefits to be obtained thereby.

The 1972 Amendments to the FWPCA inaugurated a radical shift away from the foregoing approach. The goals to which the 1972 Act ostensibly commits the nation are (a) restoration of the chemical, physical, and biological integrity of all water; and (b) elimination of all discharges of pollutants into navigable waters by 1985. In addition, an interim goal prescribed to be achieved by 1983 is (c) sufficient water quality everywhere to protect fish and wildlife and to support water-based recreation. Use of waterways for waste disposal will hereafter be tolerated only until technology makes possible the elimination of that use. "Assimilative capacity" is no longer an acceptable concept. Whatever degree of water pollution control is technologically attainable must ultimately be implemented, regardless of cost. Evidently, the benefits of zero discharge are deemed to be worth more than whatever it may cost to achieve them. A reasonable question for the public to ask in 1985 will be, What have we achieved for this expenditure and what will we continue to achieve at the ongoing operation and maintenance costs?*

But the 1985 goals are not yet operating standards. Indeed, the National Study Commission established under Sec. 315(a) of the 1972 Act has been now inquiring whether even the more modest water quality goals set for 1983 can be achieved by technologically based effluent limitations calling for "best available technology economically achievable" to treat industrial wastes and for "best practicable waste-treatment technology over the life of the works" for municipal wastes. The commission reported to Congress in 1975 on "all aspects of the total economic, social, and environmental effects" of attaining or not attaining such limitations, which fall short of zero discharge. For the present, the commitments toward the 1983 and 1985 goals can be viewed as conditional.

*The 1985 "zero-discharge" objective was not altered by the 1977 Federal Water Pollution Control Act Amendments. The 1977 legislation does, however, allow communities greater flexibility in the choice of pollution control technologies. In addition, it permits the continuation of certain marine discharges if it can be shown that they do not significantly degrade receiving waters. [Ed.]

The uncertainty is compounded, moreover, by the difficulty of defining "integrity" of waters and "zero discharge." It may be impossible to return any waterway to the condition it was in some centuries ago—if that could even be known. And does "zero discharge" imply the absence of any residue, or only of any residue that interferes with a receiving-water use? What is a pollutant? Is it solely a residue in a waste discharge or is it a residue that interferes with a water use? Is a pollutant's hydraulic residence time a sufficient measure of its presence or absence in the waterway, or should its chemical residence time be measured as a more relevant parameter?

Water quality objectives, then, are still in need of definition, and some flexibility may be allowed in undertaking the task. For some parameters, within limits and with various degrees of certainty, it is possible to plot instream waste concentrations against marginal benefits in terms of uses, and to identify a few critical threshold points along the spectrum. Perhaps this approach makes sense for waters that are already grossly polluted, that cannot be restored to their physical or biological "integrity" except at exorbitant cost, but that can sensibly be improved by incremental steps. For pristine waters, on the other hand, a strict antidegradation policy might well be justified. In any event, there is a need to reexamine the *purposes* of water pollution control from all relevant perspectives—practical as well as idealistic—and to specify defensible goals with particular reference to the Hudson River basin.

Efficiency in Implementation of Water Quality Objectives

Technologically based treatment standards are now being prescribed for all point sources, despite the absence of reliable indications that the prescribed treatment will improve water quality sufficiently to realize desired uses. Advanced treatment (i.e., secondary) plants everywhere may not be the most cost-effective strategy. For example, an advanced secondary treatment plant on the West Side of Manhattan may not have been the best way to spend the $700 or $800 million that became available for cleaning up the lower Hudson.

The issue is whether cost-effective strategies can be identified and acted upon. Their identification depends on having better information than is currently available concerning both costs and impacts of alternative control strategies. Even if the most efficient strategy could be identified, its implementation may be foreclosed by rigid federal requirements. For example, EPA will not permit primary treatment at at one location even if it was balanced by tertiary treatment at another, nor construction of swimming pools instead of treatment works designed to make the river itself swimmable again. Finally, there are bureaucratic/institutional obstacles to accepting cost effectiveness as a guiding principle for decision-making, particularly when the supporting data are incomplete or useless—as they inevitably are in many respects. "Cost-effectiveness" is now a fashionable term in water quality management. What are the prospects for applying it to the Hudson?

Allocation among Competing Uses

Up to now, water resources in the Hudson River basin have been sufficient to satisfy all demands upon them, virtually without limit. Such abundance cannot be expected to last indefinitely, however. Continuing demographic and economic growth in the basin is bound to cause scarcities of supply and competition among desired uses, each of which makes its own demands upon the resource in terms of quality, quantity, time, and place.

Competition between Instream and Take-Out Uses   The heavier the demands of New York City on the Hudson River and its tributaries for water supply, the further upstream the salt water intrudes, interfering with the freshwater component. Moreover, those demands accentuate low flows in the northerly tributaries, thereby interfering with recreational and aesthetic uses and possibly affecting the stability of the biological system. Instream pollution from a variety of waste sources requires treatment on intake for freshwater uses. High degrees of waste treatment before discharge, followed by return of treated effluents to upstream reentry points for flow augmentation, could mitigate these conflicts, but only at great expense.

Competition among Instream Uses   The Hudson is an unusually navigable river, and transportation by water supports the economy of the basin while consuming less energy than other modes. But navigation can interfere with recreational and other uses. Recreational uses themselves, such as motorboating and fishing, may also conflict with one another. Stream zoning may be a desirable technique for regulating such conflicts.

From Albany down, the river is water-quality limited—i.e., achievement of the prescribed, technologically based, effluent limitations will still fall short of meeting acceptable water quality standards, so they must be supplemented by further control measures. The nation is committed to eliminating all discharges that interfere with freshwater uses, but the costs of doing so, in terms of both higher degrees of waste control and possible brakes on development, may prove unacceptable, at least in the short run. It may therefore be necessary to strike tentative balances between restricted use of the waterway for waste disposal and other instream (as well as take-out) uses.

Competition among Take-Out Uses   Waters in the Croton area are currently committed for New York City's water supply. But the Croton area, as it develops, may lay claim to the same supply. Such conflict would be avoided or reduced if the city took its water instead directly from the lower Hudson ("flood-skimming") and treated it intensively upon intake, or imported additional water from outside the basin.

The Issue   How should these problems of allocation be resolved? The suggestions offered above are only a beginning; they will have to be explored, along with many other possibilities. On the procedural side, part of the answer may lie in development of (a) criteria for decision-making, including practical ways of applying the principles of Pareto optimality and equity between upstream and downstream interests; (b) criteria for distributing the costs of making the resource available for one or another use; and (c) authoritative institutional processes for making and implementing allocational policies that satisfy criteria of efficiency and equity. Would it be desirable to vest in a single institution the functions of regulating both water quality and water quantity?

Coordination of Water-Related Land Use with Water Resource Objectives

A river physically reflects and derives its cultural significance from the uses that are made of riparian and other lands in the watershed. Viewing the land around the Hudson River, one can readily identify the following needs:

1. Urban waterfront renewal: restoration of the waterfront as a major element of urban design
2. Preservation of open space for access to the river, aesthetic enjoyment of it, and recreation alongside it
3. Identification and preservation of unique and/or special-value areas such as wild and scenic rivers
4. Restrictions of development on critical water-related lands such as wetlands, groundwater recharge areas, riparian properties, and steep tributary slopes
5. Restrictions of highways, railroad tracks, and bridges that cut access to the river, disrespect its function as a natural barrier, and spur unregulated development in its vicinity
6. Restrictions on power-transmission-line crossings in areas where they constitute major conflicts with aesthetic and social values
7. Performance standards for controlling nonpoint-source pollution from various types of development or activity on land
8. Maintenance of the diversity of existing land uses that contribute to the aesthetic values of the rivers
9. Control of increased uses of waters for recreation so that water quality and amenity values of related lands are not reduced (e.g., traffic-generated pollutants or uncontrolled land development)

As the Storm King case lets nobody forget, the siting of power plants in the basin is also a problem, in part because of their impact on water quality and water-related scenic values. New sites may also have to be acquired for water storage. Should they be permitted to include land that is now open, recreational, or wild?

Despite the recognized need to coordinate water resources with land use planning, no effective coordinating mechanisms have yet been fully tested in this or any basin. Generally, land use decisions continue to disregard water use objectives and water-related impacts. Section 208 of the FWPCA (PL 92-500) requires establishment of regional programs for regulating the location of any facility that may result in wastewater discharges and for controlling polluted runoff from nonpoint sources. No such program yet exists in the Hudson River basin, nor is there any mechanism for ensuring that the locations and capacities of new wastewater management facilities (or facilities of any other kind) will conform to any regional land use and development plans.

How to harmonize decision-making in the respective areas of land use and water resource management is an institutional issue of great sensitivity. State or regional controls over land use in relation to water use may be desirable, but will local governments ever willingly relinquish their traditional autonomy in matters of land use within their borders? If mutually exclusive local governmental controls are no longer acceptable, then what is the most appropriate allocation of functions, powers, and duties among the different levels of government concerned? These and similar questions need to be explored in detail.

Regionwide Institutional Structures for Regulating Overall Basin Development Consistent with Environmental Standards

A Hudson River Basin Authority might be the most efficient vehicle for managing water quality, water supply, and, possibly, related land use in the basin. But can such an authority be structured to ensure adequate local representation on its governing bodies and accountability to the public? Even if it could be so structured, is there any likelihood of its gaining political acceptance? Localities in the basin will fear loss of sovereignty to it; state agencies will fear loss of regulatory control over it. Moreover, it may be inadvisable to vest powers over both water and land use throughout the basin in any one agency. On the other hand, if the authority's functions are confined to water, it may become too specialized an agency, to the detriment of other environmental and economic values.

One possibility that needs to be explored is the division of the entire basin into perhaps six or eight regions, each with its own coordinated set of regional planning and environmental management agencies. If local communities are to lose their autonomy over land and water uses of extralocal impact—as inevitably they must—participation in a regional entity may be the least unpalatable alternative to them.

The major questions comprising this issue are (a) whether there are sound bases for regionalization, considering socioeconomic, hydrologic, and other factors; (b) how regional government should be structured and defined to reflect both local interests from below and state and federal mandates from above; and (c) how interregional coordination will be achieved on matters of basinwide or transregional significance.

Equity in the Distribution of Water-Related Benefits

Many factors enter into the consideration of the equity of the distribution of water-related benefits, including those of geography or location, the socioeconomic characteristics of the populations to be served, and the planners' assumptions about the needs, attitudes, and preferences of these populations. The locations of population concentrations, and the locations of water of suitable quality and quantity for municipal uses or of potential sites for its storage, are disparate. An impoundment site in an upstream community, for example, may be valued by the members of that community for its wilderness or recreation qualities more than for its potential to help alleviate downstream municipal water demands.

The planning for water-oriented recreational opportunities and other amenities has frequently assumed a univariant set of needs, attitudes, and preferences for all sectors of society regardless of socioeconomic status or ethnic background. But these benefits are not equally available to all sectors and, in fact, favor those with greater economic well-being. Access to waterfronts in urban settings, for example, is clearly easier for those capable of paying the high rents of waterfront or waterview apartments.

This issue is to devise ways of compensating local communities for the social and aesthetic cost, as well as the economic costs, which they incur in providing out-of-community benefits. Also, the assumption about a univariant set of needs, attitudes, and preferences must be investigated. If the assumption is confirmed, the task will be to devise means of providing equal opportunity of access; if not confirmed, it will be to satisfy the diversity of needs and preferences of different socioeconomic and ethnic populations.

Data Base for Water Resource Planning

An improved and statistically relevant data base and information system are needed to meet the predictive requirements of the National Environmental Policy Act of 1969 and to satisfy the 1973 Water Resources Council Standards and Guidelines for planning. The National Environmental Policy Act (NEPA) requires that the environmental impact of every major project be assessed, and the standards and guidelines subsequently adopted under NEPA require an accounting of economic as well as environmental costs and benefits. Several significant issues can be identified: (a) what resource data are required, and at what time intervals, to describe the water system and to develop a predictive model for impacts on water quality; (b) what resource data are required and what system is to be used to measure environmental costs (i.e., aesthetic costs) and benefits; and (c) how reliable, and how prescriptive or descriptive, are the population and economic projections used in water resource planning?

Water-Oriented Recreation

Water is a primary attraction for outdoor recreational activities. Whether it is valued as a component of a scenic view from a hiking trail or roadway, or as a setting for contact activities such as swimming or water skiing, it is probably the single most important natural resource recreational use in the Hudson Basin. It is used for active and passive sport and is the magnet for resort and second-home developments.

Conflicts exist, however, among water-oriented recreational activities and between recreational and other users of water. Examples of conflicts include the following. (a) There are differences in movement and rates of speed between commercial-user traffic and recreational boating. (b) Highways, railroads, and other forms of development along waterways prevent public access to the water for recreational users. (c) Poor or mediocre water quality adjacent to major metropolitan areas precludes use for contact activities. (d) Facilities for contact forms of water-oriented recreation are frequently remote from major concentrations of users and are primarily accessible only to those with private automobiles. (e) Regulation of upstream waterways for flood-control purposes or downstream water supply conflicts with or alters existing recreational patterns of use.

7.5   Selected Examples of Significant Issues

Introduction

This section illustrates the points and issues raised in the preceding discussion. Goals, objectives, issues, and applicable technology, together with the interrelationship of water policy and other policy areas, become real and tangible in specific examples. The six examples discussed below reflect the criteria given in Section 7.4 for assigning priorities to issues for further investigation. There is no intention in this brief review to explore each area in minute detail. Rather, the aim is to provide an overview of goals, issues, available controls, and alternative futures.

The Issue of Water Quality in the Lower Hudson River and in the New York Bight

Introduction

This example illustrates several of the issues outlined in Section 7.4. Specifically, the example addresses the issue categories of (a) the definition of water quality objectives; (b) efficiency in implementation of water quality objectives; and (c) allocation of the water resource among competing uses. In addition, the example touches on most of the other issues, including the difficulty of the present institutional structure to assess adequately and implement a rational and cost-efficient water quality improvement program. But more importantly, the water quality in the lower Hudson provides a real-life setting for the issue of equity in the distribution of water-related benefits (see Section 7.4). As shown below, meaningful and penetrating questions can be asked about the present direction of expenditures for water pollution control. Are such expenditures aimed in the direction of improving the environment for a relatively small affluent sector of society? Should such expenditures be directed toward water pollution control programs (such as specific control technology to open up new bathing beaches), which would benefit a much larger, albeit less affluent and therefore less vocal, sector of the society?

Area

The region considered in this issue is the Hudson River from about Tarrytown, New York, south, including New York Harbor and extending out to the New York Bight, i.e., the offshore region from Montauk Point, Long Island, to Cape May, New Jersey. The lower 30 miles of the Hudson River represent the general area of water quality depression as a result of waste inputs and urban runoff from the metropolitan area. Figure 7-1 shows a schematic of the area and the general problem setting.

General Issue

The primary problem in this area of the Hudson Basin is the poor quality of water resulting from the discharge of significant amounts of wastes from metropolitan New York and New Jersey. Further complications exist because of the interaction of waste removal programs in the Harbor area proper, and the disposal of residues resulting from such treatment into the New York Bight.

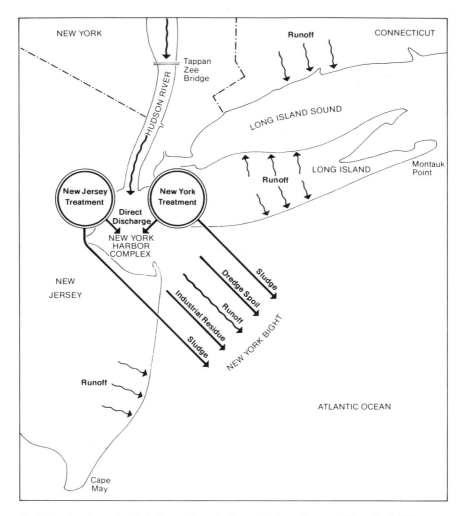

Fig. 7-1. A schematic of discharges into the lower Hudson River and New York Bight.

Present expenditures for residuals control in the region are significant: over $920 million in capital construction costs in New York alone, of which $774 million is for the plant on the West Side in New York City. In addition to expenditures of this order for conventional treatment, suggestions are also being made for further degrees of treatment to reduce nutrient discharges from the plants as well as to stop the discharge of residual sewage sludges into the New York Bight. One of the more important questions then is, What is a reasonable overall water quality management plan for this area—a plan that views the region as an integrated whole and a plan that properly reflects the technical and economic complexities of the problem? This question takes on an added urgency when one examines the projected costs for this area to, say, the year 2000, a reasonable 25-year time horizon. For secondary treatment alone, it has been estimated that about $2.7 billion in capital costs will be required (U.S. Water Quality Office, 1972). Simply stated then, the general issue is to ensure that these moneys are wisely spent, i.e., that the decision-makers at all levels are fully aware of the consequences of proposed water pollution control programs.

Specific Issues

New York Harbor Water Quality   Numerous studies have examined the water quality of the New York Harbor area. Water quality data of a traditional variety are abundant, although data on variables representing more recent concerns are somewhat lacking. In the latter category are data on biological communities, nutrients, and metals. At present, approximately 1.4 million pounds per day of organic matter (BOD) are discharged into the entire Harbor region. Additional quantities of other substances, such as heavy metals and nutrients, are also discharged. For example, about 295,000 pounds of total nitrogen per day and 200,000 pounds of total phosphorus per day are discharged in this area (Tofflemire and Hetling, 1969).

Various water-use goals have been established for the area, including swimming and protection of biological life. The latter objective has been translated into a dissolved oxygen standard of greater than 50% saturation at all times (DO of about 3.9 mg/liter). Other quality criteria are also associated with the goal of improving and maintaining a "balanced" ecosystem. The technology applied to date was first concentrated on treatment of point sources. As indicated above, these controls have involved substantial expenditures. Only recently has attention been directed toward controlling combined sewer overflows, as for example, in the Spring Creek project on Jamaica Bay in New York City. Recent water pollution legislation requires even higher degrees of waste treatment over the next 15 years. Such treatment includes advanced processes to remove nutrients and other substances. The question at this point then is, Should additional levels of waste treatment be required for point sources or should selected environmental controls (e.g., local combined sewer overflow treatment and control) be used to maximize water use? This directly relates to the issue of equity in distributing the benefits of water quality management.

The consequences of demanding advanced treatment levels and subsequently discovering that such a decision was "wrong" can be substantial.

At a projected waste discharge level of, say, 2000 mgd, the added capital costs to go to advanced treatment may be about $1 billion, with annual operation cost of $100 million, not including the cost of borrowing. At present, there appears to be a deficiency in the application of available analysis technologies to answer the question posed above in a comprehensive way. For example, expenditure of $1 billion may only marginally improve the sport fishery, which is largely a middle and upper-class activity. One reason for this is the increasing importance of discharges from combined sewers and from uncontrolled urban runoff. Should such an expenditure be made to benefit that sector of society, or should attention be directed toward local control to open up beaches, which would benefit the economically deprived sector of the society? A *rough* estimate of the improvement in dissolved oxygen in New York Harbor waters indicates that we could expect an increase of about 0.1 to 0.3 mg/liter at advanced levels of treatment. Is this worth the expenditure? How do we decide?

The New York Bight   This region, encompassing the offshore waters from Montauk Point, Long Island, to Cape May, New Jersey, has been a topic of extensive and increasingly heated discussion in recent years. (The New York Bight is a general concavity or indentation in the coastline that is considered a type of large open bay.) At present, about 13,000 cubic yards per day of sewage sludge is dumped in the New York Bight, about 10 miles equidistant from the New Jersey and Long Island shorelines, in water depths of not less than 72 feet (Buelow, 1968). This represents about one million pounds of solids discharged per day. There are also several treatment plants now under design or construction in the New York metropolitan area that will generate additional solids as part of the treatment process. For example, the completion of the West Side plant for New York City at a flow of 200 mgd will generate an additional 300 to 500,000 pounds of solids per day. This interaction, schematically depicted in Fig. 7-1, is important. It represents a trade-off between removal of solids now being discharged by the river into New York Harbor and transporting these reduced and digested solids to the New York Bight.

These solids are, of course, high in bacteria concentration, organic matter, and, in some cases, heavy metals. For the most part, however, these solids have been treated by the anaerobic digestion process, which breaks down the initial raw-sewage solids into more innocuous products. But this is only one step in the possible sequence of technologies that might be applied to handle this sewage sludge. The bacteria in the wastes have been cited as a possible source of contamination of shellfish, and the organic material has contributed to the depletion of dissolved oxygen in the offshore waters immediately over the dump site (Buelow, 1968). The metals in the sludge have been implicated as possible biological toxicants. For example, the load from New York City sludges from January 1972 to September 1973 was 950 pounds per day of copper, 600 pounds per day of chromium, and 50 pounds per day of cadmium, among other metals. However, as carefully documented by Klein et al. (1974), one should put these numbers into the proper perspective that recognizes the other sources of metal discharged into the New York Bight.

As indicated in Table 7-10, the sewage sludge contains, on average, only about 15% of the total mass of the five metals discharged to the region. The difficulty, of course, is that the 15% is discharged into an area that has only a limited assimilative capacity. This may result in localized degradation in terms of high metals concentration in bottom-dwelling organisms. The organic matter in the sludge may also contribute to low dissolved oxygen values and to possible sources of bacterial and/or viral infections.

In addition to the sewage sludge being dumped into the Bight, industrial acid wastes of about three to four million gallons are discharged on an average schedule of about 1.6 trips per day. These industrial wastes are now under temporary dumping permit under the 1972 Marine Protection Research and Sanctuaries Act (PL 92-532). It is now clear, however, that unless an industry can demonstrate conclusively to the Environmental Protection Agency the necessity for ocean dumping, the permit will not be renewed.

Finally, about nine million tons per year of dredge spoil from the New York area are discharged into the Bight with possible effects on bottom-dwelling aquatic organisms. Portions of this dredge spoil from the inner New York Harbor areas are mixed with raw sewage discharged from sewers and from overflows from combined sewers.

In the light of this background, what is the issue? Why not just promulgate an edict banning all discharge of material into the ocean? The issue is simply stated: If not in the ocean, where? The question of sewage solids merely reflects the principle of the conservation of mass. It is not clear that the discharge of *properly treated* sewage sludge in the ocean need be detrimental. For example, what is the trade-off between further treatment of the sludges (e.g., high-pressure oxidation) with subsequent ocean disposal and incineration?* What are the air pollution and local social problems attendant on building large sewage-sludge incinerators? (Land disposal of sewage sludge in the New York metropolitan area is essentially infeasible because of the large amounts of land required.) The issue, then, is to examine critically all the technologies available for coping with the solids problem in the Bight and to examine dispassionately the feasibility of continued discharge of

---

*Under a 1977 amendment to the Marine Protection, Research, and Sanctuaries Act, ocean disposal of sewage sludge must end by December 31, 1981. [Ed.]

TABLE 7-10.   Metals Discharged into New York Harbor and the New York Bight from
Various Sources[a]

Metal	Pounds per day from				Percentage sludge in total mass
	Plant effluents	Sewage sludge	Runoff	Untreated sewage	
Copper	1410	950	1990	980	18
Chromium	780	600	690	570	23
Nickel	930	145	650	430	7
Zinc	2520	1360	6920	1500	11
Cadmium	95	50	110	60	16

[a] Adapted from Klein et al. (1974).

sludge at sea in the light of the other available technological, social, economic, and political alternatives.

Water Resources Issues in Rural Regions of the Hudson Basin

The Problem Setting

The Hudson Basin covers much of the northern and eastern sections of New York State and small areas of Vermont, Massachusetts, Connecticut, and New Jersey. It is an area of great natural beauty and many of its rural regions offer resources for recreation and potential second-home development not found in many places throughout the nation. However, growing populations, often seasonal, have resulted in demands for advanced technology and an expanded economy that impose increase pressure on these native resources.

Specific Issues

Benefits are usually seen initially from second-home developments. Upsurges in economic activities occur throughout the particular locale. These are possibly due to factors such as the construction of the new homes themselves, the demand for various building components, and the demand for an increased number of skilled workers. Such benefits, however, are often short-lived; secondary effects begin to appear which are not beneficial and tend to be more long-term. One of these is the rather exaggerated demand it created for land, water supply, and high-quality water. The price of land becomes vastly increased in these areas, especially where the predevelopment price is very modest. This results in an adverse impact on the local population, who are generally lower to lower-middle income people. Further conflicts arise because of the lower purchasing power of the majority of people in the local communities compared with the resources of the second-home owner.*

Second-home development creates jobs, but these are primarily in the service industries (e.g., house cleaning, yard care, road maintenance), which are traditionally rather low paying and usually seasonal. What happens is that a few prosper at the expense of many. The few who do usually are those who need financial help the least—bankers, contractors, chain stores, professional people, and the developers.

The relationship between water supply and proposed land development is evident to the developer; water quality for nonsupply uses, however, often escapes his concern. In the upper Hudson Basin, treated or untreated wastewater is discharged directly or indirectly into the soil. Since the discharge of this effluent into the soil often occurs adjacent to lakes and streams, second-home developments, which historically have been directly allied to water bodies, accelerate and further perturb the problem.

If one considers the soil-cover-to-bedrock problems throughout the upper Hudson Basin, as well as the indirect routes by which nutrients from point sources enter aquatic systems, the issues associated with water-quality debilitation from vacation homes or permanent developments are numerous. Seasonal residences rather dramatically, and often unexpectedly, increase or decrease the flow and nutrient loads to the "natural filter biosystem" associated with subsurface wastewater disposal mechanisms, thus creating the potential breakdown in treatment efficiency or capability of the system. Although engineering technology can correct these inconsistent flow patterns, and possibly upgrade the quality of the treatment process, the conflict between the developer and the quality of the aquatic resource appears to reflect the developer's scramble for economic gain with a disregard for the disbenefits to the aquatic system.

Ton-Da-Lay—A Case in Point

In Franklin County, Ton-Da-Lay, Ltd., proposed construction of a water supply and distribution system to serve 1000 acres in the northeast corner of the 18,500-acre Town of Altamont. On account of the issues raised, the commissioner of the New York State Department of Environmental Conservation at that time, Henry L. Diamond, called a hearing to assess the potential impact of this proposed second-home development.

*For further discussion of the socioeconomic impacts of second-home development, see Section 11.2. [Ed.]

Although the DEC and the DOH disagreed with the developer on some minor issues, the Sierra Club presented strong evidence that often contradicted the experts from DEC and DOH, as well as the developer, in support of its claim that water-quality despoilation, among other environmental impacts, was very probable. Not only could this have occurred from the seasonal and intermittent discharge of wastewater via the proposed septic system, but also other subsurface, nondiffuse sources of nutrient enrichment were possible and probable when the proposed development was expanded to an eventual population of nearly 20,000. Such a population would require both improved sewage-treatment facilities and the creation of an adjacent sanitary landfill for environmental, sanitary, and economic reasons alone. Owing to the terrain and soil irregularities found in this portion of the Hudson Basin, the proper development of these operations and their maintenance could be unexpectedly costly to the town and county, and the potential for rapid leachate flow to the surrounding water bodies would be greatly increased.

Obviously, many impacts can occur from any development trend, but certain impacts are likely to be neglected for longer periods, solely because of the issues associated with economic gain and so-called public necessity. Second-home developments may, in fact, be characteristic of the latter category, and it may be necessary to establish truly effective regional institutions, with regulatory as well as taxation authority, to maintain and monitor the quality of water resources in the Hudson Basin.

The Case of the New York Metropolitan Area Water Supply

The Problem Setting

The New York metropolitan area is well endowed with water resources. Major surface-water quantities are available from the Hudson, the Hackensack, the Raritan, the Passaic, the Navesink, the Sharp, and the Housatonic rivers. Major groundwater supplies are available in Long Island and along the coastal plain of New Jersey. In addition, importation from the Delaware Basin is an important resource. Average quantities appear sufficient for a long time to come. Usable safe yields are restricted by seasonal and random variations in natural flow, by pollution, and by the location of the saltwater wedge in the Hudson.

At present, the area is served by about 500 water supplies, including municipal systems, water districts, and investor-owned water companies. They range in size from the New York City system, serving over eight million people, to scores of small systems serving as few as 50 persons. The total amount delivered exceeds 2.3 billion gallons per day (bgd) on the average. Of the total of 2.3 bgd, more than 1.9 bgd are produced and delivered by the 11 largest systems in the area. Except in parts of New Jersey and on Long Island, the principal sources of water are rivers or impounded streams. The largest system in the area is that of the City of New York. The Board of Water Supply reports an average annual delivery and use of 1528 mgd. Water is collected by the Croton System, consisting of 17 lakes and reservoirs put into use between 1870 and 1911; the two reservoirs of the Catskill system, completed in 1915 and 1926, respectively; and the Delaware system, consisting of four reservoirs completed between 1951 and 1967. In addition, there is an emergency supply, first used in 1966, from a 100-mgd pumping station on the Hudson. Total usable storage in these systems is 547.5 billion gallons. Total safe yield was estimated at 1804 mgd but had to be revised downward to 1295 mgd following the 1961-1967 drought period. Thus, the present average annual use exceeds the safe yield of the system.

The Institutional Setting   The dominant water development agency in this area is the New York City Board of Water Supply. It is responsible for investigating, planning, and constructing new water supply services for New York City. Operation and maintenance are performed by the Bureau of Water Supply of the Department of Water Resources of the City of New York.

Water in highly urbanized northeastern New Jersey is distributed by a conglomeration of municipal, regional, and investor-owned companies whose service areas cross political jurisdictions. In addition, the state's Bureau of Water Supply operates state-owned water supply facilities. Ninety water supply systems operate in the area. Many sources are jointly owned and many water suppliers buy their water from other supply systems.

The bulk of the water supply in the Connecticut portion of the Hudson Basin project area is supplied by the Bridgeport Hydraulic Company, an investor-owned system.

The Dimensions of the Problem   Continued growth of the area's population and economic activities underlie the problem of water supply. Although there is considerable agreement on this fact, estimates differ on the amount and distribution of this growth. The estimates shown in Table 7-11 are those developed in the NEWS study (NEWS, 1971), based on 1965-1968 data. It should be noted that New York City, in 1971, exceeded the amounts projected for 1980. Water deficiencies, based on estimated safe yields and on the demand data on Table 7-11, are shown in Table 7-12. The deficiencies assume that Hunterdon County, New Jersey; Ulster, Dutchess, and Suffolk counties, New York; and Middlesex County, Connecticut, will solve their problems through local supplies. Other projections, both higher and lower,

TABLE 7-11. Estimated Future Water Consumption from Public Water Supply Systems[a]

County	Present		1980		2000		2020	
	Total (mgd)	Per capita (gpd)	Total (mgd)	Per capita (gpd)	Total (mgd)	Per capita (gpd)	Total (mgd)	Per capita (gpd)
New Jersey								
Bergen	79	93	111	109	162	188	220	136
Essex	135	140	158	156	209	172	274	186
Hudson	97	158	109	169	138	203	171	224
Hunterdon	2	82	4	89	7	99	13	109
Middlesex	90	183	129	180	187	189	262	197
Monmouth	38	101	63	107	116	125	180	144
Morris	28	92	52	110	100	124	154	138
Passaic	61	145	81	171	105	198	133	226
Somerset	11	84	26	134	49	146	77	150
Union	86	160	115	200	146	220	182	138
Total	626	133	848	150	1219	162	1666	175
New York								
Bronx	191	125	211	140	223	148	244	157
Kings	299	111	399	150	441	159	488	168
New York	298	190	356	225	392	242	434	264

Queens	233	119	334	161	375	169	424	178
Richmond	33	124	54	154	88	154	123	155
Total for New York City	1053	132	1354	166	1591	175	1713	185
Dutchess	16	132	25	131	47	126	82	126
Nassau	1151[b]	109	201[b]	130	248[b]	139	296[b]	148
Orange	16	118	27	112	59	112	117	117
Putnam	2.1	100	6	100	13	103	25	106
Rockland	15.6	100	23	103	23	108	47	114
Suffolk	122	150	226	151	308	157	417	167
Ulster	9.6	110	12	113	17	116	23	121
Westchester	96	115	145	139	200	149	276	159
Total New York State	1482	127	2019	154	2445	160	2996	167
Connecticut								
Fairfield	108	167	152	183	223	196	293	208
Middlesex[c]	4.2	95	7	108	14	119	20	127
New Haven[c]	100	145	127	151	180	161	122	173
Total	212	154	286	165	417	176	546	187
Total study area	2321	131	3153	154	4081	161	5208	171

[a] From NEWS (1971).
[b] Approximately 40 mgd of water used is recovered by recharging the underground aquifers in Nassau County.
[c] Part is not in the Hudson Basin Project area.

TABLE 7-12.   Water Deficiencies To Be Met by Regional
              Systems (mgd)[a]

	1980	2000	2020
New Jersey	120	400	820
New York	150	450	840
Connecticut	40	100	240
Total	310	950	1900

[a] From NEWS (1971).

have been made by other interests. These are detailed in the reports of the
State Commission on Water Supply Needs of Southeastern New York, the
Board of Water Supply of New York City, and other sources.

Specific Issues

Population and Demand Projections   The only thing that can be said
with certainty about projections is that they will not be accurate. Projections,
unlike forecasts, are extensions based on sets of assumptions that allow past
experience to be projected into the future. Three basic assumptions underlie
most of the uncertainties over the demand in the future. One is population
distribution. The second and third major uncertainties involve the per capita
use of water. Assumption two deals with the behavioral pattern of people
and their consumption habits. Views range from depending on pricing and
education for a significant and permanent reduction in per capita use to
accepting demand restrictions as a temporary crisis condition only. The third
assumption is the degree to which people in this generally humid region will
accept restrictions without pressure on the political process to redress the
shortages.

Universal Metering in New York City   Metering has long been proposed
as a device to reduce consumption, control leakage, increase revenue, and
distribute cost more equitably. There is little doubt that it may do all these
things. There is, however, the question of how great the savings in consumption would be and how large the leakage problem in New York City really is.
Metering as a management tool appears to be acceptable to all professionals. This issue is more an emotional and public relations issue than a technical one. The lack of universal metering is taken either as proof of the waste-
fulness of the city or as a sign of how well the city provides its citizens with
one of the essentials of life.

Financing of New York City Water Supply   All capital outlays for water
supply are paid for by general obligation bonds. These bonds, interest and
redemption, are paid for from real property taxes. Water bonds are not

limited by a debt ceiling and the cost of servicing them is not subject to the legal limitations of the ceiling on real estate taxes. On the other hand, operation and maintenance are paid from the general fund, which also receives all water revenues. Thus, the general fund makes an apparent profit, since revenues exceed operation and maintenance costs. These moneys are available and needed for other city uses. The result of this financing arrangement is likely to bias decisions on water projects in favor of capital-intensive, low-operating-cost schemes.

Upland versus Hudson Supply   Upland supplies are viewed as being relatively risk-free, since the water has not received wastes, and it flows to the city by gravity, thus being independent of a power supply. However, the danger of power outages is mitigated by more than 10 days of storage capacity in the Kensico Reservoir. The use, as a water source, of water that has received waste, and therefore requires treatment, would be a significant change in policy for New York City. A further possible problem could develop from the introduction of nutrient-enriched Hudson water into Kensico Reservoir. The use of Hudson water would also prohibit interconnections with supplies in Connecticut under present laws there. Connecticut regulations forbid the use of surface waters that receive wastes as sources for water supply, even after treatment. Economic, energy, conservation, and financial considerations also play a part in this issue.

The Upstate–Downstate Controversy   Since water sources lie upstate and most water use occurs downstate, there are long-standing differences between the administrations of the state and the city on issues of water supply. There is distrust and often hostility between the two groups. Upstaters see the city as a careless and rapacious devourer of state resources; the city sees the upstaters as a force seeking to control the city to the city's disadvantage. These views color the reaction to most proposals that are made by either side.

Narrow Views   The maintenance of the institutional and technological status quo is an important part of the objective functions of the existing water supply agencies. This is not because they are bad or mean but because of the rather narrow views these agencies, both public and private, have of their role. Again this is not because the legal, political, and economic realities define their roles in a narrow sense. To satisfy customers with abundant, healthy, and cheap water is the only objective that is rewarding to water suppliers in the existing system, be they public officials or managers of investor-owned water companies. These views are reinforced by the obvious past successes of this policy in satisfying customers and political forces.

A Problem of Equity   The Temporary State Commission on the Water Supply Needs of Southeastern New York (TSCWS, 1973) has recommended the establishment of a public corporation to plan, build, and operate a regional water supply for southeastern New York, including New York City. The commission, in making this recommendation, felt that no regional focus exists now and that such an organization is needed to establish equity in resource availability between areas, particularly between New York City and the counties from which the city receives its water. The regional corporation would take over New York City's upstate reservoir and aqueduct facilities which, in the words of the commission report are "properties that already belong to the public. . . ." This is undoubtedly true, but the question is *which* public, the public of New York City, which has paid for much of the system, or the larger public of the entire region? The issues opened here are (a) what real equity, if any, does the city have in its water properties and (b) what are the legal rights of a city, whose corporate charter exists at the pleasure of the state, versus changes that the state might wish to make?

New Jersey State Involvement   The State of New Jersey is in the water supply business with two state-owned reservoirs at Spruce Run and Round Valley. The state, however, has not been able to sell all its water at the sites, and the legislature has, to date, not funded a statewide transmission line. Thus, water from these reservoirs is spilled into the Raritan to the benefit of downstream users without payment for this service. A water supply committee, consisting of legislators and gubernatorial appointees, has been trying to solve this impasse.

Water Reuse   New Jersey plans to use treated effluent as low-flow augmentation on streams serving as raw water sources. Although this is a large and imaginative step toward conservation through reuse, it raises issues of public acceptance and public health. Similar problems are raised by plans on Long Island to return treated wastewater to the aquifer rather than disposing of it at sea.

Interconnection between Water Systems   This problem is particularly acute in New Jersey, where a very large number of water systems exist. Many are totally isolated from each other. Others are interconnected by lines based on sales from one utility to another. There is no mechanism that, under drought conditions, would be able to allocate the water fairly among the many competing systems.

Ramapo, Petaluma, and the Mid-Hudson Development Guide

The Town of Ramapo, situated in the Rockland County portion of the Hudson River basin, has lent its name to the most important case in the field of zoning law since *Euclid* v. *Ambler*. On May 3, 1972, *Golden* v. *Town of Ramapo* (1972) was decided by the New York Court of Appeals. In an effort to regulate its own development, the town adopted a master plan, a comprehensive zoning ordinance, and an 18-year capital budget to provide the necessary municipal services for maximum projected growth in conformity with the plan over that period. In essence, the ordinance provided that residential development was to be permitted only as adequate municipal facilities and services became available, with the assurance that any concomitant restraint upon property uses was to be only of a temporary nature. The purpose (apart from the effect) of this technique was not to restrict population growth per se but to implement "a sequential development policy commensurate with progressing availability and capacity of public facilities."

Noting the municipality's recognized authority to determine the lines along which local development shall proceed, and assuming that the town would in good faith develop the facilities prescribed in its capital plan, the court held that the town's ordinance was authorized by the state's zoning enabling law, and that the development restrictions imposed by the ordinance were not takings of property for which compensation would constitutionally be required.

> In sum, Ramapo asks not that it be left alone, but only that it be allowed to prevent the kind of deterioration that has transformed well ordered and thriving residential communities into blighted ghettos with attendant hazards to health, security and social stability . . .

> We only require that communities confront the challenge of population growth with open doors. Where in grappling with that problem, the community undertakes, by imposing temporary restrictions upon development, to provide required municipal services in a rational manner, courts are rightfully reluctant to strike down such schemes.

Ramapo is a landmark case. It is apparently the first in this country that upholds the right of a community to restrict its own development through careful exercise of its planning and zoning powers, without having to compensate property owners for losses in current property values occasioned by forced postponement of their development rights. No longer need the pace and pattern of development in a community be decided by private developers and speculators in the free exercise of their own profit motives. If a community commits itself to a long-range capital investment program that does not appear to be a mere guise for halting growth or excluding people, it may limit development to areas served by public facilities and thereby regulate the rate and direction of growth in accordance with such a program. Moreover, as in the case of *Ramapo,* a community may regulate its development in accordance with a master plan that identifies areas to be preserved in their natural state, with concurrent requirements respecting average density, cluster zoning, and development easements designed to preserve open space and facilitate the provision of public amenities.

The majority opinion in *Ramapo* was criticized by Judge Breitel in his thoughtful dissent. He characterized the town's ordinance as a "moratorium on land development," and noted that some of the needed facilities would not be installed for 18 years, with the consequence of freezing some owners' property uses for an equally long time. In his opinion, the zoning enabling law did not authorize such severe temporal restrictions. Principally, Judge Breitel objected to letting mere local ordinances deal ad hoc with conflicts that have arisen on a much larger scale between population pressure and environmental quality. He believed these issues should be resolved "at a regional or state level, usually with local administration, and not by compounding the conflict with idiosyncratic municipal action." Municipalities were in no position to consider the far-reaching social and economic impacts of a series of Ramapo-type ordinances; their adoption by all towns might well have the effect of "destroying the economy and channeling the demographic course of the state to suit their own insular interests."

Even the majority opinion conceded that local autonomy over land use had distorted metropolitan growth patterns and crippled efforts toward regional and statewide problem-solving in a variety of related fields, including environmental quality control, housing, and public transportation. Only state or regional controls could ensure a sufficiently broad focus in charting land use policies. Arguably, the majority opinion, by upholding Ramapo's unusual ordinance, will make it more difficult to enact better state legislation for land planning, precisely because such legislation would require some reduction in the degree of local control currently exercised under zoning enabling laws.

In January 1974, a U. S. District Court in California handed down another decision of far-reaching implications in this field. Not far from San Francisco lies the City of Petaluma, whose population had mushroomed in a manner and for causes similar to Ramapo's. In a special election held in 1972, the city's residents approved by a vote of 4 to 1 an ordinance declaring that for the next 5 years, the city would permit the addition of, and extend water and sewer services to, not more than 500 new units per year. The ordinance was defended on grounds similar to Ramapo's—that the city was entitled to regulate its growth consistently with its capacity to provide the necessary utilities.

But when a group of land and real estate developers, claiming to represent the region as a whole, challenged the ordinance in a suit against the city, the court found in their favor (*Construction Industry Association of Sonoma County* v. *City of Petaluma*, 1974). "No city," it held, "may regulate its population growth numerically so as to preclude residents of any other area from traveling into the region and settling there." People have a constitutional right to travel and live wherever they wish, and every city has to accept its fair share of the population explosion. The court evidently bought the plaintiff's argument that, just as a telephone company could not decline to install more telephones, so a city is obliged to provide public utilities for whatever population it in fact acquires. The purpose of government, so the court implied, is to serve immediate human needs, not to control them in favor of longer-range objectives.*

One month before the District Court's decision in the *Petaluma* case was announced, The Regional Plan Association and Mid-Hudson Pattern for Progress (1973) jointly issued a development guide for the seven-county mid-Hudson region. Dr. John P. Keith, president of the RPA, announced that this was "the first time we have issued a report emphasizing ways of inhibiting growth. We've always spoken of inducing growth." In essence, the guide calls for concentrating new growth in the region into and around existing urban centers, and discouraging growth in the open countryside, so that 1300 square miles, or one-quarter of the region's land area, can be preserved as public open space despite an expected increase of half a million people by the year 2000. With new regional facilities (such as universities, hospitals, and department stores) located mainly in the seven major urban centers, renewal of downtown areas, expressways leading into them rather than around them, high housing densities closer to these centers and low densities farther away, and cluster development, there would be created "compact markets of people, money and jobs while conserving land, travel and energy." The guide recognizes, however, that such a regional strategy cannot be implemented if control of land remains exclusively in the hands of the 168 separate municipalities that occupy the region. It proposes that counties, with state approval, establish housing densities which would become legal requirements of municipal zoning ordinances; that local zoning controls be overridden by higher authority if they conflict with areawide interests; and that the interests of numerous municipalities be coordinated through strong county plans. In addition, localities are urged to use their zoning powers and other land use controls to discourage development of prime agricultural, scenic, and recreational areas, and of other areas whose natural resources, geological or topographical features, or "nonurban" character makes them unsuitable for development. It is implied that if localities fail to discourage development that is incompatible with the nature of such areas, the needed controls should be imposed from above by county or state authority.

The proposals advanced in "The Mid-Hudson: A Development Guide" are enlightened and intelligent but they raise some difficult questions, particularly in light of the *Ramapo* and *Petaluma* cases. The guide carefully refrains

---

*The decision was subsequently reversed by the U.S. Court of Appeals for the Ninth Circuit. Petition for review was denied by the U.S. Supreme Court [522 F.2d 897, 8 ERC 1001 (9th Cir. 1975) *cert. denied*, 96 S. Ct. 1148 (February 23, 1976)]. [Ed.]

from recommending population quotas for areas outside the existing urban centers, but its antagonists may be expected to argue that it would have such an effect if its recommendations for channeling growth and protecting environmentally sensitive areas from development were adopted. If, in the words of the *Petaluma* decision, every locality has to "take its fair share of the population explosion," could a major part of any still-unspoiled locality be designated for nondevelopment or for low-density housing? If the locality itself cannot so restrict its growth, for reasons stated in the *Ramapo* and *Petaluma* cases, will the county or the state be permitted to do it, as both cases imply it might; or will development restrictions imposed by the county or state appear equally impermissible at one or two steps removed from the local scene? Some localities have learned to use large-lot zoning as an exclusionary technique. Should they be permitted to continue doing so, if environmental objectives such as those advocated by the development guide were to be promoted? Other localities have welcomed all the development they can attract to strengthen the local tax base and economy. Will the county or state now step in and say that some localities may continue to do so because they are already highly developed, while others must refrain from similar action, despite their depressed economies, because they contain natural resources of benefit to the region as a whole?

The major challenge posed by the guide and by the *Ramapo* and *Petaluma* cases will be to develop an acceptable institutional design for channeling growth along lines that preserve and promote the quality of life as expressed inter alia in man's relationship to his physical surroundings.

Okwari Park

On May 19, 1972, the Chairman of the Montgomery County Board of Supervisors filed an application with the New York State Department of Environmental Conservation, pursuant to the State Environmental Conservation Law, to build two dams on Fly Creek and one dam on Flat Creek. The dams would create one large recreational lake and a small wildlife pond, which would form an important part of the county's projected 3700-acre Okwari Park.

Montgomery County is in the Mohawk Valley, approximately 35 miles west of Albany, and is included in the Albany–Schenectady–Troy Standard Metropolitan Statistical Area (SMSA). The New York Thruway and Mohawk River bisects the county. Over half of the 58,000 residents of Montgomery County reside in its northeastern portion.

Okwari Park was to be located in the south-central part of the county, almost on the boundary with Schoharie County, in the towns of Root and Charleston. The site is on the upper reaches of Fly Creek, which flows in a southeasterly direction, emptying into Schoharie Creek and then into the Mohawk River. Flat Creek flows in a northwesterly direction, also emptying into the Mohawk. Both creeks are classified "D," the lowest classification in the DEC's set of Classifications and Standards, with the best usage as agricultural water.

The plan itself called for the development of Okwari Park as a 3700-acre public outdoor recreational facility having, as a central feature, three lakes with about 1335 surface acres of water for swimming, fishing, and boating. Additional recreational facilities to be provided included a ski area, a golf course, camping areas, a hunting preserve, a conservation education center, picnic areas, riding trails, and a conference center. According to a spokesman for the County Board of Supervisors, Okwari Park was to be the largest outdoor recreation facility in New York State. If not that, it would be the largest county park in the State, if not the world, for the park was to be financed by the people of Montgomery County with financial assistance from the federal government.

The idea of a major lake on Fly Creek had been conceived as early as the mid-1960s by a private developer of vacation communities. The firm planned to use the lake as the basis of the construction of up to 3000 vacation homes. Owing to a number of factors, including the cost of construction of the lake and the uncertainties of water supply because of the low flow of Fly Creek, private development plans for the region were abandoned in 1966. The county then picked up the idea and began investigating its feasibility. Okwari Park was the result of their deliberation.

Numerous goals for the park were mentioned in public statements and in the written materials developed for Okwari. The park was to provide a wide range of clean, safe, and sanitary outdoor recreational facilities for all people, including the elderly, the physically and mentally handicapped, and the economically and socially deprived, regardless of sex, race, religion, national origin, or place of residence. The park would be developed in a manner that would sustain and enhance the unique and sensitive ecological and natural resource potential of the site. The park would also be designed to provide "optimum potential revenue sources to the county for maintenance and operation, as well as to stimulate maximum possible levels of ancillary economic development to all parts of Montgomery County." In public discussions, stimulation of the economic growth of the county became the major reason for the development of Okwari, and it was expected that the park would serve as the focus for substantial second-home development (estimated as up to 2000 homes). Clearly, the park was to offer many things to many people, and was to be of significant social and economic benefit to the people of Montgomery County.

A draft "environmental impact statement" for the entire Okwari project was submitted by the county to the DEC in November 1973. The applicant's case was supported by seven technical witnesses; the opponents by six technical witnesses and four witnesses resident in the area; and the State of New York was represented by seven technical witnesses. After delays in filing briefs, the hearings were closed by the DEC on September 7, 1973. The applicant's request was rejected by the commissioner on October 30, 1973. In November 1973, residents of Montgomery County voted upon the Okwari Park project in a special referendum and soundly defeated the project.

In making his negative decision, the commissioner held that the county, as applicant, had been unable to prove that the project would be in the public interest, and that the project did not meet criteria established in the applicable state regulations (6 NYCRR §608 and §615), namely, that:

> The proposal is reasonable and necessary.
>
> The proposal will not endanger the health, safety, and welfare of the people of the State of New York.
>
> The proposal will not cause unreasonable, uncontrolled or unnecessary damage to the natural resources of the state, including soil, forests, water, fish and aquatic and land-related environment.

Rejection of the application was based upon broader criteria than just the technical aspects of dam safety, and of the quantity and quality of surface water of the proposed lakes. The DEC held that, given the nature of the proposed project, the "piecemeal" approach used by the applicants did not represent the sound comprehensive environmental planning called for. And, because of this approach, the applicants were unable to provide sufficient evidence to counter the department's determination that the park would have substantial detrimental impact on the environment of the state. The DEC also held that the applicant was unable to indicate sufficient "need" by the residents of the county for a project of such size and diversity, and hence the requested dams were not reasonable or necessary. The applicant was unable to show that a sufficient potable water supply was available, or to provide acceptable information concerning sewage facilities to be provided for users of the park. In addition, cost analyses for key elements of the project were incomplete, making projections of alternatives impossible; and the lake created would inundate Little Bear Swamp, the most important and unique ecological asset of the entire area. These issues were paramount among the opponents to the project, the most vigorous and vocal of which was the Okwari Park Committee for Fair Play.

A goal of the county was to promote economic growth through the development of a regional recreational facility: to generate income and employment through increased tourist expenditures and the growth of a significant second-home development. The park was also to provide for the recreational needs of the county residents while keeping environmental trade-offs to a minimum.

Opponents contended that the county had failed to indicate in any meaningful manner that the park would create significant increases in county revenues and employment and that, in fact, the county had failed to do any analysis that would allow a comparison of the costs of the project with the supposed benefits.

Closely allied with this conflict was the issue of the distribution of benefits from the project. Okwari was to be a county park, financed largely from county property tax revenues (though no adequate analysis was provided by the county to actually establish total park funding), whereas the bulk of park users would come from outside the county and would not generate revenues adequate to cover the full costs of their recreational experience, passing the burden on to Montgomery County residents. Persons purchasing second homes tend to have higher incomes, it was argued, than those who would be paying the taxes to provide the park. Similar distributional concerns exist because skiing and golf, two activities planned for the park, are high-income-related activities. Funding would come from a broad-based property tax on residents of Montgomery County, with its per capita personal income level lower than the average for New York State. Therefore, it appeared that benefits from the park would favor the wealthier at the expense of the less wealthy. Although the issue of distribution equity must be considered in all resource allocation decisions, it became particularly evident in this case.

Joint and Regional Strategies for Wastewater Management: A Case History of Institutional and Technical Obstacles*

As late as May 1970, the Village of Castleton and the Brown Paper Company discharged raw wastewaters to the Hudson River south of Albany, where the river is grossly polluted by the numerous municipal and industrial sources in the capital region. Castleton had been previously scheduled by the New York State Department of Health (DOH) to complete construction of municipal sewage treatment facilities by February 1970, but was at that time one of many municipalities which failed to meet abatement deadlines.

Health codes, federal and state, have prohibited the draining of raw sewage into the Hudson for decades, but these requirements were treated

*The factual material for this case report was largely drawn from Greene (1970).

lightly, both by polluters and by the health agencies that were supposed to enforce the codes. When a state official contacted Castleton in 1955 to ask what it was planning to do about its discharges of raw sewage, the villagers told him they would do nothing until the much larger copolluting cities upstream—especially Albany and Troy—had taken steps to abate their wastes, besides which those of Castleton (population, 1768) were insignificant. The village took the same position in discussions with DOH in 1964. Finally, in the face of threatened court actions, the mayor signed a consent order agreeing to a timetable for constructing a village treatment system.

But the timetable specified in the order was scrapped shortly thereafter by DOH itself, which had belatedly decided, under some prodding from the Federal Water Pollution Control Administration, that comprehensive regional surveys should be made before treatment plants were built to determine where facilities for joint treatment of municipal and industrial wastes would be more cost-effective than a separate facility for each discharger. At this point, a typical problem arose: how to persuade different units of local government to cooperate in an interlocal enterprise for an objective so expensive, and so lacking in political appeal, as wastewater management. An engineering report was commissioned to define the available alternatives. Based on this report, and motivated in part by a desire to annex outlying areas, Castleton voted for a treatment system of its own, which would also handle wastes from the paper company and from a group of houses lying just outside the village. The town of Schodack, on the other hand, within whose borders the Village of Castleton and the Brown Paper Company were located, wanted to include them both within a larger system which Schodack would dominate and which it would use both to promote its own economic development and to keep Castleton's acquisitive instincts at bay. Brown was on the fence between hooking up to the town or village, or building a separate facility of its own to handle its industrial discharge.

State and federal officials favored an interlocal sewer district embracing Castleton, Brown Paper Company, and a sizeable part of Schodack. Reluctantly, Castleton consented to join such a district under threat of losing government aid to treat its wastes.* But the Schodackians were not so cooperative. On November 5, 1968, they rejected the proposed sewer district on a referendum, evidently preferring to continue their nonpolluting septic tanks rather than to undertake the expense of sewering their town and treating their wastes in a centralized facility. Under applicable health laws,

*The 1972 Federal Water Pollution Control Act Amendments eliminated the federal-aid "bonus" for intermunicipal sewage treatment systems. [Ed.]

the state could legally force Castleton to treat its sewered wastes, but had no power to force Schodackians outside of Castleton to participate in an inter-local sewer district.

Faced with this setback, DOH ordered Castleton to build its own treat-ment plant with sufficient capacity to service outside areas that might join in at a later time. Protracted negotiations between Castleton and Brown, to decide whether the latter would go in with the village or build its own separate plant, delayed progress toward compliance with the abatement order—no doubt a welcome delay to both parties. The company wanted to know what its cost share would be; the village engineer claimed he needed time for clay borings at the proposed site before he could estimate founda-tion costs. The village wanted the company to guarantee payment of a full share of debt, principal, and interest costs on the treatment facility even if the company should later reduce or shut down its operations. There was dis-agreement over where the treatment plant should be located. After a year of haggling over the issues, DOH finally told the village to proceed at once with a solo project, not waiting for an agreement with Brown, on pain of forfeiting government aid if there were further delay.

Originally, Brown had been ordered to control its effluent, which exerted six times the BOD of Castleton's sanitary sewage, by July 1970. But the company had developed no more than a preliminary plan for a treatment system by that date. Most other paper companies in the state also showed themselves in no hurry to comply with abatement schedules issued under the Pure Waters Program, nor was the Health Department inclined to take vigorous enforcement action. First it let Brown's schedule slide while the company explored the possibility of a joint facility with Schodack. Then, after Schodack's voters rejected this idea, DOH tolerated further delay while Brown negotiated with Castleton. In each case a host of difficulties, uncer-tainties, and excuses obstructed progress toward joint agreement. Moreover, the company's financial problems may have extended DOH's patience in dealing with it. Finally, the department ordered Brown to go it alone accord-ing to a new timetable, and Brown indicated that it would comply.

Castleton also began to move at last. On March 19, 1970, 2 months after the date by which it had agreed in the consent order to have its treatment system completed, the village formally submitted preliminary plans to DOH for a system excluding Brown. Final plans and specifications followed in due course. From the time the preliminary plans were approved to completion of the system would have taken 3 years, a measure of the extent of Castleton's noncompliance with the order to which it had consented.

But the situation took yet another turn when Brown and Castleton finally came to agreement on a joint facility. The agreement was prompted in large measure by Brown's threat to go out of business, depriving the locality of jobs, unless a cost-saving arrangement with Castleton could be concluded. When the parties reached agreement, the engineering report and final plans for a separate Castleton facility were accordingly scrapped, and the engineers went back to their drawing boards. A new engineering report for a joint facility was approved in February 1973 by the State Department of Environmental Conservation, which had taken over the environmental-protection functions of the DOH. Plans and specifications followed soon thereafter.

But then another obstacle was encountered: the requirement under the new Federal Water Pollution Control Act that municipal grant applicants with sewer systems in place, such as Castleton, complete infiltration and inflow studies before deciding upon the capacity of the treatment plants for which federal and state funds were to be requested. Pending completion of the necessary study, the project is currently being held in abeyance. Brown has agreed to construct pretreatment facilities prior to completion of the municipal plant, but will not have to begin construction until Castleton receives a grant offer from the Environmental Protection Agency, which will in turn be conditioned upon whatever conclusions the village, the state, and EPA may agree upon in light of the infiltration and inflow. Castleton could avoid the infiltration and inflow problem by separating its combined sewer system, but the cost of constructing new sanitary sewers would be high and, under existing priorities for allocating scarce construction grant funds, would not be met even in part by federal and state subsidies.*

It cannot be said that the Castleton–Brown–Schodack case, as summarized above, is typical of communities and industries in New York State or in the Hudson River basin. But it does show how much effort can be wasted even on a few such cases. And the lessons to be learned from this case history probably are of general applicability. They can briefly be summarized as follows, with a view to both present and likely future circumstances;

Over the past two decades, the state has not consistently taken effective

---

*As of December 1978, Castleton's sewage treatment plant is still unbuilt. The village's grant application was approved by the U.S. Environmental Protection Agency, but that agency is now questioning the final design of the treatment plant, which would require the filling of about one-third of an acre of wetland. The necessary state permit to place fill in the wetland, which totals about 20 acres, has been issued by the Department of Environmental Conservation. Meanwhile, Brown Paper's pretreatment plant is virtually complete, but there is no municipal treatment system for it to feed into. [Ed.]

enforcement action against water polluters. They have slipped abatement deadlines again and again, and with impunity. Recently, however, the fine that DEC may assess by civil administrative process against a polluter was raised to $10,000 per day plus $500 for each day of continuing violation. DEC has wielded this enforcement weapon effectively in a number of cases, but the Attorney General has been slow to collect such fines in cases that DEC has had to refer to him. Nor has the Attorney General's office compiled an impressive record in seeking and securing equitable relief—mandatory and prohibitive injunctions—against recalcitrant polluters. The Attorney General's political independence of the governor and the line agencies of state government, combined with the politically sensitive and prosecutionally unappealing nature of enforcement actions in the courts against polluters, may lie at the heart of the problem.

There is much to be said for avoiding a punitive approach toward habitual polluters who are being asked to make substantial new investments in control equipment and to operate it conscientiously over time. Invoking adversarial process may demolish the good will on which continuing progress will depend. On the other hand, there comes a point in every difficult case where negotiations must end and the full force of law be asserted; otherwise, its regulatory efficacy will be seriously eroded.

But even stiff penalties, consistently applied, would not solve the inherent difficulty of securing interlocal and municipal-industrial cooperation in constructing regional or joint facilities for wastewater management. Towns and villages value their local autonomy, compete for ratables, and are not easily convinced that the savings of regionalization are worth the political costs. The state lacks the power to declare the mandatory formation of interlocal sewer districts and to compel connection of municipal and industrial waste sources. The threat to withhold construction grants unless joint arrangements are concluded for wastewater treatment has proven largely ineffective. In time, cost-effective solutions may emerge, but only after considerable friction and delay.

Difficulties with regionalization may be expected to recur, as needs become apparent for new and larger sewer districts to provide advanced waste treatment or to employ reserve capacity built into current treatment plants. As long as voluntary cooperation remains the exclusive means of securing joint and regional arrangements for waste treatment, the principle of local and individual autonomy will be preserved, but only by indefinitely postponing the goal of clean water.

Inconsistencies within federal and state programs for abating water pollution, and frequent shifts in their ground rules, have been another major part of the problem. The pressure to build treatment plants by deadlines pre-scribed for individual polluters conflicts with the belatedly recognized need for planning wastewater management strategies on a cost-effective, area-wide basis.

This conflict is currently expressed in the tension between the federal discharge permit program (NPDES) and the federal requirements for basin, regional, and areawide planning under Sections 303, 208, and 201 of the FWPCA. A rational sense of priorities—abating the major sources of pollu-tion first, before requiring lesser ones, such as Castleton, to fall into line— has yet to be realized in the official program. Successive impositions of requirements for regional planning, infiltration and inflow studies, and even higher degrees of waste removal, may have been justified, but could not and cannot be achieved without delaying construction of treatment facilities far beyond applicable deadlines.

Insufficiency of funds has always been, and probably will remain, a fun-damental obstacle to meeting water quality standards. The federal share of eligible construction costs for treatment facilities has risen to 75%, to which New York State will add another 12.5%, leaving the applicant community with only 12.5% to raise on its own. But the construction cost index has continued to rise at an inflationary pace, and grant assistance will continue to be unavailable for costly new collection systems and the repair or exten-sion of existing sewer lines. Nor will the risk of putting some industrial discharges out of business be ignored in deciding upon the pace of future enforcement action. Scarcity of funds will be the best argument for ordering priorities for pollution-control expenditures in accordance with assessments, depending on where the greatest marginal benefits lie in terms of improved water quality and expanded water uses.

7.6 Summary and Conclusions

In Section 7.4, issue categories were selected which, in the opinion of the task group, represent significant influences upon water resource decision-making in the Hudson Basin Project area. In Section 7.5, selected site-specific problems were described and illustrated in case form. Table 7-13 displays the interrelationships between the case examples cited and the issue categories selected. The issue categories most important in any one case are designated as primary (P), and those of secondary importance as (S). This does not mean that in any one of the cases cited in Section 7.5 no other

TABLE 7-13. Summary of Water Resource Issue Categories[a]

	Growth versus environmental values	Definition of water quality objectives	Efficiency in implementation of water quality objectives	Allocation among competing uses	Coordination of land and water use objectives	Institutional structures	Equity in distribution of benefits	Data base for planning	Water-oriented recreation
Water quality in the Hudson River and New York Bight	—	P	P	P	—	S	S	S	S
Water resources issues in rural regions	P	—	—	—	P	P	S	—	—
New York metropolitan water systems	—	—	—	P	—	P	P	S	S
Ramapo, Petaluma, and "The Mid-Hudson: A Development Guide"	P	—	—	—	—	P	S	—	—
Okwari Park				S	P	—	—	—	P
Joint and regional strategies for wastewater management	—	—	P	—	—	P	P	—	—

[a] P = primary; S = secondary.

issues are involved; it is meant only to highlight the most important issues. Even from such a small sample of selected cases, some conclusions can be drawn: institutional structure and equity in the distribution of benefits (and costs) stand out among all the other issues considered. The examples, however, show one more important point: none of the issue categories occurs independently from the others. Thus, it is clear that interrelated analysis is required to gain a basic understanding of all the important issues. Areas of study and research suggested by this display are given below.

Development of the Best Practicable Institutional Design for Managing the Land and Water Resources of the Hudson River Basin, Compatible with Both Environmental and Economic Objectives

This design would allocate various powers, functions, and duties among the different levels of government, from federal agencies on down to villages, and among different agencies at each level of government. All relevant functions would be covered, including planning, financing, building, operating, and monitoring environmentally sensitive properties or facilities as well as employment of remedial techniques against violators of environmental standards. Techniques to be explored and evaluated would include master planning, regulation, subsidies, fiscal incentives, user fees, and government acquisition and management of properties or facilities. Special attention would be given to (a) how existing agencies might be made to function more effectively, and (b) the possibility of establishing intercounty districts—perhaps half a dozen or so throughout the basin—for multipurpose environmental planning and management, pursuant to state guidelines and with inputs from included localities.

Development of Techniques for Resolving Problems of Fiscal and Economic Equity Incident to Environmental Management

For example, if New York City's water supply system were to be taken over by a larger regional entity, how should the city be compensated, if at all? By what criteria should scarce natural resources be allocated among competing demands? Should a system of transferable development rights be instituted or should windfall gains accruing to some property owners as a result of government decisions be captured and used by the government to compensate other property owners who experience windfall losses in consequence of other decisions?

The Development and Analysis of an Improved Decision Process to Ensure That Scientific Information and Data Reach the Decision-makers and Are Utilized in the Decision Process

The major thrust in this investigation should center on recruitment and training to develop the type of staff that will filter the information flow to the decision-makers to remove extraneous and unimportant material, but will not consciously or unconsciously distort data by selective filtering.

The Development of an Interfunctional Monitoring and Assessment Policy That Allows the Water Resources of the Hudson Basin to Be Consistently Evaluated Relative to Their Quality and Multiple Use Needs

Such a plan would include the refinement of cross-disciplinary technical or analytical procedures to ensure a relevant and quantative data base as a resource for coordinating interdisciplinary policy development and implementation. It would also include development of data-gathering and dissemination mechanisms to facilitate information transfer and social–technical feedback for improved structural and nonstructural implementation of water quality and supply objectives, as well as for the allocation of water for other multiple uses.

The Determination of Current Relationships That Can Be Established between Available Chemical and Physical Information and Biological Integrity in Order to Implement Assessment Techniques for Water Quality Objectives in a Whole-System Framework for All Waters of the Basin

This action would require the utilization of readily quantifiable characteristics by several classes of analyses in order to establish natural baselines for various aquatic environments.

The Development of an Integrated Analysis of Water Quality Demands for the Waters of the Hudson Basin, Considered as a Single, Albeit Complex, Unit

Because of the magnitude of the problem, both in terms of potential water pollution control expenditures and the interrelationships with other en-

vironmental aspects (e.g., land use, recreation, and transportation), it is recommended that such an investigation be a continuous effort throughout the
area. Such an analysis should respond to changes in problem perceptions,
control technologies, and levels of scientific understanding.

Chapter 8

AIR RESOURCES

8.1 Air Quality

Air Quality Standards

Public awareness of the effects of air pollution increased dramatically in the 25-year period following World War II. This awareness was caused by numerous factors, including increases in source emissions from automobiles and electric-generating facilities, episodes of air pollution in which mortality and morbidity showed significant rise, and increasing social concern for the quality of life.

The Clean Air Act Amendments of 1970 set the achievement of clean air as a national goal. This legislation gave the Environmental Protection Agency certain powers, including the authority to promulgate national air quality standards, standards of performance for new stationary sources, and requirements for new automobiles. Other actions under the Amendments were left to the states. But if they failed to carry out their responsibilities, the EPA administrator was empowered to assume them.

In April 1972, the EPA promulgated national air quality standards for six air contaminants whose control was deemed essential to protect the health and welfare of the nation's populace—standards for suspended particulate

Members of the Air Resources Task Group: Philip L. Bereano, Edward Davis, Michael R. Greenberg, Robert E. Laessig, P. Walton Purdom, and Alexander Rihm, Jr.

matter, sulfur dioxide, carbon monoxide, nitrogen dioxide, hydrocarbons (nonmethane), and photochemical oxidants. The national primary standards were established to protect health; the national secondary standards were established to safeguard property, vegetation, and animal life, as well as to promote the general public well-being. The primary standards were to be achieved by 1975 with extensions possible to 1978.* The secondary standards are to be met within a reasonable time. Except for sulfur dioxide and suspended particulate matter, primary and secondary standards are set at the same values. For these two, the secondary standards are more stringent. Table 8-1 lists these national standards as of 1972.

The Clean Air Act does not prevent lower orders of government from having more stringent standards of their own. New York State, for example, adopted its first-in-the-nation standards in 1964. Where these were not as stringent as the federal standards, they have been either amended or dropped; those that were more stringent have been retained. Thus, much of the New York portion of the Hudson Basin has air quality standards for suspended particulates that are higher than those set by the EPA. The classification for New York is shown in Fig. 8-1. The New York standards, including those for some additional parameters such as dustfall, are listed in Table 8-2.

The Clean Air Act requires each state to prepare an implementation plan showing how national standards will be achieved. To assist the states in meeting the requirement, the Act authorized the establishment of Air Quality Control Regions. Regions within the Hudson Basin Project study area are shown in Fig. 8-2. The required implementation plans have been or are being prepared by the states of Connecticut, New Jersey, and New York. Revisions are encouraged under the Act, making change an almost constant process.

Air Quality Monitoring Systems

Air quality monitoring has been an essential component of virtually every air pollution control program in the nation. In fact, an effective control program is virtually impossible without base information on current air quality and past trends. The Clean Air Act did not precipitate new monitoring activity in the Hudson Basin Project study area; rather it served to reinforce an already developed program. The monitoring networks and the principal contaminants measured are shown in Figs. 8-3 and 8-4.

---

*Under the 1977 Amendments to the Clean Air Act, the primary standards are to be achieved by January 1, 1983, with extensions to January 1, 1988 for carbon monoxide and photochemical oxidants (ozone) if certain preconditions are met. [Ed.]

TABLE 8-1. National Primary and Secondary Ambient Air Quality Standards

Pollutant	Type of standard	Averaging time	Frequency parameter	Concentration $\mu g/m^3$	ppm
Carbon monoxide	Primary and secondary	1 hr	Annual maximum[a]	40,000	35
		8 hr	Annual maximum[a]	10,000	9
Hydrocarbons (nonmethane)	Primary and secondary	3 hr (6 to 9 AM)	Annual maximum	160[b]	0.24[b]
Nitrogen dioxide	Primary and secondary	1 yr	Annual arithmetic mean	100	0.05
Photochemical oxidants	Primary and secondary	1 hr	Annual maximum[a]	160	0.08
Particulate matter	Primary	24 hr	Annual maximum[a]	260	—
		1 yr	Annual geometric mean	75	—
	Secondary	24 hr	Annual maximum[a]	150	—
		1 yr	Annual geometric mean	60[c]	—
Sulfur dioxide	Primary	24 hr	Annual maximum[a]	365	0.14
		1 yr	Annual arithmetic mean	80	0.03
	Secondary	3 hr	Annual maximum[a]	1,300	0.5

[a] Not to be exceeded more than once per year.
[b] As a guide in devising implementation plans for achieving oxidant standard.
[c] As a guide to be used in assessing implementation plans for achieving the annual maximum 24-hr secondary standard.

Fig. 8-1.   New York State air classifications.

Systems within New York State

State System   New York State's monitoring network is divided into two systems: the intermittent system, which collects samples over a finite sampling time, with analysis performed at a laboratory; and the continuous system, which analyzes at the sampling location and yields results by telemetry and computer at the Albany reception center.

The continuous system is the more sophisticated part of the network. Its monitors analyze a variety of pollutants and meteorological conditions at primary, secondary, and satellite locations. Primary sites monitor SO_2, NO, NO_2, CO, hydrocarbons, soiling, ozone, and up to 11 meteorological parameters, including wind speed, wind direction, ultraviolet radiation, rainfall, temperature, pressure, and gustiness. Secondary sites are scaled-down versions of the primary, usually analyzing several contaminant and meteorological parameters. Satellite sites are designed to sample for only one or two contaminants. None has been established in the Hudson Basin.

TABLE 8-2.   Summary of New York State Ambient Air Standards

Contaminant	Interval	Concentration ppm	Concentration g/m³ (25°C)	Level(s)
Sulfur dioxide	Arithmetic mean (annual)	0.03	80	All
	24-hr concentration	0.4[a]	365	All
	3-hr concentration	—	—	—
	1-hr concentration	0.50[b]	1,300	All
Particulates (suspended)	Geometric mean (annual)	—	75[c]	IV
		—	65[c]	III
		—	55[c]	II
		—	45[c]	I
	24-hr concentration	—	250	All
Carbon monoxide	8-hr concentration	9	10 mg/m³	All
	1-hr concentration	—	—	—
Photochemical oxidants	1-hr concentration	0.03	160	All
Hydrocarbons	3-hr concentration	0.24	160	All
Nitrogen dioxide	Arithmetic mean (annual)	0.05	100	All
Fluorides				
(a) Total fluorides	Growing season	40	—	All
as F (dry weight basis)	(6 months)			
	Any 60 days	60	—	All
	Any 30 days	80	—	All
(b) Gaseous fluorides	12-hr concentration	4.5 ppb	3.7	All
as F (volume basis)	24-hr concentration	3.5 ppb	2.85	All
	1-week concentration	2.0 ppb	1.65	All
	1-month concentration	1.0 ppb	0.8	All
Beryllium	1-month concentration	—	0.01	All
Hydrogen sulfide	1-hr concentration	0.01	14	All
Settleable particulates (dust fall)	—[d]	—	—	—

[a] Also 99% of 24-h4 values shall not exceed 0.10 ppm (260 g/m³) on an annual basis.

[b] Also 99% of 1-hr values shall not exceed 0.25 ppm (650 gm³) on an annual basis.

[c] New York state also has an annual 84% value of the 24-hr average concentrations in the four levels

[d] During any 12 consecutive months, 50% of the 30-day average concentrations shall not exceed 0.30 mg/cm² at levels I and II; 0.40 mg/cm² at level III; and 0.60 mg/cm² at level IV. During any 12 consecutive months, 84% of the concentrations shall not exceed 0.45 mg/cm² at levels I and II; 0.60 mg/cm² at level III; and 0.90 mg/cm² at level IV.

One is planned for Nassau County. The Long Island Lighting Company network will be incorporated into the satellite system.

New York's intermittent monitoring system was initiated in 1957 with sampling for suspended particulate matter at about 15 locations. This network is still in existence and filters collected still receive the same special analyses at this time—analysis for sulfates, nitrates, benzene solubles, and

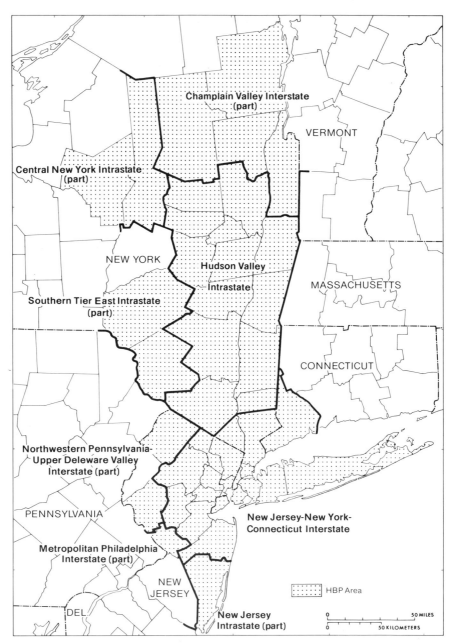

Fig. 8-2.   Federal air quality control regions in the Hudson Basin Project region.

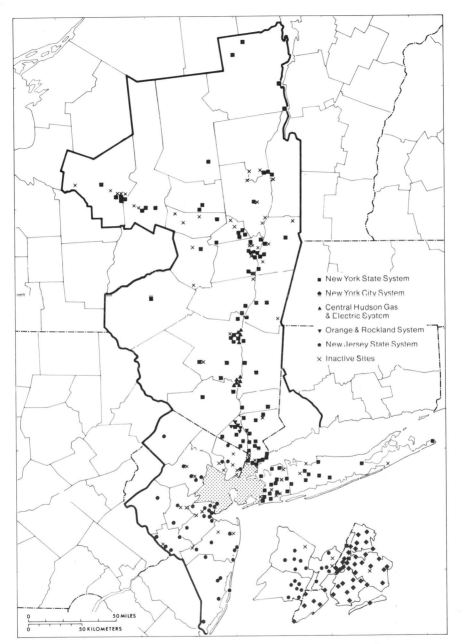

Fig. 8-3.   Air monitoring networks in the Hudson Basin Project study area.

• Suspended Particles

0 _____ 50 MILES

0 _____ 50 KILOMETERS

− Sulfur Dioxide (SO₂)

ı Nitrogen Dioxide (NO₂)

+ Both

− Carbon Monoxide (CO)

ı Oxidants

+ Both

Fig. 8-4. Contaminants measured by air monitoring networks.

pH. The intermittent system has expanded with the need for air quality data. As of 1974, there were about 107 locations, including some that are associated with the continuous system.* All but a handful collect high-volume air samples for suspended particulate matter. Most stations have sampled for sulfur dioxide in the past using sulfation techniques. Those shown in Figs. 8-3 and 8-4 sample for sulfur dioxide using accepted bubbler techniques. Nitrogen dioxide is sampled at a few sites.

New York City System   The city air sampling system is similar to the state's in many ways. Much of it is intermittent; however, the heart of the system employs telemetry to a central reception station. The current system comprises 38 rooftop sites and 3 street-level locations. The street-level sites are intended to monitor traffic-related contaminants, particularly carbon monoxide.

The rooftop system provides adequate coverage throughout the city for sulfur dioxide and suspended particulate matter. Greater coverage, however, is needed for nitrogen dioxide and photochemical oxidants, with em-

*While new stations have been added over the years, stations are also discontinued from time to time, either because a particular study has been terminated or because a sampling site can no longer be used.

phasis on the use of federally approved methods. Expanded coverage must also be provided for carbon monoxide at street level.

Private Systems For the past several years, the state has required electric utilities to monitor existing air quality prior to receiving an operating certificate for a new facility. Three such systems have been established in the Hudson Basin—two by Central Hudson Gas and Electric and one by Orange and Rockland Utilities. These networks have been established just north of Kingston, north of Newburgh, and around Haverstraw. Meteorological and concentration data from these systems are reported to the state, becoming part of the public record.

Since the private networks are specifically oriented to generating facilities, sampling equipment is confined to the plant vicinity, and contaminants associated with fossil fuel combustion are the only ones measured.

Despite their expansion in recent years, the state, New York City, and private systems still do not provide sufficient sampling to give an accurate picture of air quality in the Hudson Basin's New York portion. This is true for even the most common sampling parameter—suspended particulates. Noticeable areas where more data are needed include most of Orange County, lower Saratoga County, and additional sites around some of the urban areas. Peculiarly, although not nearly as much sulfur dioxide data are available as particulate matter, it appears that ample sampling is performed to supply adequate definitions of areas with potential problems. Sampling for other gaseous contaminants is extremely deficient and must be supplemented at least fivefold to provide an adequate data base.

New Jersey System

New Jersey's monitoring system has evolved along much the same lines as New York State's. Less emphasis, however, has been placed on intermittent systems, particularly for suspended particulates. Thus, the ability to establish trends is limited by insufficient data prior to 1970.

Within the New Jersey portion of the Hudson Basin, 62 sites for suspended particulates have been established, 44 of which were in operation as of 1974. Unfortunately, the 18 that had been discontinued were among those with the longest periods of data collection. In some instances, the equipment was relocated at a new site in the same community. Continuous monitors have operated at 14 locations, with monitoring for sulfur dioxide, carbon monoxide, photochemical oxidants, and nitrogen dioxide at most sites.

As with New York, there are probably too few samples in the basin to project air quality patterns accurately, especially for suspended particulates. For gaseous pollutants, adequate information is probably available for contaminants associated with motor vehicles. Additional sulfur dioxide measurements would be useful in defining more accurately the potential problem area(s).

Connecticut System

Connecticut has established a sampling network in Fairfield County. Although this discussion will not address measurements in Connecticut, it appears that there are sufficient stations to determine where problems exist.

Air Quality Levels and Trends

Suspended Particulates

At the end of 1973, most of the Hudson Basin region was meeting the federal primary standard (Fig. 8-5). Areas in excess of this standard were a good portion of the New York metropolitan area, including most of the city and adjacent New Jersey, and areas around Trenton, Newburgh, Kingston, Catskill, and Albany. Considerably more area was in excess of the 60 μg/m^3 to be used as a guide for achieving the national secondary standard. Extensive areas around those places exceeding the primary standard were in excess of the secondary standard.

This was a totally different picture from that which existed in 1970 (Fig. 8-6), the data on which the implementation plan was based. At that time, virtually all of the City of New York exceeded the primary standard, as did most of Nassau County. The lower portion of Westchester County, comprising the cities of Yonkers, Mt. Vernon, and New Rochelle, also exceeded the standard. Most of adjacent New Jersey, comprising large portions of Hudson (all), Bergen, Essex, Union, and Middlesex counties; much larger areas around Newburgh, Kingston, Catskill, and Albany; as well as a portion of Utica also were higher than 75 μg/m^3. The 60-μg/m^3 figure was also exceeded throughout a significantly larger area than in 1973. In 1970, 68 of the 134 stations in the region were above the 75-μg/m^3 annual average. Another 33 were over the 60-μg/m^3 value. In 1973, only 29 of 196 exceeded the national primary standard, while 47 were between 60 and 75 μg/m^3. Clearly, significant progress has been made in abating air pollution in the Hudson Valley, particularly in those areas where the federal standards were grossly exceeded in 1970. From the data presented, it appears that greater reductions have occurred in New York than in New Jersey.

As shown in Table 8-1, the national primary and secondary standards for maximum 24-hr suspended particulate values are 260 and 150 μg/m^3, respectively. A review of the 24-hr concentration data for July 9, 1973, a day which showed high values at virtually all stations, showed three stations exceeding the short-term primary standard of 260 μg/m^3 (East Orange, New

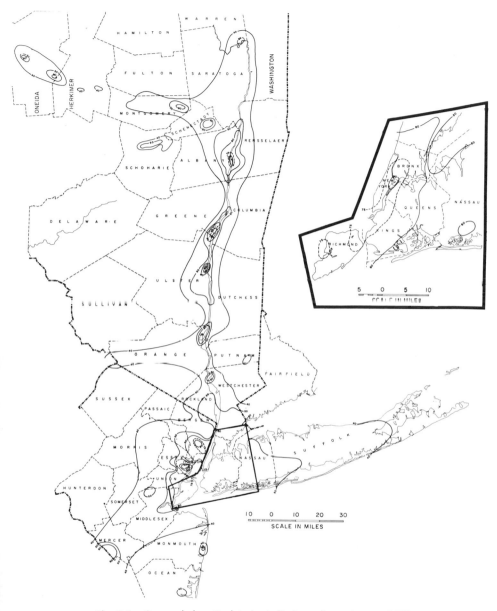

Fig. 8-5.   Suspended particulate (μg/m³) air quality estimates, 1973.

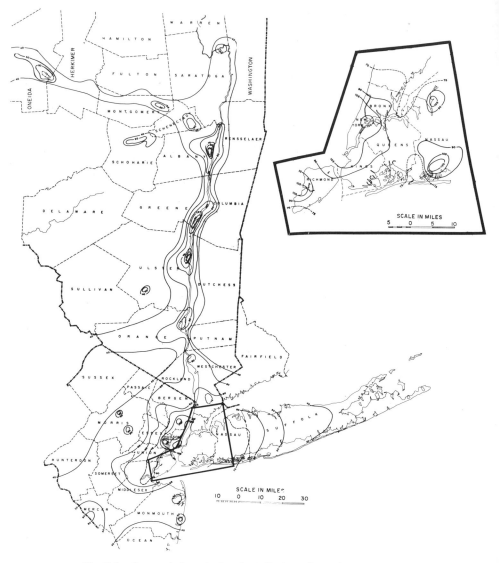

Fig. 8-6.   Suspended particulate (μg/m³) air quality estimates, 1970.

Jersey, at 282 μg/m³; a location in the Central Hudson system at 437 μg/m³; and a location in Brooklyn at 273 μg/m³). However, many more exceeded the national secondary standard of 150 μg/m³. For many of these stations, this date would be the one day that would be allowed to exceed the 150-μg/m³ value. At most stations, other values over 150 also occurred during 1973. Yet, at some of them, the 60-μg/m³ figure was met. From a statistical perspective, even if the 60-μg/m³ value is achieved, the probability of exceeding 150 μg/m³ is high, particularly under conditions of high wind speed and a dry day. In this instance, much of the suspended particulate matter is not due to the activities of man at all, but rather to the erosion phenomena of the wind acting upon the earth. Control activities within the region have been aimed at reducing annual emissions so that the national secondary standard for particulate matter will be achieved. Evidence on hand indicates two related issues: (a) maintaining an annual value of 60 μg/m³ most likely does not provide for meeting a second highest 24-hour concentration of 150 μg/m³ to be exceeded only one time, and (b) emission abatement activities have not been directed to source contributions on peak days and, therefore, may not suffice to attain standards.

Sulfur Dioxide

Through 1970, New York City was the only area in the region where sufficient sulfur dioxide data were available to provide a picture of areawide air quality (Figs. 8-7 and 8-8). Isopleths of annual sulfur dioxide concentrations for 1970 (Fig. 8-8) for New York City show all areas well above the national primary standard of 0.03-ppm annual average. Values as high as 0.10 ppm were found, yet these were significantly improved from those reported in 1965–1966. As can be seen in Fig. 8-9, most of the region met the standard in 1973. Exceptions are portions of New York City, Newark, and Albany.

During the period from 1969 to 1973, sulfur dioxide has shown the greatest air quality improvement of all the major pollutants. Reductions of over 50% from 1970 levels have occurred in New York City. Most of this reduction can be directly attributed to fuel sulfur restrictions in the New Jersey–New York–Connecticut Air Quality Control Region (See Fig. 8-2). As a result of this action, the use of coal has been almost terminated and heavy oil sulfur content has been reduced by over 80%.* Further compliance with existing state regulations is felt to be sufficient to achieve the 0.03-ppm standard.

Nitrogen Dioxide

Although nitrogen dioxide data have been collected at relatively few sites in the Hudson Basin, it appears that the entire region, except for the New York metropolitan area, is well below the national primary standard of 0.05

---

*Although the shift from coal to oil has resulted in cleaner air, it has also made the region very dependent on costly imported oil. Fuel supply considerations, as well as improvements in pollution control technology for coal-fired plants, have led to a revival of interest in coal-fired power generation in the Hudson Basin region. [Ed.]

Fig. 8-7.   Sulfur dioxide (ppm) estimates for New York City, 1969.

ppm. Because nitrogen dioxide is not source-specific (concentrations are rather uniformly dispersed in all of the region), the limited data for the urban areas appear to approximate the worst locations. Outlying areas would exhibit appreciably lower annual averages.

In the New York metropolitan area, it appears from the results at Newark and Elizabeth that achievement of the standard may occur sometime in the 1975–1977 period, primarily as a result of lower emission from newer automobiles.* The sampling method used in the continuous monitoring system is not the method prescribed by the EPA, because its method does not lend itself to continuous monitoring. Thus, the results at Newark, Elizabeth, and

*Compliance with the NO_2 standard was achieved in 1977. [Ed.]

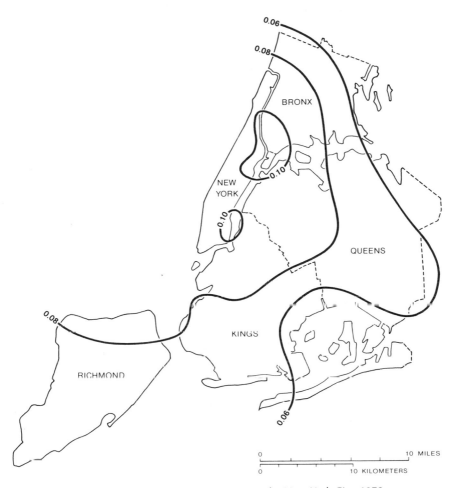

Fig. 8-8. Sulfur dioxide (ppm) estimates for New York City, 1970.

the New York State systems may be somewhat different in relation to the federal reference method. Correlation studies appear to be needed. The establishment of additional NO_2 sampling sites within the region is probably unnecessary.

Carbon Monoxide

Of all the contaminants considered in this discussion, the problem of carbon monoxide is the one most difficult to delineate. Concentrations are extremely source-oriented. They disperse to significantly lower levels within very short distances (about 100 yards). Thus, carbon monoxide mea-

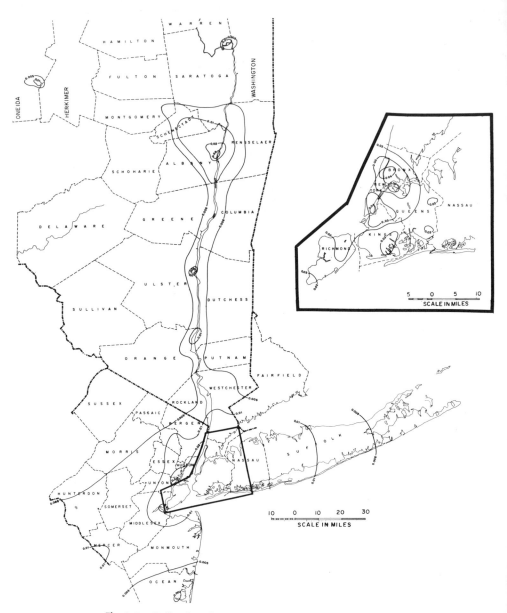

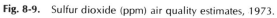

Fig. 8-9. Sulfur dioxide (ppm) air quality estimates, 1973.

surements in the region are essentially illustrative, rather than definitive, of a particular problem.

Carbon monoxide measurements have been taken in most urban areas in the Hudson Basin. Many of these, however, particularly in the New York State and New York City systems, have been taken in conjunction with other contaminant measurements at rooftop sites or away from areas of suspected high concentrations, and have therefore yielded results that are considered low. Most of the New Jersey system, as well as the New York City traffic-monitoring network, exhibits results significantly higher. From these data, it appears that in virtually all the region's downtown areas, the 8-hour national primary standard will be difficult to achieve without the imposition of additional controls beyond the federal new-vehicle standards. Restraints on vehicle movement (reducing the number of vehicle-miles traveled) seem to be insufficient. The only reasonable available alternatives are the reductions in per-vehicle emissions. But this suggestion would require a massive vehicle retrofit program—a program that cannot be implemented in time because the service industry could not install such devices, nor could the manufacturers supply them in sufficient numbers.

Escape from this dilemma will require either modification in the Clean Air Act or a determination by the EPA that 8-hour carbon monoxide values in downtown street level locations do not constitute a health problem, in that no susceptible receptors are subjected to these concentrations for an 8-hour period.

Photochemical Oxidants

Photochemical oxidant data within the region are rather limited, but they indicate that the federal standard is not being achieved throughout much of the region. During 1972, the federal reference method was changed from a potassium iodide method to one employing chemiluminescence. This charge has had a pronounced effect on reported values (compare the 1972 and 1973 data in Table 8-3). The values have generally risen, markedly in some cases; yet it cannot be stated that air quality has worsened. In fact, air quality should be improving as hydrocarbon emissions—the alleged precursors of photochemical oxidants—are reduced within the region.

The change in method will have a pronounced effect on programs within the Hudson Basin region. It must be emphasized that the standard of 0.08 ppm 1-hour value, not to be exceeded more than once a year, was based on effects noted using the potassium iodide method. No supportive health studies have been performed using the chemiluminescence method, which measures only ozone, not photochemical oxidants. Many agencies, including the New York State Department of Environmental Conservation, have postulated that photochemical oxidant concentrations (ozone) are not en-

TABLE 8-3.   One-Hour Maxima of Photochemical
Oxidants in the Hudson River Basin[a]

Station	1970	1971	1972	1973
Hempstead	—	0.127	0.106	0.178
Utica	—	—	—	0.095
Rensselaer	—	0.054	0.087	0.170
Schenectady	—	—	0.095	0.191
Babylon	—	—	—	0.149
Kingston	0.060	0.080	0.084	0.161
Glens Falls	—	—	—	0.115
Mamaroneck (Town)	—	0.095	0.136	0.183
New York City	—	0.174	0.207	0.179
51 Astor Place	0.120	0.090	0.080	0.250
Bayonne	0.140	0.113	0.108	0.283
Newark	0.130	0.109	0.101	0.264
Elizabeth	—	—	0.096	0.171

[a] Expressed as parts per million.

tirely a function of urban hydrocarbon emissions. This is evidenced by the fact that rural maxima are about as high as those found in urban areas. This theory was evaluated during the summer of 1974. If studies indicate that reduction of urban hydrocarbon emissions will not significantly reduce ozone measurements, then the EPA will be asked to reevaluate its air quality standard and control techniques for this contaminant.*

8.2   Issues and Illustrative Situations

Five case studies were undertaken by the Air Resources Task Group. They illustrate some of the complex issues and interrelationships encountered in the planning and implementation of public and private actions affecting the environment. The cases studied were the Storm King pumped-storage project, a deepwater oil terminal for northern New Jersey, *Boomer* v. *Atlantic Cement,* air quality and natural resources in the Catskills, and air pollution and transportation in the New York City area.

Storm King

The proposed Storm King pumped-storage project is designed to meet intraday peaking requirements. During off-peak hours, water would be

*The Environmental Protection Agency has proposed a change in the photochemical oxidant standard to 200 μg/m^3 or 0.10 ppm. [Ed.]

pumped to a storage reservoir at higher elevation. This water would be released as necessary to drive turbines to generate electricity for the peak period. The storage reservoir would be located in the Hudson Highlands, filling a depression between hills and covering about 240 acres.

The environmental questions raised by this proposal are numerous:

1. What will be the damage to scenic vistas by the flooding of the land between the hills?
2. What will be the effect on the ecology of the region by removal of this land from its current use and flooding it?
3. Will the pumping of water to the reservoir kill fish and other life in the river?
4. Will there be any compensating recreational value in the new reservoir or will fluctuating water levels negate such use?
5. Fifty percent more energy will be required to pump the water than will be generated. Is this acceptable?
6. If the additional energy use is supplied by fossil fuel rather than nuclear, what additional air pollution will result from the system?
7. The electricity will benefit people in New York City and vicinity. Should the area remote from New York City bear the brunt of environmental degradation for the benefit of other areas?
8. What will be the impact of the transmission lines?

Ancillary issues raised include the following:

1. Should the consumer demand for electric energy be uncontrolled or checked in some way?
2. Should environmental impacts be concentrated in urban and other areas where benefits accrue, or should impacts be dispersed so that their effect at any one place will not be so great?
3. Should New York City's planning exclude those in remote areas who receive impacts from sustaining the city?

This case also raised issues concerning institutional arrangements. The government agencies concerned included the Federal Power Commission, the State Department of Environmental Conservation, the City Department of Air Resources, fish and wildlife agencies, water resource agencies, local agencies concerned with land use, agencies concerned with the construction of the reservoir dam, and the AEC. There may be others.

In addition to the official agencies, there would be the interest of investors in the utility and its management, the financial institutions loaning the money for the project, fuel suppliers, and the citizens groups concerned with air quality or fish and wildlife. Not to be overlooked are the publics in New York City and in the area of the reservoir.

This project illustrates the great role of sunk costs in perpetuating a plan, even if it is a bad plan. Conditions have changed since this project was first proposed and approved.* Nuclear plants have not been built as originally envisioned to provide clean energy for pumping. The fossil-fuel situation is critical and, in the short range, changing from day to day. How can projects of this type be reviewed after the lapse of time to update the evaluation of the plan? How can the sunk costs in a bad plan be discounted so as not to overwhelm efforts to reevaluate the situation with freedom to select more desirable alternatives?

Deepwater Oil Terminal**

To facilitate the unloading of large supertankers for oil, it has been proposed that a floating facility be located off the Atlantic Coast. Supertankers reduce the shipping costs about 50%. At the national level, a critical goal is to import sufficient oil to maintain the economic health and security of the nation.

Much of the productive capacity, population, and need for petroleum is in the Northeast. One proposed location for such an offshore oil terminal is near northern New Jersey, an area already plagued with industrial development (especially petrochemical), population congestion, and waste disposal problems.

An oil terminal of the magnitude proposed would stimulate regional development through the use of oil as an energy source and as a raw material for the petrochemical industry. Indirectly, it would stimulate the development of a new, or the enhancement of an existing, infrastructure and regional market.†

The following environmental issues are raised by this case:

1. Will the offshore facility contribute to air pollution from escaping vapors of hydrocarbons, or to water pollution from accidental spills and intentional cleaning of tankers, etc.?
2. What will the onshore impacts be, including the effects from the

*As of November 1978, the project was awaiting further hearings before the Federal Energy Regulatory Commission. Con Edison plans to have it in service by the mid-1990s. [Ed.]

**For additional discussion of the deepwater oil terminal, refer to Volume 1, Chapter 1, Section 1.4.

†The deepwater oil terminal proposal is now dormant. The Corps'of Engineers study of the project concluded that there was a need for such a facility and that it was "economically, engineeringly and environmentally feasible. . . ." However, citing strong local opposition, the report recommended against federal participation "at this time" (U. S. Army Corps of Engineers, 1973). [Ed.]

induced growth of industry, population, and transportation, and the resulting wastes?

3. Air quality data are collected by inconsistent sampling procedures and under different site conditions. How can the data be related to health and environmental concerns?

4. It is assumed that a low level of growth comparable to normal past growth can be obtained. Is this so, or will economic pressures force a high level of growth? Is a "normally" low level of growth acceptable in an area already burdened with population and pollution?

5. Is a small increment of pollution linearly additive in its impact on health or environmental quality? Is there a threshold beyond which even small increments of pollution are unacceptable?

6. Is there a limit on the capacity of an area to absorb, e.g., pollution, population, or industrial development?

7. Is there need for a centralized, computerized, standardized data bank?

8. What are the implications of development at the microspatial scale? Are improved models required for single-source plumes, network (transportation) sources, and multiple sources (e.g., residential and commercial areas)?

9. Should plans be based on normal conditions or should abnormal conditions also be considered, as done by the AEC (probabilistic simulation of malfunctions)?

10. Is the developmental philosophy of concentrating pollution in areas already burdened an acceptable one?

This case illustrates the inadequacy of the uncoordinated decision-making process concerning land use. At present, land use is generally determined at the smallest civil division. In this case, the construction of the superport would unlease economic and political forces beyond the capability of these small units of government to handle.

However, in some ways the small civil division protects local interests. If national and multistate regional interests are served, environmental burdens may be thrust upon a local area without its consent or any concomitant compensation. This raises questions about the most appropriate level for decision-making where the issues involve international, national, regional, state, local, and private interests.

A very serious question raised by this case is the capability, or even desirability, of attempting to accomplish complex decision-making in an overall planned fashion. Should independent decisions be made in the interests of economic development, environmental quality, or social goals, and should provision be made for competition of interests on the battlefield of political action?

With respect to institutional arrangements, this case involved the following federal agencies: the Coast Guard, the U.S. Army Corps of Engineers, the U.S. Maritime Administration, the National Oceanic and Atmospheric Administration, the Department of Transportation, the Department of the Interior, the Council of Economic Advisers, the Office of Emergency Preparedness, and the Council on Environmental Quality. Other agencies that should have interests, but have apparently not had a significant role in the decision-making, include the Tri-State Regional Planning Commission, the Regional Plan Association, the Port Authority of New York and New Jersey, and Region II of the Environmental Protection Agency (EPA II). TSRPC and EPA II have attended meetings. A report of TSRPC has not been released and EPA II has not made detailed studies. RPA and the Port Authority have not actively studied the issue.

Boomer v. Atlantic Cement

Boomer v. *Atlantic Cement* not only illustrates the relationship between land use and air pollution but also brings to the fore the role of the courts in decision-making. In this case the court, in effect, directed that there be some degree of air pollution in the public interest.

A combination of natural resources—deposits useful in the manufacture of cement and access to transportationalong the Atlantic seaboard via the Hudson River—made southern Albany County an ideal location for the cement plant. Air pollution control equipment was installed, but it did not remove all of the pollution. Sometimes there were operating problems, and miscellaneous sources of fugitive dust were not adequately controlled. Affected neighbors brought suit against the company. The courts considered the school tax and other benefits to the community in allowing the company to continue operating after paying permanent damages. The air pollution was considered to be a nuisance and not a direct health hazard. The right of the state to control air pollution emissions was not questioned.

Environmental issues raised by this case are

1. How are the interests in natural resource development, environmental quality, and regional economic development balanced in site selection for industry?
2. Does the award of nuisance damages to private individuals protect environmental quality? Is it an acceptable approach to land use that degrades the environment for all subsequent populations in the area?
3. Is it ever in the public interest to degrade environmental quality?

4. Should health values or property values be superior?
5. Does air pollution control rest on proven health hazards of a specific, short-term, acute nature, or is an effect detrimental to the quality of life also considered to be a health hazard?
6. Should ambient air quality or emissions be the basis for air pollution control?
7. Should the courts be the final arbiter of the public interest in determining how much air pollution is acceptable?
8. Should taxes paid by an industry be a determinant of how much air pollution is to be controlled?
9. Is it all right to pollute the air if compensation is paid to property owners for the financial damage?
10. Do all citizens have a constitutional right to a clean environment? If not, should there be a constitutional amendment to that end?
11. Are natural resources a public trust?
12. Should local environments be degraded in order for a larger population to receive the benefits of a natural resource?
13. What standing should the interests of individual citizens have in matters concerning their environmental quality?
14. Should environmental impact statements be required for all major developments, whether public or private ventures?

Interests in this case, aside from the litigants, included the State Department of Commerce (which helped select the site), the State Department of Environmental Conservation, the State Attorney General's Office, the Coeymans Town Board, the Ravena–Coeymans–Selkirk School Board, and the Albany County Department of Health.

Air Quality and Natural Resources in the Catskills

About 10 million people in New York State alone live within 2 to 3 hours' driving time of the Catskills. Millions more live in nearby areas of New Jersey, Connecticut, and Massachusetts. Travel to the Catskills, and tourist activity within the area, induce pollution from autos and ancillary development. But the Catskills may also be affected by pollution generated in remote areas. Previous studies have not considered the interactions between a natural area, tourist influxes, and air quality. Because it contains no major sources of pollution, there is a dearth of baseline information about air quality in the Catskills. Furthermore, little is known about the interactions of the forests and other wildlife with air pollution.

More research is required to ascertain the effects of air pollution on vegetation, especially secondary effects in combination with other factors such as disease and insects. Little or nothing is known about the effects of air pollution on disease and insect susceptibility, genotypic and phenotypic evolution, responses of plants to stress, agricultural productivity and timber yields, quantitative dose response from acute and chronic exposure, and quality of plant-derived food and fiber.

Environmental issues raised by this case include

1. Should recreational areas in a state be available to persons from outside the state? How can the overwhelming of a natural area be avoided?
2. Forested land in New York State is increasing. Why? Is this increase desirable? Is marginally productive agricultural land being returned to a use for which it is better suited? If so, are geology, topography, etc., determinants of basic land use potential?
3. Is commercial forestry compatible with recreational pursuits?
4. Is mining compatible with preservation of forestlands?
5. Air pollution from northern New Jersey and New York City may be transported at times to this area. What is the potential for damage? What can be done to control air pollution generated in areas remote from the receptor?
6. Should major highways be constructed in the vicinity of such an area?
7. Is industry compatible with natural recreational areas?
8. Are there benefits from forests other than recreation, such as the release of oxygen in the fixing of carbon?
9. How can air pollution effects on vegetation be minimized?
10. What is the long-term effect of air pollution on the natural succession of flora and fauna?
11. What are the interactions among land use, regional economy, recreation, and air quality? How will further development affect trees, etc.?
12. Air quality data are lacking in the Catskill area. Are they necessary for proper planning?
13. What is the effect on forests and vegetation of low-level exposures to air pollution over a long period of time? What is the effect of economic and population growth (e.g., power plants, cement plants, transportation) on the extent of forests?
14. Of the institutions concerned with development of the recreational potential of the Catskills, are any concerned with air pollution?

In the Catskills case, there appears to be little interaction between the interests concerned with wildlife and recreation, on the one hand, and the New York and New Jersey air pollution control agencies on the other. Furthermore, interaction is also lacking with those concerned with transportation planning, land use, and regional economic development as they may relate to air pollution generation.

Air Pollution and Transportation in the New York City Area

From the standpoint of the Air Resources Task Group, transportation systems in urban areas and transit corridors are of interest because of their impact on air quality. Of course, dust and other air pollutants may be generated in the construction of facilities, but it is the pollution resulting from day-to-day operations that is of major concern.

In urban areas, motor vehicles are a major source of certain pollutants— carbon monoxide, oxides of nitrogen, and hydrocarbons. Motor vehicles may also be a significant source of particulates, but little attention has been given to this possibility.

If electric power is substituted for internal combustion engines, pollutants from generating stations must be considered. If nuclear fuel is used, air pollution is virtually eliminated but the potential hazards of ionizing radiation must be considered. If fossil fuel is used at electric power stations, the pollutants of concern are different from those generated by internal combustion engines. They are primarily oxides of sulfur and particulates, along with some oxides of nitrogen, carbon monoxide, and hydrocarbons. Both nuclear and fossil-fueled generating stations produce waste heat, which must be considered both in its potential impact on atmospheric conditions (e.g., vapors from cooling towers), and in its impact on water resource (e.g., consumption, alteration of flows, and temperature changes).

Community air sampling data show excessively high levels of carbon monoxide, which could be a problem in other communities over 25,000 population. Carbon monoxide was therefore selected to illustrate this case.

A number of strategies have been advanced for controlling vehicle emissions and traffic. On a short-range basis, emissions from mobile sources may be reduced by three general approaches: by reducing the rate of emission of pollutants, by reducing total vehicle-miles of travel, and by shifting travel to modes of lower pollution potential. On a longer-range basis, the need for travel and transport can be reduced through design of land use and through changes in spatial arrangements and living habits.

This case raises a variety of issues of great complexity, both from the standpoint of environmental impacts and institutional interactions. Among the environmental issues are

1. How well defined are the health effects from levels of pollution permitted from motor vehicles?
2. Are the pollutants from motor vehicles more or less hazardous to health than the pollutants produced by electric generating stations?

3. Is the thermal pollution from electric generating stations more acceptable than air pollution from motor vehicles?
4. Is it possible and feasible to control emissions from motor vehicles without restricting travel?
5. If exhaust emissions are controlled, will particulates from, e.g., tire wear, pavement wear, or wear of brake shoes be a sufficient problem that travel will have to be restricted?
6. If alternate mass transit is made attractive, will people forego use of a personal car? How can they be encouraged to do so?
7. Will people accept industry in residential areas if the industrial plant is designed to have no pollution, noise, or other objectionable features? If so, will people elect to live close to work (within walking distance)?
8. Should land use patterns in cities be restructured to encourage walking and cycling?
9. Can mass transit systems be developed which do not require the use, in part of the trip, of a personal car?
10. What kinds of deterrents to travel in a personal car would be effective in reducing polution levels? Will people accept such restrictions?

Auxiliary issues raised include

1. Who or what agency should plan for transportation? Should air pollution control agencies determine acceptability of transportation strategies in a control function or in the actual transportation planning role.
2. Should it be left to government agents and professional planners to decide what is "good" for the population at large?
3. How can and should ways of life and habits be changed?
4. How much personal choice should there be in selecting a mode of transportation; a location to live with respect to work?
5. Can a majority choice for air quality be imposed to restrict actions by a minority of polluters?
6. Should air quality, land use, transportation, and energy be the responsibility of one super and ineffective agency?
7. Should density of workplaces be restricted?

Among the public agencies involved in these issues are the EPA and its Region II office, the U.S. Department of Transportation, the Interstate Commerce Commission, the New York State Department of Environmental Conservation, the New York City Division of Air Pollution Control, the Interstate Sanitation Commission, the Port Authority of New York and New Jersey, and the New Jersey Department of Environmental Protection. Indirectly concerned are the planning agencies controlling land use, utility commissions concerned with transportation and energy, real estate developers, highway departments, investment bankers, industrial planners, and a host of others.

Analysis of Issues

Criteria

The cases studied reveal uncertainty with respect to the phenomena to be observed and evaluated in determining environmental quality.

With respect to air quality, federal legislation has mandated the Environmental Protection Agency to establish primary air quality standards to protect health. Secondary standards are also to be set, and there is some uncertainty about them. For example, are levels of NO_x too severe and levels of CO and hydrocarbons too lenient? Furthermore, only acute physiological responses are considered in the primary standards, not the effects of air pollution on the mental health and well-being of man. In the analyses in this chapter, the task group did not examine the basis for the federal standards, referring such questions to the Human Health Task Group.

The effect of air pollution on ecology is assumed to be potentially detrimental because damage to vegetation in specific locations or test situations has been cited. The case of the Catskills, however, reveals a lack of generally applicable knowledge for evaluating effects of air pollution in a large region with diverse species. Although acute effects may be forecast under certain conditions, their interaction under natural conditions of climate, disease, or insects is not fully understood. It is also not known how air quality might favor the dominance of certain species over others and the resulting impacts on ecosystems. With the transport of air pollution over great distances, from urban–industrial locations to more primitive areas, and the location of transportation corridors through agricultural and forested areas, these matters demand more attention.

One of the parameters evolving in the evaluation of air quality is the energy investment in "clean" or "dirty" air. This is not just the influence that air quality standards have on the selection of energy conversion and energy transportation systems, but includes the energy requirements to meet air quality standards (or to restore damage caused by air pollution if standards are not met). Such analyses may be compared with benefit–cost analysis of the economic type, but with energy, a criterion other than the dollar is needed.

Strategies to preserve or enhance air quality affect aesthetic considerations directly and indirectly. In the *Boomer* case, the dusty operations that depressed land values were objectionable but not necessarily detrimental to health. In the Storm King case, a scenic vista was to be altered and a reservoir substituted for a valley. The social and economic value of aesthetic considerations in such cases is somewhat elusive, but nevertheless real. Aesthetics, as such, may have value in mental health and in stimulating mental development. This, too, is an area for further research.

All of these factors—health, ecology, energy and economic investment, and aesthetics—are parameters in the evaluation of environmental quality. Proposed actions should be evaluated to determine their impact on each factor. Further refinement of these parameters is sorely needed for use in decision-making.

Measurements

Where there is agreement or legislation on criteria and standards (e.g., the EPA primary standards for air pollutants), planning and decision-making rest on measurements. In several of the cases reference is made to the need for uniformity, or at least consistency, among jurisdictions on parameters to be sampled, test procedure, sampling locations, frequency of sampling, number of samples, time period, and other aspects of sampling methodology. Standardization is essential to permit comparability of data between areas. In most cases data were lacking or were inadequate for evaluation and planning purposes.* In addition to measurements of air quality, other indicators of environmental change should be observed to determine indirect effects of air pollution and to see what other environmental and social conditions lead to air pollution.

Community air monitoring systems are costly, but when compared with investments in air pollution control by the private sector, these outlays for data gathering are warranted. Unfortunately, monitoring activities have little dramatic appeal. Appropriating bodies are more prone to support expenditures for direct action programs.

It is also possible that data currently collected are not utilized to the extent that they might be. Samples may not be in the location most representative or useful for evaluation or planning. The relationship between pollutant emissions from multiple sources and community air quality is not precisely understood to the point of predictability. Accordingly, much control is on a "trial and error" basis, following the rules of thumb of "best practice" or "available technology."

Indirect and Subtle Effects

Where air pollution from an isolated exhaust stack causes acute responses in the immediate vicinity, the relationships are readily recognized and ap-

*This is especially true when considering the effects of a given project, or potentially detrimental activity, at distances somewhat removed from the immediate site of the project. This point is exemplified in the Catskills case study.

propriate action can be considered almost immediately. In the cases cited herein, the causal relationships are more subtle or indirect and require more thoughtful examination.

Examples include the following:

1. The transport of pollutants from point of generation to remote areas, such as from northern New Jersey and New York City to the Catskills
2. The effects on air quality of increasing population density and industrial and commercial activity, as in the onshore activity stimulated by the development of a deepwater oil terminal
3. In a similar vein, the ultimate effects on air quality of "normal" growth of population and economic activity
4. The effects on air quality of decisions pertaining to such matters as energy or transportation systems. Similarly, the impact of air quality regulations and standards on choices in these other areas

The examples reveal even more remote relationships that involve land use, regional and national economic development, resource utilization, and the like. Decisions in all of these areas influence air quality, and achievement of air quality goals may ultimately require changes in these other areas.

There appears to be considerable knowledge which could be brought to bear on the examination of these issues, but there are also significant constraints on the utilization of that knowledge:

1. The lack of a centralized, coordinated, computerized environmental data bank based on a uniform sampling and measurement system
2. The fact that land use planning and control is done at the level of the smallest political unit with little or none at the regional, state, and federal levels
3. The lack of attention to environmental determinants for decision-making with respect to growth patterns, land use, energy systems, transportation systems, and the like
4. The lack of environmental impact analysis where NEPA does not apply, or inadequate breadth of focus where NEPA or similar requirements do apply

These constraints might be eased by reorganization of governmental activities at various levels and by legislation. But those steps would not be easy because of existing strong relationships between agencies and the nongovernmental interests that they deal with.

Policy Issues

These cases raise policy questions typical of other situations in other locations. These questions include the following:

1. Should air quality be a major determinant in policy formulation for, and control of, land use, transportation, and energy sources and systems?
2. Should developments that tend to degrade the environment be situated in areas already degraded to a degree (concentrated) or in areas relatively free of pollution (dispersed)?
3. What growth policies should be pursued—maintenance of "normal" growth, economic expansion, zero growth, deconcentration?
4. What relative weight should be given to environmental quality, resource development, economic expansion, and energy investment in decision-making?
5. How should economic and human values be balanced? Where do private property values fit?
6. To what extent should personal freedom of choice be restricted in the interest of the whole population?
7. To what extent should public and private discretionary decisions be subject to public scrutiny, review, and control?

These questions are interwoven with people's concepts of their personal relationships to their government and society. Habits, culture, and behavior must also be considered.

There is the very sensitive question of whether judgments of government technical experts are based on limited professional criteria or consider the values of the people affected. Questions such as these can only be resolved in the political arena. The problem then becomes one of whether information and knowledge are available to, and conveniently assembled for, analysis by those making decisions, be they the electorate or their representatives. Accordingly, the major concern here is the satisfactory resolution of questions related to criteria and measurements, and the understanding of indirect and subtle relationships so that more informed decisions are possible.

The social, economic, and health implications of these decisions are important in the evaluation of alternative proposed actions, including the "no-action" alternative. One may raise the question of the extent to which a public agency should assume an advocacy role with respect to these matters. If so, is the agency assuming multiple, and possibly incompatible roles, e.g., responsibility for the promotion of energy production facilities and simultaneously the protection of public safety and health from hazards associated with these facilities?

Where decision-making responsibilities are vested in a government agency, communication between the agency, the principals, and the public must be considered. The agency may be able to communicate its findings and determinations, but may lack the means and opportunity to ascertain public feelings and to communicate them to government officials in the process of formulating decisions. Since the implementation of decisions is frequently delayed, it is important to provide a mechanism for reviewing and updating past decisions to make sure they are still economic, in the public interest, and represent the best available alternatives.

Coordination

These cases all involved a multiplicity of agencies at various levels of government. It appeared as though these agencies operate at times as adversaries or competitors. It is apparent also that agencies designated as "planning agencies" are not the only ones doing planning, and the planning they do may be very restricted in scope.

One of the problems in planning is moving from the analysis and planning phase to the implementation phase. Where planners conduct their activities without the direct involvement of the change agents, implementation may flounder from lack of support.

The forecast of private planning and decisions in public planning exercises becomes difficult. However, government is not without persuaders to influence private decisions. Taxes, subsidies and other incentives, eminent domain, and laws and regulations are devices that may be invoked to promote or deter certain decisions. More subtle withholding of utilities, transportation, and other services can stimulate or deter development.

Even so, problems of level of jurisdiction, branch of government, and unit therein all become issues. Should courts be the final arbiter in issues of environmental quality? Should the smallest political unit determine land use? What is the role of private citizens and citizen activist groups in government decision-making?

It has been suggested that the level of jurisdiction should encompass sufficient territory that implementation of the plan of action will have a significant effect on the air quality. One may postulate that this territory should also contain sufficient taxable resources to provide financial support for an adequate program. It is also necessary to coordinate with other decision-making processes in the same territorial jurisdiction.

Satisfaction of these criteria may mean a shift to larger jurisdictional areas. The hazard in this process is one of aggregating majorities that will impose or add to the environmental stress of some segment of the area.

Interdependencies

There are numerous illustrations of the interaction between areas of the environment, as well as with other areas of social concern. These matters will be explored in the next section.

8.3   Priority Policy Interdependencies

Interrelationships and interdependencies between air resources and other areas of environmental concern fall into two categories. One relates to activities that generate air pollution and that have to be restricted in some way to achieve air quality goals. Another category of interdependencies deals with actions or activities adversely affected by air pollution.

Air quality goals might restrict activity in various categories of land use (commercial, industrial, high-density residential), as well as in transportation, solid waste disposal, resource extraction, and energy conversion. Uses adversely affected by air pollution, but not considered major sources of air pollution in themselves, include natural forests and similar areas, agriculture, low-density residential neighborhoods, resort development, and certain types of industrial development such as electronics and food processing.

Generators of Pollution

Land Use

A feature that threads through practically all the case studies is the interdependency between land use and air pollution. When one considers the normal meteorology and topography of an area, it is suggested that there is a carrying capacity of that area to receive air pollution within prescribed limits based upon the ventilation rate. Accordingly, the quantity or tonnage of air pollutants which the atmosphere could handle without exceeding standards has a limit. In other words, the land area has a carrying capacity for sources of air pollution. The density of sources has to be restricted, as well as the amount of emissions by individual sources. Thus, the future development or dispersal of various activities should consider the assimilative capacity of the air and the area's existing burden.

Such an approach raises the additional question of whether or not air pollution control activities should be based on normal conditions or extreme adverse conditions. In urban areas with a diversity of pollution sources, individual adjustments based on meteorological conditions and forecasts become extremely difficult, if not impossible, to manage. Consequently, it appears that the control effort in such areas would have to be based upon extreme conditions.

If land use were used as an instrument in air pollution control, then an area with excessive air pollution might be discouraged or prohibited from further development that would introduce more pollutants into the atmosphere. For example, the Hudson Valley should not be used as the location of any more fossil-fueled electric generating plants. Similarly, the Arthur Kill should not be the site of additional petroleum refining facilities. On the other hand, natural resources, such as those used in manufacturing cement, are site-specific and their use may result in some unavoidable local degradation.

The question has been raised previously whether industrial sources should be dispersed so that some sources go into relatively clean areas with some degradation of the atmosphere. The alternative is to place industries that produce air pollution in an area with similar industry, thereby aggravating an already degraded environment. The resolution hinges on value considerations, related to air quality goals, economic development aspirations, etc.

Transportation

Transportation is obviously also related to land use. Most transportation-related air pollution, of course, is from mobile sources. Even so, the many small sources of pollution do tend to be concentrated in certain areas or corridors. These areas of concentration are transportation corridors, parking facilities, and major traffic generators such as sports stadiums and shopping centers. Topography obviously can influence the concentration of pollutants from these mobile sources. In addition, certain man-made features, such as tall buildings and tunnels, tend to aggravate this situation. The location of a transportation corridor in a natural area will introduce air pollution and may disturb existing ecosystems. The routing of traffic and the arrangement of buildings will influence the concentrations of pollutants within the urban area.

There has been previous discussion of the possibility of controlling emissions from these sources, as well as restricting or facilitating vehicular movements to reduce the amount of air pollution. On a longer-term basis, rearrangement of spatial relationships between place of work, recreation, and residence could do much to reduce emissions from mobile sources.

If electric power is substituted for the internal combustion engine, air pollution from electric generation must be considered. Substitution of mass transit for autos will also reduce overall pollution, but may also tend to concentrate it.

Solid Waste Disposal

No cases were developed to illustrate problems associated with solid waste disposal. Some communities, however, use incineration to reduce the volume of solid waste that must be disposed of in landfills. Incinerator feed may consist of garbage and combustible refuse and may also include the solids resulting from treatment of liquid waste. The burning of sewage sludges presents special problems not necessarily associated with the burning of garbage and combustible refuse. Problems most frequently associated with the combustion of solid waste are those of odor and fly ash. There is some concern about the possibility of producing carcinogens in the burning of plastics, and there is not much known about other chemical by-products resulting from combustion of the many things that go into a municipal incinerator. Federal research in this area has been curtailed in recent years.

Aside from generating air pollution, the burning of solid wastes simply to reduce volume neglects the potential for recovery and recycling. Even where resource recovery is practiced, the heat value of the combustible solid waste may be recovered to produce low-quality steam to heat buildings and for other purposes.

Resource Extraction

The *Boomer* case illustrates a type of problem associated with the extraction of site-specific natural resources. If these resources are to be exploited, there may be air pollution problems. Since the location of these resources is not under human control, it may be necessary to restrict or prohibit some types of development near the point of resource extraction to avoid air pollution problems. If this is impossible, it may be necessary to alter the existing use in the vicinity of the resource so that resource extraction can proceed.

Electric Energy Generation and Air Pollution

Most contemporary electric power plants use either fossil or nuclear fuel. Air pollution standards tend to restrict the use of fossil fuel because of the sulfur content of fuel oil and coal. There are practical means of stripping sulfur from fuel oil, but this has thus far not been proved for coal. Crushing can remove pyrites, but there would still be about 2% sulfur left in the coal unless the supply of coal were unusually low in sulfur to begin with. The removal of sulfur from stack gases is only now moving beyond the experimental and pilot-plant stage. Trial commercial installations have reported considerable difficulty in maintaining consistent operations.* If nuclear fuel is substituted for fossil fuel to avoid air pollution problems, we are faced with an evaluation of the effects of the ionizing radiation that results from operation of the nuclear plants. Whereas the levels of ionizing radiation resulting from the operations of nuclear facilities are generally below those of background radiation, there are individuals who are concerned about this minimum amount, as well as the possibility of catastrophic emissions due to system failure.

Whether the plant is nuclear or fossil-fueled, there is waste heat to be absorbed by the environment. Nuclear plants are less efficient than fossil-fueled plants, so there is more heat to be disposed of per kilowatt-hour

---

*Since this chapter was written, there have been significant improvements in the reliability and efficiency of SO_2 scrubbers. [Ed.]

generated. This hot water, if discharged to streams, can produce changes in aquatic ecosystems that may be considered detrimental. An alternative is to dissipate the heat to the atmosphere through cooling towers or cooling ponds. This procedure may alter the immediate climate, perhaps resulting in some greater frequency of fogging. The large cooling towers necessary for natural draft may have a visual impact which some people might wish to avoid.

Because of concern for the safety of population, the tendency is to locate nuclear plants remote from populations. This requires construction of transmission lines. The broad rights-of-way that must be cleared for such lines may cause ecological changes where they pass through forested areas.

Receptors of Pollution

Natural Resources

We do not know the extent to which air pollution will change the ecology of forests or other natural areas. However, the transport of pollution from urban areas could introduce a significant quantity of sulfates to such an environment. These sulfates result from the combustion of fossil fuels containing sulfur. The likelihood would be that the rainfall in such circumstances would be acid in nature. This too, could alter the ecology in such areas.

Many truck crops are adversely affected by various pollutants—oxides of nitrogen, oxides of sulfur, hydrocarbons, and so forth. Thus, the transport of pollutants from urban areas is also of concern in agricultural areas.

Neighborhoods

Apart from its adverse health effects, air pollution can adversely affect the quality of life in residential neighborhoods. Odors are disturbing; particulate matter will dirty the linens and automobiles and other things in the neighborhood; sulfates will have an adverse effect on paints and statues and promote rust. Particularly severe problems can be caused by lead, fluorides, other metallic compounds, and acid fumes from smelters.

In addition to the direct health effects and the direct economic damage from pollution, one must consider the effect on the mental health and mental development of persons living in neighborhoods subjected to air pollution. Little is known about this and suitable research attention might be applied to this area.

Special Developments

One frequently hears about the retarding effect of air pollution control requirements on some types of economic development. Little consideration is given to the fact that air pollution also retards economic and industrial development. An example was the stagnation of Pittsburgh before the cleanup. This is particularly true if the industries require clean air to maintain the quality of the product, as in electronics and food processing. Furthermore, employees of a relatively clean industry are sometimes unwilling to work or live in a dirty community.

Recreation

Recreational values are particularly sensitive to air pollution, whether generated by visitors or transported from other areas. Scenic vistas have already been desecreated in the Los Angeles area, where the beautiful foothills are no longer visible from the boulevards and valleys on days of photochemical smog accumulation. Yosemite National Park has suffered from the great number of visitors in automobiles. If these problems are anticipated, they can be controlled to a degree to protect the natural beauty of areas such as Lake Tahoe and the Catskills. Once such areas are disturbed, it is difficult, if not impossible, to regenerate them.

Other Interdependencies

In evaluating alternatives between the use of the personal automobile and mass transportation, the suggestion is offered that this is a comparison between pollution created by the internal combustion engine and pollution created by an electric generating station which may burn fossil fuel. In actuality, the environmental and social impacts of the decision are much more extensive. In evaluating alternative sources of power, one should consider the environmental pollution and other hazards from the extraction, transportation, and storage of various fuels.

The air pollution in the actual processing of the fuel to generate electricity has been discussed, but one should also consider the disposal of the wates resulting from the combustion. In the case of coal, there are the ashes and collected fly ash. In the case of nuclear plants, there is the problem of radioactive waste. Thus far, we do not have a final disposal method for radioactive waste. The present method of handling has to be considered a temporary holding until a more satisfactory method of recycling or other disposal is developed. True, the amount of radioactive waste from nuclear power plants is insignificant compared to the wastes from weapons manufacturing.

Not to be overlooked, and equally as important as physical and biological impacts, are the social impacts of the decisions. If the choice is made to burn petroleum products rather than coal, then coal miners are unemployed and the petroleum refineries employ very few people. The question might also be raised, Is it better for uranium miners to be unemployed than for coal miners to be unemployed?

The fallacy of this reasoning is that people should be employed in some task that is not socially dysfunctional. If make-work projects are to be undertaken, they might better be considered with respect to projects of great social value. To do otherwise would be to protect those who have investments in a particular way of life or mode of operation rather than to protect the great number of individuals who might be employed in that kind of operation. It would be similar to suggesting that one should smoke cigarettes in order to keep farmers employed in raising tobacco and other individuals employed in manufacturing cigarettes. It would be of much greater value to society to have the farmers engaged in raising food and the cigarette manufacturers engaged in processing the food.

Recommendations

In general, it does not appear that new, innovative institutions are necessary. What may be necessary is a reorientation of the institutions' objectives and modes of operation, a greater utilization of available knowledge, a search for additional knowledge for purposes of decision-making, and a possible rearrangement or reallocation of functions among existing institutions.

Environmental Ethics

The adoption of what might be termed a code of environmental ethics by both public and private institutions could lead to a more sensitive evaluation of the environmental impacts of decisions and to the formulation of attitudes that would lead to a better quality environment. As an example, it is understood that the Maine Bankers Association adopted a code of ethics to use in developing their lending and investment policies. It is also understood that some of the large New York investment banks have hired consultants to advise on the environmental and ecological impact of large-scale projects seeking investment capital. To develop fully this "voluntary" approach to better environmental quality, it is necessary to have knowledge upon which decisions can be based. This suggests the incorporation of appropriate course work in the curricula of institutions that train engineers, scientists, business administrators, public administrators, and other potential decisionmakers. If the electorate is to exercise its opportunities in an informed way, then it would be necessary to incorporate environmental concerns in the high school curricula. This might best be done, not in special courses, but by training high school teachers in science and civics so they could use environmental examples in their classroom work.

Obviously there will be continued need for specialists who can advise on unusual problems, foresee future events, and correct the mistakes of the past. Unfortunately, in recent years the federal government has withdrawn its support for such educational activities. Since the financial rewards in this field are not as great as in some others, there is a continuing need to subsidize scientific education to provide government and industry with the expertise necessary to conduct sound environmental programs.

Coordination of Planning

In the government sector, the critical area of concern seems to be that of planning, particularly the planning of land use and associated transportation. What we have seen in the cases outlined previously is land use planning by the smallest civil divisions. These local governmental units cannot begin to cope with the ramifications of large-scale developments, such as a deepwater oil port, whose effects are felt on a regional scale.

Unfortunately, land use planning seems to consider primarily physical and economic development concerns. Little attention is given to the ultimate impact on air quality or other environmental concerns in land use planning as practiced by the small civil divisions. To be effective, land use planning would need to be conducted at several levels of government with various purposes receiving primary attention at respective levels. The level should be such that it can materially influence the end results. For purposes of air pollution control, planning would have to be on some regional basis encompassing more than townships and small cities. Because of the intimate relationship between transportation and air quality, the planning process must include transportation along with land use and concerns for air pollution control. It is apparent from the case studies that there is a lot of fragmentary planning occurring in the transportation field. Elements at various levels of government are not fully coordinated, nor is there adequate coordination among those planning for various modes of transportation. This lack of coordination is detrimental to the end goal of improved air quality.

Monitoring

Government interventions to improve air quality have been focused on establishing air pollution control agencies to monitor environmental conditions and to propose remedial action, employing legislative sanctions where necessary. Unfortunately, the monitoring systems are neither sufficiently uniform nor sufficiently extensive to allow the optimum use of monitoring data in planning air pollution control programs.

What is needed is a centralized, computerized data bank with uniform methods of sampling, location of samplers, test methods, data processing, and the like. Other environmental parameters must be measured along with those relating to air quality so that meaningful decisions can be made.

Air Quality

A factor generally overlooked is the role of the courts in the question of air quality. The *Boomer* v. *Atlantic Cement* case brings out the very important role of the courts in air quality and other environmental issues. One might raise the question whether the courts are adequately prepared to act in such a role and whether or not the value systems used in adversary proceedings employed in most courts should be applied in determining social policy with respect to environmental quality. If courts are to be used in this manner, there should probably be more extensive research into the matter of providing information so that informed decisions are made.

Consideration might be given to some other approach to the resolution of contests involving air quality. The difficulty is that such questions do not rest on matters of air quality alone, nor do they rest on the protection of the health of individuals and populations. Also to be considered are the rights of individuals and the compensation of interested parties when their use of property is denied or taken for higher purposes of society in the interest of environmental quality.

Not to be overlooked are the rights of groups of people to the amenities of life, the need to preserve and protect ecosystems, and the rights of populations to a healthful and stimulating quality of life. To pursue these interests of the people, a role could be created for a public defender, because individuals may not have the knowledge or resources to assess adequately environmental quality issues and the impacts of proposed actions.

8.4 Strategies for Utilizing Knowledge and Establishing Research Priorities

Technical Issues

Two items of technical concern, already apparent from previous discussions, are significant in the examination of policy analyses and determinations. One has to do with the data base used for decision-making purposes. It has been previously indicated that, at present, the methodologies, parameters, and location practices of sampling networks vary between jurisdictions. An effort should be made to develop a centralized, computerized, integrated, environmental data collection system and data management information system that would serve the several states and jurisdictions in the region.

If there were concurrence and uniform implementation of agreed-upon procedures, each state could manage its own system, providing the data obtained are readily available to the other states, to all decision-making authorities, and to the public. Experience would indicate, however, that it would be better if this were centralized rather than handled by the several states independently.

If there were an adequate data base, it would be possible to proceed with the development of a computerized simulation model. The purpose would be to examine the physical impact of alternatives before investments were made which would preclude feasible alternatives. For example, one could propose a location of a particular electric generating station, a manufacturing process, a resource extraction operation, a transportation system, or other similar action and, using the model, evaluate the impact of these actions without actually having to experience them and to make expensive corrections. Such a model could help avoid the problem of what to do about Storm King. It would also help to examine locations for an offshore oil terminal. Other similar problems could be handled by this means.

These two proposals would require considerable research and investment. But in considering priority, one might compare the cost of these efforts with the cost of all the installations which might be constructed in future years. It would certainly be worthwhile to invest in these kinds of efforts and to avoid some very costly mistakes, both in terms of human value and economic investment.

Another area of investigation which might be included under technical issues is the determination of the carrying capacity of a geographic region for various kinds of human activity. How much water pollution, air pollution, population density, traffic, and other pollution can an area assimilate before the resulting impairment of health, destruction of social values, degradation of the quality of life, or other costs exceed tolerable limits? Although a general concensus is developing that there are limits to the amount of pollution or other environmental stress that can be absorbed by an area, these limits are yet to be defined.

Social Issues

One of the critical items in connection with social issues is the definition of public interest. This involves the articulation of important social values that people in groups desire to have effectuated. Every public decision may have costs and benefits, but a crucial—and frequently overlooked—aspect of the decision is the distributional effect. In other words, which groups bear the costs and which groups reap the benefits? This thesis is generally accepted, but problems arise in developing the parameters or indicators to be measured and the method of measurement for considering these social values. Are the social values to have one system of concern paramount over others? In other words, are environmental quality and the health of people superior to economic values? What about the aesthetics and the enjoyment of a clean environment? Should these considerations be subservient to employment or to the generation of capital wealth? Should one area accept an environmental stress so that another area can receive the benefit of a resource extracted from the first area? Better articulation of social values is needed, as well as greater precision in the indexes used to measure the achievement of these values.

In addition, it is impossible to engage in meaningful policy analyses without directly considering the normative aspects. What social values are public laws, regulations, and institutions effectuating in terms of the evaluation of options? What are the criteria for deciding which set of effects of a given outcome is "good" and which is "bad"?

Justice Brandeis once expounded the idea that a chief virtue of federalism as a mode of national organization is that it allows the existence of numerous social laboratories to test out policies. The social laboratories theory is working in many ways in the environmental area: Vermont, Florida, and Hawaii are experimenting with new land use schemes; Michigan and other states are investigating new legal relationships; the federal government led the way with the idea of environmental impact statements; Oregon has pioneered in solid waste legislation regarding returnable bottles and containers. One might propose innovative methods be attempted in the Hudson Valley region to handle the social issues associated with decision-making in matters which impact on environmental quality.

In formulating the public interest in environmental quality decisions, the question arises about the appropriate role for special interest groups. In particular, the question may be raised what is the appropriate role for public environmental organizations in decision-making at state and local levels. At what stage or stages can the public be most effective? Are the National Environmental Policy Act and other formal citizen involvement mechanisms means of involving the public, or are they a means of keeping the public dissenters busy shuffling papers? Are public forums a more effective means of developing public opinion? One might also explore whether or not these environmental organizations really reflect the public interest or the interests of a very narrowly oriented group of individuals.

Summary

This chapter has outlined a variety of issues associated with decision-making on matters affecting environmental quality. These issues have ranged from technical questions, such as the indexes to be measured and methods for measuring them, to the balancing of social values among interest groups. This task group has also outlined deficiences of governmental institutions for dealing with the current problems. In some instances, strategies which may overcome some of these deficiencies are suggested either for investigation or implementation.

This task group did not come away from this exercise with any feeling of doom. There do seem to be institutional capabilities within the present organization of society and government to handle environmental issues in a rational manner. There are areas of technical knowledge that need to be extended. There are methods of information management that would improve decision-making, and there are arrangements of governmental institutions that might be more effective. It does seem possible, however, within these considerations, to provide a model of decision-making that would come closer to achieving the intended results.

Chapter 9

BIOLOGICAL COMMUNITIES

9.1   Introduction

A biological community is an assemblage of populations of species inhabiting a prescribed area and set of environmental conditions. Communities have a functional unity with respect to food and energy-flow relationships among the components. They also have compositional unity in that there is a certain probability that certain species will occur together. But species are, to a large extent, replaceable in time and space, so that functionally similar communities may have different species compositions.

The concept of biological communities is broad and may be used to designate assemblages of various sizes, from the biota of a spring to that of the entire Hudson Basin. For the purposes of this chapter, we have divided the biota in the Hudson Basin study area into two communities—the aquatic and the terrestrial, and each of these may in turn be divided into several smaller biotic communities.

The populations of biological communities, in their struggle for survival, strive to convert as much of their environment as possible to biomass of their own species. The more similar the habitat and environmental requirements of any two species, the more competitive they are likely to be. Each organism is part of the environment for other organisms.

Members of the Biological Communities Task Group: Gerald J. Lauer, Angus MacBeth, David Pimentel, Bert Salwen, and John Seddon.

Biological communities interact with the physical and chemical components of the environment that they inhabit so that flow of energy leads to a clearly defined trophic structure, biotic diversity, and material cycles between the living and nonliving parts of the system. The biotic and the physical/chemical factors, taken as a whole, comprise an ecosystem. This definition is applicable to small-scale units such as ponds and to large-scale units such as river basins—or even to the entire planet.

The interactions of a biological community with its abiotic environment induce changes in both the biotic and abiotic components. Modification of the environment by each successive assemblage of species eventually leads to its replacement by a new assemblage of species, as when mosses and lichens "pioneer" on rocky substrates and, in their processes of growth and decay, form soils in which higher plants can take root. The rate and general direction of environmental modifications by biological activity are governed by the physical characteristics. Man, too, is a member of the biological community and a component of the ecosystem. He is affected by it and can affect it, deliberately or inadvertently, to alter the interactions of biotic and abiotic components.

All biological communities have two major components. The first component is made up of the *primary producers,* mostly green plants, which are able to convert light energy to chemical energy and to synthesize food from simple inorganic substances, including carbon dioxide. In the process, they produce oxygen and give off heat and other wastes. The second component consists of the *consumers,* which utilize, rearrange, and decompose the complex material synthesized by the plants and, in the process, consume oxygen and excrete carbon dioxide, heat, and organic and mineralized wastes. Macroconsumers (chiefly animals, including man) ingest other organisms or particulate organic matter. Microconsumers (chiefly bacteria and fungi) decompose dead protoplasm and other wastes. The mineralized wastes are then reused by plants. In this way chemical substances such as carbon, hydrogen, oxygen, nitrogen, phosphorus, and many others that are essential for growth are repeatedly recycled through biological communities. On the other hand, energy is not recycled but rather is dissipated as heat. Because of this one-way flow of energy, biological communities cannot exist without the continued conversion of light energy to chemical energy by green plants.

It follows that humans could not continue to exist without the food energy made available by green plants and the other consumer species in the biological community. Being among the more versatile of consumer species, man can utilize every trophic level—from plants through herbivores, carnivores, and decomposers—as food. Because of the energy loss that occurs in transfer through successive trophic levels, man can obtain the maximum quantity of food energy by eating plants.

Man derives many other important benefits from interactions with biological communities. These include building materials, fiber for clothing, medicines, recreation, temperature and light modification, degradation of wastes, soil and water conservation, aesthetic enjoyment, information on the origin and role of man in the natural order of our universe, and many others. On the other hand, many interactions with biological communities that cause human discomfort, disease, and death are certainly not beneficial for the individual victims, although the survivors may benefit by the reduced competition for limited resources.

Man is a natural component of the Hudson Basin ecosystem, but his interactions with other parts of the ecosystem are unique in kind and magnitude. One of his principal environmental concerns—indeed, perhaps the principal concern underlying the entire Hudson Basin Project—is that man may inadvertently modify the environment on such a scale or at such a rate that he may disrupt processes vital to the continued existence and well-being of his own species.

Compared to alterations of biological communities occupying the Hudson Basin since the recession of the last glacial ice sheet, during the period from 8000 to 17,000 years ago (caused by changes in climate, sea level, and other nonhuman influences), the effects on habitation have been quite small. The relative influence of man, however, has been increasing during the past 3000 years, so that, particularly in the last 200 years, the major changes in the biological communities and ecosystem of the Hudson Basin study area have been the result of human activity. Modern man intrudes on and changes the natural biological system for human use (as in agriculture and fishing); by incidental intrusion resulting primarily from land use for nonbiological purposes (as in the development of cities); and from the disposal of industrial and human wastes (as in toxic and sewage pollution).

This chapter attempts to describe the major components of the Hudson Basin ecosystem; to describe how man has and is interacting with other components of that ecosystem; to delineate those interactions and interdependencies that are substantially within or beyond man's capacity to control; to explore whether or not the institutional management mechanisms exist and are adequate to manage those interrelationships; and to identify major information needs and research priorities.

9.2   The Ecosystem

A biological community is a consequence of all the factors of the environment. Soil, water, and air comprise the medium in which, in the presence of light and heat from the sun, living things can develop. The composition of biological communities is ultimately determined by climate and by the physical and chemical characteristics of water and soil. But living things also affect climate, water, and soil in the network of physical and chemical ineractions that we call an ecosystem (Fig. 9-1).

Abiotic Components

Climate

The climate of the bulk of the Hudson Basin study area is of the humid/continental type, subdivided into warm and cool zones. The humid/continental regime extends over most of the northeastern United States east of longitude 100 and north of latitude 35. Weather conditions within this area are relatively similar, varying mainly with respect to latitude and major water bodies. Subdivisions affecting the study area are the transition between warm and cool summer regions, which occurs in the vicinity of the Capital District, and the coastal region, which is moderated by ocean water temperatures. These subdivisions are hundreds of miles wide throughout most of their extent, but are relatively narrow in the Hudson Basin and to the east. Consequently, the study area exhibits a relatively wide spectrum of biologically significant conditions. An example of this is found in horticultural manuals, which divide the Hudson Basin into four or five plant-hardiness zones while few regions in the country of similar size encompass more than two.

The principal factor determining the subdivisions of the humid/continental regime is maximum summer temperature. These subdivisions can be further divided into microclimates on the basis of elevation, relief, and continuity of terrain features.

Water

The weather system, modified by terrain, determines the quantity and time distribution of precipitation. The characteristics of the terrain and the action of water on it determine the structure of the drainage system. Within this framework, biological communities exist and further alter the rate and distribution of water within the hydrological cycle.

Compared to other major river systems of North America, the Hudson is small in terms of both basin area and discharge. The Hudson estuary is relatively long, however, and the total estuary watershed is comparable to that of other Atlantic Ocean basins such as the Delaware, Connecticut, and Potomac. Only about 60% of the total discharge entering the Hudson estuary is through the main stem of the Hudson. This is a direct consequence of the length of the estuary and implies a very gradual transition from freshwater to marine conditions.

Within the study area, glaciation completely obliterated the drainage system responsible for much of the previous landscape. Throughout the

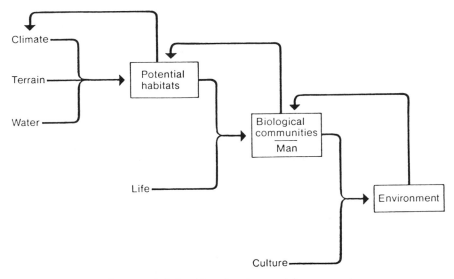

Fig. 9-1. Relationships of environmental components.

glaciated area there are many places with no positive drainage network. Glacial valley impoundments are common, whereas natural lakes and wetlands are a rarity outside of the glaciated area (except in some floodplain and tidal areas). All streams are in a youthful or rejuvenated stage. Disrupted or immature drainage increases with northerly latitude (as the postglacial drainage system becomes younger). The study area includes all of the main components of the Hudson River and estuary drainage basin, as well as the headwaters of several other major drainage basins, and several small watersheds of Long Island Sound, the New York Bight, and the Atlantic Ocean. The study area is therefore involved in the hydrological cycle of a much larger area of the northeastern United States and Canada. Water utilization by biological communities within the study area has the effect of transferring water spatially and temporally within the hydrological cycle and can have a profound effect on net flow and water quality throughout the system. Throughout this system, impoundments, both glacial and man-made, provide water storage which moderates extremes of flow downstream. Impoundments also cause deposition of suspended particles, which fill up the impoundments and create wetlands—marginal terrestrial habitats occasionally subject to flooding or ponding.

Soil

Earth provides the substrate for all biological processes. Variations in the earth's surface provide variations in the habitat available to organisms.

Within the study area, terrain features are the result of the chemical and physical characteristics of the bedrock (which determine its susceptibility to weathering and erosion); glaciation and processes of deglaciation; and the erosive action of water and, to a lesser extent, of wind.

The study area encompasses five major geologic regions: the Appalachian, the Taconian, the Laurentian, the Central Lowland, and the Atlantic Coastal Plain. As a result of geologic structure and events, there are characteristic types of terrain and sequences of landforms with each. With the exception of the southern New Jersey portion, the entire area was glaciated, and its terrain considerably altered from the prior fluvial–bedrock physiography. All valleys were filled with glacial debris and lake sediments. The present drainage pattern was established during the process of deglaciation. The glacial landscape is relatively unstable with respect to the current forces of climate and weather which are acting upon it. The present drainage regime is in the process of eroding and redistributing many of the deposits of unconsolidated material resulting from glaciation.

Soils in the study area are almost entirely derived from glacially transported parent material, and so do not necessarily reflect the bedrock beneath them in their texture and their mineral and chemical content, although the bedrock may be responsible for their physical position. Most of the study area is dominated by soils derived from glacial till. Many valleys are filled with coarser soils developed from glacial outwash. There are numerous depressions and basins with very fine-textured soils derived from lake bottom sediments. The southern New Jersey area is characterized by sandy soils derived from coastal plain deposits.

These variations in soil texture determine the water-holding capacity of the soil and thus greatly influence the type of vegetation that can grow. The soils in many parts of the study area have been exposed to weathering and erosion for long periods of time, which has greatly affected the soil structure and its fertility.

Biological Communities

Climate, water, and soil form the abiotic matrix in which biological communities develop, but these nonliving components of the ecosystem have been shaped, in turn, by cosmic and geophysical processes that are beyond man's power to affect—or even, in some cases, to detect.

Seventeen thousand years ago—a wink in the scale of geologic time, and not very long ago in the span of man's existence as a species—virtually all of our study area was covered by the Wisconsin ice sheet. The present biological communities of the Hudson Basin, as well as its landforms and drainage patterns, have all developed since then.

As the ice retreated, it uncovered a landscape of raw rock, sand, and clay, laced by expanses of intricately shifting meltwaters. Spores and microorganisms were carried into the area by winds and water currents. The first plants to take hold on the barren terrain were those characteristic of arctic tundra—hardy mosses and lichens. Meanwhile, as new drainage systems took shape, linkages with older drainage systems were constantly being formed and broken, permitting colonization by those fish able to tolerate waters that were both very cold and very poor in nutrients.

By 13,000 years ago, the ice sheet had retreated northward to about the latitude of Albany. The mid-Hudson Basin was by then a posttundra type of environment, dominated by spruce and pine. The stream systems, developed in the topography left by the receding ice sheet, delivered huge volumes of glacial meltwater to the lower Hudson channel. The aquatic life that populated the lakes, tributary streams, and the lower Hudson itself was almost certainly made up of species characteristic of fresh, cold-water environments.

Sea level 1000 years ago was approximately 100 feet below its present level, and the Atlantic coastline was 20 to 30 miles south and east of its present position. Both the present lower Hudson and Long Island Sound were then freshwater bodies inhabited by freshwater species.

As the ice sheet receded further, what had been tundra was generally taken over by conifers, while the subarctic coniferous forest was replaced by deciduous species. These shifts in vegetation were accompanied by corresponding changes in fauna.

While the dominant trend in the Hudson Basin has been toward a warmer climate and a northerly movement of temperate-zone species, it would be incorrect to view the biological changes of the last 17,000 years as a simple progression. Important differences in climate can be observed with changes in altitude, wind exposure, or proximity to large water bodies. Thus, small areas of tundra still exist on the cold higher elevations of the Adirondacks, while a species as "southern" as the prickly pear can be found in places along the lower Hudson as far north as Iona Island.

The long-range forces that shaped the Hudson Basin are still at work. The climate and habitats continue to change, and species continue to invade, adapt, compete, and, in some cases, become extinct.

The Hudson River itself has undergone marked changes in its elevation and its relation to the sea. The composition and location of aquatic communities in the Hudson River estuary are largely determined by the extent of saltwater intrusion. Many species are sensitive to differences in salinity of a few parts per thousand (⁰/₀₀). The location of the "salt front" is not so much a function of sea level as of the volume of freshwater flow available to oppose the press of salt water from the ocean. The salt front—more accurately, a long mixing zone in which salinity decreases progressively from south to north—shifts seasonally and, of course, with the tides. However, there have been large-scale changes in salinity with changes in climate and vegetation.

Sea level 9000 years ago was still 80 feet below its present level, and the entire lower Hudson of today was then probably still a freshwater habitat. Yet between 6000 and 4000 years ago, though sea level was 20 or more feet below its present position, salinity intrusion up the Hudson as far north as the present Bear Mountain Bridge was probably greater than it is today. The lowest levels of huge oyster-shell heaps (middens) dated at about 5650 to 5850 years ago—located on the east bank of the Hudson at Croton Point and at Montrose Point—indicate a minimum salinity of about 5‰, with the likelihood that the salinity was closer to 10‰. This marked increase in salinity may have been the result of a decrease in freshwater runoff, caused by a combination of decreased precipitation and increased evapotranspiration that was also reflected in the change in the composition of the tree cover from oak–hemlock to oak–hickory. By 3000 years ago, sea level was rising at the rate of 3 feet per 1000 years, and apparently is continuing to rise at that rate.

As we approach historic times, the effects of human intervention are difficult to distinguish from changes wrought by long-term natural forces. Centuries before their first contact with Europeans, the Indians of the Hudson Basin practiced forest burning to clear land for the cultivation of crops. Within the last two centuries, the vast oyster beds of upper New York Bay and the lower Hudson River estuary have disappeared. The effects of pollution, landfill, and overfishing cannot be denied, but a long-term decrease in salinity may have been a major contributing factor. And if salinity has, in fact, declined, has that decline been due to long-term climatic changes or to man-made changes in the environment that have increased runoff and reduced evapotranspiration? The next section deals further with man's impact on the environment of the Hudson River basin.

9.3   Man's Use and Impact

The human populations of the Hudson Basin study area (like any other biological populations) from 9000 B.C. until very recently, have tended to live up to the carrying capacity of their habitat, using the technologies at their command. Until relatively recently, the limits of these technologies in turn limited the rate of population growth and the rate and extent of modification of the habitat. After the introduction of efficient large-scale water transport in the seventeenth century, and particularly after the fossil-fuel revolution of the nineteenth century, it became possible for the human population of the region to expand explosively through the importation of ever larger amounts of energy and material in a variety of forms.

Indian Culture

The best estimate for the Indian population of the Hudson Basin circa 1600 is about 65,000. This is only 0.3% of the current population (20.1 million) of the basin.

At the time of the first European contact, the Indians were in relative balance in the Hudson Basin ecosystem and almost no input from adjacent ecosystems in the form of food or other goods was necessary. All of the Indian groups in the basin at this time subsisted by combining maize-beans-squash horticulture with hunting, fishing, and the collecting of wild plant resources in a complex pattern that involved seasonal changes of residence by at least some members of the society to permit harvesting of seasonally available resources. The groups differed, however, in their emphasis on different combinations of resources. Those on Long Island and at the mouth of the Hudson could depend heavily on marine and littoral resources, including shellfish, that were not available to groups farther upriver, and it has been suggested that the availability of both land and sea resources in coastal areas accounted for the relatively high density (about 525 per 100 km²) of the tribal groups that resided nearest the coast. Food, water, and fuel were obtained for the most part by living near or traveling to the location of the needed resources. Travel was by foot and by small craft on water.

The Indian settlement system focused on villages that were relocated at intervals of 10 to 20 years as the soil declined in fertility, as the local supply of firewood became exhausted, or as weed infestation of fields, scarcity of game, or accumulation of trash and vermin made the site uninhabitable.

Sizable clearings were created for agricultural use, and forest cover in the vicinity of villages was also reduced by setting fire to woods to improve traveling and visibility, to drive or enclose game, and to destroy vermin (Day, 1953).

Medical practices were very limited, consisting primarily of the use of medicinal plants. Early Dutch accounts frequently refer to the general and good health and robust appearance of the Hudson Basin Indians. Wounds and sickness were treated with a wide variety of medicinal plants, through extensive sweating in small huts in which water was poured over hot stones, and, in more difficult cases, through the intervention of religious practitioners who strove to drive the disease-causing spirits from the patient's body.

European Culture

The first recorded European visit to the New York Coast was the very brief one by Verrazano in 1524, when he spent only a few hours in New York Bay before heading back to sea in fear of an approaching storm. The first extended reports on the natives of the region come from the explorations of

Henry Hudson in 1609. Dutch fur traders were in the area between 1612 and 1623, and have left us bits of ethnographic information and a few maps. Dutch settlement began in 1624, and with it, major disruption of the pre-contact way of life. Indian populations declined very rapidly under the combined influence of disease, massacre, migration out of the area, and general demoralization. By 1675, very few Indians remained anywhere in the basin east and south of the Schenectady–Albany settlements.

Since the Dutch West India Company was more interested in the fur trade than in extensive settlement, the population of the colony grew quite slowly. A 1673 estimate places the population—men, women, and children—at about 6000 (O'Callaghan, 1849). After the final English takeover in 1674, immigration increased sharply from about 18,000 in 1698 to about 163,000 in 1771. Almost all of this population was concentrated on Long Island, in the New York City and Albany areas, and in the smaller towns strung along the Hudson River between New York and Albany. The combination of continued immigration, high birth rate, and a death rate reduced by improving health services resulted in a dramatic increase in the human population of the Hudson Basin to the present level of about 20 million.

Transportation capability increased rapidly with the addition of the horse, larger self-propelled watercraft, railroads, automobiles, trucks, and aircraft. The mechanical means of transportation were at once products of the industrial revolution and means to further industrialization and expansion of agriculture. Large amounts of food, fuel, and materials could be transported from far-away sources to support rapidly increasing human populations around centers of trade and industry.

Present Culture

Several of modern man's activities change biological communities directly and indirectly in the basin. The major activities that impact on biological communities include (a) construction, (b) chemical industries, (c) other industries, (d) personal wastes of man, and (e) agriculture. The criteria employed in making this judgment include the permanence of the effect on the environment, the sensitivity and/or severity of effect, and the extent of effect and/or limitation of the biological resource. These activities involve three types of use of the biological system: nonbiological land use (construction, particularly urbanization); waste disposal (industrial pollution and human waste disposal); and exploitation of the biological system for human use (agriculture or fishing). Regulatory institutions tend to control use of biological systems along these functional lines. We shall describe briefly what is included in the activities mentioned and how they influence biological communities.

Construction

Construction includes the building of roads, parking lots, sidewalks, and family, institutional, and industrial structures. Construction of these items is normally associated with urbanization. Road and other construction has a particularly severe impact upon biological communities because it permanently changes the environment, is significant from the standpoint of the nearly total destruction of life, and is quite extensive in impact.

Chemical Industries

This activity includes the production, use, and disposal of chemicals such as petroleum, pesticides, fertilizers, or SO_2. Chemicals have high biological activity (severe) and are particularly widespread in use and impact on the environment. Some chemicals, such as lead, cadmium, DDT, and PCBs, endure in the environment and therefore may have a long-term effect.

Other Industries

This activity includes steel, auto, power, and other industries. Production, use, and disposal of the product may cause significant changes in biotic communities, e.g., the automobile. The extent and severity of this activity rate it as having an important impact on biotic communities.

Personal Wastes of Man

Each person produces about 1200 pounds of feces annually. Hence, for a population of 20.1 million in the basin, the total annual waste produced is about 12 million tons. These wastes enrich our aquatic ecosystems and often directly and indirectly alter the aquatic biotic communities.

Agriculture

This activity includes the replacement of forests with crop monocultures. Agriculture does not totally eliminate the biotic community; it is not generally a permanent change, but it is relatively widespread. Also, cropping is probably the main factor contributing to soil erosion and stream sedimentation, which are fairly widespread.

Terrestrial Communities

Before the Europeans arrived, about 92% of the Hudson Basin was covered with forests and 8% with water and wetlands. Since then, significant changes have been made in the basin ecosystem by man. Urban land (including residential, commercial, industrial, extractive, transportation, institutional, and recreation) is now 14%, agriculture 11%, open vacant areas

14%, and forest only 53%. The changes in the biological community of the basin relative to intensity of human occupation and use can be well illustrated by comparing the quantitative and qualitative differences among four biotic communities in the Hudson Basin, Stony Creek, Stillwater, Tarrytown, and Manhattan (Fig. 9-2).

Stony Creek comes close to being typical of the original biotic community before the Europeans invaded the basin—mostly woodland; only 2% is urban. If the biomass (pounds of living protoplasm) of the various kinds of living organisms is estimated and compared, we observe that the plant material is dominated by trees, bacteria, and fungi (Fig. 9-3). Note that the biomass (pounds per acre) is given on a log scale. There is little livestock present. The earthworms and insects dominate the animal biomass. Deer probably dominate the mammal biomass, and the birds of New York State woodlands would be the primary species in this region.

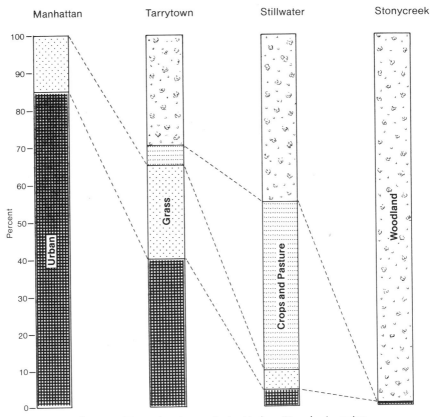

Fig. 9-2. Vegetational types in the Hudson River basin region.

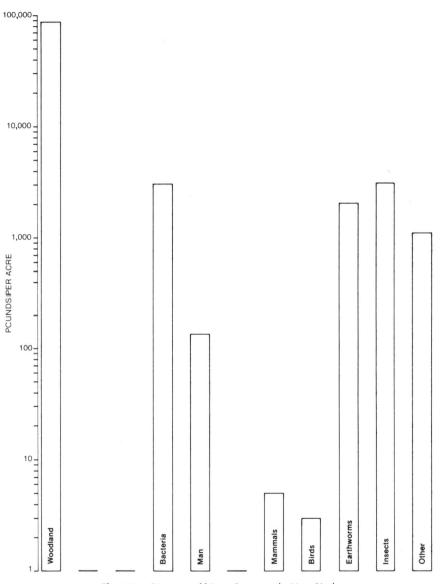

Fig. 9-3.   Biomass of biota, Stonycreek, New York.

In the Stillwater region, urban land uses increased to about 5% and grass to about the same (5%) (Fig. 9-2). This region is now dominated by agriculture and woodlands. The dominant plant materials are trees, crops, bacteria, and fungi, followed by grass (Fig. 9-4). The makeup of the animal community includes a large proportion of livestock, encompassing farm animals, such as cows and chickens. Wild mammals include deer, which in biomass would dominate all other wild mammals in the region. Of the animals, the insects and earthworms are exceedingly abundant. The bird species are those typical of New York State woodland and grassland.

The Tarrytown region, in contrast to Stillwater, is now 40% urban (Fig. 9-2). The amount of grass increased to 25% and woodland decreased to about 30%. Agricultural land use is only about 5%. In the Tarrytown region, there is a change in the biomass dominance. Among plants, trees still dominate, followed by crops, bacteria (including fungi), and grass (Fig. 9-5). The earthworms and insects dominate as far as animal matter is concerned. The livestock in this case includes some dairy animals as well as dogs and cats. Wild animals include rats, mice, squirrels, raccoons, and rabbits. The birds now include many introduced pigeons, sparrows, and starlings, but also several wild birds common to New York State woodlands and grasslands.

Manhattan is about 85% urbanized and the land is covered with roads, buildings with very little grass (estimated at 15%), and a few trees (Fig. 9-2). Manhattan man contributes the largest quantity of biomass (Fig. 9-6). The livestock in this situation refers primarily to dogs and cats. The wild mammals in this case include rats, mice, and squirrels. The resident birds are primarily imported species of pigeons, sparrows, and starlings.

Aquatic Communities: The Hudson River Fish Fauna

Because of morphometry and geographical location, the Hudson River drainage is inhabited by an extraordinarily rich fish fauna. About 120 fish species have been recorded in the literature as occurring in the Hudson River system, and recent collecting has pushed the total to more than 130. Despite the changes brought about by human uses and abuses of the river, there are more different kinds of fishes in the Hudson now than there were when Henry Hudson arrived in 1609. There have been a number of successful introductions, but there are no convincingly documented examples of any species becoming extinct, although some have not been reported for a long time and the ranges of others have been severely restricted.

Like other large rivers, the Hudson has been badly neglected and our knowledge of its fishes is far from complete. Large rivers are singularly difficult to sample because depth and current prohibit some types of gear, and rough bottom restricts the use of others. Furthermore, there are political and

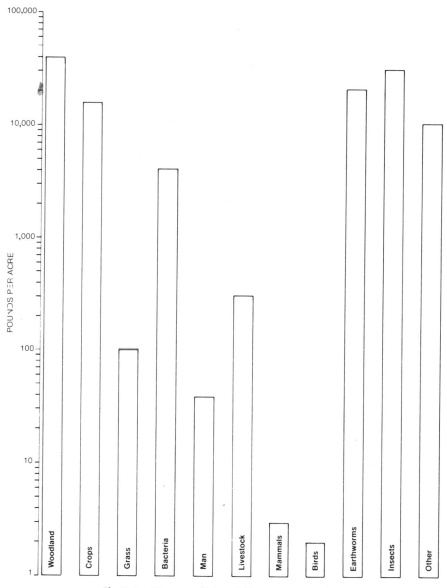

Fig. 9-4.   Biomass of biota, Stillwater, New York.

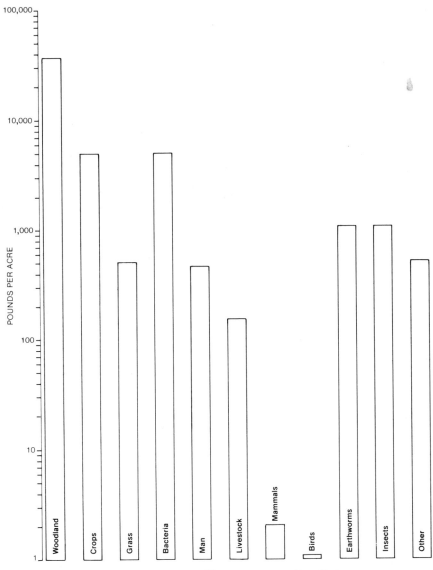

Fig. 9-5.   Biomass of biota, Tarrytown, New York.

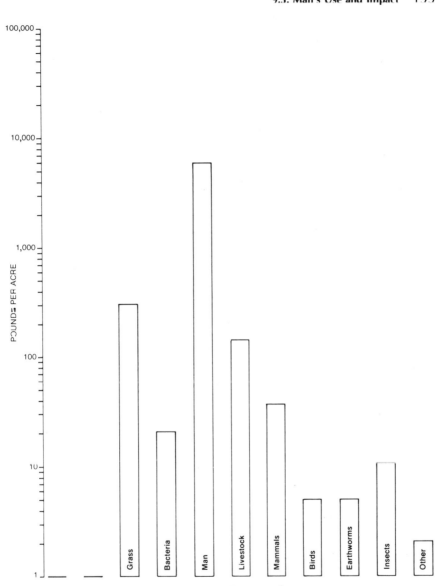

Fig. 9-6. Biomass of biota, Manhattan.

economic reasons why little effort has been directed to the scientific study of its fishes.

The Hudson River fish fauna is a young one. The entire drainage was covered by glaciers during the Wisconsin glacial interval, hence the fauna can be no older than 8000 to 10,000 years. It has, however, been pointed out that sections of what is now the Hudson Canyon would have been uncovered by Pleistocene sea level lowering and may have served as a refugium from which some fishes could have repopulated the present day basin as soon as the glacial front began to retreat (Cole, 1967). Glacial drainage patterns also provided access to the Hudson Basin from the Gulf of Mexico drainage, and this, more than any other single factor, accounts for the richness of the Hudson River fish fauna.

Hudson River Geography and Fish Habitats

The upper Hudson, from its source streams in the Adirondacks to about the Glen, is a fast flowing, cool, oligotrophic stream. The granitic rocks are poor in calcium and relatively insoluble so that minerals are limiting. This region lies within the boundaries of the Adirondack Park and is well forested, so that runoff is naturally controlled.

Between the Glen and Troy, the river flows more slowly and the underlying rocks provide more nutrients. Between Warrensburg and Troy, a series of natural waterfalls has been augmented and harnessed for hydro and hydroelectric power and this has created a series of slow water environments. Major tributaries including the Schroon, the Sacandaga, the Batten Kill, the Hoosic, and the Mohawk provide still more diverse fish habitat. Here, too, the Hudson is joined by two major canals, the Champlain Canal (opened 1819), which connects it with the St. Lawrence River, and the New York Barge Canal, the present-day version of the Erie Canal, which first connected the Hudson with the upper Great Lakes in 1825 (Hubbs and Lagler, 1947).

From the Troy lock to the Verrazano Bridge, the Hudson River is a long narrow tidal estuary. Except for the Cornwall to Verplanck section, where it passes through the Hudson Highlands, it proceeds southward in almost a straight line. All of the estuary is tidal but the salt wedge extends upstream only to the vicinity of Newburgh, its exact limit varying according to the amount of freshwater coming downstream.

Despite its straightness and austere appearance on the charts, the lower Hudson presents a wide spectrum of fish habitats. Islands, tributary streams, shallow flats, deep channels, and bays that have been partially walled off by railroad beds provide rich and varied cover for fishes and their food organisms. Much of the shoreline is protected by stone riprap that provides excellent shelter for small fishes.

Although it would appear that the Hudson River is divided into well-defined fish habitats, the fishes themselves do not recognize such sharp distinctions. While it is generally true that the small creeks of the Adirondacks are dominated by brook trout and blacknose dace and the lower Hudson contains such marine species as anchovies and bluefish, there are no really pronounced faunal breaks. Many species have a wide range in the river—the yellow perch, white suckers, and golden shiners, for example, are taken in small Adirondack streams and also in the main river at Haverstraw. Most species have preferred habitats in which they reach their greatest abundance and marginal habitats where they exist as minor components of the community. Thus, a complete study of their distribution must also include information on relative and absolute abundance. Unfortunately, it is frequently the unusual or stray individual that finds its way into museum collections, and for this reason a plot of recorded occurrences often does not give a true picture of the species range.

Fish Distribution Patterns in the Hudson River

Marine and Euryhaline Fishes Numerous marine fishes enter the lower Hudson and travel upstream various distances, depending on their ability to tolerate freshwater. Some are present throughout much of the year; others come in only at certain seasons. Still others are strays or wanderers and are recorded only sporadically. In theory almost any species from the North Atlantic or even the West Indies might at some time enter the lower reaches of the Hudson, and new records will appear as long as we continue to study the river.

The jack crevalle (*Caranx hippos*) is an example of a marine fish that is frequently taken in the river during late summer and early fall. Like the bluefish (*Pomatomus saltatrix*), the weakfish (*Cynoscion regalis*), and the silver perch (*Bairdiella chrysura*), it appears to enter the river in numbers only when young. Most of the jack crevalle are less than 6 inches long and presumably less than 1 year old. Other marine and brackish water fishes common in the lower Hudson are

Brevoortia tyrannus	Atlantic menhaden
Anchoa mitchilli	Bay anchovy
Strongylura marina	Atlantic needlefish
Fundulus heteroclitus	Mummichog
Menidia menidia	Atlantic silverside
Menidia beryllina	Tidewater silverside
Syngnathus fuscus	Northern pipefish

Apeltes quadracus	Fourspine stickleback
Morone americanus	White Perch
Gasterosteus aculeatus	Threespine stickleback
Leiostomus xanthurus	Spot
Mugil cephalus	Striped mullet
Paralichthys dentatus	Summer flounder (fluke)
Pseudopleuronectes americanus	Winter flounder
Trinectes maculatus	Hogchoker

Of these, *Apeltes quadracus, Morone americanus,* and *Trinectes maculatus* are able to tolerate fresh water for extended periods and range well upstream.

In contrast to these regular inhabitants, some other marine species are rare or sporadic in the lower Hudson and have only been taken on one or a few occasions. Examples are

Carcharhinus obscurus	Dusky shark
Raja laevis	Barndoor skate
Gadus morhua	Atlantic cod
Merluccius bilinearis	Silver hake
Fundulus majalis	Striped killifish
Membras martinica	Rough silverside
Hippocampus erectus	Lined seahorse
Myoxocephalus octodecemspinosus	Longhorn sculpin
Rachycentron canadum	Cobia
Lutjanus griseus	Gray snapper
Micropogon undulatus	Atlantic croaker
Peprilus triacanthus	Butterfish

Lutjanus griseus is a West Indian species, once recorded from near Tarrytown (Boyle, 1968).

Some of the best known Hudson River fishes are diadromous forms that spend part of their life cycle in fresh water and part in salt water. The American eel, *Anguilla rostrata* is a catadromous species that must return to the sea to spawn. Juvenile and adult eels are extremely abundant in the lower Hudson and even up into the Mohawk River, where there was formerly a considerable fishery for eels.

Three herrings, the American shad (*Alosa sapidissima*), the blueback (*Alosa aestivalis*), and the alewife (*Alosa pseudoharengus*), are well known for their spring spawning runs, as is the striped bass (*Morone saxatilis*).

During the late fall and winter months the tomcod (*Microgradus tomcod*) moves into the river to spawn. Other anadromous fishes are

Petromyzon marinus	Sea lamprey
Acipenser brevirostrum	Shortnose sturgeon
Acipenser oxyrhynchus	Atlantic sturgeon
Osmerus mordax	Rainbow smelt

Although there are a few early records of Atlantic salmon (*Salmo salar*) entering the river, it is doubtful that the Hudson was ever a salmon stream (Boyle, 1968).

Freshwater Fishes   The freshwater fishes of the Hudson River pose some interesting distribution problems. Introductions—both deliberate and accidental—occurred early in our history, in many cases long before there was any attempt to determine the original ranges of the species in question.

Among lake-dwelling species, the lake trout (*Salvelinus namaycush*), the round white fish (*Prosopium cylindraceum*), and the lake whitefish (*Coregonus clupeaformis*), and the cisco (*C. artedii*) are apparently native species, having invaded the region through glacial outlets and lakes at the end of the Pleistocene. Their habitat requirements restrict them to lakes rather than streams.

The following list includes species that are generally distributed on the Atlantic coast and occur on stream drainages on each side of the Hudson. Their presence is therefore expected, and in general they offer no clues as to the corridor by which they invaded the Hudson River drainage.

Lampetra lamottei	American brook lamprey
Dorosoma cepedianum	Gizzard shad
Salvelinus fontinalis	Brook trout
Esox niger	Chain pickerel
Esox americanus americanus	Redfin pickerel
Erimyzon oblongus	Creek chubsucker
Catostomus commersoni	White sucker
Hypentelium nigricans	Northern hog sucker
Notemigonus crysoleucas	Golden shiner
Exoglossum maxillingua	Cutlips minnow
Semotilus corporalis	Fallfish
Semotilus margarita	Pearl dace
Semotilus atromaculatus	Creekchub
Rhinichthys cataractae	Longnose dace
Rhinichthys atratulus	Blacknose dace
Phoxinus eos	Northern redbelly dace
Pimephales notatus	Bluntnose minnow

Notropis hudsonius	Spottail shiner
Notropis cornutus	Common shiner
Notropis bifrenatus	Bridle shiner
Hybognathus nuchalis regius	Silvery minnow
Ictalurus nebulosus	Brown bullhead
Ictalurus natalis	Yellow bullhead
Percopsis omiscomaycus	Trout-perch
Fundulus diaphanus	Banded killifish
Culaea inconstans	Brook stickleback
Enneacanthus obesus	Banded sunfish
Lepomis auritus	Redbreast sunfish
Lepomis gibbosus	Pumpkinseed
Perca flavescens	Yellow perch
Stizostedion vitreum vitreum	Walleye
Percina caprodes	Logperch
Etheostoma olmstedi	Tessellated darter
Cottus cognatus	Shiny sculpin

The gizzard shad (*Dorosoma cepedianum*), is of particular interest because it has only recently been taken in the river (Dew, 1973). Whether it arrived via the Champlain Canal, the Barge Canal, or along the coast is not obvious.

Some northern species reach their southern limit in or near the Hudson. Certain of these species occur only in headwater tributaries and were presumably able to become established through glacial outlets as the ice receded. Probably they are habitat (temperature?) limited. The range of *Hybognathus hankinsoni* Hubbs, for example, extends from the Missouri drainage of Colorado, Wyoming, and Montana across Nebraska and the Dakotas, Wisconsin, Iowa, northern Illinois, Michigan, and southern Ontario to the Adirondack region of New York (Bailey, 1954). Others have even broader ranges. The longnose sucker (*Catostomus catostomus* Forster) occurs in eastern Siberia as well as most of Canada and the northern United States.

Esox lucius	Northern pike
Catostomus catostomus	Longnose sucker
Moxostoma macrolepidotum	Shorthead redhorse
Couesius plumbeus	Lake chub
Phoxinus neogaeus	Finescale dace
Pimephales promelas	Fathead minnow
Hybognathus hankinsoni	Brassy minnow
Notropis heterolepis	Blacknose shiner
Notropis heterodon	Blackchin shiner

There are species of the Atlantic coastal plain that have not extended their range north or east of the Hudson Valley. Possibly they are temperature limited but other explanations cannot be ruled out at this time.

Umbra pygmaea	Eastern mudminnow
Notropis chalybaeus	Ironcolor shiner
Ictalurus catus	White catfish
Noturus insignis	Margined madtom
Noturus gyrinus	Tadpole madtom
Acantharchus pomotis	Mud sunfish
Enneacanthus gloriosus	Bluespotted sunfish

Two other species, the rosyface shiner (*Notropis rubellus*) and the spotfin shiner (*Notropis spilopterus*), have wide ranges in the Mississippi and Great Lakes drainage and on the Atlantic coast. *Notropis spilopterus* occurs in the Susquehanna, Delaware and Hudson basins, and *N. rubellus* is found south to the James River. They have not, however, extended their ranges to the east.

Species that are not native to northeastern North America are clearly introduced, but there are some species that occur in nearby drainages and may or may not have been introduced. It is probable that the following species were intentionally introduced into the Hudson River system:

Salmo salar	Atlantic salmon
Salmo trutta	Brown trout
Salmo gairdneri	Rainbow trout
Carassius auratus	Goldfish
Cyprinus carpio	Carp
Micropterus dolomieui	Smallmouth bass
Micropterus salmoides	Largemouth bass
Pomoxis annularis	White crappie
Pomoxis nigromaculatus	Black crappie
Ambloplites rupestris	Rock bass
Lepomis macrochirus	Bluegill

The restricted occurrence of the green sunfish (*Lepomis cyanellus*) in the New Croton Reservoir and the warmouth (*Lepomis gulosus*) in the Sawkill near Annandale strongly suggests that they were accidentally introduced (Greeley, 1937).

Finally, there are several species whose presence in the Hudson drainage may have resulted from their moving through canals. Most canals, however, follow ancient stream connections and glacial outlets, and we cannot always be certain that the species was absent before the canal was built. Thus, Gibbs (1963) interpreted the presence of *Notropis analostanus* in the Mohawk-Hudson as "evidence in favor of a formerly wider distribution in New York, for the species probably entered that river system when it was the outlet for the waters of glacial Lake Lundy or Lake Iroquois." In contrast, Snelson (1968) states "there are two alternate explanations for the widespread occurrence of *Notropis atherinoides* in the Mohawk-Hudson system. Transfer could have been via Mohawk outlet which shunted water from glacial Lake Vanuxem down the Mohawk-Hudson Valley . . . Just as likely, however, is the hypothesis that *Notropis atherinoides* more recently entered the Hudson drainage via the Erie Barge Canal system which was opened . . . in 1825."

Western species that probably gained access through the Erie Canal are

Umbra limi	Central mudminnow
Notropis atherinoides	Emerald shiner
Clinostomus elongatus	Redside dace
Labidesthes sicculus	Brook silverside
Etheostoma blennioides	Greenside darter

Species that could have entered through the Erie Canal or through the Champlain Canal, since they occur in the St. Lawrence River are

Noturus flavus	Stonecat
Morone chrysops	White bass
Etheostoma flabellare	Fantail darter

The hornyhead chub (*Nocomis biguttatus*) reaches its eastern limit in the Mohawk system, where Hubbs and Lagler (1947) considered it to be native.

Three species are known only from western tributaries of the lower Hudson with a few records from the river itself. They are *Notropis amoenus, Notropis analostanus,* and *Percina peltata*. These may have entered the Hudson drainage by stream capture, where the Wallkill reversed its flow from the Delaware drainage to the Hudson drainage. One must also consider the possibility that they gained access through the Delaware and Hudson Canal.

Summary

In addition to its well-known commercial and sport fishes, the Hudson River Basin contains a wide variety of small fishes that serve to indicate the dispersal routes through which the fishes repopulated the river after the retreat of the last Wisconsin glacier. More than 100 species live in the Mohawk-Hudson system and 22 additional species have been reported so

TABLE 9-1.   Taxonomic Distribution of the Hudson River
Fish Fauna[a]

Family	Number of species
Petromyzontidae	2
Carcharinidae	1
Rajidae	1
Acipenseridae	2
Anguillidae	1
Clupeidae	5
Engraulidae	1
Salmonidae	8
Osmeridae	1
Esocidae	3
Umbridae	2
Catostomidae	5
Cyprinidae	28
Ictaluridae	6
Percopsidae	1
Gadidae	4
Ophidiidae	1
Belonidae	1
Cyprinodontidae	3
Atherinidae	4
Syngnathidae	2
Gasterosteidae	4
Percichthyidae	3
Lutjanidae	1
Centrarchidae	13
Percidae	7
Pomatomidae	1
Rachycentridae	1
Carangidae	3
Scianenidae	4
Labridae	1
Mugilidae	1
Stromatidae	1
Cottidae	2
Bothidae	3
Pleuronectidae	1
Soleidae	1
Tetraodontidae	1

[a] This distribution includes some data from unpublished
records.

infrequently that they can be considered visitors, although our present knowledge is so sketchy that this judgment may be modified in the near future.

The origin and distribution of Hudson–Mohawk fishes can be summarized as follows*:

1. Marine and brackish water species
   a. Common (residents at least part of the year)   20 species
   b. Rare (transients)   22
   c. Diadromous   10
2. Freshwater species
   a. Lake-dwelling species   4
   b. Wide-ranging species   34
   c. Northern species   9
   d. Atlantic drainage forms that reach their northern
      limit in the Hudson   7
   e. Western (Mississippi Drainage)   2
   f. Introduced species
      1. Deliberately introduced   11
      2. Accidentally introduced   2
3. Canal introduction
   a. Erie Canal   5
   b. Champlain or Erie Canal   3
   c. Erie Canal or native   1
   d. Wallkill or Delaware and Hudson Canal   3
                                                      ̄ ̄ ̄
                                                      133

Although introductions have increased the faunal list, other human influences (such as impoundments and eutrophication due to domestic sewage and other fertilizers) have tended to favor the most tolerant species at the expense of others. The concept of diversity should include equitable distribution of numbers. Although there are more kinds of fish in the river today (Table 9-1), the overwhelming preponderance of a few species (carp, white perch, striped bass, sunfish) means that the fishes are actually less diverse than they were in primeval times. Lower diversity is generally a sign of deteriorating environment.

9.4   The Biota and Man's Survival

An estimated 200,000 species of plants and animals make up the biotic community of the United States (probably 40,000 species in the Hudson

*More recent collecting has added approximately 20 species to this list. [Ed.]

Basin). The biotic community is vital to man, for he depends upon the life system for his food, maintenance of a functional ecosystem, and environmental amenities. We will illustrate briefly the importance of the biotic community to man.

Food Supply

Several hundred species of plants and animals are consumed by man as food. The mean caloric consumption per day per person is 3300 thousand calories (kcal), or 1.2 million kcal per person per year. Since there are 20.2 million humans in the Hudson Basin region, total yearly demand is 24.4×10^{12} kcal. As one might expect for an area such as the Hudson Basin, which contains a major metropolitan area, food production falls far short of consumption. The basin produces only about 5% of the annual needs of the human population or only an estimated 1.1×10^{12} kcal per year. Delaware and Schoharie counties come the closest to producing food equivalent to their demand, but even these counties produce about 60% and 48% of their population's needs, respectively.

Air Quality

In the presence of sunlight, plants take in carbon dioxide and water and release oxygen, which is vital to man and other animals. It takes about 360 square feet of land area with mixed vegetation to supply the annual oxygen requirements for one person. Oxygen produced by plants also contributes to the control of some air-polluting gases through the process of oxidation. The free movement of air allows these exchanges to operate over wide geographic areas.

Weather and Light Modifications

The presence of plants modifies the effect of weather and sunlight. For example, grass and trees make summer environments cooler and more humid. Temperatures over grassy surfaces on sunny summer days may be 10 to 14°F cooler than those over exposed soil. Also, ambient air temperature near the tops of trees may be about 96°F on a sunny day but only 71°F in the deep shade of a tree near the ground.

Of particular importance to man is the screening of lethal solar ultraviolet light. Oxygen, produced by plants as both oxygen and ozone, screens out these lethal rays, significantly reducing the amount reaching the earth's surface.

Soil Erosion Control

About four billion tons of soil annually are washed into our streams and ponds in the United States. This valuable topsoil is lost from cropland, home-building sites, and other areas where soil is left with insufficient plant cover. The sediment in water causes mortality to fish and other aquatic organisms, and eventually fills ponds and slow moving streams. On bare soil such as at construction sites, about 500 tons of soil per acre may be lost. The value of various types of vegetation is well illustrated by the following data from Miller (1936):

Crop	Average annual loss of soil per acre (tons)
Corn	19.7
Wheat	10.1
Corn, wheat, clover (rotation)	2.7
Continuous blue grass	0.3

Degradation of Biological and Industrial Wastes

The biological wastes produced by a human population of 20 million, and by the livestock maintained to produce meat for this population, totals about 200 million tons annually. Without the microorganisms that are involved in the degradation of this matter, we would eventually be buried in our own wastes. Most industrial wastes are broken down by the same processes. The breakdown of the wastes is vital for another reason: the release of life-making elements, e.g., carbon, oxygen, hydrogen, nitrogen, and phosphorus, for reuse by the biotic community and man.

Pollination of Crops and Other Plants

Despite man's many technological advances, substitutes for general insect pollination of plants, cultivated and wild, have not been found. The production of fruits, vegetables, and forage depends upon the activity of bees and other insects that pollinate or fertilize the blossoms.

A single honeybee may visit and pollinate 1000 blossoms in a single day (ten trips with 100 blossoms visited per trip). In New York State, with about three million beehives and each with 10,000 worker bees, honeybees could visit 30 trillion blossoms per day (Pimentel, 1974). Wild bees pollinate as many or more blossoms than do honeybees. In fact, on a bright, sunny day, more than 60 trillion blossoms may be pollinated.

Indicators of Toxic Pollutants

Some species of organisms are quite sensitive to various pollutants. Hence, when various species in the surroundings of man start dying, the suggestion is clear that pollutant dosages may be reaching dangerous levels in the environment. For instance, when raptors such as peregrine falcons and osprey were dying, this was an indication of the accumulation of DDT and its metabolites in the environment.

Aesthetics

Plants and animals have always constituted an extremely important part of the environment visually and from the standpoint of experiences, education, recreation, cultural heritage, and aesthetics. It is important to see that these biota continue to be incorporated into future living environments in the study area. This was dramatically recognized in the nineteenth century by the creation of the Adirondack Forest Preserve and Central Park.

Antagonistic Interactions

Several species of organisms pester humans, cause disease, destroy our food, eat our clothes, and attack our homes. The loss of life caused by microorganisms is the most significant problem. Some of the most serious diseases of mankind include typhoid, smallpox, black plague, malaria, schistosomiasis, and syphilis. Nothing can compare with the number of infections and discomfort caused by the common cold virus.

In addition to disease-causing organisms, there are many species that simply pester man, including mosquitoes, fleas, lice, flies, ticks, and bedbugs. These organisms may also be important in transmitting some of the diseases mentioned above, such as malaria and the plague.

Few people are aware that insects, plant pathogens, and weeds destroy about 43% of the food we produce and store. About 33% is destroyed by these pests before harvest and nearly 10% after harvest. These losses are especially serious in light of the world food shortage and rising prices. Pests such as clothes moths and carpet beetles eat our woolen clothes and cause other losses. Other pests, such as termites and carpenter ants, destroy our wooden structures.

The annual losses of life, food, clothes, and shelter to pests in the United States are tremendous. The losses of food, clothes, and shelter from pests in the Hudson Basin alone total several million dollars annually, which does not even include the high costs of control.

The notorious ragweed and other plants produce pollen, which could be termed a pest. Pollen can cause asthma, runny eyes and noses, and other cold-type discomforts.

9.5   Interactions, Management, and Environment

Given the framework of the Hudson Basin Project, the interaction of biological communities with the other nine policy areas constitutes a policy analysis of man's use of his environment. Biological communities is a holistic subject; it is comprehensible only in relation to all of the other policy areas as it both affects and is affected by the functioning of each of them. Basically, this interaction centers on the policy areas of human health, and leisure time and recreation. These constitute man's essential use of the environment to provide for his physical and emotional requirements.

The desire for a healthy, safe human environment presumes an ample supply of food and water. The additional desire to achieve and express a sense of well-being and a high quality of life requires a high consumption of energy, intensive and extensive transportation linkages, and highly organized social systems to process elements of the natural environment into forms usable by man. These two policy areas, and their attendant economic and social systems, summarize or underlie man's relationship to his environment and are basic to the policies by which man regulates and manages his environment.

To this perspective should be added one other factor basic to man's use of his environment: the total extent or magnitude of demands made on the environment, i.e., the intensity of the man–environment interaction, which is a corollary of population and of cultural and industrial development. All organisms convert elements of their environment into biomass of their own species. But because man is able to concentrate and transport great amounts of energy, he has become highly successful in this endeavor relative to other species. He has also become relatively free of localized environmental constraints and balances, and consequently has the ability to create more extensive environmental changes. Both the tradeoffs in uses and the absolute limits of the environment to support the human species are matters of concern. So, too, are the more immediate consequences of changing and generally increasing the intensity of demands made on the environment. The biological communities of the land and water are harvested for human use and affected by competing human use of their habitat, i.e., withdrawals of water, disposal of wastes, etc. In addition, there are significant amenity or cultural values associated with many of the biological communities in the Hudson Valley.

Thoughout this chapter we have considered biological communities as subdivided into terrestrial and aquatic biota. The system of institutions and laws by which the biological communities are influenced or managed also reflects a division between the terrestrial and the aquatic.

Land is held primarily in private ownership and is not generally seen as a resource in which the public has a direct interest. Therefore, most land is subject to use directly for the production of private economic gain. Land use is controlled by local units of government. The water and its biota are generally perceived as a public resource. Water bodies, except for very small ones, are not privately held. There is a recognized public interest in the waters such that no riparian owner may degrade or obstruct the water to the damage of other riparian owners. Government control of water is primarily the province of state and federal governments.

Problems in the management and regulation of terrestrial biological communities principally come from the use of land for constructing of human facilities and as direct or indirect results of the harvest of the communities. On the aquatic side, the management and regulation problems spring primarily from waste disposal, with its consequent effects on the biota and, again, from the harvest of biological communities for human use.

An example of a problem which brings all of these factors into play is the controversy between the fishing groups, which have sought to ensure the protection and development of the Hudson for sport and commercial fishing, and the power companies, which have sought to use the river for powerplant cooling. Their uses of the river differ, but both crop the Hudson's biological communities, and any overly exploitative cropping can have a major impact on the size of the fishery. The conflict caused by these competing uses raises the issue of the appropriate use of the river and the alternatives open to both fishing interests and the power industry.

The resolution of these controversies requires meeting four conditions: (a) an institutional framework with the appropriate power to make decisions, (b) principles by which decisions will be made, (c) sufficient knowledge to apply the principles to the factual situation, and (d) sufficient funds and staff to enable the institutions to fully carry out their mandates.

On the terrestrial side, both the scale of institutions and the private nature of land are obstacles to effective policy. On the aquatic side, the institutional framework is present, but the principles of decision-making, the political will, and adequate funds and staff are not sufficiently developed.

In evaluating the impact of other policy areas on biological communities, it is essential to consider both direct effects on the biota and effects on the other components of the environment on which biological communities depend. In most cases this distinction is a function of geographic scale: direct effects on biota occur as a result of competition for the same land areas and are usually confined to a single site or local area surrounding a project. Effects on biota due to changes in environmental systems occur on a wider scale such as a region or subregion. These effects are typically less apparent and less dramatic but they may be more pervasive and more significant to the ecosystem.

The following are brief discussions of the interaction of biological communities with each of the other policy areas.

Land Use/Human Settlement

Human settlements have permanent and severe effects in changing the biological systems on which they are imposed. The local effects of human settlement involve removal or radical change in the existing biological system, owing to the removal of water and vegetative biomass from the ecosystem, and the introduction of large areas of paving and structures, causing destruction of the soil medium. The net result of urbanization, particularly the unorganized sprawl typical of the Hudson Valley, is a reduction in primary productivity and a major drop in the recycling of secondary and tertiary productivity within the ecosystem. On a regional scale, human settlements affect the entire water system on which all biological communities depend, through alteration of the water balance and the use of water for water supply and waste disposal. Alternative development plans can influence the severity of the local impact, but usually to only a minor degree, because the basic conflict is the occupancy of land. Alternatives can have a major influence on the wider indirect effects, which involve the integrity of systems that function on a regional scale.

Currently, land development decisions are controlled by local government and made on a fragmented, incremental basis. Regard for biological communities requires management in a broader spatial context based on data which take account of both direct and indirect effects on the productivity of the land, species composition, future alternative biological communities, and the management of the land as a long-range productive medium. For example, the filling of wetlands should not be allowed on an ad hoc basis but should be seen in the context of the total area available as wetland habitat, its absorptive capacity for waste, and its importance to parts of the life cycles of aquatic species and birds, much of which may occur outside the wetland area.

Equally important to direct regulation is indirect or incidental regulation through the conjunction of the economic and legal systems. This is most obviously seen in the scheme of property taxation, which can force degrading development despite careful analysis and review. Indirect forms of regulation are as important as direct regulation and should also be subject to some type of policy guidance.

Land Use/Natural Resource Management

This subject area focuses on the fact that there is little management by any level of government of terrestrial biota. The basic reasons for this probably lie in society's perception of land as a resource in which the public has little direct interest, one that is privately owned and to be privately exploited. There are a few major exceptions to this situation: the Adirondack and Catskill preserves; the regulation of certain wild animals (not habitat areas so much as the organisms themselves); and the provisions for agricultural districts. None of these schemes involves very much active management, but they restrict the major forces that threaten to impair the use or condition of the resource.

The issues of terrestrial natural resources revolve around the land from which all of its biomass is derived. No existing institutions operate from this fundamental perspective, so the basic problems of natural resource management are largely unaddressed by government. For example, major changes in biological structure result from changes in land and production economics. The change from an undisturbed natural-resource system to agriculture, changes from one type of agricultural use to another (e.g., from multicrop to single-crop production), and the retirement of agricultural land are all influenced by changes in technology, in transportation, and in the demand for agricultural products as expressed in the economic system. They are not themselves, however, the subject of overt governmental regulation. If natural resources were positively managed rather than regulated on a limited basis, a comprehensive philosophy of use would have to emerge. This is very unlikely to occur without dramatic changes in society's perception of the status of land as a natural resource and of the existing systems of land ownership.

Water Resources

In contrast to terrestrial resources, the waters of the study area are seen as a public resource. The larger water bodies are held by the state in trust for the people and no riparian owners may degrade or obstruct a water body so as to impair the use of the water by others. Water resources are important to biological communities as the habitat of aquatic biota and a habitat requirement of terrestrial biota. The public management of the waters is undertaken for a variety of ends: providing water supply; protecting the land from flooding; exploiting the aquatic biota for recreation and food; and allowing the use of water for municipal and private waste disposal. The wastes may either be directly harmful to aquatic biota (as are toxins), or they may increase biotic production (as with nutrients), or they may be selectively harmful, beneficial, or neutral.

Both the regulation of flow (for water supply, power production, and flood protection) and the use of water for waste disposal can have major impacts on the aquatic biota. Waste disposal will be increasingly controlled by the 1972 Federal Water Pollution Control Act Amendments, which endorse the principle of minimizing the impact of disposal from all sources while also concentrating the impact of municipal disposal by encouraging fewer but bigger discharges to the water.* There remains a choice whether disposal will be to the water or the land (as with sewage wastes), or the air (as with heat wastes from steam-electric plants). The legislation cited above puts little emphasis on the use of the biological system to recycle organic wastes as opposed to neutralizing and simply removing all wastes. The opportunities for using waste material as a source of energy and nutrients merit greater efforts in analysis and development.

Alteration of the water flow regime is caused both by projects directly related to water use, such as dams and interbasin water exchanges, and also indirectly, and more pervasively, by changes in land use, particularly the introduction of urbanization and intensive agriculture. Direct changes are more thoroughly regulated than indirect changes but both have major effects on the habitat and aquatic biota. As with alterations to terrestrial systems, both should be seen in the context of the productivity of the biotic system, the species composition, the future alternative biological communities, and the management of the water as a productive medium. Most effort is needed in developing control over indirect impacts that are land-use related.

Focusing on the direct use of the biota, as in fishing, the mechanisms for the regulation of human exploitation exist. But for most of the waters, particularly the marine and estuarine portions, what is lacking is either the knowledge or the political will to manage for sustained yield, recreation use, or economic advantage. Investment in fishery knowledge and decisive administrative direction is needed to produce an effective management scheme.

Environmental Service Systems

The major linkages between this area and biological communities have been touched on in the discussions of land use and water resources. This area puts into clear focus the choice between impacting the air, land, or water systems and their dependent biota in the disposal of wastes such as sewage or heat from steam-electric plants. It also emphasizes the management alternatives of each resource. For instance, the issue of stormwater management focuses on policy choices for avoiding flood damage (a) by emphasizing the indirect cause and by adopting a land use scheme preventing construction in flood-prone areas; or (b) by concentrating on the direct issue and effecting major alterations of the water flow by dams and stream channelization. A scheme of management emphasizing biological communities would seek solutions to each problem in which the impact on the biological system could be absorbed. For instance, stream channelization optimizes efficiency of runoff and tends to be destructive of biotic habitat. Thus, from a biological standpoint, flow management by means of land use schemes is preferable in dealing with flood damage problems. Another significant policy issue is that the state condones use of both water and air as media for disposal at little or no cost to the disposer. If the government permits these costs to be externalized, they are passed on to the public either in the form of degraded environmental quality (partly due to disturbance of biological communities), or as taxes necessary to maintain environmental quality.

Air Resources

Atmospheric cycles occur on such a large scale that the present quality of the basin's air resources has fewer impacts on its biological communities than does the use of land or water. Assuming present institutions are effective in maintaining and improving the quality of the air, major impacts on the biological system from air quality are not expected. There are and will continue to be local adverse effects to particularly sensitive species, as seen at the New York Botanical Garden's research station in Dutchess County, or in the dust accumulations around cement plants in the mid-Hudson area.

Energy Systems

Energy systems are intimately linked with biological communities. The fossil fuels responsible for 80% of the energy produced in the study area are all products of biological communities. Our ability to transport and utilize these fossil fuels is fundamental to our industrial technology and economy. In other words, our level of energy consumption is a prerequisite to our standard of living. Historically, the transition from the use of charcoal, wood, and peat (standing crop) to coal, oil, and gas (fossilized biomass) caused a tremendous reduction in the cropping of current biological production. Cropping for fuel now has an insignificant impact on biological communities in the study area. However, energy conversion, utilization, and transmission have major impacts. Present competition over fossil fuels for energy production and the operation of machines, for fertilizers and machinery to increase biological productivity, and for the production of plastics and chemicals, poses a problem of global concern—one with potentially devastating consequences in the study area, which has an intensive demand for all of these products. The major regional effects of energy systems on biological communities involve the alteration of habitat, as in the construction of hydropower dams, the addition of waste heat to water, and the passage of aquatic organisms through power-plant cooling systems. The relatively greater capacity of the air to absorb heat without major effect on the biota makes preferable use of air rather than water as a heat sink. The construction of hydropower stations involves the same distinct alteration of habitat and has the same effect on biota as is discussed in both the water resources and environmental services task group chapters, with the additional factor that many modern projects are of enormous scale so that the greatest care in analysis of probable effects and in siting and design is required. The construction of nuclear stations involves the added impact of radioactive waste products, which can have profoundly damaging effects on biological organisms and communities and therefore cannot be discharged into the environment at all.

Transmission corridors, whether for wires or pipelines, cause changes in terrestrial habitats through control of vegetation. The philosophy of least-cost, single-purpose planning customarily disregards biological communities. Although the transmission corridor itself is not necessarily damaging to biological communities, the location of the corridor can have major consequences on man's use of the environment. Thus, both the locational decision as well as management of the disturbed area have a potentially great impact on biological communities.

Transportation

Transportation, along with energy systems, has the greatest impact on biological communities because it is the prime determinant of the location of human settlement and activity. Transportation facilities, such as roads, railroads, navigation channels, and airports, do not in themselves have large-scale impacts on biological communities. In many cases, they function as barriers to movement or define the limit of a habitat. There are also direct effects such as road kills and gross discharges from ships and barges. But indirectly, transportation is the man-made system that is most significant in structuring biological communities.

There is usually a close relationship between transportation systems and river systems. In the study area, however, the transportation linkages along river systems are so potent that the major valleys have become strategic transportation corridors. This has had great consequences, both adverse and beneficial, on the land-water edge, which is a very critical interface to biological communities. The main beneficial effect is the creation of wetlands behind diked-off coves of the Hudson. But in causing the filling of other wetlands and by bulkheading shorelines, the net effect of transportation on land-water edge has been decidedly destructive.

Human Health

The most serious issues of human health revolve around the control of biological pathogens, vectors, and pests. This is accomplished directly by chemical agents such as pesticides and antibiotics, or indirectly by manipulation of the population-controlling factors of the environment. This sort of problem occurs in the case of insects such as mosquitoes and flies that may carry diseases; bacteria and fungi that are parasites of man or of essential food crops; bacteria and invertebrates that contaminate drinking water or food; plants with irritating pollen, toxic foliage, or fruit; birds that may be disease vectors; and mammals that may be disease vectors or direct predators to man.

In addition, there are problems of the concentration of pathogenic bacteria or toxic agents, such as heavy metals and chlorinated hydrocarbons, in the human food chain. This occurs through the agency of biomagnification. It is most significant in aquatic ecosystems and may render shellfish and certain fishes toxic. Biomagnification of certain persistent toxins occurs in terrestrial ecosystems also, but these are not a serious problem to human health because man does not extensively utilize the natural terrestrial food chain. The main issues concerning terrestrial food supplies, other than basic quantity, are the potential effects of cropping, fertilizing, and other management practices on the nutritional value of foods.

The importance of biota as indicators of environmental quality should not be disregarded. Certain species are widely used as general indices of the condition or health of streams and lakes. Other species reliably indicate certain aspects of air quality. The higher trophic levels in food chains usually show the first symptoms of biomagnification of toxins. As a general principle, all organisms respond to their environment. Therefore, by analyzing the presence and behavior of threshold organisms, which are likely to be the most sensitive, environmental quality can be understood in functional terms of the effect on the health of species, including man.

Leisure Time and Recreation

There is an increasing demand for the use of biological communities as an amenity of life. This is demonstrated by the increased use of parklands, development of second homes in the country or on fresh- or saltwater shores, recreational hunting and fishing, hiking, and even suburban development. All of these activities aspire to a strong relationship to biological communities and their environment. Many of the recreational and leisure time uses of biological communities compete with other forms of exploitation of resources. For instance, the use of several of the Hudson's tributary stream systems for New York City's water supply competes with their use as recreational trout fisheries. Exploitation of visual amenities usually results in destruction of the view. Biological organisms themselves may inhibit recreational usage, as in the case of black fly swarms in the Adirondacks, or growths of algae and water hyacinths in fresh and brackish waters. Some of these biological detriments can be minimized by management techniques. Many, however, are either fundamental to the ecosystem or cannot be controlled without major side-effects, and are perhaps accepted as a component of the recreational environment.

HUMAN HEALTH

10.1 Introduction

The Definition of "Health"

The term "health" has various meanings in various contexts. As used by members of the health professions—by people in medicine, public health, and allied fields throughout the world—"health" refers to the biological integrity of each person as an individual, or of many people as a population of individuals. That is to say, the health professions are concerned with maintaining the health of individual people. They are not concerned with the health of "the family," "the city," "the nation," or "the environment," except in the somewhat general sense that these entities affect the health of people who live within them.

In modern terms, the concept of *mens sana in corpore sano* implies that a healthy person will live out his natural span of life without disease or impairment; that he will be able to attain his full biological potential for physical and intellectual growth and development; and that he will be able to live harmoniously and productively with his fellow men, if the circumstances that he encounters allow him to do so.

Members of the Human Health Task Group: Merril Eisenbud, Amitai Etzioni, Lawrence E. Hinkle, Jr., Stanislav V. Kasl, and Mary McLaughlin.

By this medical definition, health represents the absence of premature death, illness, disability, and impairment, and the absence of any failure of growth or development. Just as the concept of cold represents the absence of heat, the concept of health by this definition represents the absence of illness, impairment, and premature death. The perfect state of health is rather like absolute zero in the Kelvin scale—it is a state that can be approached, but is not likely to be attained. Whether or not there may be a state of positive health beyond the complete absence of disease, disability, impairment, or failure of development is a moot question.

The Relationship of Attitudes and Perceptions to Health

The term "attitude," as we have used it in this chapter, refers to a "mental set," a "tendency or orientation of mind," the "propensity of a person for reacting in a certain manner." Attitudes are often the outgrowth of individual experience, but often they are shared by groups of people in a quite systematic way. Mothers are likely to see virtue in their own children, and Scotsmen to find beauty in the music of bagpipes, that other people may have difficulty in perceiving.

Shared attitudes are important in determining people's reactions to their environment, because so much of men's reaction to their environment is determined not by how it impinges upon them physically, but upon the information they obtain from it through their sense organs.

To a certain extent, attitudes help to determine health and behavior. People who view smoking as a harmless pastime, or drinking as an acceptable way of escaping from the cares of daily life, are likely to suffer certain consequences to their health. People who regard their work as dull and monotonous may find that their emotional health is adversely affected by it, while others who regard the same work as interesting and varied may experience no adverse effects.

Attitudes toward the number of people who can live together in a confined space are major determinants of the effects of crowding. People living very closely together with other members of their own families in Hong Kong slums, in very densely packed communities in Melanesia, in the crews of submarines, or in house trailers on family vacations suffer no ill effects when they regard the arrangement as acceptable, traditional, necessary, or transient, and when they subordinate some of their desire for comfort and privacy to attain other goals. Equal degrees of crowding occurring under similar circumstances but among people who have different attitudes may be accompanied by quite disruptive social effects.

The idiosyncratic attitudes of individuals growing out of their own particular experiences have no special concern to this chapter; but attitudes that are widely shared by members of social groups are of great concern, because these attitudes may markedly influence the reaction of many people to the environment. We have decided to deal with socially determined attitudes at some length for this reason.

A "perception," as we use this term, is a "cognition," an "apprehension," an "identification." To "perceive" a part of the external world involves not only seeing, hearing, feeling, smelling, and tasting, but also "recognizing," "understanding," and "sensing the implications" of it. Since a major goal of environmental programs is to improve the beauty of the environment and to increase the pleasure and satisfaction that people attain from it, we have regarded human perceptions and their measurements as being closely relevant to the task of our committee. We are also aware that what David Mechanic has called "the illness behavior" of people may be seriously influenced by their perception of their environment (Mechanic, 1962, 1968, 1972). That is to say, people exposed to conditions which they expect may cause illness are likely to experience some of the symptoms of illness, to visit physicians and hospitals and complain of these symptoms, and to attribute any illness that they develop to the condition that they presume may have caused it.

At the present time, with the widespread awareness of air pollution, periods when air pollution is present and visible, even though materials are at quite low concentrations, might easily be accompanied by many more complaints and much more visiting of physicians and hospitals than used to be the case, although it has not been established that this actually happens. Similar phenomena of perception have been involved in people's refusal to eat swordfish or tuna, and in their temporary turning away from low-calorie soft drinks when the possible carcinogenic effects of cyclamates were published.

It has become increasingly important to attempt to determine when aspects of the environment affect human health or behavior because of their intrinsic qualities; when they do so because of the symptomatic complaints related to people's perceptions of the environment; and when they do so because of changes in illness behavior that result from people's perceptions of their environment.

General Measures of Health

To estimate the level of health of the population at any time, and to determine the extent to which environmental programs may alter health, both general and specific measures of health are needed. General measures of health include rates or indicators of *mortality, morbidity, impairment,* and *growth and development.*

General Measures of Mortality

Crude mortality rates reflect all causes of mortality within a population, including those that are genetically determined and those that are the delayed effects of environmental agents or conditions which may have acted many years in the past, during infancy, childhood, or youth. They also reflect immediate causes of mortality, including sudden changes in environmental conditions such as periods of very hot weather or contamination of water supplies.

Infant mortality rates reflect the mortality of a segment of the population that is especially vulnerable to environmental factors such as nutrition, infection, injury, and maternal care.

Expectation of life at birth measures duration of life based upon age-specific mortality rates, and thus overcomes some of the difficulties associated with crude mortality rates. This, too, measures all causes of mortality; but if two populations are genetically comparable, and there is no significant migration into or out of these populations, then the life expectancy of their members generally reflects environmental conditions. However, this measure is not as rapidly responsive to changes in environmental conditions as are crude mortality rates.

The expectation of life at 1 year of age is a small refinement that eliminates the unique problems of infancy, but otherwise it remains a nonspecific measure.

The Swaroop Index is the proportion of deaths at 50 or more years of age among total deaths. The community with the higher index is considered "healthier," since deaths are concentrated at the older ages.

General Morbidity Rates

Morbidity refers to the amount and kind of illness present in a population. It generally reflects what is happening to the health of a population at any given time more closely than does mortality, especially if the population is one such as ours in which mortality rates are low.

However, data on morbidity are usually less exact than data on mortality, and they are more difficult to come by. Data are less exact because death, in the quaint terminology of the epidemiologist, is "an exact endpoint" whereas "illness" and "disability" are not so clearly delineated. Data on morbidity are harder to obtain because they must be gotten by surveys (with examinations, if they are to be exact) or inferred from behavior, such as going to a doctor or staying away from work, which depends upon motivation and is compiled and reported with varying accuracy. Deaths, on the other hand, are recognized and reported quite completely, even though the reported causes of death may be somewhat inaccurate.

Disability, the most commonly used measure of morbidity, is a general term used to describe any temporary or long-term reduction of activity as a result of an acute or chronic condition (NCHS, 1958). *Disability days* may be further classified according to whether they are days of restricted activity, bed days, hospital days, work-loss days, or school-loss days. Restricted activity days and bed days must be estimated by surveys, but other indicators of disability are more easily available.

Hospital days generally reflect the amount of severely disabling illness in a population, but this measure is clearly influenced by the availability of hospital beds. *Work-loss* days caused by illness are a more useful measure of morbidity in the employed population, and respond quickly to changes in environmental conditions. The spread of an epidemic of influenza from city to city can be more closely followed by watching the sickness absence rate among employed people than by any other means. Long-term sickness absence (7 days or more) reflects the prevalence of severely disabling illness more closely than shorter-term absences, but both are significantly influenced by illness behavior and worker attitudes.

School-loss days share some of the problems of attitude and behavior that are associated with work-loss days.

Visits to physicians and clinics are a general indicator of morbidity which, however, is markedly influenced by the availability, ease of access, and cost of these visits, as well as by individual attitudes, motivations, and sickness behavior. However, this can be very useful for the detection of certain kinds of specific morbidity.

The incidence and prevalence of acute and chronic conditions must be obtained by surveys such as the National Health Survey. It has the advantage that it measures the prevalence of conditions such as hypertension, obesity, or arteriosclerosis, which may cause little or no disability for long periods of time, but which may nevertheless make a serious contribution to mortality.

General Levels of Impairment

Impairments are the residual abnormalities of form or function that remain after illness or injuries—loss of sight, loss of hearing, absence of teeth, paralysis of extremities, and so on. The general level of impairments in a population is an indication of its past as well as its present health. However, in the study of environmental effects upon health, impairments are most useful when they can be specifically related to environmental conditions— as, for example, hearing loss in relationship to exposure to noise.

Growth and Development

Humans, like animals and plants, grow larger and develop some of their capacities more fully when they are in environments suited to their needs.

Children who are well nourished and protected from infectious microorganisms grow larger and mature at a rate different from that of otherwise similar children who grow up in a less benign environment. Among the useful measures of growth and development are the following.

Measures of physical characteristics include height, weight, and various anthropometric measurements such as the circumference of the head and chest. All of these are related to norms for age. *Indicators of maturity* include physical indicators such as age of dentition, age of menarche, and age of closure of epiphysis, and some behavioral indicators such as the age at which an infant turns over, creeps, sits, walks, or talks. *Indicators of intellectual development* usually take the form of psychological tests. An additional measure of intellectual development is the school achievement of children. However, performance on tests can be significantly influenced by the past and present environment of the child. School achievement, in addition, is influenced by the availability and cost of schools, culturally determined attitudes toward schools, and varying academic practices.

Specific Indicators of Health

A "specific" indicator of an environmental effect upon health may be thought of as one for which the causal links between an environmental agent or phenomenon and a specific manifestation of morbidity, mortality, or impairment of growth and development has been established with evidence sufficient to satisfy the majority of the scientific community. The indicator is most useful when the linkage is direct, obvious, and well demonstrated. It is less useful when two or more environmental agents (such as air pollution, cigarette smoking, allergenic agents, and infectious agents) interact in a complex manner to produce conditions such as respiratory illnesses that are not distinctly related to any one cause. When an indicator such as this is also influenced by differences in individual exposures and in individual susceptibilities, and when it may be significantly influenced by illness behavior, it may be very difficult to ascertain just which of several environmental causes has the greatest influence upon the indicator at any given time.

Specific Mortality Rates

Even when mortality arises from conditions known to have several causes, it can be a useful indicator of environmental effects if one cause is of overriding importance (as, for example, cancer of the lung and cigarette smoking), or if the acute intervention of one factor causes a rise in mortality, as in the deaths of people with chronic cardiovascular and respiratory disease in London or Donora during the severe air pollution episodes. In view of the usefulness of this measure, remarkably little has been done to utilize it to quantify the relationships between certain environmental factors and human health.

For example, it has been about a decade since it was first suggested that the increasing exposure to asbestos fibers was resulting in higher incidence of mesothelioma in the general population (New York Academy of Science, 1965). There is known to be a long latent period for the development of this disease in asbestos workers or in other exposed people. If the exposure of the general public was beginning to be reflected by an increasing incidence of mesothelioma a decade ago, it was reasonable to assume that the increasing exposure during the previous several decades had already committed the members of the general population to a relatively marked increase in the incidence of mesothelioma during the next 10 or 15 years—regardless of what might be done for control measures during that time.

In the 1930s and 1940s, the use of asbestos increased markedly, and a parallel curve of increasing mesothelioma might have been expected 10 to 20 years later. By a systematic use of mortality data, coupled with careful epidemiologic studies, it might still be possible to determine if the incidence of this condition is increasing.

Specific Morbidity

Most environmental agents or conditions are much more likely to cause illness or injury than to cause death. When a specific environmental condition or agent produces an illness or injury of a characteristic sort, the very appearance of this illness or injury in population, or an increase in its incidence, may lead immediately to an inference about the potential environmental cause.

The sudden appearance of first degree burns of the skin in a large portion of the young population immediately after the Memorial Day weekend suggests that a great many people have been to the beach and have exposed themselves to the sun. The absence of a parallel rise in acute gastrointestinal conditions suggests that, whatever may have been their exposure to fecally polluted water in beaches, river, and swimming pools, it was not sufficient to produce significant illness in them.

Visits to physicians and clinics are better indicators of severe and prostrating conditions, such as typhoid, heat stroke, or automobile accidents, than of less disabling conditions. There may be marked differences in the illness behavior of people in reaction to minor illnesses.

For example, there is reason to believe that a large proportion of people who are bitten by dogs or who suffer from dirty puncture wounds do go to physicians, even though the wounds are small, because there is a widespread fear of rabies and tetanus. On the other hand, relatively few people who suffer from sunburn visit physicians, and these only in the more severe cases, because first degree sunburn is known to be a self-limiting condition, and it is usually tolerated by people who seek it because of the "suntan" that follows.

Specific Impairments

When impairments can be specifically related to environmental agents or conditions, they can be useful indicators of exposure to those conditions. A good example is the finding of hearing loss among people exposed to loud noise. Other examples are characteristic deformities created by prenatal exposure to thalidomide and to German measles virus.

Specific Effects on Growth and Development

When environmental agents or conditions have clearly identifiable effects on growth and development—such as the intellectual deficiencies resulting from protein-calorie malnutrition in early childhood, the rickets that results from inadequate exposure to sunlight or vitamin D, or the mottled teeth resulting from excessive exposure to fluoride—these also can be very useful indicators of environmental effects.

Specific Indications of Exposure to Environmental Agents

Specific indications of exposure to environmental agents can be obtained by survey procedures. Tests such as the tuberculin test and other indications of acquired hypersensitivity can determine which members of a population have been exposed to environmental agents such as bacteria, viruses, or pollens. Measurements of chemical substances, such as lead in blood or arsenic in hair, can be used to determine exposure to heavy metals. However, there is an important distinction between evidence of exposure and evidence of disease. The number of exposed people in a population may far exceed the number that actually develop the disease.

Availability of Health Indicators

In general, mortality statistics are available on a national basis, on a statewide basis, and on a countywide basis throughout the Hudson Basin region. Morbidity statistics are more difficult to obtain. General levels of morbidity and of impairments for the nation as a whole, and for certain broad geographic regions and social and economic categories, have been obtained by survey procedures such as the National Health Survey. Specific morbidity figures usually depend upon specific reporting procedures set up for that purpose. Physicians and hospitals are required by law to report certain infectious diseases and certain injuries such as those caused by gunshot. Most other illnesses are not systematically reported. Some idea of the prevalence of many diseases can be obtained from hospital records, but information about others, which are not disabling, depends upon the development of adequate survey procedures.

In recent years a great deal of public discussion has been generated about environmental pollution and the health hazards it poses. Some poll data exist which bear directly on how the average citizen feels about this threat: to what degree people are worried about pollution, how high it ranks on their list of priorities for problems to be solved, and how willing they are to have government money spent to solve pollution problems.

Available poll data, of course, provide information about the attitudes of a nationwide sample of Americans—or in some cases residents of a particular state, such as California. While we cannot say for certain that the attitudes of Hudson Basin residents would echo those of Americans in general, there is little reason to think that they do not.

Perceptions of the environment are likely to be influenced by mental health, which is itself a troublesome concept. Disagreements in the approach, the definition, and the measurement of mental health are the rule rather than the exception. Indeed, any single measure that might be chosen (such as hospitalization in a mental institution or a psychiatrist's rating) is always going to be too narrow and too broad: too narrow because it will not reflect all of the underlying dimensions of mental health, and too broad because it will be "contaminated" by other influences as well—reporting biases in questionnaire measures, readiness for self-referral in treatment-based indexes, and so on.

Despite these problems, it is possible to organize the multiplicity of criteria of mental health into several categories: (a) functional effectiveness, (b) well-being, (c) mastery and competence, (d) psychiatric signs and symptoms, and (e) evidences of treatment. Altogether, these categories of criteria can serve as a working definition of mental health. No one category can be considered preeminent, nor can the categories be seen as additive, in the sense that a summary index (based on averaging the scores for the various components) can be treated as an overall measure of mental health. The criteria are best treated in a profile approach, with each person characterized by a pattern of high and low scores on the various indicators.

To the reader with strong convictions about how mental health should be defined and measured, this eclectic approach may appear to have more weaknesses than virtues. On the other hand, given the broad concerns of this report, the approach we have adopted still may not be sufficiently inclusive where we consider questions such as satisfaction with housing or neighborhood, reports of noise interference with conversations and recreation, or concern or unhappiness about levels of air pollution around one's residence.

One may fairly ask whether these are indicators of mental health or simply variables that may or may not prove to be correlates of mental health or processes (intervening variables) which link environmental quality and mental health. Clearly, there is something arbitrary in considering satisfaction with oneself (self-esteem) as an unchallengeable indicator of mental health, whereas satisfaction with one's job may be a dubious indicator, and satisfaction with the size of one's apartment may be an unacceptable one.

Yet the answer to a question such as, Does housing affect mental health? is very much dependent on whether or not housing satisfaction is considered "part" of mental health (Kasl, 1973). The answer is a clear yes if housing satisfaction is included; but if housing satisfaction is excluded, the answer is probably only weakly, if at all, since it has been difficult to show that improved housing improves mental health (e.g., Wilner, 1962), or that there is even a positive association between housing satisfaction and mental health (e.g., Kasl and Harburg, 1972, 1974; Wessman, 1956).

"Health Effects"

The effects of the environment upon human health may be either beneficial or adverse; however, the term *health effects* is usually applied to the adverse effects. These may be immediate or delayed. An epidemic of influenza or typhoid, a heat wave, a loss of jobs resulting from the closing of a factory, or a loss of homes resulting from the demolition of a neighborhood may lead to an immediate upsurge of morbidity and mortality among people who are exposed to these agents or conditions.

Delayed health effects occur when the damage created by an environmental agent acts slowly, or accumulates over time. For example, the "rheumatic fever" reaction to an infection with streptococci in childhood may damage the valves of the heart so slightly its function is not impaired for many years, and the "heart disease" becomes apparent only after several decades. *Potential health effects* are those that might be produced by an environmental agent or condition, but which may not have occurred up to the present and might not occur at all. It is important to distinguish between these potential effects and delayed health effects, which are known to occur in a certain proportion of people who are exposed to an environmental factor at a known intensity for a known period of time.

Examples of potential health effects are the effects of cyclamates and DDT on human health. The ingestion of cyclamates in food in the amounts usually used has not been known to cause human illness. Cyclamates were banned from use in foodstuffs because it had been shown that they might cause tumors in laboratory animals if fed to these animals in high concentrations over long periods of time. DDT has not caused any significant human illness, even in those who have worked with it most closely and have been most heavily exposed to it for many years. The effect of asbestos particles in drinking water is also a potential health effect. It is known that the inhalation of asbestos fibers may ultimately cause mesotheliomas in the lungs of a proportion of those so exposed—a true delayed health effect; but the ingestion of asbestos fibers in food or water and the exposure of the endothelial lining of the gastrointestinal tract have never been known to lead to the occurrence of a cancer. There are theoretical reasons for supposing that it might not; but there are also good theoretical reasons for supposing that it might.

Many decisions on environmental policy have been made in the past because of known health effects, either immediate or delayed. Recently, more and more decisions have been made on the basis of potential health effects—effects that might occur but have not been known to occur. These decisions are based both upon experience and upon fear—experience with the delayed effects of cigarette smoking, exposure to X rays, thalidomide, vinyl chloride, and the like, and a legitimate fear that exposure of human populations to substances demonstrated to be carcinogenic, such as cyclamates or asbestos fibers, or to protoplasmic poisons such as DDT, might have disastrous effects.

In this connection, it is worth remembering that the amount and duration of exposure are very important determinants of adverse health effect. Cancer of the lung occurs not simply in those who smoke a few cigarettes for 20 years of more; it occurs primarily in those who smoke one, two, or even three packs of cigarettes a day for 30 years or more—people who have inhaled the concentrated smoke from 200 to 600 kg of tobacco during that time. Leukemia from exposure to X rays has occurred primarily in those who received an overwhelmingly large dose of radiation in a short period of time at Hiroshima or Nagasaki, or among radiologists who have been exposed day after day to many times the daily exposure of ordinary people. Mothers whose children developed abnormalities of their extremities had taken thalidomide not just in trace amounts but in gram amounts at a crucial period of their pregnancy. The vascular tumors in those exposed to vinyl chloride have not occurred among those who were casually exposed, but among workmen who have been exposed to this substance in large amounts and for many years.

One can never be absolutely sure that an exposure to a damaging agent or condition in the environment will not cause a serious disease or death, but there is very good reason for believing that as the intensity, concentration, and duration of exposure decline the likelihood of an adverse effect declines almost to the point of being a great rarity. There are two good reasons for this.

First, the large majority of adverse environmental effects depend upon chemical or physical reactions that must be either widespread enough to damage a biochemical process essential to life or health, or frequent enough to cause a cancerous change in a sufficient number of susceptible cells to initiate a tumor. As Dinman (1972) has pointed out, such physical and chemical processes require a finite concentration of molecules or ions acting within a finite volume—a single molecule or ion (or even a very few) is not sufficient to initiate or sustain a significant reaction. Even highly potent chemical substances such as botulinum toxin or hydrocyanic acid, when diluted in a large volume of water or air, become too attenuated to cause disease when introduced into the human being. Ionizing radiation can be a highly potent mutagenic agent, but a few cosmic rays passing through a human body each day are unlikely to damage the nuclear material within a sufficient number of strategically placed cells to lead to a cancer or a mutation in any given person—even though they may occasionally do so in a large population of people.

Second, like other animals faced with the necessity of surviving in a hostile environment, man has evolved many protective mechanisms to cope with toxic or damaging agents or challenging environmental conditions. These mechanisms enable people to deal with most of the threats from the environment that occur under most circumstances. When bacteria or viruses are ingested or inhaled from the environment in small numbers, they are contained and killed by the immune processes and other defense mechanisms. When dangerous chemical substances are taken in, they are buffered, conjugated, detoxified, and excreted through a variety of biochemical mechanisms that work to this end. Most of the cancer cells that appear sporadically seem to be recognized as such and dealt with by defense mechanisms which contain or destroy them. When mutant genes are produced (by radiation or other causes) and become a part of fertilized ova, they usually lead to significant abnormalities of developing embryos which are "recognized" and rejected by the uterus long before birth can occur.

Life in an environment containing a modest amount of threatening or damaging material is the natural condition of all living organisms, including men. This is a point worth remembering. The effort to remove from the human environment a potential hazard to health which is likely to affect, at most, only a very few people may be self-defeating. It may be accomplished not only at great monetary cost, thereby diverting societal resources that might be put to other uses, but also at the cost of an immediate adverse health effect for a number of other people which outweighs any potential gains in health that might be accomplished. Examples of this idea will be cited.

Apocalyptic effects are those that might be created if there were a widespread poisoning of photosynthetic organisms in the ocean, a drastic increase in the amount of carbon dioxide in the air, or widespread climatic changes. They are, in this sense, potential health effects of a catastrophic nature, except that they are probably an order of magnitude more remote than the threat presented by cyclamates or by asbestos in drinking water. They are different from other potential health effects both in the magnitude of the threat and in its remoteness, but from the human health point of view, the same considerations enter into weighing the cost of dealing with such apocalyptic threats to health that enter into evaluating other potential health effects.

"The Environment"

The environment of a building, a city, or a river basin is different from that of a person. The distinction is important because the term "environment" has different meanings when used in different contexts. The environment that is relevant to human health is that which surrounds a person as an individual.

Men, like other living organisms, depend for their lives upon a continuous interaction with their environment. The metabolic activity that sustains life within the human organism is maintained by this interaction, which takes place on the surfaces of the human body. It consists primarily of the interchange of gases on the surface of the lungs; of food and water on the surface of the gastrointestinal tract; of heat on the surface of the skin; of fluids, salts, and waste materials on the surfaces of the kidney; of information through the eyes, ears, nose, and other sense organs; and of an output of physical energy through muscular activities.

The parts of the environment of greatest importance to human health are those that are closest to a person and come into the most intimate contact with him: the air he breathes, the food he ingests, the water he drinks, the temperature and humidity of the air around him, the clothing he wears, the house he lives in, the place where he works, and the light and radiation that fall upon him. In the last analysis, most of the environment does not act at a distance. It acts through those agents which immediately impinge upon a man, and it acts in relation to the intensity of their impingement and its duration. It is this action which affects human health.

The one important exception to this is the information that a man receives from his environment through his sense organs. This information enables him to react to that part of his environment which is at a distance. No small part of the information that people obtain from their environment is concerned with other people in their environment and their relationship to these other people. Men, like most of the other higher animals, are social creatures. They always exist as members of groups of animals of the same species. They depend for their livelihood, safety, comfort, happiness, and reproduction upon the other people who surround them. In other words, the so-called social environment is an essential part of the environment of every person, which must always be considered in efforts to determine how the environment affects health.

Environmental Indicators Relevant to Human Health

It has become customary to measure or describe aspects of the environment that are relevant to various human activities such as agriculture (e.g., rainfall) or home heating (e.g., degree days) or to broader environmental concerns (e.g., CO_2 content of air). Because such measures can be used to help determine the effectiveness of programs that may be set up to control or change the environment, they are often called "program indicators."

During the past century, indicators have been established for various aspects of the environment considered relevant to human health. One of the oldest of these is the number of colon bacilli present in a milliliter of water. This has been a very useful indicator of the relative safety of public water supplies. Its use was based on the rationale that the limiting factor for the safety of public water supplies is potability—safety for drinking—because most waterborne human diseases in the United States and in Western Europe are acquired by drinking water, and most of the human pathogens in public water supplies come from contamination by human feces. The colon bacillus is one of the less pathogenic fecal bacteria, but it is so much more common and abundant than the other fecal pathogens that it is much easier to detect when present in water supply.

Like most other "environmental indicators" or "program indicators" that are selected because of their supposed relevance to human health, the *Escherichia coli* count of water is a measure that is empirical. Its usefulness as an indicator of the safety of public water supplies is limited to the circumstances under which the assumptions behind it are probably true. It is not an adequate measure of the safety of water in places where major hazards to health arise from uses other than drinking (as in Egypt where much of the hazard comes from wading or swimming in canals); when the major contaminants of water are not from human feces (as when contamination is primarily from industrial wastes); and when colon bacilli, or other bacilli quite like them, are present in water, but may not come from human feces.

In the sections that follow, each of the other nine "policy areas" of the Hudson Basin Project will be viewed in turn from the perspective of human health. Our discussion will include consideration of some of the major "environmental indicators" in each area that has been used because of its presumed relevance to health. The concluding section will address a troublesome question, that of the ultimate benefits to human health that can be expected from current efforts to improve the environment.

10.2   Land Use/Human Settlement

Where a man lives does not determine his health so much as his income, his education, and his position in society. The type of dwelling and the people with whom he lives are more important to his health than the place where he lives. The variables most strongly associated with health throughout the United States are age, income, and education (NCHS, 1964, 1966, 1969, 1972b, 1973c). The upper- and middle-class residents of suburban communities in the Hudson Basin region are among the healthiest people in the world, not because of where they live, but because of their level of education and income.

There are, to be sure, differences in the patterns of illness between cities and countryside, even in the United States. In rural areas the rates for dysentery and other waterborne diseases tend to be much higher, and the death rates in infancy, childhood, and youth also tend to be higher (Lew, 1974). Acute conditions, brief episodes of illness that affect each of us about twice a year, are in general slightly more common in urban than in rural regions, but apparently are much more frequent among central city residents than among farm families. The difference is accounted for almost entirely by differences in acute upper respiratory conditions (colds and sore throats) and other infectious conditions caused by highly contagious microorganisms. Lower respiratory conditions, including bronchitis, tracheitis, and bronchial pneumonia, which are thought to be especially affected by air pollution, are apparently more frequent among farmers than among central city residents (NCHS, 1974a). In cities, especially in the Northeast, the death rates from cardiovascular and renal diseases are among the highest in the world. Death rates from cancer, including cancer of the lung, from respiratory diseases, and from cirrhosis are also very high. Within these urban areas, all of these diseases show a marked social-class gradient. Popular belief to the contrary notwithstanding, the rates for these diseases are significantly higher among lower-income and blue collar people than among the upper-income and white collar groups (NCHS, 1972b).

The United States is so large, the social, economic, and ethnic differences among its people are so great, and the effect of immigration and internal migration upon its population so important that it is difficult to determine what, if any, effects upon health are the result of geography alone or of urban, rural, or even national differences. Much has been made of the high infant mortality rates in the United States, as well as the high rates for cardiovascular diseases, cancer, and cirrhosis, compared with certain other nations, notably the Scandinavian countries and the Netherlands. However, Edward Lew (1974) has pointed out " . . . the dubious validity of ranking . . . a continent of over 200 million alongside . . . nations of 2 to 10 million people. . . . If one compares the United States death rate from all causes with the corresponding rate for all of Western Europe, the differential is relatively small."

Those who take part in a migration may suffer from the injuries and illnesses that are associated with it, but their children and grandchildren often display the beneficial effect of the new environment. The American children of recent immigrants from eastern and southern Europe, from Puerto Rico, and from Japan, are all taller and more robust than comparable children in their native land (Greulich, 1957). Internal migration has had a similar effect. Although the condition of the blacks in the slums of our northern cities is often deplorable, their health and that of their children seem to be much better than the health of those they left behind in the rural South. They are larger and better educated. They have avoided much of the malnutrition and infection that they might have encountered as children, and they have avoided many of the injuries of youth, and some of the hypertension of older age. On the other hand, like the American-born Japanese of California and Hawaii, the urban blacks of the Northeast have begun to develop conditions such as coronary heart disease and cancer of the bowel, which seem to be characteristic of our modern urban society (Buell and Dunn, 1965; Haenszel and Kurihara, 1968).

The desire of low-income residents of cities to move to suburban areas may be expressed as a desire for clean air and green grass, but it seems to represent the traditional American thrust toward places where one may attain higher social status, better economic opportunity, and better human facilities, such as schools and housing.

Among the aspects of land use/human settlement that are within the purview of this study, the density of human settlements is considered relevant to health. In connection with this, it is customary to distinguish between population density (persons per unit of land area) and crowding (persons per dwelling unit). However, neither population density nor crowding has any simple relationship to health. High population density places heavy demands upon food supply, housing, and services such as sanitation and transportation, but where these are adequate, as in the Upper East Side of Manhattan, health may be excellent. The health effects of crowding seem to depend upon the circumstances under which one is crowded and with whom one is closely associated. Military units made up of new recruits living closely together in barracks are notoriously susceptible to respiratory disease; but veteran military units living under similar circumstances may be quite healthy. The psychological consequences of five people sharing a small apartment may be quite different if the people are members of one family or of two families.

The general properties of the design and organization of cities have not been amenable to measurement in the past because of the lack of any organized system for measuring or counting them. Recently, architects, urban planners, and sociologists have attempted to remedy this (Doxiadis, 1968, 1970; McHarg, 1972; Gutman and Geddes, 1974). Although it has been proposed that studies be carried out to relate various aspects of the man-made environment to human health, few such studies have been made, and there is little evidence one way or the other that some of these aspects of the environment do have any significant relation to health.

Noise, a general feature of human settlements, has been a matter of considerable concern in recent years. "Noise" in common parlance is "unwanted sound" (American Standards Association, 1954). A person talking on the telephone, a recording of a Beethoven sonata, or even the soft dripping of a faucet may be noise to a person who is trying to sleep, whereas the literally deafening sound of a rock band may be music to those who are enthusiastically standing nearby and listening to it. Noise does have a proven relationship to health, but this is in terms of the loudness of sound, and the relationship is to hearing loss (American Standards Association, 1954; Glorig and Davis, 1961; Karplus and Bonvallet, 1953). Unwanted sound interferes with many important human activities, such as teaching in schools, church services, interpersonal conversations, and even sleep; but the relationship of these to mortality, morbidity, and other measures of health is by no means clear.

Another feature of human settlements that is sometimes overlooked, but which may have major implications for health, is their location. For various reasons, usually economic or political, people have always been prone to locate cities and towns in places peculiarly subject to natural disasters, such as floodplains, in earthquake zones, along low-lying seacoasts, and on the sides of volcanoes. Within the Hudson Basin region, there are a number of sites potentially subject to flooding by rivers or storms, but none peculiarly susceptible to earthquakes or volcanic eruptions.

Indicators of Land Use/Human Settlement Relevant to Human Health

A Committee on Planning for Environmental Quality Indices, which was recently convened by the Environmental Studies Board (sponsored by National Academy of Sciences) under the chairmanship of Dr. Merril Eisenbud, has made these tentative comments about indicators of land use (National Research Council, 1975):

> While it is generally appreciated that land use can have pervasive effects on environmental quality, indices useful for assessing these impacts have not been developed. The issues and policies important to land use are conceptually different from those important to air pollution or radiation. . . . Indices on the impacts of land use present a conceptual problem.
>
> For example, in the case of urban land, data are available on densities of population; number and type of industrial and commercial establishments; municipal services such as schools, libraries, and post offices; green space and recreational area; tax revenues and transportation systems; and many other factors. But a means of translating these various data to a common scale is not available. In many cases, the relative importance of the various factors is not known. Perhaps the most important factors have not as yet even been measured.

Indicators of Population Density and of Crowding

Population density is usually expressed as number of people per square mile. Crowding is usually expressed in numbers of people per dwelling unit or per room in a dwelling unit. Crowding usually refers to dwellings rather than workplaces or modes of transportation, even though crowding may be significant in all of these places.

Indicators of Housing

Although housing is outside the purview of this study, it would be desirable to have a system of indicators of the quality of the houses, buildings, and communities that make up the major part of the human habitat and within which people spend most of their time. Indicators that might provide a useful insight into housing would be the number of indoor toilets per person in each dwelling unit, the percentage of families with indoor bathing facilities and with indoor washing facilities, the percentage of rooms having walls or ceilings that are peeling or fragmenting, and the number of dwelling units in which vermin droppings or other evidence of infestation can be seen.

Federal law now prohibits the production of paint having more than 0.5% lead. It is possible that this standard may be reduced substantially in the near future. Many dwelling units, particularly the older buildings in ghetto areas, have multiple coats of lead-bearing paint. These peel and become available to infants, who have a tendency to nibble on window sills or ledges, or to eat the paint chips. A useful indicator of the potential for community lead poisoning would be the number of dwelling units with surfaces containing more than 1% lead or more than 0.5 mg of lead/cm^2 (NAS, 1973b). The number of children in the general population having lead concentrations in the blood above 40 μg/100 ml (NAS, 1973b) would also be a useful indicator.

Indicators of the State of Neighborhoods

Indicators of the state of neighborhoods would also be desirable. For example, there are as yet no indicators of the extent to which a neighborhood is littered. Many other measures could be devised which would be in part indicators of potential environmental health problems, and in part indicators of socioeconomic status. These might include the rate of reported rat bites, and the rate of reports of forcible rape, homicide, and felonies. These are clearly matters that affect health and they are certainly due, in part, to the conditions of human habitation.

Indicators of the Design and Organization of Human Settlements

Gutman and Geddes (1974) have proposed a scheme for the analysis of the major properties of the "man made environment." It includes measures of spatial organization, circulation systems, communication systems, ambient properties, visual properties, amenities, symbolic properties, and architectonic properties. Some of these properties have been related directly to human health, and it seems reasonable that others of them may be. (Gutman and Geddes, 1974). Among these are circulation systems, which include the means for the transport of both people and goods; communication systems, architectonic properties, and "amenities," which includes facilities for recreation.

Indicators of Noise

Loudness of sound is related to sound pressure or to the amplitude of sound waves. The range of sound pressures varies from 0.0001 to 100,000 dynes/cm^2. The mathematical scale most useful for measuring variation of this magnitude is a logarithmic one, which is commonly referred to as the decibel scale. The *pitch* of sound is related to the frequency of sound waves. This also varies over a wide range, from 20 to 20,000 Hz. The *loudness of sound as perceived by a person* is in part based upon his psychological judgment. By definition, the *loudness level* of a sound is the sound pressure equal to a 1000-Hz pure tone stimulus that has been judged to be equally loud as the stimulus to be defined. *Loudness,* which is distinguished from loudness level, is also based on a judgment of tones. *Noisiness,* yet another psychological measure of noise, is based on the perceived noise decibel level (PNdB). All of these measures are founded on the principle that if the octave or one-third octave spectrum of a noise is known, one can calculate the perceived noise decibel level and can also calculate loudness and loudness level (Rudmose, 1969). The *speech interference level,* as the term indicates, is the level at which speech is interfered with.

The concept of the *Noise Exposure Forecast Level* (NEF Level) has been developed to deal with the problem of noise around airports (NAS/NAE, 1971). It is generally agreed that the noise exposure forecast level for residential environments should be less than 30 on an arbitrary scale that ranges from 0 to 100. In an NEF-30 area, the sound of a jet plane is intrusive. It intrudes upon sleep, prohibits conversation, and interrupts many kinds of relaxing activity.

Location

The health effects of the location of human settlements can be expressed in terms of the frequency of the occurrence of flooding, storm damage, damage from volcanic activity or earthquakes, or from other natural phenomena.

Storm damage within the Hudson Basin region does occur with computable frequency in some communities along the ocean shore and the shore of the Long Island Sound, and flooding from rivers has occurred with computable frequency along the shores of some rivers in New Jersey as well as in upstate New York. Damage from earthquakes has been negligible in this area, and damage from volcanic activity has not been known to occur within the human history of the region. On the other hand, there are occasional natural phenomena that produce threats to health. These include damage from forest fires in outlying areas, which sometimes occurs in outlying communities in the Adirondacks and Catskill regions; and threats to health from severe episodes of air pollution, which are more likely to occur in communities located in low areas of valleys in which damp air and pollutants can accumulate in excessive amounts.

The Effects of Some Aspects of Land Use/Human Settlement upon the Health of People in the Hudson Basin Region

The Effects of Population Density and Crowding

A cursory review of the vital statistics of the counties of New York State in the Hudson Basin region, based on the vital statistics for the state in 1972, shows the general death rate is lower in counties where the population is greater than 200,000 (median death rate is equal to 8.6); more in counties in the 100,000 to 200,000 range (median, 10.8), and highest in counties with a population of less than 100,000 (median, 11.5). This gives us no real information about the effects of population densities since we do not have age-adjusted death rates, socioeconomic information, and information about the accessibility and availability of medical care in various regions (Table 10 1).

There has been discussion whether there is a "critical urban mass" (Kilbourne and Smillie, 1969) and whether there is a critical space requirement for humans similar to that which appears to be true for some species of animals. However, there is no documentation of this, nor is there any documentation of the effect of population density per se upon human health in the Hudson Basin region.

Past studies in various parts of the nation show that census tracts high on overcrowded living conditions (persons per room) yield higher numbers of chronic conditions and cases of disability (Hochstim, 1970), tuberculosis (McMillan, 1957; Stein, 1954), and diverse pathologies, such as suicide, infant mortality, mental disorders, and VD cases (Schmitt, 1955, 1966). Studies dealing specifically with juvenile delinquency (Gordon, 1967; Landner, 1954; Shaw and McKay, 1969) and hospitalization for schizophrenia (Dunham, 1965; Faris and Dunham, 1939; Hare, 1956; Weinberg, 1968) confirm this general picture. However, the "crowding" variable is heavily confounded by its association with social and psychological variables. When these are controlled, the effect of crowding per se largely disappears (see below).

The Effects of Design Properties of the Man-made Environment

In this country, according to Gutman and Geddes (1974), "the study of circulation and movement systems . . . has tended to focus on economic effects. One does not find the kind of concern that is so evident in various French discussions that emphasize the way in which transportation inefficiency contributes to worker fatigue, and the costs imposed upon health and family solidarity."

The Effects of Noise

It has been established that a noise level above 40 dB can lead to changes in the threshold of function of the organ of Corti. The level of exposure considered a risk for permanent damage to hearing is 90 dB. Recently, the Environmental Protection Agency determined that for purposes of hearing conservation alone, the level that will protect practically the entire population is an L_{eq} of 70 dB over a 24-hour day. (L_{eq} represents the sound energy over any given time period.) The EPA opinion is that "as an individual moves from a relatively quiet home through the transportation cycle to a somewhat noisier occupational situation, and then back home again, his hearing will not be impaired if the daily equivalent of sound energy in his environment is no more than 70 decibels" (Anonymous, 1974b).

TABLE 10-1. Basic New York State Statistics by County in Hudson Basin Area, 1972[a]

| | Population | Live births[c] | Fetal | Adult[d] | Infant | Neonatal | Death rates[b] | | | | |
							Heart disease	Malignancies and neoplasms	Cardiovascular	Accidental	Motor vehicle
Albany	288,000	12.6	17.4	10.8	17.4	13.8	456.6	212.8	96.2	42.4	15.3
Albany City	111,600	16.9	17.7	14.8	22.3	18.6	604.8	291.2	113.8	49.3	10.9
Columbia	52,100	14.4	18.4	12.8	17.4	13.4	504.8	234.2	157.4	82.5	40.3
Delaware	44,850	13.3	23.0	11.7	11.8	8.4	573.0	198.4	115.9	51.3	26.8
Dutchess	218,500	13.4	14.8	7.9	16.8	13.0	348.7	137.3	73.7	45.8	28.8
Essex	34,350	15.7	14.6	12.7	16.6	14.8	538.6	200.9	116.4	81.5	43.7
Fulton	52,850	15.3	14.7	13.5	14.9	8.7	592.2	257.3	153.3	49.2	24.6
Greene	33,150	16.2	16.5	15.4	13.1	13.1	684.8	298.6	132.7	84.5	42.2
Hamilton	4,800	12.3	16.7	11.7	—	—	500.0	208.3	166.7	20.8	20.8
Herkimer	67,900	14.7	15.7	11.4	15.0	11.0	537.6	195.9	114.9	48.6	29.5
Montgomery	55,700	13.8	25.4	13.1	20.8	18.2	502.7	226.2	206.5	43.1	16.2
Nassau	1,400,000	8.1	20.5	8.0	17.2	13.8	346.8	172.6	70.7	28.3	13.1
New York City	7,843,200	NA[e]	NA	11.2	NA	NA	454.2	218.7	79.9	31.7	13.1

County										
Oneida	266,500	14.6	14.0	10.3	15.7	12.4	460.4	176.4	110.3	48.4	17.6
Orange	227,800	15.2	10.0	10.3	15.0	11.3	455.2	188.8	97.5	43.9	24.1
Putnam	63,700	13.3	15.1	7.0	23.6	18.9	270.0	157.0	48.7	45.5	23.5
Rensselaer	154,700	14.8	20.2	11.1	16.7	13.6	463.5	195.2	119.2	45.9	23.9
Rockland	243,000	10.9	14.8	6.5	23.7	18.1	259.7	124.3	63.8	39.9	18.5
Saratoga	133,700	17.2	9.5	7.9	13.9	10.0	323.9	138.4	70.3	47.1	25.4
Schenectady	162,800	13.1	18.8	10.9	14.0	11.2	498.8	202.7	87.8	40.5	12.9
Schenectady City	77,600	19.9	19.7	15.2	15.6	13.6	698.5	271.9	130.2	55.4	15.5
Schoharie	25,250	16.1	19.3	12.4	9.9	2.5	526.7	162.4	162.4	106.9	59.4
Suffolk	1,200,000	13.7	17.7	7.0	15.1	10.8	290.8	144.9	63.8	35.7	21.0
Sullivan	53,650	13.7	36.8	13.1	17.7	10.9	617.0	218.1	89.5	55.9	31.7
Ulster	144,800	13.6	14.0	10.6	17.7	15.7	415.1	198.2	143.0	64.9	31.8
Warren	50,700	17.1	5.7	11.7	26.5	19.6	451.7	242.6	126.2	65.1	23.7
Washington	52,500	10.0	5.9	11.4	20.2	15.5	544.8	165.7	108.6	66.7	41.5
Westchester	910,500	9.7	19.5	9.3	18.0	14.6	375.2	199.0	85.2	38.2	16.3

[a] Source: New York State Department of Health (1973).
[b] All death rates are given per 100,000 population, except for adult death rates, which are given per 1000 population.
[c] Live births per 1000 births.
[d] Total death rate, exclusive of fetal deaths.
[e] NA, not available.

There is a general decrease in auditory acuity in our population which appears with age (Glorig and Davis, 1961; Lasser and Master, 1959; Rosen, 1966). It especially affects the hearing for high-frequency sounds and it appears to affect men more than women. Although it has been reported that such loss of hearing does not occur among the members of certain tribal communities in Africa and elsewhere (Rosen et al., 1962, 1964a), it is not yet proven that the loss of acuity that occurs in the American population is related to noise in the environment. One of the more generally held theories has related it to the development of atherosclerosis (Rosen et al., 1964b; Rosen and Olin, 1965; Lawrence et al., 1967).

Although noise at the community level has not been shown to cause any increase in morbidity or mortality or any impairment of development, it clearly does interfere with many important human activities (Broadbent, 1957; Cohen, 1968). Noise around Kennedy Airport in 1969 within the NEF-30 area was estimated to interrupt the sleep of 371,000 people, to interfere with the schooling of 275,000 children, to prevent 525,000 people from using their front yards for ordinary family recreation, and to interfere with the household conversation of 560,000 people (Kryter, 1966; NAS/NAE, 1971).

The Effects of Residential Mobility and Rehousing

Even in the best designed rehousing studies (e.g., Wilner et al., 1955), the change is not only in the residential environment, but also in possibly large numbers of known and unknown factors as well. Schorr (1968), for example, has noted that moves to better housing for poor people are frequently accompanied by segregation, unfamiliar surroundings, and unknown new requirements, inadequate schools and police service, or rigid and unfriendly management. Often they also require spending more money on rent. A related issue is that rehousing represents to many individuals a major life change, which, as the recent developments in pyschosomatic medicine and psychiatry suggest (Jacobs et al., 1970; Myers et al., 1972; Rahe, 1972; Rahe and Arthur, 1968), can be stressful.

Even voluntary residential moves can have a disruptive influence on existing social networks, socializing, and mutual help. The same effect should be even stronger and more apparent from studies of involuntary residential moves. (Fried 1963, 1965; Gans, 1959). The studies of involuntary relocation of the elderly (Kasl, 1972; Niebanck, 1968) suggest that this is a particularly vulnerable group. The relocated elderly are generally less mobile and have lived in the old neighborhood longer than the average person. For the elderly, the move frequently represents an added financial hardship because their economic circumstances are already quite precarious.

The literature on involuntary change in residence because of urban renewal or highway construction is clearly sufficient to mount an attack on the way the federal and local governments have managed this social problem. For example, relocated slum residents generally pay higher rent without necessarily getting better housing (Lichfield, 1961; Pozen et al., 1968). Sometimes they scatter throughout the city (Thursz, 1966), but more often they move to similar housing in adjacent areas. Since such housing is also usually substandard, the relocatees experience additional moves later. Several studies have specifically tried to evaluate the health and psychosocial benefits of improved housing. The expected mental health benefits appear to be discouragingly small. In the best known and best designed study (Wilner, 1962), the results lead one to conclude that the consequences of rehousing were quite modest: aside from some effects on housing satisfaction and on evaluative perceptions of the neighborhood, very little was found—certainly no effects on mental health or well-being, or life goals or aspirations.

Attitudes toward Land Use and Human Settlement

There is an apparent discrepancy between the attitudes of Americans toward the places where they now live and their concept of the ideal place in which they would like to live, if they had a choice. Today, more than 70% of Americans are urban residents, and only 10% express dissatisfaction with their present neighborhoods; yet 38%, asked if they could live anywhere they wanted to, said they would choose a rural area (Watts and Free, 1973).

Attitudes toward Density and Crowding

Census tract studies of density and crowding (Mintz and Schwartz, 1964; Shaw and McKay, 1969; Short, 1969; Wechsler and Pugh, 1967; Weinberg, 1968) generally provide support for what has been called the "social fit" or "social homogeneity" hypothesis: persons with a certain social characteristic, living in an area where the characteristic is less common, will have higher rates of juvenile delinquency or hospitalization for mental illness than people with that social characteristic who live in areas where it is more common. The characteristics investigated most often have been race and ethnic origin, but support is also found for age, occupation, and place of birth.

The basic problem with the census tract approach is that when one contrasts census tracts which differ on a housing variable (e.g., crowding or general housing quality), one is simultaneously also contrasting on all the other variables which are part and parcel of poverty: race, age, education, work status, family structure, nutrition, medical care, and so on. There is no way to pinpoint the role of the residential environment, and observed differences in rates of mental or physical illness and disability are not interpretable.

Attitudes toward Properties of the Man-made Environment: The Neighborhood

In general, it would appear that the nature of the dwelling itself is a more important source of satisfactions and dissatisfactions than is the neighborhood location (Foote et al., 1960), although the situation appears reversed for elderly residents (Carp, 1969; Hamovitch and Petersen, 1969), and does not hold in all studies (Michelson, 1966). Moreover, social characteristics of neighbors appear to be a chief determinant of satisfaction with neighborhood (Foote et al., 1960); evaluating neighbors as "friendly" is an especially good predictor of neighborhood satisfaction, much more so than actual frequency of interaction with those neighbors (Lansing and Hendricks, 1967; Lansing and Marans, 1969; Zehner, 1971).

The traditional description of urban slum areas has been in terms of poor housing, high rates of crime–delinquency–disease, and a high proportion of broken families and of individuals living alone. However, later studies of slum communities (Fried and Gleicher, 1961; Gans, 1962; Hollingshead and Rogler, 1963; Marris, 1963; Ryan, 1963; Whyte, 1943) began to correct this old picture: (a) slums were shown to be well organized, with a good internal social structure; (b) the typical slum dwellers were not newcomers or transients and residential mobility was low; (c) slum dwellers liked their neighborhood much better than dwellers in public housing; (d) they had a strong sense of spatial identity, which is based on extensive networks of interpersonal contacts and overlapping role relationships.

The importance of the social networks in slum communities is especially apparent when one examines low-income public housing as a contrast (Hollingshead and Rogler, 1963; Kriesberg, 1968; Levin and Taube, 1970; Rainwater, 1970; Yancey, 1971). Public housing, it appears, is a definite barrier to social interaction, especially when there is an absence of semipublic spaces and facilities which can normally promote informal social networks.

Attitudes toward Noise

Somewhere between 25 and 40% of adult residents of large cities are annoyed by noise or consider noise of high environmental concern (Cameron et al., 1972; Koezkur et al., 1963; Kryter, 1970). Traffic noise is the most frequently cited source of annoyance (Goldsmith and Jonsson, 1973; Koezkur et al., 1963; Kryter, 1970), with construction equipment a distant second. The public is bothered by noise at home and while commuting to work, but seldom at work. There is some evidence that long-term residents near an airport have loss of hearing at high frequencies; however, the most solid evidence on hearing loss comes from studies of specific industrial and military settings. Second, there is evidence from one British study (Abey-Wickrama *et al.*, 1969) of a greater number of admissions to a mental hospital from the residential area near Heathrow airport with the greatest amount of noise, than from other surrounding areas. The excess in admissions was specific to one category of people: women over 45 who were widowed, divorced, or unmarried. While it is not clear to what extent the slightly lower average social class of the residents closer to the airport could explain this finding (and the specific effect on one subgroup), the results certainly call for replication for many different cities.

Most studies of residents near airports deal with complaints and their determinants. Knowing neighbors who moved out because of noise, and being of higher social class also raises complaint level. There seems to be no long-term adaptation to aircraft noise: the longer a person lived in a given neighborhood, the more he was bothered by the noise (Borsky, 1961).

Perceptions of Land Use and Human Settlements

Perceptions of Density and Crowding

Studies of crowding (Keller, 1953; Michelson, 1968; E. D. Mitchell, 1971; Tulkin, 1968) do not reveal striking effects of crowding on mental health. However, they do suggest that *forced interaction* (with members of another household sharing the same unit) and the *inability to escape* (living on upper floors, low income) are more significant variables than the sheer limitation on space.

The literature on high-rise living (Cappon, 1971; Havranek, 1969; Power, 1970; Reynolds and Nicholson, 1970; Wekerle and Hall, 1972) represents another approach to the study of residential density. In general, families with small children are the most unhappy tenants, if they live on the upper floors. There is some evidence (Havranek, 1969) that children of preschool age living on upper floors of high-rise buildings stay in open fresh air for considerably shorter periods of time and are delayed in motor development.

Perceptions of Neighborhoods

In relatively new, homogeneous communities of middle-class and upper-middle class residents, the perception of the neighborhood as "well kept up" is a major determinant of neighborhood satisfaction (Lansing and Marans, 1969; Lansing *et al.*, 1970; Zehner, 1971). Other, lesser determinants of neighborhood satisfaction are privacy in one's yard, low neighborhood noise level, and adequate space for family activities. Satisfaction with the community itself seems to depend in large part upon proximity to work, shopping areas, and other facilities (Lansing et al., 1970; Zehner, 1971). Comparing planned and unplanned suburban communities, one finds that the extent of planning is more often a reason for moving to a community rather than for level of satisfaction, once the move is made (Lansing et al., 1970).

The two variables that most strongly influence residential perceptions and satisfactions are social class and stage of life (Cutler, 1947; Keller, 1966; Michelson, 1966, 1970). These two variables are reflected in the results of the above-cited studies: the respondents were predominantly middle- and upper-middle class, young-to-middle-aged residents for whom basic residential needs were well satisfied. Different results may be expected with different subgroups.

Data on the elderly suggest that, because of limited mobility, proximity to services such as shopping facilities, transportation, and medical services is a major determinant of residential satisfaction (Donahue and Ashley, 1965; Hamovitch and Peterson, 1969; Lawton, 1969; Niebanck and Pope, 1965).

Studies of slum residents (e.g., Kasl and Harburg, 1972; Rainwater, 1966) reveal the strong concern with crime, violence, and dangers such as rats, poison, fire, trash, and unprotected heights. Wolfe et al. (1968) found that perception of human dangers in the neighborhood was strongly related to the level of the respondent's integration into informal networks: persons who were not integrated were more likely to express concern over allowing children out of the house, felt more vulnerable to strangers entering the neighborhood, and felt unsafe on the street at night.

Perceptions of Noise

The study of 22 United States communities near military airfields (Borsky, 1961) reveals the role of mediating psychological variables in the perception of noise. Individuals who (a) considered the airbase to be important, (b) saw airbase officials and pilots as considerate, and (c) had little fear about crashes could tolerate, without complaint, about four times as much noise exposure per day as respondents whose attitudes toward these items were all negative.

Studies of noise effects under laboratory conditions have shown that an unpredictable noise, even if soft, has a bigger effect on task persistence and efficiency than a loud but predictable noise. Most interestingly, perceived ability to control noise wiped out the adverse effects of unpredictable high intensity noise (Reim et al., 1971), even though none of the subjects ever actually used the switch designated as control switch for shutting off the noise.

In an excellent review of the noise literature, Kryter (1970) concluded that long-term harmful effects (whether nonauditory physiological or psychological) of noise per se have not yet been demonstrated. Indeed, the possibly harmful effects which have been found appear to be due "to psychological factors related to stimulus and response contingencies as associated with the noise by individuals." In other words, it is the meaning of the noise to the individual that appears to produce the major effects. For example, noise on the job may mean threat of bodily harm from machinery, and it is this interpretation of the noise, rather than the noise per se, which may have long-term effects. [The results of the recent Glass *et al.* (1973) study do not fit this conclusion.]

Goldsmith and Jonsson (1973) feel that the long-term effects of noise may be underestimated because of the lack of definitive studies. They suggest four areas of possible effects yet to be documented: (a) symptoms of aggravation or disease—headache, muscle tension, anxiety, insomnia, fatigue, and drug consumption; (b) impairment of functions—impaired hearing, altered threshold; (c) interference with activities—communication, rest, relaxation; and (d) feelings—fear, resentment, distraction, and need to concentrate.

Perhaps the relationship between noise and sleep is a good illustration of the dangers of underestimating the adverse effects of noise. Most residents around airports do not report problems with sleeping, not because noise does not affect their sleep, but because the volume of air traffic drops off markedly during the night hours. But if we zero in on specific vulnerable populations living in vulnerable settings, such as shift workers in poor housing (Thiis-Evensen, 1958), then the link between noise and insomnia is clearly seen.

Finally, we must not underestimate—in the absence of evidence—the possible effects of noise on some aspects of well-being via curtailment of valued activities. For example, interference with conversation and with listening (radio, TV, phonograph) may ultimately lead to a reduction of social contacts and socializing. Less mobile groups, such as the elderly, are not only less able to cope with such adverse effects of noise, but also their life satisfaction may be more strongly affected because of the close association between social interaction and well-being (e.g., Burgess, 1954; Clark and Anderson, 1967; Maddox, 1963; Palmore, 1968; Tobin and Neugarten, 1961).

Limitations to Understanding Perceptions of the Urban Environment

The limitations of the various measures of housing preferences and satisfactions (and, by extension, of environmental perceptions in general) are suggested by Riemer. They can be stated as follows: (a) housing attitudes are related to the housing conditions with which the respondent is familiar and/or to the conditions to which he aspires; (b) preferences are not absolute and permanent; (c) as some needs are satisfied, other needs become paramount; (d) housing attitudes are not based on full information; (e) housing attitudes and satisfactions are more volatile after rehousing.

10.3   Land Use/Natural Resource Management

Adequate access to natural resources, and to the goods and services that these can provide, seems to be an ultimate key to the attainment of a high level of human health. This message can be read in because, except for age, income is the single variable most closely associated with good health, not only in the United States, but also throughout the world. In our country, as in other countries, mortality, morbidity, impairments, and relative failures of growth and development are not just higher, but often much higher, among the lowest income groups than among the highest groups (Metropolitan Life Insurance Co., 1972; NCHS, 1964, 1972b). Throughout the world, the level of health of whole populations rises in parallel with per capita income (Brown, 1971; Candau, 1971; United Nations, 1966a, b; WHO, 1971b) (see Fig. 10-1).

It may be argued that the vast expenditure of energy and resources in modern industrial societies is far above that needed to maintain a high level of human health, and that this is demonstrated by the Chinese experience. Indeed, not only in this country but also in China, very little of the total amounts of energy and resources utilized are expended directly upon the health of the individual. However, the apparent Chinese success in combat-

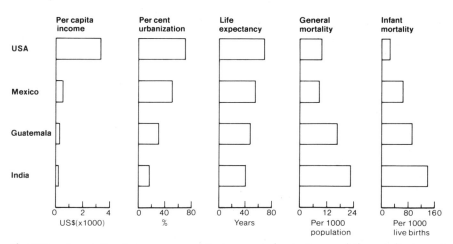

Fig. 10-1. Association between per capita income, urbanization, and three indicators of health. (From WHO, 1971b.)

ing schistosomiasis, malaria, and trachoma is based upon a technology implying that, somewhere in the world, there are scientific laboratories utilizing sophisticated instruments, as well as complicated industrial installations which, in turn, use large amounts of energy and resources, and which are capable of synthesizing complex chemical substances in ton amounts. The Chinese success in improving the nutrition of their population is in part based upon the importation of many shiploads of wheat, which are grown in Canada on heavily mechanized farms enriched by artificial fertilizers. These fertilizers are manufactured by large petrochemical complexes out of oil from distant places such as Nigeria and Venezuela. In the last analysis, improving the health of the Chinese, like improving the health of Americans or Indians, involves an increased per capita access to goods and services, and implies, to a large extent, the existence of a modern, energy- and resource-demanding technology.

Conservation of resources is one of the keys to intelligent management. However, those who benefit by the conservation of resources may not be the same as those who pay the cost of this conservation in terms of restricted access to resources. This may be especially true if the conservation is carried out primarily for the maintenance of beauty, or for the protection of natural systems that are not in themselves ultimately relevant to human health. This consideration applies, for example, to the preservation of some wilderness areas, scenic views, and wildlife habitats. It even applies to some extent to the preservation of wetland and estuarine areas, despite the fact that these have a more or less clear relevance to fisheries and therefore to human food supply.

Modern agriculture is heavily dependent on the use of artificial fertilizers, soil conditioners, pesticides, herbicides, and fungicides, and also on the use of machines. The net effect of these uses has been highly beneficial to human health because it has vastly increased the yield of agriculture and has thus improved the supplies of food and clothing that are available for the population of the world. This effect is not so immediately apparent to most Americans because its impact on our own population has occurred over a period of generations in the past, while its present effect in preventing malnutrition and starvation occurs among the people of Asia, Africa, and Central America who receive our excess food. The occasional adverse effects of modern agricultural technology are more apparent to us, and they have been a matter of more concern recently, even though they produce more damage to natural systems than they do to people. (USDHEW, 1969a; WHO, 1969, 1971a, 1972a).

Artificial nitrogen fertilizers tend to build up the level of nitrogen in groundwater and runoff. The adverse effects of this on plant life and streams are apparent. In theory, there may also be adverse effects upon humans.

Infants who ingest nitrates may develop methemoglobinemia. Investigations of such cases generally reveal the use of well water to make up artificial feedings for nursing infants (Knotek and Schmidt, 1964; Lee, 1970; Walton, 1951; Wolff and Wassermann, 1972). But the nitrogen in the well water appears to have originated primarily from decaying natural products and not from artificial fertilizers. The net health effects of the making up of infant formula from well water have been very small up to now. However, there are parts of the Hudson Basin region where contamination of well water with nitrates must be considered.

Many pesticides used in agriculture are toxic to humans. This is not very true of DDT, which has been the most widely used. In fact, illnesses and deaths have occurred when attempts were made to replace DDT, which is highly damaging to plant and animal life, with other pesticides that are less damaging to the environment but more damaging to people (Davis et al., 1969; Reich et al., 1968; USDHEW, 1969a). Similar considerations apply to herbicides and fungicides.

Forestry is more of a threat to the environment than it is to people. The manufacture of paper from forest products is associated with a considerable stench, and may be accompanied by heavy pollution of water. However, the hazard in paper manufacturing is more to human aesthetic sensibilities than to human health (Hall, 1974).

Mining in all forms is accompanied by major hazards to those who participate in it. These hazards arise particularly from accidents and from the inhalation of toxic dusts. The pathogenic effects of inhaling dust act in combination with the effects of other respiratory irritants and infectious agents such as tobacco smoke, tubercle bacilli, and radioactive minerals. Open pit mining and strip mining offer fewer hazards for the participants, but create greater hazards for the environment at large.

Indicators Relevant to Human Health

In the area of natural resource management, the indicators most relevant to human health are measures of access to natural resources, i.e., measures of income expenditures and of consumption. Other indicators are measurements of specific natural resource management activities and their effluents.

Residents of the Hudson Basin region are fortunate that there is relatively little mining in this area. However, large amounts of minerals are imported into the region for processing and manufacturing. If improperly controlled, these activities can produce air and water pollution capable of affecting health.

For many decades, public health authorities have used specific indicators, such as the concentrations of certain known toxic substances in air, water, or food, to gauge the adequacy of control measures or the need for additional controls. Many of the present indicators were established on the basis of rather flimsy scientific evidence. As epidemiological techniques improve and as knowledge of the toxicological properties of the trace substances is increased, these indicators, published in the form of maximum permissible concentrations for the individual substances, will carry a higher degree of credibility than they do now. The criteria used to regulate trace substances in air, water, and food have value for public health protection, even though the administration of these standards does not always reflect the limited information on which they are based, or the conservative approach taken in establishing them.

The hazards of certain pesticides, fungicides, herbicides, and rodenticides used in agriculture have already been noted. With the development of tree farms and scientific forestry, some of these pesticides and herbicides have been used by foresters. In addition, substances such as cacodylic acid (dimethyl arsenic acid) have been used, exposing certain forest workers to arsenic (Wagner and Weswig, 1974). Other substances such as sulfites and sulfones have been used in paper-making (Hall, 1974).

Mining, quarrying, crushing, and smelting are notoriously associated with exposure to dusts and fumes that are health hazards. Among the dusts of greatest interest in the Hudson Basin region is asbestos, used widely in the building industry (roofing, sheets, wallboard, and pipes) and in other manufacturing processes. There is also the possibility of the exposure of the general public to very low concentrations of asbestos in ambient air, drinking water, and possibly beverages that have been filtered through asbestos filters. However, exposure of members of the general community to asbestos in ambient air at such very low concentrations, or in drinking water in beverages has never been shown to be a health hazard, either in animals or in man.

Indicators of Health Effects of Aspects of Natural Resource Management

Deaths, illnesses, and injuries occurring as unintended side effects of exploitation of natural resources in the Hudson Basin region appear to have a minimal effect upon human health when compared to the major effects associated with inadequate income.

Detectable amounts of nitrites have been found in the drinking water of some communities, and some pediatricians have warned mothers against using this water to prepare infants' formulas, but so far as we know, no cases of illness have occurred from this source.

Poisoning by pesticides, herbicides, and fungicides is relatively uncommon in the Hudson Basin region. Nearly all of the substantiated cases occurred among people who were engaged in using these substances and were exposed to high concentrations of them. There were also a few cases among people, especially children, who accidentally ingested these substances.

So far as is known, there have been no reported adverse health effects of forestry in the Hudson Basin region.

Adverse effects of mining, quarrying, crushing, and smelting have been reported. The significant occupational exposures to dust particles and fumes in this region have been associated with the mining and quarrying of limestone, zinc, talc, and silicates.

Attitudes toward Natural Resource Management

In the field of public health, as well as in the environmental sciences, there has been a remarkable dichotomy of attitudes toward the health effects of the use of natural resources. It is widely recognized by those in public health that poverty and inadequate income are strongly associated with disease and death.

Efforts to improve the health of underdeveloped nations by education, physicians, and building hospitals have been generally ineffective. Efforts to introduce sanitation, inoculation, and the suppression of diseases such as malaria through public health measures have been only partly successful.

Success, by and large, has been dependent upon increasing the per capita income and the level of education of the population. This, in effect, has meant increasing the level of essential goods and services available to the members of the population, which in turn is based upon the exploitation of resources.

Despite this observation, people in the field of public health, when asked to consider how the exploitation of natural resources affects health, nearly always consider only the unintentional adverse side effects that result from the processes of resource management. Environmental scientists often have the same view—possibly because human biologists have not acquainted them with the facts on the other side of the equation. Regardless of the explanation, the failure to recognize that the exploitation of resources is important to the maintenance of human health has had a very significant influence upon many decisions with regard to environmental policy.

Very often, when it has been proposed that the use of some substances such as artificial nitrogen fertilizers or DDT be discontinued because of the damaging effect upon the environment, or when it is suggested that some process of mineral extraction be discontinued for the same reason, it is assumed that any health effects of this discontinuance will be entirely beneficial. The removal of the potential toxicity is thus seen as a benefit to human health not outweighed by any costs. The magnitude of the harm that may be done to human health by decreasing the available supply of food or other important goods or services is often overlooked, and no attempt is made to compute it, nor is any account taken of the additional fact that this cost falls most heavily upon those people and nations whose access to resources is already most limited.

The concern for conservation and preservation often arises primarily from those whose homes or investments in land would be adversely affected by the exploitation of nearby resources. Without entirely articulating the basis upon which their attitudes are formed, members of communities do seem to understand that the appearance of a community and the activities that go on within it reflect upon the social status of people who live there—a reflection long embodied in popular characterizations of people as coming from "across the tracks" or living "down by the gas works."

Perceptions of Natural Resource Management

Even before the present concern about the environment developed, there was a widespread view that strip mines, gravel pits, smelters, and the like were ugly and undesirable in proximity to residential communities. Recent publicity has caused many people to view these as "unhealthy" also. Publicity has also raised pesticides, herbicides, and smelter fumes to the levels of major health hazards in the eyes of many people, increasing the negative attitudes toward manufacturing processes that produce them.

Often the context in which people confront environmental issues is a general political one. For example, people may have to confront an environmental issue in the context of how much tax money they are willing to see spent on efforts to clean up the environment, or what kinds of personal sacrifices in terms of money or convenience they are willing to make to accomplish the cleanup. Answers to such questions are particularly important in order to tap the actual salience of environmental issues in the mind of the average citizen. Damaging the environment is like sin. Everyone is against it in the abstract; but in any concrete instance, there may be some doubt about whether people's attitudes will remain the same.

In general, it must be noted that the methods used to assess environmental perceptions tend to be biased themselves in exaggerating the inaccuracy of such perceptions. To illustrate: if the objective measure of an environmental hazard, such as brush fires, is based on the numbers of such fires for different residential areas and for a certain period of time, then the most appropriate measure of perceived hazard is to ask the respondent how many brush fires there were in his area for that period. Any other measure of percentage (How concerned are you about brush fires? or How worried are you that your home will be caught in a brush fire?) tends to bring in the perception of the objective reality *plus* something else which may be an evaluation of or a reaction to his perception (e.g., the respondent is not worried because his house is overinsured and he does not like it anyway), but is not properly a part of the environmental perception. And to the extent that most studies use these perceptions-plus-evaluations types of measurements, they tend to exaggerate the inaccuracy of environmental perceptions.

10.4   Water Resources

Under ordinary circumstances, a man must ingest about 2 liters of water a day to sustain his health. He gets much of this water from his food, from beverages, and usually rather little in the form of drinking water as such, except during very hot periods or when he is quite active. Water is necessary also for cooking, washing, and bathing. The good health of residents of modern societies is not simply based upon their having pure drinking water and sanitary food. It is also related to the fact that they wash their cooking and eating utensils, bathe themselves regularly, and wash their clothing. Before such bathing and washing became common in our society, bacterial and fungal infections of the skin were much more frequent; infestations with body lice, head lice, crab lice, scabies, and human fleas were common; and the population was subject to epidemics of diseases such as typhus and plague, which may be transmitted by these parasites.

Ingested water causes diseases when it contains microbial agents or harmful chemicals. The waterborne microbial and viral agents that cause disease nearly all arise from contamination of water with human feces, and the diseases they most commonly cause have predominantly gastrointestinal manifestations. Nonspecific indicators of potential fecal contamination of drinking water have served well to protect from disease arising by this route. There are also microbial agents that can infect humans by direct invasion through the skin and that might, therefore, gain entry through washing, bathing, or swimming. Fortunately, these agents are not present in the Hudson Basin region.

People can wash or bathe with impunity in water that is contaminated with human fecal material to a degree that would make it entirely unsafe for drinking; but just how much fecal contamination is permissible for bathing water and recreational water has not yet been agreed upon. The contamination of water with industrial wastes is another matter altogether. In general, drinking water supplies have been protected from this hazard largely by the great dilution that occurs. There remains a nagging issue of whether or not substances such as chloramines, which might be generated in drinking water that has been treated with chlorine, may cause significant mutation in genetic material even though they are present in very small amounts. At the present time, this is a potential rather than an acute health hazard.

Indicators of Water Resources Relevant to Human Health

Water quality is generally described in terms of standard permissible concentrations of trace substances, suspended solids, dissolved oxygen, or turbidity. Under the 1972 amendments to the Clean Water Act (Anonymous, 1973; U.S. Health Services and Mental Health Association, 1973), the Administrator of the EPA is required to identify toxic substances being discharged into streams and to establish effluent limitations for these substances. As in the case of air, this is a somewhat different approach from setting standards of ambient quality.

The significance of a discharge of x pounds per day of a given substance depends on the physical and biological properties of the receiving body of water. The volume of water, the flow rate, the nature of the sediments, the salinity, and the use to which the body of water is put all influence the significance of a given discharge. In the Hudson River, when the element manganese is introduced to the freshwater reaches in ionic form, it promptly precipitates to the sediments which, because of the high clay content, have a substantial capacity to bind this element. However, in the saltwater reaches of the estuary, manganese may be released from the sediments and tends to remain in suspended or colloidal form, where it is more available to biota. The fact that the manganese is bound to the sediments does not of itself mean that the element is out of harm's way; this example simply illustrates one simple difference that should influence effluent limitations for manganese, depending on whether the receiving body of water is saline or not.

Drinking Water

The classical method for monitoring drinking water for infectious agents and trace contaminants appears to be adequate. Unfortunately, such measurements are made routinely in vast numbers, and no effort is made to aggregate the data for a given water source to characterize its relative quality. It is important that a system be developed to combine the various biological and chemical measures into a single indicator of quality. In the absence of any such system of aggregation, the present numerical standards and protocols for drinking water analysis appear adequate to protect public health (USDHEW, 1969b).

The freshwater reaches of the Hudson River will become increasingly important as a source of water supply toward the end of the century. It is estimated that 20 million people may obtain their potable water from the Hudson River. Thus, apart from aesthetic and recreational considerations, it is important that the quality of the river water be maintained. It is conceivable that neglect of the river could result in its becoming contaminated with toxic chemicals to such an extent that it would be impractical to purify by artificial means. Similarly, should the load of organic materials increase to the point where eutrophication occurs, it might not be possible to purify the billion or more gallons per day that will be required of the river. The blue–green algae that currently appear during the summer months in parts of the freshwater reaches suggest that early eutrophicational changes may in fact be taking place at the present time. However, the pure waters program should reverse this trend during the next few years.

Swimming and Bathing

The estuarine portions of the Hudson Basin are endowed with many miles of sandy beaches, some of them among the most beautiful in the United States, and many of them within walking distance of places where New Yorkers live and work. Some of these beaches are closed because they do not meet the present bathing water standards. The indicators that determine the fitness of water for bathing are promulgated at various levels of government, but there has been little effort to determine whether these indicators, which have been in use for many years, are still valid in light of present scientific knowledge.

The Committee on Bathing Beach Contamination of the Public Health Laboratory Service in Great Britain (PHLS, 1959) came to the following general conclusions:

> (i) That bathing in sewage-polluted sea water carries only a negligible risk to health, even on beaches that are aesthetically very unsatisfactory. (ii) That the minimal risk attending such bathing is probably associated with chance contact with intact aggregates of fecal material that happen to have come from infected persons . . . (iii) That the isolation of pathogenic organisms from sewage-contaminated sea water is more important as evidence of an existing hazard in the populations from which the sewage is derived than as evidence of a further risk of infection in bathers, and . . . (iv) That, since a serious risk of contracting disease through bathing in sewage-polluted sea water is probably not incurred unless the water is so fouled as to be aesthetically revolting, public health requirements would seem to be reasonably met by a general policy of improving grossly unsanitary bathing waters and of preventing so far as possible the pollution of bathing beaches with undisintegrated fecal matter during the bathing season.

A committee of the American Society of Civil Engineers has also found "little, if any, conclusive proof that disease hazards are directly associated with large numbers of coliform organisms" (ASCE, 1963).

The waters of the estuary are increasingly free of visible sewage. On the other hand, the coliform counts in the lower estuary have for some years actually been increasing, and it is not certain that this tendency will be reversed (Eisenbud, 1973b). The reason for this is not known, but it has been proposed that coliform clumps may be broken up by phosphates in the water. Thus, the increase in coliform counts reported during the past decade may be an artifact resulting from the observation that what once appeared as a single colony on an agar plate now shows as many colonies because of the deagglomeration process. The inhabitants of the lower estuary thus face the dilemma that the beaches may not be available to them for recreational bathing, even though the community has spent billions of dollars to treat its sewage. It is quite possible that, in an effort to eliminate a potential health hazard that has not been demonstrated, a greater risk is imposed upon a community: the risk associated with depriving the population of the use of beaches during the hot summer days and nights. There is an acute need to reexamine the indicators of water quality that are the basis for denying the public access to bathing beaches in places such as the upper East River, western Long Island Sound, the shores of the Hudson, and some of the beaches of Brooklyn and Staten Island, which have been closed to bathers for years.

Groundwater

In many parts of the Hudson Basin region, water supplies are from private wells located on property on which there is also a septic system. In general, present sanitary procedures are such as to ensure that the sewage from the septic tank will not get into the well under most but not all circumstances. Also, with the increasing use of detergents for dishwashing and for washing clothes, these substances have tended to get out of septic systems and into the groundwater and streams. In general, they have not created a significant hazard to human health, nor has there appeared to be a significant hazard from the nitrogen fertilizers, nor from the heavy metals or pesticides in groundwater. A possible exception is in Nassau and Suffolk counties where the public water supply comes from groundwater.

Health Effects of Aspects of Water Resources

Gastrointestinal diseases are the second most common form of acute illness that occur in the American population; respiratory diseases are the most common. The average adult who has two or three colds a year has at least one episode of acute gastroenteritis. Most often, this is associated with a respiratory infection and is caused by one of the viruses that also cause respiratory illnesses. Other common causes of gastroenteritis are the contamination of food by bacteria or viruses from food handlers, the ingestion of toxic substances such as alcohol, and the functional disturbances of the gastrointestinal tract that are often called "nervous diarrhea."

Outbreaks of gastrointestinal disease traceable to the contamination of public water supplies are quite rare in the Hudson Basin region.

The rule that such diseases are more common in rural than in urban areas also seems to hold in the Hudson Basin region. This is related to the fact that water supplies and sewage systems in rural areas are often private and sometimes dependent upon privies or septic tanks and wells on the same property, an arrangement notoriously subject to cross-contamination. By far the greatest amount of gastrointestinal disease caused by fecal contamination is the result of the direct contamination of food or drink and not the result of contamination of public or even private water supply. An exception is the contamination of shellfish with hepatitis virus. In 1972, there were 83 cases of infectious hepatitis traceable to the eating of raw shellfish taken from fecally contaminated water; in 1973, there were 45 cases reported (NYC Department of Health, 1974).

The relatively few cases of infectious hepatitis from eating shellfish are probably the only readily identifiable cases of human disease that one might eliminate by treatment of the sewage flowing into the waters around New York City, even if this sewage were rendered sterile. People do not drink the water in the harbor and the bay, and available data suggest that the British attitude toward the relative harmlessness of bathing in such fecally contaminated waters is correct.

Attitudes toward Water Resources

Even if people were entirely assured that bathing in sewage is safe, a great many would not wish to bathe in water that has sewage in it; and even if people never intended to bathe outside of their own bathrooms, a great many of them would object to dumping sewage or industrial waste into streams and rivers.

Dislike of water pollution, like some other important environmental attitudes, is stronger among the well-to-do and the well-educated than among the poor. The published literature on attitudes toward problems such as water pollution is very limited. A survey of Toronto residents (Koezkur et al., 1963) revealed that 55% considered water pollution to be a high environmental concern to them; this was a lower concern than air pollution but higher than noise. In a study of environmental perceptions in the Hudson River region (Capenar et al., 1973) water pollution was the most frequently mentioned issue.

Attitudes toward direct reuse of reclaimed sewage (Johnson, 1971) were shown to vary with perceived need for water, beliefs about pollution, trust in technology, and educational level. Past experience with water shortages was only minimally related. That there may be strong latent attitudes toward chemical alterations of the water supply is suggested by the fluoridation controversy of the past (Gamson, 1961; Kirscht and Knutson, 1961; Knutson, 1960; Simmel, 1961). Opponents of fluoridation were found to have lower income and lower occupational status, as well as lesser upward mobility, in the previous 10 years. Moreover, opponents were found to have stronger feelings of helplessness and a lower sense of political efficacy. Finally, while opponents of fluoridation were not substantially more opposed to science as such, they were nevertheless quite concerned with the diffuse, unanticipated, but vaguely threatening consequences of scientific and technological advances. Various professional groups tend to see water pollution in different terms (Sewell, 1971). Engineers perceive it as an economic problem, which can be solved by applying appropriate technology, while public health officials see it mainly as a health problem to be corrected by regulations to maintain standards of specific chemical and biological quality. Each group is skeptical about the involvement of the general public, or of any other professional group, in decision-making. A study of viewpoints of lay public and professional water managers in Waterloo County, Ontario (B. Mitchell, 1971), found that the public is more likely to see water problems in terms of water pollution, while the managers are much more likely to define water problems in terms of water supply. Interestingly, agreement with the statement, The average person does not know enough to make useful suggestions, was found more among the lay public than among the professionals.

Perceptions of Water Resources

As indicated above, there is often a wide discrepancy between the presence of an environmental hazard and an individual's perception of whether or not a hazard is present. This undoubtedly applies to the question of health hazards related to water pollution. We have no data on the proportion of the population who believe that water pollution constitutes a major hazard to public health, but there is good reason to believe that the perception far outstrips reality. Undoubtedly, this perception is reinforced by the tendency of the press and of regulatory authorities to speak of water pollution problems primarily in terms of health. In an article in *The New York Times* on pollution of the beaches (Bird, 1974), one government investigator (who has been strongly rebutted by federal officials) is quoted as speaking of the sewage sludge dumped offshore as if it constituted a significant potential health hazard, and another is quoted as being concerned about viral contamination of bathing waters, implying that a significant hazard of diseases such as infectious hepatitis exists for the bathers at the New York beaches. If there is a potential health hazard from either of these, it is very small. There is, of course, a large aesthetic hazard from sludge on bathing beaches, but this is another matter.

10.5   Energy Systems

The human use of extrametabolic energy is as old as mankind. *Homo erectus* used fire to protect himself from predators, to drive the game that provided his food, to sharpen the spear with which he killed it, to cook some of the meat it provided, and to warm the cave or windbreak in which he sought shelter. All of this helped to reduce his mortality, to improve his nutrition, and to prevent some injury and disease. When later men developed agriculture and began to live in villages and cities, they accomplished this with the help of labor from domesticated animals, and later with energy from wind and falling water.

During the present century, the application of power-driven machinery to farming has greatly enhanced the productivity of agriculture, and has greatly improved the supply of food for all people; and the application of energy to transportation has made it possible to carry this food to distant places where it is needed, a process that has helped not just those in other countries that are "underdeveloped," but people in our own society also. Within the memory of many people now living in the Hudson Basin, the growth and development of children have been greatly enhanced by the development of rapid, cheap, and sanitary means of transporting milk, meat, and citrus fruits from distant places.

The primary sources of extrametabolic energy for human use in our region today are oil, coal, and nuclear fission. Draft animals have all but disappeared even from farms, and wood fires are used more for aesthetic reasons than for any other. Coal and nuclear fission are used primarily to generate electricity. The energy package that is delivered to the final consumer in the Hudson Basin region comes in the form of oil, gasoline, or electricity. All three of these have had an important impact on health and an important social impact as well.

In 1968, Americans expended approximately 210,000 kcal of energy per day per person. If we allow 3000 kcal per day as a reasonable estimate of the amount of energy that an active adult man obtains from his own metabolism, then we can estimate that in 1968 each American enjoyed the energy equivalent of 70 men from extrametabolic energy. Many people living today have a vivid recollection of the impact of new sources of energy upon their pattern of life and their health.

The benefit of electricity to health has not only been for men and only on farms and in the factory. When the electric motor moved into the house, it provided the first really effective method of home refrigeration. It made possible the storage of many fresh foods with a beneficial effect on diet, both by improving the variety of food and preventing the spoilage of food. Electricity also provided improved facilities for washing dishes and clothing, and provided undoubted though unmeasured benefits to health by this means also. Yet its biggest impact was on the lives and the health of women. For the average woman in the nineteenth century, the care of a household was a never-ending round of menial drudgery—of sweeping floors, making beds, hauling wood or coal, building fires, preparing food, cooking food, boiling water, washing dishes, washing diapers, scrubbing clothes, and—between all of this and the care of children—finding the time to shop daily for small amounts of perishable food which she could not store. It was accepted that the beauty of a woman faded within a few years of her marriage and that husbands often outlived not one wife but several. If a family was fortunate enough to have servants, this meant only that the burden of labor for the household was transferred to some other woman who had to bear this as well as that of her own household.

One could make a good case that the emancipation of the American woman came not so much from giving her an education and the right to vote as from the introduction of the electric vacuum cleaner, the dishwasher, the clothes washer, the clothes dryer, the refrigerator, the freezer, the water heater, the automatic oven, and a variety of other electric appliances. In many ways, it was these mechanisms which freed the female half of the American population from millennia of drudgery, and allowed women fortunate enough to have these mechanisms to turn their minds and talents to more rewarding activities.

This relief from drudgery has been extended to most women in our society, but not to all. Many households in the region still lack adequate facilities for refrigeration or for washing clothes, not to mention the many other accurately named "labor-saving devices." The provision of adequate supplies of electricity for these households would undoubtedly provide health benefits for many people in this segment of society.

A large and generally unrecognized health benefit from electricity can be provided by the much-maligned air conditioner. On a cost-effectiveness basis, the best way to reduce the excess mortality associated with high levels of air pollution and with heat waves would be to air-condition the dwelling places of the very old and of those who are chronically and seriously ill—especially those with cardiovascular and respiratory diseases—and to air-condition very hot, humid, and poorly ventilated working places. Nearly all of the excess deaths that occur during severe episodes of air pollution occur among the old and chronically ill (Carnow and Meier, 1973). In the New York region, these are relatively few compared to the excess deaths associated with heat waves. Excess deaths during heat waves can amount to several thousand per annum in the large cities of the United States in the summertime (see Section 10.6). A major heat wave can lead to a thousand excess deaths in New York City alone. Most of these deaths also occur among the very old and the ill, but some are the deaths of otherwise robust younger people who work in hot and poorly ventilated places such as laundries.

The air-conditioning of dwelling places and hot working places would undoubtedly prevent many of these excess deaths. In New York City, if this required 2000 MW of electric power, and if it were supplied by a coal-burning power plant that increased the level of SO_2 in the city back to the level of the late 1960s, the net gain in excess deaths prevented would be overwhelmingly in favor of the air-conditioning, since the reduction of SO_2 levels in the last several years appears to have had little or no effect on general mortality (see Section 10.6). The widespread air-conditioning of dwellings has been seriously advocated as a health measure in some communities that are very hot in the summertime. Questions can be raised about the wisdom of spending large amounts of money and resources to delay the deaths of terminally ill people by any means. Nevertheless, it is important to point out that a society which is used to heating dwellings to prevent deaths and illnesses caused by cold has not yet accepted the idea of cooling dwellings to prevent deaths from heat.

One of the major catastrophic threats to health in the Hudson Basin region is the possibility of a collapse of the electric power supply at a crucial time. A total power blackout, a few of which have occurred in recent years, might cause a disaster if it took place during the rush hour of a very hot afternoon, and if it lasted for several hours. A disaster could also occur if such a total power breakdown took place during very cold winter weather and lasted for 72 hours or more. A very large number of the suburban and rural households in the Hudson Basin region are entirely dependent upon electricity. Their water is pumped from a well by electric motors. Their heat is provided by an oil-fired furnace, and powered by an electric motor, and their light and cooking are entirely dependent upon electricity. Within 48 hours after power breakdowns occurred on Long Island and Connecticut in December 1973, the temperature within many of the affected houses had fallen below the freezing point. There was no water, no facilities for cooking, and no sanitary facilities. Fortunately, the breakdown was spotty, and those seriously affected could move to warm buildings in the same community. If the breakdown had been general, however, and there had been no warm places of refuge, there would undoubtedly have been a significant upsurge of mortality within the next few days.

The immediate health effects associated with the generation of electricity are quite small so far as the general public is concerned. Some of the potential health effects could be large, but all of these seem to be quite distant. When fossil or nuclear fuels are used for the production of electrical energy, a number of substances are released into the environment which can potentially affect human health. The health hazards of fossil fuels have been less studied and less publicized than those of nuclear fuel. In the case of electrical generating stations burning oil or coal, these emissions include the sulfur oxides, nitrogen oxides, trace metals and other particles, and a minor amount of unburned hydrocarbons. If the power stations utilize nuclear fuel, traces of radioactive materials are released, and there is always the possibility of a major nuclear accident.

Radioactive substances can be expected to be released in both liquid and gaseous forms to some extent whenever nuclear reactors are operating. In the course of their daily lives, people are exposed to ionizing radiation from various sources, including those from nature and from medical practice as well as those from nuclear power generation. The effect of the dose from nuclear power generation is insignificant compared to the effects of other sources of ionizing radiation, as is seen from Table 10-2.

There have been seven deaths from nuclear accidents since the first nuclear power was activated in 1942, but none from civilian power plants. The potential hazard of a major nuclear accident has been estimated to be one in 10 million (Eisenbud, 1973a). By way of contrast, there were 27 pressure-vessel (boiler explosion) deaths in New York City in 1965 and 1966 alone; and 10 fatalities statewide from 1967 through 1971 (New York City Medical Examiner's Office, 1974).

The internal combustion engine has had health effects and social effects as great as those associated with the introduction of electric energy. Its use has led to an increase in farm productivity and a great improvement in transportation, thereby making food, clothing, and other goods and services more available and cheaper in terms of human labor. The health of people in

TABLE 10-2.   Per Capita Ionizing Radiation Dose Rates for 1970 and 2000[a]

Source of exposure	1970 (mrem/year)	2000 (mrem/year)
Natural	130.0	130.0
Occupational	0.8	0.9
Nuclear power	0.002	0.2
Nuclear fuel reprocessing	0.0008	0.2
Weapons fallout	4.0	4.0
Medical	72.0	72.0

[a] From U.S. EPA (1972).

general has benefited by this through mechanisms that we have already discussed. An indication of the magnitude of the contribution of gasoline and oil to the cheapness and abundance of "the essentials of life" is reflected in Slesser's estimate that a quadrupling of energy prices in the next 40 years would bring about a sixfold increase in the price of food in England (Slesser, 1973).

A special impact of the internal combustion engine from the point of view of both health and social change has been in its effect on transportation. The influence of the automobile and the airplane are more appropriately discussed in Section 10.7 under Transportation and in Section 10.6 under Air Resources. However, it is worth pointing out that whereas the immediate health effects of the generation and transmission of electric power are minimal, the immediate health effects of the internal combustion engine, in terms of automobile accidents, have been major.

Indicators of Aspects of Energy Systems Relevant to Human Health

So far as we know, no one has derived any indicator of those aspects of energy systems that are probably beneficial to human health. However, on the basis of what we have just said, three measures might be the cost of gasoline, of home heating oil, and of electricity delivered to the household. Each of these enters into the cost of many activities that are essential to health and well-being. Their cost to the householder relative to his income is an indication of their general availability for him. Other indicators that might be applied to populations would be the percentage of households having adequate central heating, hot water heating, refrigeration, facilities for clothes washing and drying, dishwashing, cooking, and air-conditioning.

Yet another set of indicators might be based upon the relative adequacy of electric power for rapid transit systems, perhaps using some of the measures proposed under Transportation (Section 10.7).

The emissions of fossil fuel power plants include sulfur oxides, trace metals and other particulates, and a minor amount of unburned hydrocarbons. With respect to these emissions, environmental quality is judged on the one hand to meet standards of ambient air quality (see Section 10.6), and in certain other cases by the need to meet "emission standards." The standards of ambient air quality are used as indicators of the state of the atmosphere, whereas the emission standards are used mainly because of the relative ease with which they can be administered by regulatory authorities. The fact that emission standards are being exceeded does not of itself mean that ambient air quality standards are similarly being exceeded. There may not be any one-to-one relationship between the emission rate of a given facility and the ambient air quality in a given area.

Nuclear power plants release traces of radioactive materials into the environment. The potential risk to the population from these plants is estimated by the rem, a unit that permits aggregation of the dose from various sources and types of radiation exposure. The relative biological effectiveness of radiations having different physical qualities (such as alpha, beta, and gamma radiation, neutrons, and so on) can be normalized according to a system that has been developed for that purpose.

This simplifying assumption can be made because of the functional model that has been developed to describe the effects of ionizing radiation on the general population. In brief, it is considered that there are two major effects, genetic and carcinogenic. It is further believed that, regardless of the cause of the ionizing radiation, the potential effect can be evaluated by the use of the rad, a dose unit that describes the amount of energy deposited in the "critical organ." The critical organs for genetic effects are the gonads. For carcinogenic effects, either the blood-forming tissues or other organs of the body are critical. It is further assumed that, for purposes of defining the upper limit of risk, the dose–response curve is linear, without a threshold and independent of dose rate. Finally, risk coefficients have been developed which describe the number of genetic effects or the number of cancers per unit of dose per million of population. These coefficients have been derived from extensive epidemiological studies of irradiated populations on a scale that is without parallel in the field of chemical toxicology. It is generally believed that these assumptions greatly overestimate the effects (United Nations, 1972). The data in Table 10-2 indicate that the per-capita radiation dose from nuclear power plants might average a fraction of a millirem per year by the year 2000. The dose expected from medical uses of ionizing radiation will be very much higher. It is from information such as this that one can state that the hazards from the generation of electric power by nuclear generating facilities are distant and appear to be very small (Eisenbud, 1973a; Hammond, 1974). The hazards of nuclear accidents, as mentioned earlier, are also estimated to be quite small.

Indicators of gas delivery systems relevant to health include adequacy of procedures for detecting gas leaks; frequency of breakdowns or leaks; and rapidity of response to breakdowns. Another aspect of energy systems relevant to health is the adequacy of street lights. Data on numbers of vehicular accidents, and numbers of accidents involving pedestrians, related to given roads, walkways, or intersections are collected in many areas. There are standards of street lighting adequate for the reduction of vehicular accidents, and standards have been suggested for public safety and the prevention of crime. The Street Lighting Engineering Division of the Bureau of Gas and Electricity establishes standards for adequate street lighting in New York City, patterned after the guideline published by the Illuminating Engineering Society (1972). Probably the best indicator of the beneficial effects of adequate energy supplies is hidden within the overall differences in health that are associated with differences in annual income. One might also derive, by inference from statistical studies, indications of the health effects of increasing the cost of gasoline, and the effect of this cost upon the price of food delivered in urban regions. One might also estimate the health effects of the price of home-heating oil or electricity in terms of the proportion of the budget of people in low income groups that is taken up by this cost at various price levels.

Health Effects of Energy Systems

The mortality from cancer has been rising steadily in the Hudson Basin region during the past several decades, as it has in the rest of the country. Much of this rise has been in carcinoma of the lung and the bowel, but there has been some increase in the amount of leukemia. Although it is theoretically quite possible that some of this rise in carcinogenesis may be related to exposure to radioactivity in some manner, there is no reason whatsoever to relate it to any effect of generating nuclear energy within the Hudson Basin region. There has, in effect, been no clearly demonstrated morbidity or mortality from this activity up to now, nor have there been any accidents during which people were injured by radioactivity (Eisenbud, 1974a).

The major health hazard from the transmission and utilization of electrical energy is accidental electrocution. Between 1967 and 1971, there were 75 statewide closed compensation cases for electrocution fatalities (NYSWCB,

1974). Since 1972, there have been 15 cases in the New York metropolitan area, primarily among workers exposed to high-voltage lines (New York City Medical Examiner's Office, 1974).

Adverse health effects of the combustion of fossil fuel will be discussed under Air Resources and to a certain extent under Transportation.

Attitudes toward Energy Systems

Access to energy and to the various appliances that make use of it is not equally distributed throughout the Hudson Basin region. In general, the determinants are social and economic—the poor get less. Since members of lower social and economic groups are largely concentrated in the cities, the breakdown is also somewhat along an urban–suburban axis, with the suburban groups having a relatively greater access to energy for household uses on a per capita basis.

In general, those who have access to adequate supplies of energy are more likely to worry about the environmental cost of its production, while those whose access to energy supplies is inadequate are more likely to worry about their low income or whatever else they see as the cause of the inadequacy.

It is also the urban groups and the lower social and economic groups who have less access to automobiles and who are more dependent upon public transportation, including rapid transit systems. The problems of automobile exhausts are of less consequence to these people than the availability of automobiles, which they perceive as the key to their access to many amenities otherwise denied to them (see Section 10.8, Leisure Time and Recreation). Similarly, they are more concerned with adequate rapid transit systems to reduce the delay and the discomfort that they experience during the hour and a half or more that they spend in getting back and forth to work, than they are in the possible environmental costs of generating the electricity to make this possible.

The costs for electric power, gasoline and other fuels, and home-heating fuel fall differently upon different social and economic groups as well as upon rural and urban groups. If the cost of electricity is increased, either because of scarcity or because more expensive grades of fuel are used to decrease air pollution, the greatest increase in the burden is among the urban poor, whose utility bills are a relatively large proportion of their total budgets. Those hardest hit by the increase in the cost of gasoline are a somewhat different group, at a somewhat higher economic level, located less often in urban areas, and more dependent upon automobiles for earning a living or for other important personal uses.

Perceptions of Energy Systems

The dramatic rise in the cost of gasoline, fuel oil, and electric power has made people aware that these once cheap and plentiful commodities are now costly and potentially scarce. Although shortages have eased, the awareness of cost and scarcity remain. The tendency has been to place the blame upon electric utilities, oil refineries and marketers, the federal government, and the oil-producing states.

Few Americans have ever regarded electric power plants or oil refineries as aesthetically pleasing or as desirable members of a community. However, these attitudes have become much stronger during the past decade, as people have become more aware of the potential damage that these installations can do to the environment and possibly to human health. The hostility to them has become so strong that it has become difficult to find new sites upon which they can be located. The controversy is aggravated because these installations are not usually located in the middle of cities, but in suburban or rural areas, and usually alongside bodies of water which might otherwise be beautiful and undisturbed. The opposition to them is strongest in or near the communities in which they will be located, and among the better educated, higher income, and often younger members of the population.

Environmentalists have attacked the private corporations attempting to build or expand facilities for the production or transportation of energy. At the same time consumer activists have attacked the corporations for their excessive profits. Undoubtedly, there is some truth in both sets of charges. Many energy producers have been demonstrably neglectful of the aesthetic qualities and social impacts of their installations, and there has been much serious and apparently well-founded criticism of their pricing policies. Nevertheless, these arguments obscure the primary problem. Even if all of the electric, oil, and coal production and transportation facilities were operated by nonprofit authorities acting in the public interest, the fundamental difficulty would remain. These facilities are, indeed, often unattractive, space-consuming, and associated with some hazard to the environment and to the people who live near them and work in them; but a failure to create them may lead to much greater human costs.

10.6   Air Resources

An adult breathes about 12 times a minute, 500 cm^3 at a time—6 liters of air/minute, 360 liters/hour, 8640 liters/day. It is this air which passes through his nose and into his lungs that is the vehicle for the environmental agents that cause airborne human disease.

Most people in the Hudson Basin region spend rather little of their time out of doors—adults not more than 5% of their time in the winter and not more than 20% in the summer. Employed men and women in the New York City area and in New Jersey spend about 13 hours/day in their homes; housewives spend several hours more and sometimes the entire day. Working people spend 7 or 8 hours/day at their place of work—usually within a building or other closed space. They spend from 0.5 to more than 2 hours in one or more vehicles—automobiles, buses, subways, or railroad cars. Even for those engaged in ostensibly "outdoor" activities—construction workers, some utility workers, and some policemen—the 8-hour working day is likely to include several hours in a vehicle or other enclosed space.

People in the Hudson Basin region also move around a great deal. Suburban and rural residents may travel as much as 50 miles to and from work. Blue collar and white collar workers in the city are similarly mobile, although they usually travel shorter distances. Even school children are often transported several miles to school, and many housewives travel several miles to shop.

There are several important consequences to all this activity. First, in the winter, people in the Hudson Basin region spend more than 90% of their time breathing the air in buildings, vehicles, and other closed spaces, and less than 10% of their time breathing air directly inhaled from the "ocean of air" that covers the airshed. In the summer, they are outdoors more, and are much more in contact with the air from outside through open windows. Nevertheless, they still spend most of their time in partly or completely closed places. Second, people move about widely within the airshed. Few spend much time in close proximity to any single air sampling station.

When substances inhaled with air lead to disease, the manifestations of this disease are likely to be predominantly in the respiratory tract. Respiratory disease is the most frequent cause of acute episodes of disability among the American people. The common cold, pharyngitis, tonsillitis, bronchitis, influenza, and pneumonia are the most frequent causes of days lost from work and from school because of sickness (NCHS, 1973a, b, c). If one includes cancer of the lung among the respiratory diseases, then these diseases fall third after the cardiovascular diseases as the largest cause of death in the Hudson Basin region. The respiratory diseases that most frequently lead to death are cancer of the lung, pneumonia, and chronic obstructive pulmonary disease. Respiratory diseases are also very common causes of chronic symptomatic conditions and one of the most common causes of severe chronic disability.

The agents in air that lead to human disease fall into three categories. First, and most common, are infectious microorganisms suspended in air. Exposure to these is acquired from close association with other people. Numerically, the viruses are the most common airborne microorganisms. More than a hundred viruses are known to be able to cause the syndrome of the common cold and often cause pharyngitis or various influenzalike syndromes (Andrews, 1965; Bell, 1965; Tyrrell, 1965). Bacteria are now less frequent as causes of very serious respiratory disease, but they are still very important. They are the major causal agents involved in pneumonia, and in chronic pulmonary diseases such as tuberculosis and bronchiectasis.

Second, and probably the second most common cause of acute and chronic symptomatic respiratory reactions, are the allergenic substances. These are usually of natural origin and usually contain a protein to which people become allergic. They include pollens, dusts, danders, molds, and spores, which occur in great profusion. They are responsible for many cases of chronic or acute rhinitis, which at one time or another affects at least half of the population, for many instances of asthma and bronchitis, and for some of the chronic severe cases of obstructive pulmonary disease.

Third are various compounds which are inhaled as gases, dusts, fumes, or mists, and are harmful in sufficiently high concentrations. Some of these, such as the carcinogenic agents in tobacco smoke, the nitrates and sulfates, have a direct irritating or damaging effect upon the lining of the respiratory tract. Others, such as carbon monoxide, carbon tetrafluoride, carbon tetrachloride, benzene, and polyvinyl chloride, exert a chemical toxic effect or a carcinogenic effect in various parts of the body after they have passed into the bloodstream. Radioactive substances inhaled in sufficient amounts can also cause cancer in various parts of the body.

Inhaled tobacco smoke is the single most important cause of chronic obstructive pulmonary disease and of cancer of the lung in the United States today. It is a very important contributing factor in the occurrence of acute myocardial infarctions and death from coronary heart disease, including sudden death. It is involved in the etiology of peripheral vascular disease, stroke, cancer of the bladder, and leukemia. It probably accounts for more mortality and more serious morbidity than any other single pathogenic environmental agent that has been identified in the United States at the present time. The likelihood that any inhaled environmental agent will cause disease is closely related to the concentration of the substance that is inhaled, to the duration of the exposure, to the total amount inhaled, and to whether or not inhalation is continuing. Although there is much concern about the potential hazards of inhaling very small amounts of toxic or carcinogenic substances intermittently over long periods, the fact is that the great majority of the people who have developed, and who are most likely to develop, disease from inhaled agents are those who have inhaled them more or less constantly and in high concentrations over long periods.

These considerations are as true in the case of infectious agents as they are in the case of allergenic, toxic, or irritating materials. One is most likely to get a cold from close association with members of his family, from people at work, or from a person riding close to him in a subway or automobile over a period of a half-hour or more. He is much less likely to get one simply from a casual passing contact with another person. The people who have developed tuberculosis in the past have been those who have lived with or worked around other people with open tuberculosis. People who are susceptible to allergic rhinitis are much more likely to develop symptoms in the spring or in the fall when there is much pollen suspended in the air. People who smoke half a pack of cigarettes a day for 10 years are much less likely to develop bronchitis or cancer of the lung than those who smoke two or three packs of cigarettes a day for 20 to 30 or even 40 years, and inhale the combustion products from several hundred kilograms of tobacco during this time.

The relative risks of cigarette smoking, occupational exposure, and community air pollution exposure must be taken into consideration in estimating the health effects of pollutants in the general body of air over an air shed. The effects of cigarette smoking or other air pollutants are directly related to their concentration in the inhalers' air. The combustion products from cigarettes, inhaled through the mouth directly into the lungs and bypassing the protective mechanisms in the nose, are 10,000 to 20,000 times as concentrated as the pollutants found in the ambient airshed. The exposure of smokers to cigarette smoke is orders of magnitude greater than their exposure to agents in the general body of outside air (NCHS, 1967; Naumann, 1973; USDHEW, 1972). Such considerations hold whether one is concerned with sulfur dioxide, carbon monoxide, or asbestos. Those who are most heavily exposed in the highest concentration and over the longest periods of time are most likely to become diseased. By comparison, transient and intermittent exposures at low concentrations are much less likely to lead to disease.

A factor in respiratory disease that is not to be overlooked is that of individual susceptibility. This is a well-known phenomenon in hypersensitivity diseases. Many people develop no symptoms of rhinitis or asthma when exposed to concentrations of pollen which lead to profuse symptoms in others. Similar phenomena are seen in relation to infectious diseases. Some people have as many as four or five colds each year. Others, living in the same community and exposed to the same range of viral agents, may have no disabling episodes of respiratory disease over periods as long as 20 years, may report that they never have colds, and when observed throughout a winter may show no evidence of having a cold. Table 10-3 illustrates this effect. These 24 women had worked side by side in an office over 5 years,

TABLE 10-3.   Disabling Colds, Influenza, and Acute Gastroenteritis during Previous Five Years

Informant	Common cold syndrome	Influenza syndrome	Acute gastroenteritis syndrome
3 F	CCCCCCCCCCC	FF	GG
4 F	CCCCCCCCCCC		GGGG
15 F	CCCCCCCC	F	GGGGGG
14 F	CCCCCC	FF	GGG
13 F	CCCCC		GGGG
1 F	CCCC	F	GG
2 F	CCC		G
10 F	CCC	F	GGG
12 F	CCC		GGG
19 F	CCC		G
20 F	CCC	F	
47 F	CCC	F	
16 F	CC	F	G
17 F	CC	FF	GG
45 F	CC	F	
9 F	C		
21 F	C		
40 F	C	F	G
44 F	C	F	GG
7 F		F	
11 F			
22 F			
23 F			
24 F			

ª From Hinkle (1965a).

traveling back and forth to work on the crowded buses and subways, and being widely exposed to the infectious agents prevalent in the community. They had quite similar exposures to infectious agents, but differed widely in the number of episodes of common cold, influenza, and gastroenteritis that they exhibited during the 5-year period. Furthermore, when a viral agent appeared among them during the course of a winter's observation, some of them developed colds, some developed influenza, and some had gastroenteritis, with each woman tending to favor the type of reaction she had shown in the past. Some women in this group developed no symptoms of illness of any sort during the winter, even though one could detect the evidence that they had been infected by the virus and that it had been present in their blood.

A similar phenomenon has been observed among middle-aged men who have smoked two packs of cigarettes a day for 20 years or more. Some developed lung cancer, many developed bronchitis and chronic obstructive pulmonary disease, a number had heart attacks, and a few had strokes. Those who have had one manifestation of disease have not necessarily exhibited any of the others. And there are some who smoked two or more packs a day for as many as 30 years with no significant evidence of disease. The phenomenon of differing susceptibility is very important in the interpretation of data from epidemiologic studies, and especially of data from studies of exposure to environmental agents such as air pollutants. Susceptibility to illness is not randomly distributed throughout the population. In any given population of similar people, some not only have more episodes of illness but more kinds of illness resulting from more different apparent causes (Hinkle, 1965b; NCHS, 1964). The medical explanation for this is not entirely abstruse, and it is not simply based on illness behavior.

The occurrence of one illness increases the likelihood that other sorts of illnesses will occur. If, for example, a person smokes many cigarettes and has chronic bronchitis with increased secretion and impaired ventilation, he may become more susceptible to the infectious agents that cause acute bronchitis and pneumonia. If, as he grows older, he also becomes more obese, as many people do in our society, he is more likely to develop an impairment of his glucose tolerance or diabetes mellitus. If this happens, he will experience greater difficulty in dealing with the infectious pneumonia that he is rather more likely to get because of his bronchitis from smoking cigarettes. Because he has become obese, his blood pressure is more likely to rise, and later, because he has high blood pressure and diabetes, and is a cigarette smoker, he is more likely to have a heart attack. The heart attack and the high blood pressure may weaken his heart and cause him to have congestive heart failure. If, under these circumstances, he has another episode of pneumonia, if he is exposed to a severe heat wave, or to a severe episode of air pollution, he is much more likely to die.

Thus, one finds that the people who are likely to die during epidemics of infectious disease, during periods of serious air pollution, or during heat waves, are usually seriously ill people with a number of cardiovascular, respiratory, and metabolic diseases, and that their deaths may be attributed to any one of these. These seriously ill people are more likely to be old, and they are also more likely to be poor. The poor, as we have pointed out, have more of all sorts of disease. This statement includes poor children and poor adults as well as poor old people. The malnourished and relatively neglected child of an uneducated and poor working mother is more likely to develop infectious illnesses, to be injured, unable to cope with his illness or injury as well, and to have permanent sequelae of various sorts.

As noted in Section 10.1, increased susceptibility to illness and death among a relatively small proportion of our population can lead to particularly malignant forms of the "ecological fallacy." Since frequently and severely ill people are more likely to be poor, to be concentrated in cities where air pollution is high, and to die if exposed to adverse environmental or social conditions of any sort, one can find an association between death and illness and the presence in the atmosphere of almost any substance that varies in its concentration in various parts of the community or from time to time. Also, if there are relatively few highly susceptible people in a census tract, and one attributes to them the median income, age, education, or state of health of all people in the census tract, a serious error can occur. The presence of a few nursing homes, a concentration of alcoholic or indigent people in one part of a community, or even a very large stand of ragweed in one area may grossly distort observations that are imputed to all people in a census tract. Causal inferences drawn from correlative studies of any sort relating human health to air pollutants are highly suspect if all of the variables are not measured in each subject and at the same time, and if the effects of confounding variables are not carefully considered and adequately accounted for.

The importance of air in closed and poorly ventilated spaces is explained by the relationship between the concentration of air pollutants and their pathogenic effects. Many substances released into the general body of air make their way into the closed spaces of houses, offices, factories, garages and mines; but when adverse health effects occur, it is much more common to find that the pathogenic agent originated *within* the closed space and was present at much higher concentration inside than outside. The respiratory viruses and bacteria that cause disease are most frequently encountered in the home, the workplace, or in the vehicle in which one travels between them. Most of the carcinogenic materials that produce lung cancer originate in the fire at the end of a cigarette at the tip of one's nose. Acutely lethal concentrations of smoke usually are caused by fires occurring within houses and buildings. Lethal concentrations of carbon monoxide occur in homes with space heaters, in closed automobiles with the engines running, and in manholes, tunnels, and garages. Lethal concentrations of chemical fumes occur in factories, laboratories, or cleaning establishments.

Temperature is an aspect of the ambient air with important implications for health that are frequently overlooked. A severe heat wave in the Hudson Basin region may be associated with up to a thousand excess deaths. Most of these occur among the old and among those chronically ill with cardiovascular and pulmonary disease, but a significant proportion of them represent heat stroke occurring among otherwise apparently healthy people who work and live in hot places. The effect of a heat wave on the death rate in New York City is usually quite evident (Fig. 10-2), while the effect of an episode of air pollution may be difficult to detect. (Buechley et al., 1973; Cassell et al., 1968; Marmor, 1974).

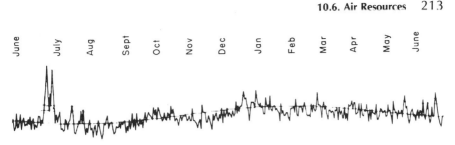

Fig. 10-2.   Seasonal effect on mortality: total deaths, all ages, in New York City, June 1, 1963, to July 1, 1964. Heat wave in late June and July. Data from the New York City Health Department.

Because the heating of homes and workplaces is generally more adequate than the cooling, deaths directly attributable to cold in the winter are less frequent than those attributable to heat in the summer. Nevertheless, the overall death rate is higher in the winter and every winter storm may be associated with an increase in mortality and morbidity (Cassell et al., 1968; Puffer and Griffith, 1967). It is possible that the brief exposures of people to the outside air in winter are more important in terms of the change in air temperature than in relationship to anything that the air contains. Moving from a warm atmosphere to a cold atmosphere and back into a warm atmosphere, with the inhalation of chilled air and some body chilling in between, is accompanied by vasomotor changes in the nose and changes in nasal secretion. This may have some relation to the fact that respiratory infections are more frequent in winter, and frequently occur in relationship to changes in the weather (Burrows et al., 1966; Lawther et al., 1970; NCHS, 1974b; Puffer and Griffith, 1967).

Indicators of Air Resources Relevant to Human Health

There is no single generally acceptable index of air quality. A number of indicators of air quality are published, and the results of these analyses individually can be compared to the standards promulgated by the U.S. Environmental Protection Agency (see Table 8-1). It is a relatively simple matter to aggregate these data into a single index of air quality. This has been done by a number of agencies (Eisenbud, 1974b). However, to say that it is simple to do is not to say that such an aggregated index is meaningful. We can develop indexes that use the air quality criteria as an arbitrary yardstick, but the relationship of these air quality criteria to human health remains to be determined.

In our opinion, the present federal air quality standards are adequate to protect people against deaths specifically caused by substances in air, e.g., from carbon monoxide poisoning or from smoke inhalation. However, they are unlikely to have any effect upon the death rate from these causes, since they are not applicable within closed spaces where almost all of these deaths occur. The standards are probably adequate to protect against major acute effects on general mortality, like those which occurred in London in 1952 or Donora in 1948. Whether they are adequate to protect against the influence of air pollution on day-to-day levels of general mortality is not known, primarily because it is not clear whether air pollution per se actually has an important effect on day-to-day mortality. Efforts thus far to control air pollution, which have reduced SO_2 levels in the New York City area by 60 to 80%, have had no measurable effect on general mortality or upon the mortality apparently associated with air pollution. Thus, it seems to us that adopting more stringent standards of the present kind would not be effective at the present state of knowledge (Schimmel et al., 1974).

The present air quality standards are also well below the level at which acute and chronic morbidity occurred in places such as London, Donora, and the Meuse Valley. At the present time, during periods of relatively high pollution levels, there are still complaints of eye irritation and, sometimes, respiratory symptoms in some people. These probably would not occur if federal standards were met at all times. That attainment of these standards would abolish all of the presumed chronic effects of present levels of air pollution is a matter that is not clear, again largely because it is not clear whether there are any major significant chronic effects at the levels indicated by the federal air quality standards. At present, it is our opinion that no change in these standards is indicated.

While we support the view that no changes in the air quality standards are indicated, it is not apparent that the air quality standards are related to emission standards on a one-to-one basis. In short, some relaxation of emission standards—particularly in the case of automobiles and stationary electrical generating stations—could be permitted without exceeding the present air quality standards.

Different approaches are needed in the establishment of air quality standards, depending on the nature of the pollutants and on their mode of physiological action. When we deal with irritant gases, carbon monoxide, or asphyxiants, we clearly need short-term standards. Upper limits that cannot be exceeded over a period of time are essential to prevent the general effects on mortality that have occurred during the well-documented smog episodes, and specific health effects such as carbon monoxide poisoning. On the other hand, when we deal with trace metals and similar substances whose effects are generally related to the burden of the total body or on a particular organ, an average annual standard is necessary to keep this burden from being exceeded by continuous or repeated exposures, none of which might exceed the standard for an acute exposure. Similar considerations probably apply to the chronic effects of many of the irritant substances, even though these do not accumulate within the body.

Would it be more desirable to concentrate or disperse sources of air pollution? So far as humans are concerned, if we have standards for both acute and chronic exposures, and these standards are being met, there is no difference in the effect on human health.

We have only begun to understand how air pollutants interact with one another to affect health, but we do know that these interactions occur. In uranium miners, the interaction between cigarette smoking and radioactive dust produces more lung cancer than would be expected from either alone (Archer et al., 1973). Similar interactions may occur in people with silicosis and asbestosis (Selikoff and Hammond, 1973; Selikoff et al., 1972). In animals it has been shown that benzo[a]pyrene exposure does not produce lung cancer unless there is an accompanying exposure to sulfur dioxide and possibly to other irritant gases (Carnow and Meier, 1973). The possibilities of interactions between sulfur oxides and particulates in the atmosphere have been the subject of much speculation, but there are few data upon which to form a conclusion.

Health Effects of Air Resources

There is no doubt that episodes of relatively massive air pollution have been responsible for sudden illness and death in a number of places in the United States and Europe. The best known of these incidents occurred in the Meuse Valley, Belgium, in 1930; in Donora, Pennsylvania, in 1948; in London in 1952 and 1962; and probably in New York City in 1953 (Logan, 1953; Schrenk et al., 1949). The number of deaths attributed to these episodes ranged from 20 in Donora to about 4000 during the 1952 London episode. Interestingly, the 1953 episode in New York City, in which 300 excess deaths were reported, did not come to light until 1962 when studies of meteorological records were shown to correlate with a transient increase in the death rate during the episode that occurred 9 years previously (Greenburg et al., 1962). However, the 1962 findings are equivocal and have been rebutted by subsequent investigators (Cassell et al., 1968). After the 1952 episode in London, a search was made of the death records, and periods of excess mortality associated with atmospheric stagnation were found to have occurred as far back as 1873 (Eisenbud, 1968). It is likely that many communities have unknowingly experienced similar episodes due to meteorological circumstances that resulted in increased concentrations of air pollutants.

These acute episodes have had a number of features in common. They were associated with periods of temperature inversion lasting 4 or 5 days. Symptoms began to develop on the second or third day. Most of the serious illnesses were in the older age groups. Increases were seen in hospital admissions for respiratory and heart disease. The most frequent causes of death were listed as chronic bronchitis, bronchial pneumonia, and heart disease. It is generally agreed that the most serious cases were among individuals who had chronic cardiorespiratory disease prior to the smog incident (Goldsmith, 1962).

There were very few measurements of atmospheric contamination during these episodes. The sulfur dioxide concentration in Donora was estimated to have ranged between 0.5 and 2 ppm. Measurements made in London in 1952 showed that the sulfur dioxide concentrations ranged up to 1.34 ppm, and were associated with suspended solids in concentrations as high as 4.5 mg/m^3. During the 1962 episode, the SO_2 concentrations were somewhat higher than in 1952, but the number of fatalities was much less. It has been suggested that this may have been due to the higher concentration of particulates during the 1952 episode.

The evidence for health impairments from atmospheric pollution in the amounts that are normally encountered in the Hudson Basin region at the present time is equivocal. Many investigators have found no association between air pollution, morbidity, and mortality. Others have demonstrated some relationships but the apparent differences are usually small, and they might be related to confounding variables.

The number of deaths that occur from day to day in the New York metropolitan region fluctuates with the pattern of human activities and with changes in the environment in which these activities occur. Deaths are more common in the winter than in the summer. They are significantly more frequent on Mondays than they are on Wednesdays and Thursdays. There is a 15% excess of deaths on Christmas and New Year's and on the days just around them, but this does not occur on Memorial Day, Labor Day, or Thanksgiving. Any change in the weather affects the death rate. An extreme heat wave can more than double the death rate for a short period of time. Any shift from cold weather to warm weather is usually accompanied by a 1-day increase in the death rate, and any shift from warm weather to cooler weather by a 1-day decrease; but a prolonged cold spell, accompanied by the passage of a cold front and by the occurrence of rain or snow, can have a transient effect almost as great as that of an influenza epidemic. Changes in air pollution are also associated with changes in general mortality (Buechley et al., 1973; Cassell et al., 1968).

Schimmel and Greenburg analyzed all deaths that occurred anywhere in New York City from 1963 through 1968 (Schimmel and Greenburg, 1972). During this period, the daily average number of deaths was 243.21, with a standard deviation of 30.45. They compared the total number of deaths each day with the average value for sulfur dioxide and smokeshade in the air as measured at a single monitoring station on the Upper East Side of Manhattan. After correcting their data for the effects of temperature and for seasonal trends, they found that there did tend to be an excess of deaths in New York City on days when air pollution indicators were high at the measuring station. Smokeshade was a better indicator of excess deaths than was SO_2. Altogether, they estimated that 10,000 deaths occur each year in New York City on days of high air pollution which would not have occurred on that day had there not been such a high level then or on the preceding day. This association appeared to affect 12% of all deaths that occurred in the city during the observation period.

These observations appear to put transient, small increases in the levels of air pollution in the same category as Mondays, Christmas, New Year's, winter, changes in the weather, influenza epidemics, cold waves, and heat waves. That is to say, people who are about to die in any case are more likely to die on a day when the smokeshade level is high, other things being equal. More recent and extensive studies by Buechley and others (1973), using more variables and a more elaborate technique, and covering the entire air quality area of New York, northern New Jersey, and southern Connecticut, have essentially confirmed a temporal association between the presence of air pollution and the day of death for all deaths in this area. They have estimated that the SO_2 level affects the day of death in about 2% of all deaths. Recently, Schimmel et al. (1974) extended the previous Schimmel and Greenburg (1972) study to include the period from 1969 through 1972, when the SO_2 levels in the atmosphere over New York City were reduced by more than 60%. They found the same temporal relationship between changes in air pollution level and the frequency of death; but the very large fall in the concentration of sulfur dioxide was not accompanied by any fall in the total death rate.

There are many interesting aspects to these studies which influence our interpretation of the findings. Daily fluctuations in the death rate from all causes, not just in New York City but in northern New Jersey, Westchester, Long Island, and southern Connecticut, show a temporal correlation with air pollution levels as measured at a single station in northern Manhattan. Yet during the period when these studies were carried out, there were more than 30 other air monitoring stations operating at one time or another throughout the area, and the levels of pollutants were often very different at different measuring places. The level of smokeshade was somewhat more consistent from station to station than the level of SO_2, even though the latter is much more irritating, and it was the level of smokeshade that was most closely associated with changes in the death rate.

Carnow and others, who studied the "excess deaths" associated with transient high levels of air pollution in Chicago, found that these deaths occurred primarily among those who were seriously ill and already near death from cardiovascular disease and pulmonary disease (Carnow and Meier, 1973). The Schimmel and Greenburg study in New York reported that the excess deaths from coronary heart disease on days of high pollution were greater in proportion than the excess deaths from chronic pulmonary disease. This observation is especially interesting because more than 80% of all deaths from coronary heart disease, even among patients in the hospital, are attributable to a cardiac arrhythmia which has no known relationship to any air pollutant at any of the levels usually encountered in New York City. On the other hand, many of the deaths from chronic respiratory disease are in chronic respiratory failure and occur among people who are especially susceptible to known irritants in the air such as sulfur dioxide.

Altogether, these data do indicate that there usually is a temporal association between the levels of SO_2 and smokeshade recorded at a single monitoring station in the New York region and the time of occurrence of all deaths of any sort in the New York metropolitan area, such that the time of occurrence of at least 2% of the deaths seems to be explained by this association. However, this association seems not to be mediated primarily by the concentration of pollutants themselves but to be an association with some aspect of the pattern of human life in the region, which is also associated with a slight excess of smokeshade throughout the region. Deaths occur even in parts of the region where SO_2 is not elevated. They affect people who are seriously ill, many of whom are already about to die, and they seem to involve diseases not greatly affected by air pollution, and mechanisms of death not related to air pollution. Reducing the level of sulfur dioxide has had no effect upon them.

One can only speculate about the mechanism behind this small but real association. Possibly the mechanism is in part like that which may lie behind the excess of deaths on Monday—an increase in the tempo of human activities with an added physiological demand accompanied by an increase in industrial and commercial activities and in the burning of trash in incinerators, which increases the amount of smokeshade in the air of eastern Harlem. Possibly the mechanism is like that which may lie behind the excess of deaths around Christmas and New Year's—a period of great significance in the lives of many people. It is a time of marked change in their pattern of daily activity, family reunions: changes in the pattern of eating and drinking, emotional excitement, and a well-known tendency for serious depressive episodes to develop among the lonely and among the emotionally and physically ill. Whatever may be involved in the mechanism, the effect is small. It acts upon lives already near termination and nothing that has been done about air pollution thus far seems to have changed it.

In general, it is our opinion that pollution of the ambient air at the levels now present in the airshed of the New York area has not been shown to have any significant causal relationship to cancer of the lung or significant respiratory disease. An effect may be present, but if present it is probably quite small.

Air Pollution and Morbidity

The summary statements of the National Academy of Science's Conference on Health Effects of Air Pollution (NAS, 1973a) describe the present state of our knowledge in this area.

Carbon monoxide. The several adverse effects of carbon monoxide on health are better documented than are those of any other pollutant discussed at the conference. Because of its preferential binding to hemoglobin, carbon monoxide reduces the ability of the blood to carry oxygen to the tissues of the body. The extent of this phenomenon due to air pollution appears not to constitute a physiological hazard in otherwise normal individuals, but may impose an additional burden on organ systems already challenged by preexisting pathological conditions. This is considered most likely to be of consequence in patients with coronary artery disease. However, the fraction of all persons with coronary artery disease whose physiological limitations are aggravated by carbon monoxide cannot be quantitated with any certainty. Studies of the effects of low atmospheric concentrations of carbon monoxide upon human behavior are still in their early phase and there is as yet little agreement as to the nature or seriousness of such alterations. It appeared to be agreed that the effects of the inhalation of carbon monoxide by cigarette smokers exceed those which may be attributed to concentrations of this gas in ambient air.

Sulfur oxides and particulates. In animals, exposure to sulfur dioxide in atmospheric concentrations many times that of the air quality standard is required to elicit any detectable adverse health effect. However, impaired pulmonary function is observed in animals at sulfur dioxide concentrations only a few time greater than the air quality standard when the sulfur dioxide is accompanied by microparticles known to emerge from certain stack gases. There is highly suggestive evidence that the mixture of acid sulfates and sulfuric acid present on these microparticles are the responsible agents. Further, it appears that in man these effects are likely to be most pronounced in the very young and in elderly individuals already suffering from preexisting debilitating disorders. Oxidation of sulfur dioxide to sulfur trioxide, precursor of the acid sulfates, occurs most readily at high humidity, seemingly in keeping with an apparent correlation between relative humidity and the incidence and extent of such health effects.

Nitrogen oxides. The nature and extent of adverse health effects deriving from the presence of nitrogen oxides, and their relation to the ambient air concentration of these chemicals, are more poorly documented than are those of any other of the pollutants under consideration. The difficulties deriving from the inadequacy of current analytical procedures for measurement of the amounts of the several nitrogen oxides in the atmosphere are well known. A reliable method for sampling and analysis of these materials in the atmosphere is badly needed. The present air quality standard rests largely on data obtained in a study in Chattanooga that indicated increased respiratory disease in both children and adults exposed to greater than usual amounts of nitrogen oxides in the atmosphere. However, the quantitative aspects of that study now appear to be suspect. Additional epidemiological studies using a reliable analytical procedure are badly needed to substantiate and extend that study.

Hydrocarbons and "oxidant." Hydrocarbons released into the atmosphere do not appear to be significant, of themselves, as noxious substances but rather are important for the role that they play in a complex series of chemical and photochemical processes leading to the production of ozone in the atmosphere. The chemistry of these processes is incompletely understood; the reaction products are as yet poorly characterized; but it appears to be accepted by those who are knowledgeable that it is ozone that is the principal "oxidant" which may give rise to significant adverse health effects except for eye irritation.

In animal studies, ozone alone, in concentrations considerably greater than those which would be encountered were the air quality standards met, has been shown to produce a decreased ability to exhale. More recent studies have indicated that ozone combined with sulfur dioxide in lower concentrations—but still 2 to 4 times that at the air quality standard—appear to produce more adverse effects in the lower respiratory system than do much higher concentrations of either when inhaled separately. Epidemiological studies have been conflicting and it has been very difficult to separate the effects of "oxidant" from the effects of high ambient temperature. It appears indisputable that eye irritation occurs when "oxidant" is present in the atmosphere at a concentration of approximately 0.1 ppm but that this effect is not due to the ozone itself.

Mutagenesis and carcinogenesis. There are substances present in polluted atmospheres which have been demonstrated in experiments on animals to be mutagenic or carcinogenic. The concentrations required in such experiments have been very much higher than those which might be encountered in polluted atmospheres. There is an urban–rural gradient in human lung cancer not attributable to cigarette smoking. The atmospheric pollutants here considered may be among the factors contributing to the higher rate in urban areas but definitive evidence is lacking.

Studies in the United States and in England generally support the conclusion that exposure to a high level of sulfur dioxide and particulate matter over long periods of time in a climate characterized by heavy rainfall, high humidity, heavy fogs, and cold winters is associated with an increased prevalence of respiratory disease. Under such circumstances, preschool children appear to have a higher incidence of tracheobronchitis and croup, and possibly more colds. School children have a greater number of respiratory symptoms. Adults have a greater number of respiratory symptoms. Episodes of asthma may be exacerbated, and the respiratory symptoms of people with chronic respiratory disease are worse. Data relating all these phenomena to moderately high levels of one agent (for example, SO_2) in the absence of the others are less reliable but generally consistent. Data relating these phenomena to differences in pollution levels within the range usually observed in New York City or northern New Jersey are highly equivocal.

An illustration of the difficulties of relating present air quality indicators to human health is shown in the data from the aforementioned 24 women who worked together in a building on East 56th Street in Manhattan and lived in various parts of New York City. These women were examined shortly after their arrival at work for evidences of engorgement and secretion of their upper respiratory tracts. Measurements of sulfur dioxide and smoke shade were obtained from the station at Central Park in the East 60s, slightly less than 1 mile northwest of the building in which these women worked. There was no significant relationship between the pollutant levels as measured in Central Park and the state of the women's nasal mucosae shortly after they arrived at work, nor was there any association between the pollutant levels and either their symptoms or their illnesses. One would not have expected that there would be. The building in which these women worked was air-conditioned and maintained at a mean temperature of 70°F and a mean humidity of 56%. When the women left the building in the evening, they walked not more than two or three blocks to a subway or bus and then rode to their homes in various outlying areas of the city. In the morning they returned to work by the same route. The temperature and humidity of the outside air were much more closely related to the state of the women's nasal mucous membranes than were the smoke shade and sulfur dioxide content. The presence of infectious agents in the community as measured by the presence of illness in other women in the building; exposure to infectious agents as measured by throat cultures, throat washings, and antibody titers; the general susceptibility of the women as measured by their past histories; and the activities of the women and their general physical and emotional states were all more closely related to the occurrence of illness than the pollutants in the outside air to which they were so slightly exposed (Hinkle, 1965a).

This study is not intended to imply that it would be desirable to measure all these aspects of human populations as well as the various air quality indicators that are now monitored. This illustration simply points out that very important aspects of the human susceptibility to respiratory disease are not being measured and probably cannot be measured in any practical sense at points where the measures would be meaningful in terms of human health.

Air Temperature and Respiratory Disease

In contrast to the equivocal effects of present levels of air pollution on mortality in the Hudson Basin region, the effects of air temperature and weather are most striking. Figure 10-2 shows the effect of a heat wave on the daily mortality pattern in New York City. While many deaths during such a heat wave are of seriously ill and old people, many others represent heat prostration and heat stroke among otherwise apparently healthy people exposed to very hot places. The role of the weather in the occurrence of acute respiratory illness is illustrated in Fig. 10-3.

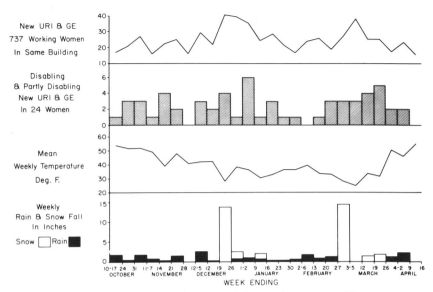

Fig. 10-3. Upper respiratory infections and the weather. From Hinkle (1965a).

Attitudes toward Air Pollution

Respondents in large cities tend to show more concern over air pollution than other environmental quality problems (e.g., Koezkur *et al.*, 1963; Van Arsdol *et al.*, 1964), while residents of more rural areas tend to put air pollution low on their list of environmental concerns (Capener *et al.*, 1973). The fairly high level of concern over air pollution among large-city residents apparently does not mean that the issue is seen as important as such non-environmental social problems as juvenile delinquency, unemployment, and police–community relations (de Groot and Samuels, 1962; Swan, 1970). Moreover, it also appears that air pollution is seldom defined in health-related terms (Crowe, 1968); instead, most respondents consider it a nuisance and define it in terms of malodors and reduced visibility. In general, upper-social-class respondents are more concerned with, and more aware of, air pollution than lower class respondents (Medalia, 1964; Smith *et al.*, 1964; Swan, 1970).

Perceptions of Air Pollution

We know of no studies that have attempted to link air pollution exposure to diverse indicators of mental health. However, there is some convergence of evidence that air pollution can be linked to a greater incidence and/or prevalence of various symptoms, such as eye and nasal irritation, headache, sore throat, shortness of breath, chest pain, and common colds. In these studies, the effects of social class have been pretty much parceled out, but it is not clear that the same can be said for weather conditions (Goldstein, 1972).

So far, then, it is only a matter of speculation that any of the above symptoms affect any aspects of a person's mental health and psychological well-being. We do not even know if air pollution per se has any effects on various daily and social activities. Perhaps the one behavioral effect that can eventually be traced to air pollution is residential mobility. For example, among Los Angeles residents who were not satisfied with their community, one-third of them gave air pollution as the reason (Goldsmith, 1968).

10.7 Transportation

Transportation is the only environmental policy area in which the Hudson Basin Project focused directly on an aspect of the human environment having a major impact upon human health. Transportation is a major cause of death, disability, and impairments in the Hudson Basin region. To be specific, automobile accidents are the most important single cause of death for men in the second, third, and fourth decades of life. They are an extremely important source of injury and of impairments such as deformed and missing limbs, loss of eyesight, and damage to the central nervous system. Deaths and injuries associated with other modes of transportation are less frequent on a passenger-mile basis. However, in a single serious railroad, subway, or airplane accident, a relatively large number of people may be killed or injured at one time.

There is an important morbidity from transportation which arises quite aside from accidents. This is the morbidity associated with the fatigue of people who use transportation, their exposure to heat and foul air, and their close exposure to each other. Long trips back and forth to work are believed to be a significant factor in worker fatigue in urban areas. The crowding in public transportation is notorious. Nowhere do people spend more time in closer proximity to each other than in the crowded subway cars, buses, and railroad cars. The air in such vehicles is subject to heavy contamination from many sources. Respiratory pathogens from human exhalation are undoubtedly in high concentration. In many buses, fumes from gasoline and diesel engines may reach high levels. During hot days, temperature and humidity within such vehicles may become very high, especially if they are enclosed and not air-conditioned, as is still the case with some railroad cars and most subway cars and buses.

The mass transportation systems used in urban areas carry a significant potential for catastrophic health effects. A subway power breakdown on a hot day during the rush hour, trapping thousands of people in dark, hot, subway cars that are stranded in tunnels, could lead to a massive loss of life from heat prostration, injury, and cardiovascular accidents. The addition of a smoky fire could add many deaths from smoke inhalation. Similar hazards exist, though possibly to a lesser degree, in railroads. Fortunately, major catastrophes of this nature have not occurred, although there have been incidents both in the subways and in the commuter railroads which offer a small foretaste of what might happen. Major bus accidents are also a possibility, and have occurred in other communities.

The health hazards associated with automobile driving are in part related to the driver and particularly related to the problem of alcohol. However, they are also related to the vehicle and to the highway. A meaningful proportion of automobile accidents occurs in relation to highways and intersections that are inadequately engineered for the traffic that uses them (Anonymous, 1969a, b). Improvements in such facilities may lead to measurable reductions in human injuries and deaths. The morbidity and the large potential mortality associated with mass transit systems are largely the result of the inadequacies of the systems. The health hazards arise from inadequate and antiquated equipment and from potential breakdowns of power supply, signaling systems, and ventilating systems.

The hazards to people who use various means of transportation are great or potentially great. Compared with these, the hazards of people who live beside transportation systems or who are exposed to them are relatively small. Automobiles introduce nitrogen oxides, carbon monoxide, and hydrocarbons into the atmosphere, and are responsible for much of the smog that afflicts many cities. These emissions have an adverse aesthetic effect. They cause eye irritation. They probably cause some difficulty to people who already have embarrassed respiratory systems, and they may have some effect upon primary respiratory episodes. Whatever effect they have is most important along very heavily traveled streets and highways, especially those in which the traffic moves slowly and ventilation is poor (Aronow et al., 1972; Ayres et al., 1973; NAS, 1973a).

Automobile emissions also contain lead, which is deposited primarily near the highways. Some of this gets into human systems and is added to the lead absorbed from other sources (NAS, 1972). However, this lead has not been a significant cause of detectable human illness in the Hudson Basin region.

The noise associated with transportation can be a source of great annoyance and constraint to those living nearby. The noise from major highways is such that preferred dwelling places are distant from these or, in central urban areas, high above them. The noise of elevated railways in urban areas is a notorious nuisance for those who live nearby. However, the greatest noise problem contributed by modern transportation is that arising from nearby airports (see Section 10.2).

Transportation systems are also associated with hazards to the health of people other than those who use them or live beside them. These hazards have been illustrated in the past by the transient effects of railroad, trucking, and tugboat strikes. A large metropolitan region such as New York City does not store a very large supply of food and fuel essential for its operation. If all transportation to the New York metropolitan area were cut off, the supplies of milk and perishable fruits and vegetables would probably be exhausted in a few days, and the supplies of all foodstuffs would probably be diminished to the danger point within a few more days. Similarly, cutting off all transportation would led to the rapid exhaustion of gasoline and heating oil supplies, and of coal supplies within a somewhat longer time.

Indicators of Transportation Relevant to Human Health

Even though transportation plays a major role in human health in modern society, it is not customary to collect data systematically on those aspects of transportation systems relevant to human health. If one is planning transportation systems for the benefit of people, it is certainly important to have such indicators. On the basis of the points that we have discussed in the foregoing section, it is possible to suggest that some useful indicators might be the following.

1. *The carrying capacity of transportation systems for people in terms of the peak load requirement.* For highways, such a measure would indicate the likelihood of delays at peak hours, as well as the likelihood of accidents. For rapid transit systems and railways, it would indicate the likelihood that riders would have to stand or wait for trains.
2. *Point-to-point travel times between various parts of the study area by various methods.* Since travel time is strongly related to fatigue, this could be a meaningful measure in relation to health.
3. *The frequency of breakdowns, with or without fatality and injury; of delays; of waiting time for buses and trains.* All of these measurements are relevant to travel time for the individual and therefore to fatigue. The frequency of breakdowns is also related to the likelihood of an accident that might cause fatility or injury.
4. *Indicators of human comfort of means of transportation:* for example, the number of standees usual at peak loads; the internal heating and cooling arrangements, and the air quality and noise levels within vehicles.

5. *The reliability of sources of electric energy and the margin of safety at times of peak load requirement.* These are related to the likelihood of a catastrophic breakdown of the electrically powered transportation system under peak load conditions.
6. *The carrying capacity of transportation systems for perishable foods in relation to available community stores of these foods.* In case of a breakdown of transportation systems, the health of the population is dependent upon the duration of the breakdown and the available stores of food within the community.
7. *The carrying capacity of transportation systems for fuel and electric energy in comparison to available community supplies of fuel and alternate sources of electric energy.* The relationship of energy to health has been discussed in Section 10.5. The implications of a possible breakdown have been pointed out.
8. *Indicators of pollution levels of ambient air caused by (a) auto exhaust and (b) tire dust,* mentioned previously in Section 10.6.
9. *Indicators of noise along highways, around airports, and around rapid transit,* as discussed in Section 10.2.

Health Effects of Transportation

Accidents

Morbidity and mortality relative to modes of transportation are usually expressed as deaths or injuries per passenger-mile. This expression originated years ago when the safety of railroads was being assessed. It has been extended to the automobile and airplane as well as rapid transit systems. It is a better way of comparing safety among railroads than of comparing safety between different means of transportation. Assuming that the average rate of progress of a driver in start-and-stop automobile traffic is of the order of 15 to 30 miles an hour, while the average speed of an airplane is of the order of 300 miles an hour, it is evident that the air traveler covers 10 to 20 times as many miles in a given unit of time. A more meaningful method of comparison would be per hour of exposure. Even these present measures indicate that automobile travel does, in fact, entail much greater risks than travel by other modes (see Table 10-4).

Other Sources of Morbidity from Transportation

There are no good estimates of the effects of the fatigue caused by the various modes of transportation, or of the chronic effects of the air quality in automobiles or subways, or the relationship between crowded conditions

TABLE 10-4.   Transportation Accident Death Rates[a]

Kind of transportation passenger deaths in 1972	Passenger miles (million)	Passenger deaths	Rate/million passenger miles	1970–1972 death rate (average)
Automobiles and taxis[b]	1,850,000	35,200	1.90	2.00
Automobiles on turnpikes	50,000	540	1.08	1.05
Buses	70,000	130	0.19	0.19
Railroad passenger trains	9,000	48	0.53	0.28
Scheduled air transport planes (domestic)	125,000	160	0.13	0.10

[a] From National Safety Council (1973).
[b] Drivers of passenger automobiles are considered passengers.

and the transmission of respiratory disease. Anecdotal evidence from hospital clinics and from dealing with patients indicates that these are seriously hampering to especially susceptible population groups, including the old, the chronically ill, and the physically handicapped.

Effects on People Not Using the Transportation

Morbidity and mortality from automobile exhaust occur primarily among tunnel workers, garage workers, and others who are exposed to automobile exhaust in closed places. People who must work outdoors in city streets with heavy traffic (toll takers and the like) may show evidence of increased levels of carbon monoxide in their blood, but rarely any evidence of morbidity resulting from this. The evidence suggesting that the people who have angina pectoris and other forms of ischemic heart disease may exhibit adverse effects from breathing automobile emissions along freeways is generally viewed with scepticism. Subjective complaints of chest pain and minor changes in electrocardiographic tracings may occur in such people for many reasons and most often by mechanisms that do not involve inhaled carbon monoxide. Studies of people with coronary heart disease up to now have not suggested that exposure to carbon monoxide plays a significant role in this disease. When high carbon monoxide levels are found in people with coronary heart disease, they are usually attributable either to cigarette smoking or to exposures in closed spaces.

Studies of exposures suggest that lead burdens are higher among people who live close to highways. Up to now, lead inhaled as dust and fumes contaminated by automobile exhaust has not been found to be a significant cause of human disease.

Hearing loss caused by noise has been a significant occupational hazard for ground crews servicing jet aircraft, but it has not otherwise caused clear-cut evidence of morbidity or mortality. The evidence of disturbed sleep, and of inability to carry on school work, conversation, and outdoor recreation among people living or working near airports, rapid transit facilities, and highways has been mentioned. These constraints upon human activities are major nuisances for people living in the urban region.

Attitudes toward Transportation

Attitudes toward transportation, like attitudes toward many other aspects of the environment, are influenced by social determinants. Negative attitudes toward automobiles and highways appear to be prevalent among the relatively well-to-do and among some suburban residents, but not necessarily among rural residents who may be heavily dependent upon highways. Positive attitudes toward owning automobiles are common among the less well-to-do and among some urban residents who see them as a key to mobility that they now lack.

The automobile has become an integral part of the social fabric of present-day American society. The suburbs, the supermarkets, the shopping centers, the family vacation, and the courtship patterns of the young are all built around it.

All of this is well known and does not need to be discussed at length. It is mentioned merely to remind us that the automobile is far more than a simple means of transportation, and that its use is no longer optional for many people. A shift to walking, bicycling, bus riding, or traveling on the rapid transit is not feasible for most people or for most activities, even though it might be helpful for some.

Concern with the difficulties, inconvenience, and discomfort of public transportation is chiefly found among urban residents, especially the working members of these populations. Other people, especially those who do not live in cities or metropolitan regions, generally seem to be unaware of the large amounts of time urban working people must spend in getting back and forth to their jobs, and the inconvenience and discomfort that they must endure in doing so.

Perceptions of Transportation

We have not carried out any special review of the literature relating to people's individual perceptions of transportation beyond those mentioned in the section on attitudes. However, it is worth repeating that many people tend to perceive their automobiles as an essential tool for themselves and their families, intimately interwoven with their daily lives, whereas public transportation of one sort of another they see as providing a special service, and useful under certain conditions.

10.8   Leisure Time and Recreation

Recreation is essential to health in the sense that people must have regular periods of rest and replenishment. Although we cannot show from morbidity and mortality statistics that it is a factor in disease and death, there is abundant clinical evidence and practical experience to support this contention. It is not accidental that a period of convalescence is required after a disease or injury, and it is well known that people return from their vacations looking fit and healthy, "feeling fine," sleeping better, and generally more relaxed than when they left. Even a weekend in the country enables one to face the next week's work better.

But granting that some form of regular recreation is essential to health, can we say that outdoor recreation is essential to health? Is there something special about activity "out-of-doors" that adds to its value as recreation over and above the value that would come from the same sort of activity indoors? We must reply in all candor that there is literally no hard scientific evidence to support a positive answer at this time.

In the late nineteenth and early twentieth centuries, it was widely believed that rest, exposure to fresh air, and a rural environment were particularly beneficial in the treatment of mental and emotional illnesses, and in the treatment of tuberculosis and pulmonary disease. It is now believed that there is nothing peculiarly beneficial about the rural setting. For many years both mental illness and pulmonary disease have been treated as well in the city as in the country. A belief that a return to a life in a setting of nature can be beneficial to mental health has become popular once again during the past decade; but there is no sound evidence that this is true. Indeed, the epidemiological evidence points in the other direction. Both mental and emotional illness in the clinical sense are somewhat more prevalent in rural than in urban regions. Many people do, of course, get pleasure and satisfaction from living in a natural setting or from visits to natural areas—but many others do not.

The biggest controversy has revolved around the question of whether or not physical exercise promotes health. Physical exercise, of course, does not have to be undertaken outdoors. If it is health-promoting, there is no reason why it should not be equally health-promoting when undertaken indoors. For most people, however, physical exercise generally means outdoor exercise, not only because opportunities for indoor exercise are more limited but also because most people find most forms of outdoor exercise more pleasurable.

Our review of the question of physical exercise and health leads us to support the conclusion stated by the Wolfenden Committee on Sport (1960), appointed by the Central Council of Physical Recreation in London, which could not find any unequivocal connection between exercise and health. As the committee stated, "It is generally accepted that, in the sense that health implies the absence of disease, and fitness is a subjective sense of well-being, both physical and mental sports, games and recreation generally exert a beneficial influence on both; but surprisingly enough, this impression can be substantiated to only a very small extent."

Since the report of the Wolfenden Committee, there has been rather convincing evidence that people who engage in regular, strenuous, and sustained physical activity, over long periods of time, are protected from the disease-producing effects of high-fat diets like those usually consumed in the industrial societies of Northern Europe and the United States (Edholm and Karvonen, 1964, 1967). However, the people who enjoy this protection are only those who engage in continuous and heavy physical labor—lumberjacks, railroad track workers, agricultural laborers, and Masai tribesmen of Central Africa, who trot 40 miles a day. The daily energy expenditure of such people is on the order of 5000 kcal, a level far above that of the average workman today, and far above the daily level that can be attained by the casual exercising of otherwise sedentary people. Some professional athletes may approach this level of energy expenditure some of the time, but most do not. And even though they do not develop arteriosclerosis, it should not be assumed that lumberjacks, track workers, agricultural workers, Masai tribesmen, and professional athletes actually live longer than other people. In fact, they do not. They are protected from coronary heart disease, but their death rates from other causes more than offset this.

Nevertheless, it does seem that the modest level of activity involved in walking regularly; in sports such as bicycling; or in other moderately vigorous activities can be beneficial to health. What evidence there is suggests that people who are moderately active in this manner, and who sustain their patterns of activity throughout their lives, may live longer as compared to otherwise similar people. Data supporting such a hypothesis have been derived particularly from the studies of cohorts of college students, some of whom were athletes and kept up a sustained pattern of athletic activity in later life as opposed to others who did not. Of course, it may just be true that healthy people are more active, but it is also possible that men who are moderately active throughout their lives live longer because of the greater physical fitness of their heart muscles. There is evidence that suggests that when active men do have heart attacks, they are more likely to survive than men who are not active. None of this evidence is conclusive, but so far as it goes, it tends to support the concept that physical activity as a part of recreation is additionally beneficial to health.

A very important aspect of all forms of outdoor recreation is accessibility. A recreational facility is of no use to a person who cannot get to it, and of little use to a person who cannot get to it conveniently and cheaply. Many facilities for outdoor recreation are distant from urban centers and are accessible only by automobile. Unfortunately, the people in the Hudson Basin region who have the greatest need for outdoor recreational facilities are those who live in central city areas, many of whom do not have access to automobiles. For such people, the only useful park or playground is the one that can be reached by a short walk, and the only accessible beach is one that can be reached by subway or bus. Regardless of what is intended, a recreational facility built in a rural or suburban area and accessible only by private automobile is a facility whose use is restricted to a relatively small, and in a certain sense privileged, segment of the population.

Another important aspect of recreational facilities is their upkeep. People at play are notoriously destructive. When the ordinary citizen is enjoying the out-of-doors, he spreads around papers, beer bottles, and cans. He tramples the grass, breaks the benches, falls into the shrubbery, and writes his name all over public facilities. This ordinary behavior of people is widely deplored, but it seems unlikely that it will change very soon—the public places of Pompeii are covered by the graffiti of the Romans. The practical consequence is that if a park, a playground, or any recreational facility is to continue to be useful, there must be an adequate budget for its maintenance. The failure to provide funds for the adequate upkeep of recreational facilities is probably a more significant cause of their deficiency than the failure to build facilities in the first place.

Indicators of Recreational Facilities Relevant to Human Health

Indicators that merely describe the size and location of recreational facilities and their potential capacities are of very limited use for estimating their effects on health. Indicators which relate recreational facilities to population requirements, and which taken into account accessibility, carrying capacity, useful season, cost to the user, and state of maintenance, would be more relevant.

For estimating the adequacy of recreational facilities in a given area, indicators which might be useful would be the number of playgrounds per thousand children aged 10 or below, the number of playing fields per thousand youths aged 11 to 18, the number of parks per thousand adults, the number of swimming pools, lakes, and beaches per thousand population, the total playground capacity per thousand children, the total playing field capacity per thousand youths, and the total capacity of beaches, lakes, and pools per thousand people.

Other important indicators might be the numbers of children, youths, and adults per thousand population living within specified walking distances of various types of facilities; and the numbers of people per thousand population, both with and without automobiles, who can travel to a swimming pool, lake, or beach within specified travel time.

The Long Island Sound Study of the New England River Basins Commission has made a good start toward providing some information of this nature for some communities on Long Island and southern Connecticut (NERBC, 1974).

Effects of Recreation on Human Health

In the raw statistics, the possible beneficial effects of recreation are confounded by the effects of many other factors of known importance to disease. The people who have the greatest access to recreation are in general those who are in the better educated and higher income segments of society. These people are more free from disease for many reasons other than recreation. Also, people who exercise regularly and who systematically engage in various forms of recreation are likely to be healthy to begin with. Often people who exercise regularly also regulate their diets, smoking, drinking, and exposure to other hazards in a way that is likely to enhance their health.

There are no clear-cut data relating health to recreation in the Hudson Basin region. The studies that have been cited of people in various parts of the world suggest that among cohorts of college graduates, those who exercise modestly but regularly throughout their later lives are more likely to be healthy (Montoye et al., 1962; Morris et al., 1973; Polednak, 1972; Schnohr, 1971). There are also studies relating the growth and physical development of children to the availability of regular exercise (Espenschade, 1960; Hein and Ryan, 1960). Recently, there have been reports of increased longevity among people with known coronary heart disease who have been involved in systematic and supervised exercise programs as well as reports that those who are more physically active are less likely to die if they suffer a heart attack (Bassler, 1974; Fox and Haskel, 1968; Fox et al., 1972). All of this information is strongly suggestive, but it does not allow one to state what kind of effect upon morbidity and mortality is produced by what sort of recreation, or what the magnitude of this effect might be.

Some forms of recreation have unintended adverse side effects upon health. These are related in part to the fact that many people deliberately seek forms of recreation that are dangerous and exciting. A certain number of sky divers, racing drivers, and scuba divers die each year while engaged in their chosen sport. Likewise, a certain number of hunters are shot, and a certain number of swimmers are drowned each year. The hazards of hunting and swimming are not deliberately sought by the participants, but are accepted by them. Significant injuries are associated with all body contact sports, and with many other activities such as skiing. Many minor discomforts such as first degree sunburn, eye irritation, and ear infections are experienced by many people who sunbathe or swim in swimming pools. The injuries occurring during contact sports and in the course of skiing are not inconsiderable. In 1973, there were an estimated 225,000 skiing injuries in the United States for a population at risk of about five million skiers (Ellison, 1973).

Attitudes toward Leisure Time and Recreation

There are important social determinants of attitudes toward leisure time and recreation. In general, tennis, golf, camping and hunting, hiking and mountain climbing, sailing, power boating, and nature walks are recreations for middle- and upper-income people. This is partly because they require costly equipment, special clothing, and sometimes a fee for the use of the facility, and partly because the facilities for these activities are likely to be accessible only by means of an automobile. However, cost and accessibility are not the only criteria. These activities also enjoy a vogue among the more prosperous and better educated members of the society. Group sports, such as softball or volleyball, picnicking in parks and at beaches, pier fishing and party-boat fishing, are forms of outdoor recreation enjoyed by the less well-to-do and less well-educated. These activities require a minimum of equipment and use facilities that are free or inexpensive and readily accessible on foot or by public transportation. Swimming when the weather is warm and going for a ride in the family car, if one is available at any time, are outdoor recreations enjoyed by all segments of society.

Preferences for recreational activities are not entirely determined on an economic basis. There are ethnic, regional, and age group preferences also. The age differences are clear enough, but they are often not taken into account. Young children require playground facilities. Youths of both sexes enjoy playing fields and opportunities for group games, as well as swimming and bathing facilities. Adults seek a variety of facilities. And old people, who are often forgotten, find a special use for sunny parks where they can sit and talk with each other, walk, and engage in quiet sports such as shuffleboard and lawn bowling. People in small towns and suburban rural areas are somewhat more likely to enjoy hiking, camping, and hunting, which many of them have done since childhood.

Individual Perceptions of Recreation

Recreation, as much as beauty, lies in the eye of the beholder. Even within families, there may be very marked differences in recreational preferences. In spite of all of the similarities of people in terms of their background and location, one finds in any group some who dislike sports and outdoor activities of every or any kind, while there are others who will not read a book, watch television, or engage in any form of indoor recreation if they can get outdoors. The practical lesson from all this is that any population requires a variety of recreational facilities if the majority of its members are to be satisfied. Surveys to determine what kinds of facilities people want and what kinds they feel they need are a very important adjunct to the planning of recreational facilities.

10.9   Environmental Service Systems

The most notable feature about all of our environmental service systems is the remarkable efficiency and reliability with which they operate. In the great majority of homes, more than 95% of the time all systems are "go." You can turn on the tap and there is an abundant flow of potable water. The toilet flushes, and the garbage disappears with more or less regularity. When breakdowns occur, these are usually at the terminus of the system within the house or building. Disruptions of water mains are few and usually repaired quite rapidly. The sewer is almost always open. Only the system for solid waste removal tends to function irregularly, and sometimes inaccurately.

In general, sewage systems operate remarkably well from the point of view of people. Human feces are a prolific source of disease when deposited on the ground near dwellings or in privies, or when left in open receptacles waiting to be carried away. The much maligned flush toilet whisks this dangerous stuff away from potential human contact as rapidly as it is excreted. The sewer to which the toilet is connected carries it off along with the dirt washed from people and their clothing, and the scraps of food from their eating and cooking utensils. Toilets and sewers thus have a major role in breaking the chain of infection that caused so much human disease in the past. The sewer, of course, causes problems, but these are problems for the environment rather than for people. These problems occur chiefly because the sewer ultimately deposits its contents into streams, rivers, and bays, to the detriment of water quality and of aquatic life.

Sewage treatment is useful for preventing infectious material from getting into water supplies used by people further downstream. Although it could be argued that this contamination might be taken care of at the point of intake, such a procedure is not yet regarded as entirely safe. Sewage treatment is also useful in preserving the beauty of natural water bodies and making them more attractive as sites for human recreation. However, its chief value lies in preserving natural waters as healthy habitats for plants and animals, and to keep them from being swamped by the vast amount of excrement from humans on the surrounding land. The problem is not one of their being infected by human microorganisms. It is chiefly a problem of the oxidation of the sewage, which uses up the oxygen that organisms need to live, and the vast quantities of nitrogenous material that are introduced which cause an overgrowth of algae and other plant life. If an effective, economic, and sanitary method can be devised for making the nutrient material in human sewage available for use in agriculture so that it can be recycled to provide food for people rather than for algae, the benefits to people as well as to the environment might be very great.

Within the Hudson Basin region, a good word might be said for the retention of adequate septic systems for individual households and small buildings in rural and suburban areas. When there is an adequate plot of land—approximately 2 acres per household—and when the septic system is properly designed and serviced, it deposits the liquid portions of human sewage in the ground where, for the most part, they cause little difficulty. Replacing septic systems by community sewage systems sometimes has the undesired effect of increasing the density of human habitation and of delivering human excrement to a nearby body of water, where it has adverse effects on the environment, whether it is treated or not. The issues here, however, are not those of public health but of public policy—the adequate design and supervision of septic systems, the control of population density, and the construction of sewers and treatment plants.

Although engineers tend to focus their attention on the disposal of solid waste, it is the collection of solid waste that creates the most immediate problems. Solid waste can be a threat to human health if it is allowed to accumulate around dwellings, where it can become a breeding place for rats, mice, flies, cockroaches, and other vermin which can become carriers of disease. The collection of solid waste is not automatic, and it is not carried out without human intervention, as is the case with sewage. It is therefore subject to both the high cost and the vagaries of human labor. In most communities, and in large parts of the cities, the collection is carried out more or less effectively, but in the central areas of cities and in the slums, the collection system has broken down in the recent past, allowing solid waste to accumulate in backyards, driveways, and hallways, and to litter streets and public parks. This has had some public health consequences, and more important social consequences. Areas that might be used for play or recreation are not available because of garbage, and the appearance of the littered neighborhood contributes to feelings of degraded social status and alienation among its inhabitants.

A study by Burden *et al.* (1971) in Boston has indicated that the breakdown in collection has been as much social as mechanical. The collection system in that city is largely manned by members of closely knit white ethnic groups. There has been antagonism between the sanitation workers and slum residents, most of whom are black. The effect of this has been to limit the cooperation between the two groups, so that the collectors do only what is legally required of them, and the residents make little effort to do anything. Burden found that in Boston slums the collection of solid waste from the curbside was essentially complete and regular. He also found that the collection of solid waste within the households was more or less complete and regular. But a large hiatus lay between the household and the curbside. This area was not accepted as anyone's legal or occupational responsibility. The landlords did not provide any service for carrying solid waste from apartments to curbsides or for cleaning it up from halls, yards, alleys, or sidewalks; nor did they provide adequate receptacles for this solid waste either within the building or at the curbside. The collectors, for their part, would collect waste only when it was deposited at the curbside in proper receptacles. As a result, garbage accumulated in halls and in yards.

There are problems related to the disposal of solid waste, but these are problems more for the local environment than for public health. The measures now in use are, by and large, effective from a health point of view. Indeed, procedures for solid waste disposal sometimes have gone well beyond the point of diminishing returns so far as health is concerned. Prohibiting householders to burn leaves or trash in the interest of maintaining air quality bears no demonstrable relationship to human health, and probably has no real relationship to the health of other living organisms. People have a high tolerance for the smoke of leaves and wood fire in the low concentrations usually encountered outdoors. Undoubtedly, they are well adapted to it. Man has been using fires and living in smoky caves, huts, and tents for many millenia. Carbon particles, unlike other dust, are notoriously well tolerated by the human lungs. Since forest fires and brush fires have always been a part of the natural system, one can surmise that the smoke from burning twigs and leaves also has little or no adverse effect on other parts of the natural system.

The characteristics of solid waste have changed dramatically in recent years, particularly those wastes that are associated with human habitation. On a per capita basis, the total amount is increasing exponentially at a rate of about 5% per year. The present per capita disposal of solid waste in New York City is about 6 pounds a day or 1 ton per year. This presents difficult engineering problems, but the health effects of modern solid waste are probably less than those of two or three decades ago. Prior to World War II, when the per capita production of solid waste was more like 2 or 3 pounds per day, a very high fraction was putrescible kitchen waste, which tends to attract vermin. Present waste contains less putrescible material because of the extent to which foods are prepared and packaged for market. The increased per capita production of solid waste has been largely due to the increase in the use of packaging materials, including nonreturnable bottles, and to a generally extravagant way of living which results in high turnover of domestic appliances, furniture, and goods of all kinds.

Indicators of Environmental Services Relevant to Human Health

Delivery Systems

Indicators of water quality have been discussed in previous sections. Indicators of water supply systems relevant to health include (a) the proportion of households served by safe, approved water supply systems; (b) the frequency of breakdown of these systems; and (c) the frequency and extent of contamination of water within the delivery systems.

The contamination of water within the delivery system is a more important public health problem than is commonly recognized. It has occurred frequently in some of the older European cities, where water in the reservoir may be highly potable but water delivered to the tap may be contaminated. Often the contamination derives from cross-connections within buildings, but it may also occur within the distribution system itself.

An important indicator of sewage systems relevant to health is the proportion of dwelling units, or of other working or gathering places, that are served by adequate, approved, and inspected sewage or septic systems.

Where sewage disposal is concerned, the ultimate test of the adequacy of a sewage system is the quality of the receiving water. This has been discussed elsewhere. Beyond this, the performance of the treatment plants themselves provide useful indicators. An annual estimate of the biochemical oxygen demand discharge from all outfalls may be a useful figure. Another useful indicator may be the weighted mean performance of all sewage treatment plants. This would, in effect, provide a measure of the percentage BOD removal from the system as a whole. It would be important to include those days or hours when, because of heavy rains, the plants are overloaded and the sewage flows untreated into the receiving body of water.

Probably the best indicator of the adequacy of solid waste disposal in a given community or neighborhood is the amount of uncontained waste per year collected from streets and vacant lots and alleys. With respect to the cleanliness of streets and parks, the best measure of the adequacy of cleaning activities might be the quantity of uncontained debris that can be collected from a sample of streets or parks on a random basis.

Health Effects of Environmental Service Systems

From the point of view of human health, the Hudson Basin region has a remarkably good record with respect to both the quantity and quality of its water supplies, and the adequacy of its sewage systems. Although people tend to complain about the deterioration of the quality of the water supplies, the fact remains that outbreaks of waterborne disease that can be traced to inadequate water supplies or to breakdowns in sewage systems have been remarkably few during the past several decades and of quite moderate severity.

The diseases related to solid waste are in general those transmitted by flies, cockroaches, and similar vermin, the gastrointestinal diseases previously described, and those transmitted by rats and mice. Epidemics of rodent-transmitted diseases are infrequent in our society, but potentially very dangerous. Rats are reservoirs of major epidemic diseases such as plague and typhus, which they can readily transmit to people by way of their fleas. The prevention of these diseases is in part dependent upon the suppression of the rat population, which in this region is thought to be free of these diseases. While there have been no cases of plague or typhus in this area for several years, these diseases do exist in many species of small wild mammals in other parts of the country, and particularly among rats and humans in the developing countries. So long as any part of the human population of our cities is living in close proximity to rats that might become infected, the possibility of an epidemic disease exists. The chief danger to humans from proximity to rats and mice at the present time arises from rat bites to children. In 1973 there were 270 reported cases of rat bites among children in New York City (NYC Department of Health, 1974). It is likely, moreover, that only a small fraction of the actual number of rat bites come to the attention of health authorities.

Attitudes toward Environmental Service Systems

Present public concerns about drinking water relate to its supposed metallic or chemical taste and to the various chemicals that are added to it in order to prevent disease. The dissatisfaction with the taste of tap water seems to be in part an expression of the current general preference for things "natural." There has been no substantial evidence of any deterioration in the taste of public water supplies in general which would account for the increase in complaints about them. The concern about additives is chiefly directed at chlorine, which is used to kill any residual pathogenic bacteria that may have passed the purification process, and fluorine, which is added in very small amounts because of its effect in preventing dental caries. The idea that these substances might have harmful effects in the amounts added is partly an irrational fear that has been directed particularly at fluorine. The concern about chlorine is based in part upon the hypothesis that this substance in time might be converted partly into chloramines (Aaronson, 1972; Anonymous, 1974c; Prival, 1974; Prival and Fisher, 1974; USDHEW, 1974), which are known mutagenic agents. No evidence has been presented to suggest that this actually does occur. There is some theoretical reason to believe that, if it does occur, the effect is so small as to be almost undetectable in the face of other mutagenic factors that act on the human population. In any case, the documented benefits of chlorinating and fluoridating water supplies in preventing serious disease in large numbers of people appears to be very much greater than any potential adverse health effects.

As we have indicated, the rapid and automatic removal of human wastes via sewer is a public health measure of first importance, which greatly reduces the likelihood of human disease and death. While the treatment of sewage after its collection has some effect in reducing human infection, it is primarily directed at reducing the degradation of natural waters which occurs when sewage is dumped into them. However, most of the public, and many public officials, apparently do not see the distinction between these two processes and regard sewage treatment as primarily undertaken in order to abate a threat to public health. This has lead many to anticipate that sewage treatment will produce large and measurable improvements in public health, which, in fact, it is unlikely to do.

Concern about the collection and disposal of solid waste is chiefly felt among the urban residents, and especially among the poor. Although the health hazard believed to be associated with solid waste is probably greater than the evidence of disease which can be shown to have occurred, the extent to which such accumulated wastes create nuisances, impede the use of areas valuable to the community, and are aesthetically repugnant cannot be denied.

Perceptions of Environmental Service Systems

To some extent, those who see great potential hazards in environmental service systems are people who are subject to irrational fears and suspicions. Various environmental services tend to become the focus for such fears. Quite prevalent today are fears of toxic substances in drinking water, fears of the adverse effects of fluoridation, fears of hidden motives on the part of people who support fluoridation, and fears of crime and lawlessness in the streets. These fears are probably something over and beyond the widespread human tendency to blame the water company, the gas company, the electric light company, the telephone company, and the garbage man for various breakdowns in their systems; for the size of their bills; for the various errors of billing; and for delays of repair. These problems do occur. Justice to the rationality of the average citizen requires one to comment that the size of many of the corporations that deliver our environmental services; the impersonality and the ineptitude of their dealing with their customers; the inefficiency, lassitude, and irregularity with which they respond to complaints; and the apparent thoughtlessness and social irresponsibility of some of their public policies invite the attitudes that the public holds toward them. In spite of this, recent surveys have indicated that a larger proportion of people feel confidence in public utilities such as gas, electricity, and telephone companies, than feel confidence in the Supreme Court, Congress, environmental protection groups, the news media, the public school system, or organized labor—possibly an indication that at least in many parts of the country their overall reliability is good, even though their behavior is irritating.

10.10   Biological Communities

The steady improvement of the health of mankind over the sweep of human history has been primarily the result of several million years of effort by men to separate themselves from the natural systems of which they were originally a part, and to create for themselves an artificial man-made environment more suited to their needs. A large part of the success of this effort has been based upon combatting, suppressing, and sometimes eradicating organisms that are predators of men, while encouraging, controlling, altering, and even inventing species that provide food, clothing, building and manufacturing materials, and energy for man. It can be said truthfully that the more man has controlled nature, and separated himself from other biological communities, the healthier he has become. This trend continues at the present time.

As the early hominids became tool users, they began to use their tools as weapons to improve their food supply. By the time our own species evolved, those tools had improved so much that they enabled men to become quite efficient in the collection of high-quality protein in the form of animal meat, which they pursued with the help of new and effective tools such as the bow and arrow. In his search for meat, man was undoubtedly responsible for the eradication of a number of species of large grazing mammals during the last hundred millenia. The destruction of these animals may have been the heedless act of precivilized people, but there is no reason to believe that it was simply a wanton act. The men involved were undoubtedly trying to provide food and clothing for themselves and their families.

Without question, the most important development in the control of the human food supply was the emergence of agriculture and animal husbandry about 10,000 to 15,000 years ago. It could be said that these were the most important public health measures in the history of our species. By providing a more stable and abundant food supply, these techniques increased not only the numbers of men, but also their life expectancy—from a level of 20 to 25 years to a level of 30 to 35 years, where human life expectancy remained essentially unchanged until the Industrial Revolution and the evolution of scientific farming.

One of the major activities of the tool-using predecessors of our species was to protect themselves from the other large predators that competed with them for food, and that occasionally preyed upon man himself. Man was highly successful at this. Long before the evolution of modern civilization, the large animals that preyed upon and competed with man had been effectively eradicated as threats.

The assault upon the "micropredators" of men—the microorganisms that have always been the major cause of human disease and death—had to wait until they were discovered in the seventeenth century after the invention of the microscope, and then wait further until it was demonstrated in the nineteenth century that they were indeed a cause of disease. The vast improvement in the health and longevity of man during the last century, the widespread alleviation of impairment and disability, and the addition of almost 35 years of productive activity to the lives of people in modern nations has been the result of our success in this assault upon the microorganisms that prey upon our species.

Until the beginning of the twentieth century, diseases caused by microorganisms were the leading cause of death throughout the world. They remain the leading cause of death in the underdeveloped nations; however, in the industrial nations, because of their successful efforts at sanitation, at prevention, and in treatment, these diseases have been superseded by cardiovascular disease and cancer. Nevertheless, in the United States today, infectious diseases—influenza and pneumonia—are still the fifth most important cause of death, and infectious diseases—acute respiratory and gastrointestinal infections—are by far the most important causes of acute disability and of days lost from work and school among our population (NCHS, 1974a, 1974b). In the industrial nations, the viruses are the cause of most of the widespread infectious diseases that continue to elude our efforts at prevention and control; but in the rest of the world, bacterial diseases and infestations with protozoa, flatworms, and roundworms, producing diseases such as tuberculosis, malaria, schistosomiasis, and filariasis, continue to be major causes of death and disability.

There are other species of animals that are not strictly speaking micro-predators of man, but are ectoparasites of man. These were well known to our ancestors: the human flea, the body louse, the crab louse, and the itch mite. They disappeared from most of our population only during the last few generations as people began to bathe regularly and to wash their clothes regularly and as facilities for doing so became widely available.

Both the parasites of man and the animals that surround man are factors in human disease. A characteristic feature of the microorganisms that cause human disease is that they are often also parasitic upon other species of higher animals, and particularly upon other vertebrates. The microorganisms that have caused the greatest amount of human disease in the past have been parasitic upon the animals that have lived closest to man. They spread with ease from one species to another because many of them are adapted to survive and multiply in the insects that prey upon both man and other animals. Tuberculosis, for example, is a disease of cattle as well as man. Its eradication among people has been in part dependent upon its eradication among cattle. Plague has a natural reservoir among the wild rodents of Central Asia. It spreads readily to the rats that are commensals of man, from rats to man by means of rat fleas, and from man to man by human fleas. The virus of equine encephalomyelitis has a reservoir primarily in birds and rodents. It is transmitted to horses and humans by mosquitoes and ticks, which in turn feed on other birds and rodents, perpetuating the cycle.

The existence of disease in species that surround man has always been a major threat to human health. Most of the major infectious diseases that have reservoirs in other animals are now in relative abeyance in the American population, but few if any have been eradicated. Most of them continue to exist. Their animal reservoirs can be identified, and from time to time human cases occur. Major outbreaks have been prevented in part by the constant vigil of the public health authorities; but we have probably been freed from them in the last few decades in large measure because we have withdrawn ourselves one step farther from the natural biological communities of which we were formerly a part. During the last 50 years, as people have moved from the farms to the cities, as the automobile and the tractor have replaced the horse and mule, as the farm animals have been removed from the farmer's door yard to the distant barn, as the milkmaid has been replaced by the milking machine, as the veterinarian has eliminated tuberculosis from the cow and trichinosis from the hog, as the washing machine and the Saturday night bath have rid us of our fleas and lice, and as the garbage collector, the incinerator, and the sanitary engineer have helped us get the rats and mice out of our households, we have separated ourselves even further from the animals that used to be our close associates. As we have done so, there has been less and less opportunity for us to be infected by them, and we have become healthier.

The fact that the major infectious diseases have become much less frequent than they used to be should not lead to a feeling of complacency. They probably will reappear when we give them the opportunity—as we sometimes inadvertently do. Two examples can be cited. Crab lice, body lice, and scabies had been absent from all but a few of the poorest members of our population for several decades until a few years ago when it became popular among young people to wear their hair long, to wash infrequently, to change clothing rarely, and to live together in close association in communal groups. Very soon, all of the human ectoparasites reappeared among some of the people who adopted this life style, and with them came risk of diseases which had hitherto been absent. In another segment of society, rapid air transportation now brings to the New York area people who have recently been in distant countries and have been infected with diseases such as typhus or typhoid. The incubation period of the disease occurs while they are en route and they develop the disease in this country among our mass of susceptible people. Only constant vigilance and a certain amount of good luck have continued to protect us against major outbreaks.

With minor exceptions (such as some of the yeasts), plants are not directly infectious for man, although some are toxic if they are eaten or brushed against. Indirectly, however, plants contribute significantly to chronic respiratory disease because of the ease with which people develop hypersensitivity reactions to some of their pollens and dusts, and develop rhinitis, bronchitis, and asthma.

Undoubtedly, there are beneficial effects which arise from man's relationship to biological communities. Many of these effects are psychological. Man and his domestic animals have been closely associated for many generations. In many respects the relationship has been a mutually beneficial one. The companionship that may exist between people and dogs, cats, and horses is proverbial. Lonely people and single people especially can obtain very meaningful outlets for their affections through a relationship with pets. It is believed by some that such a relationship has a beneficial effect upon their mental health. Certainly it can be said that large numbers of people obtain pleasure and satisfaction from animals, birds, and plants of many kinds and under many conditions.

Indicators of Biological Communities Relevant to Human Health

The communities most important to human health are the populations of domesticated plants and animals that supply most of our food. Their contribution, of course, is a positive one in the net. One might say, then, that the state of agriculture and animal husbandry is highly relevant to human health, and that the size of crops, the availability of foodstuffs, and the price of agricultural products, cattle, and dairy products at the farm are among the most important indicators of the state of biological communities that are relevant to human health.

However, when communities are considered in relation to health, the health effects considered are usually the adverse ones. At present, a number of biological communities are being observed to determine the presence or absence of conditions relevant to human health. Some indicators are in actual use, and others can be readily suggested.

Indicators of Disease in Domestic Animals

For many years, the U.S. Department of Agriculture and various local and state health departments have regularly examined certain domestic animals as well as the meat and milk from these animals for evidence of disease. There is still surveillance for such diseases as tuberculosis, brucellosis, and anthrax in cattle and sheep. These are not such frequent sources of human disease as they used to be because the careful control over the quality of meat, milk, and dairy products and the common use of practices such as pasteurization have prevented most disease from this source.

Pets are also a source of disease. Indicators of the presence of diseases in pets, such as rabies in dogs or ornithosis in pet birds, are relevant to human health. Similarly, the number of pets per capita in a human population and the type of pets are potentially useful data. Additionally, in a city such as New York, the amount of dog feces on the streets is an indicator of a condition that has no immediate health implication, but represents a nuisance to many urban residents.

Indicators of Animals That Are Commensals of Humans

Among the important indicators in this area are the number of rats and mice per unit of area, evidence of rodent infestation in buildings, and evidence of disease in rats and mice themselves. Other important indicators are the frequency of flies, fleas, bedbugs, cockroaches, mites, and other vermin in human dwellings; and the frequency of pigeons and of pigeon droppings on window ledges and air conditioners (a potential source of fungal disease).

Indicators of Other Biota Relevant to Human Health

In some suburban areas, populations of small mammals such as raccoons, opossums, chipmunks, and foxes appear to have increased during recent decades. Animals in these areas are relatively protected from hunting. To some extent they support themselves with food scraps foraged from human garbage. Their presence in proximity to people represents a potential health hazard. An important indicator is the frequency of disease in these small terrestrial mammals (for example, the occurrence of plague in ground squirrels, tularemia in rabbits, and rabies in skunks).

In the Hudson Basin area certain insects, particularly mosquitoes, generally represent a nuisance, but are also potential carriers of diseases such as encephalitis.

Indicators of the State of Aquatic Communities   Relevant indicators of fish and shellfish are the "health" of those populations that are a source of human food and also of human recreation. The infection of shellfish with viruses and the potential for the transmission of other waterborne infectious diseases by shellfish are much more immediate threats to human health than the apparent contamination of finfish with heavy metals or pesticides, which has been a matter of much more public interest during the past few years.

Indicators of the State of Terrestrial Plant Communities   In urban regions particularly, both the pollen count in the ambient air, representing the number of suspended pollen particles per unit volume of air, and the frequency and distribution of important pollen-bearing weeds, such as ragweed in vacant lots and other areas near to human habitation, are relevant to the occurrence of acute respiratory illnesses.

Indicators of the State of Microbial Communities Relevant to Human Disease   The communities of microbes themselves, the bacteria, the viruses, protozoa, the yeasts, the fungi, and other microscopic disease-causing agents are not easily sampled. Many of these forms are obligatory parasites of men and animals, and some are obligatory intracellular parasites. One measures not their frequency and characteristics as free-living communities, but rather evidence of their presence in their hosts as indicated by the occurrence of disease in animals or in people. In most cases, the measurements of disease frequency are much more precise for humans than for animals, but sometimes the opposite is true.

Health Effects of Biological Communities

Adverse Health Effects from Domestic Animals

Many of the diseases once distributed by milk and meat from domestic animals, or by contact with domestic animals, have essentially disappeared from this region. One no longer sees conditions such as milkborne tuberculosis. However, there is still an appreciable incidence of illness and injury arising from association with pets. Dog bites in metropolitan New York occur at a frequency of about 38,800 reported cases a year. There were several fatalities among children in Suffolk and Nassau counties in 1974 alone. Cases of rabies continue to occur from time to time. Phenomena such as cat scratch fever or psittacosis occasionally appear.

Adverse Health Effects of the Commensals of Man

Rat bites of children and infants have recently been the most frequent manifestation of adverse health effects caused by the rather large numbers of rats and mice in some buildings in slum areas. Scabies and crab lice still occur among the unwashed, and the possibility of major diseases transmitted by a combination of rats, mice, and vermin are still present. Pigeon droppings have caused some respiratory disease in special instances. However, the health threat from commensals today is more potential than actual.

Adverse Health Effects from Terrestrial Animals and Insects

New York had 21 reported cases of (tickborne) Rocky Mountain spotted fever statewide (exclusive of New York City) in 1974 through July, mainly in Suffolk County. Without medical treatment, mortality can be expected to run about 20%, and with treatment, about 7% (McLaughlin, 1974). Plague has not appeared in the eastern region in the ground squirrel, but is present in the West (Altman, 1974). Rabies in skunks has been reported. In this area the threat of disease remains more potential than actual.

Mosquitoes, as mentioned, are primarily a nuisance at the present time. However, in 1959 there was an epidemic of mosquito-borne encephalomyelitis in central New Jersey.

Adverse Health Effects of Aquatic Communities

Fish and shellfish are notoriously subject to secondary infection and deterioration if they are not handled in a sanitary manner and adequately refrigerated after they are caught. It is this aspect of seafood that represents the chief threat of bacterial disease. As mentioned earlier, infectious hepatitis is the only reasonably common disease directly traceable to the infection of fish or shellfish. Human toxicity resulting from eating swordfish contaminated with mercury or salmon contaminated with DDT has been essentially nonexistent.

Adverse Health Effects of Terrestrial Plants

Approximately one-quarter of adults have from time to time had symptoms suggesting allergic rhinitis and from 1 to 2% have or have had asthma. The seasonal rises in these conditions are most commonly related to plant pollens.

Adverse Health Effects of Microbial Communities

Infectious diseases remain the fifth largest cause of death in the United States, with influenza and pneumonia leading the list. Many kinds of infections with microorganisms can be fatal. Meningitis, purulent infections in any part of the body, bacterial endocarditis, pyelonephritis, and the hypersensitivity reactions to streptococci that lead to rheumatic fever and to conditions such as rheumatoid arthritis are among the most prominent of the fatal effects of microorganisms in our society. Tuberculosis and syphilis are not so widespread as they once were, but are still prevalent, and gonorrhea is thriving. Microorganisms causing acute respiratory diseases and acute gastrointestinal diseases still produce more days of disability among Americans than any other types of disease.

Attitudes toward Biological Communities

As with other aspects of the environment, attitudes toward biological communities are different depending upon the social and economic background of people and their geographic location. Middle- and upper-income people living in the suburbs or in rural areas tend to attach great value to the preservation of animals, birds, and plants, and to conservation in general. On the other hand, urban people, and especially the urban poor, find their attention called to rats, cockroaches, bedbugs, pigeons, and other near neighbors, and tend to have a less benign view of the wildlife that they encounter.

All in all, people in general show a remarkable fondness for other animals, and especially for their domestic animals and for mammals and birds. They identify with them, find them beautiful, live with them, and, even if they hunt them, often express admiration for them. There is very little feeling among people that animals are threats even when they are known to be harbingers of disease. This feeling of warmth and protectiveness has probably increased as most people have become less dependent upon agriculture, and no longer see the small wild animals of their neighborhood as potential sheep killers, hen-house raiders, or garden destroyers, as their grandfathers used to.

Perceptions of Biological Communities

There are wide differences in individual perceptions of animals, birds, and fish, possibly because the relationships between animals sometimes resemble those between men. People can see in animals traits like those of humans. Some tend to identify with animals. They develop strong emotional attachments to pets, and particularly to cats, dogs, and horses. The companionship that these animals afford seems to be a truly stabilizing factor in their lives, especially if they live alone. A general identification with animals as helpless in the face of man, and as needing protection, runs very strongly in some people. Professional people in the field of public health and medicine have found that people who are protagonists of animals, and particularly the antivivisectionists, have attitudes that are as impervious to argument as those of many antifluoridationists.

In general, there are emotional needs in many people which are partly satisfied by attachment to and identification with animals, and which are highly valuable to them for this reason. People's defense of animals, their protective attitude toward them, and their hostility to what they see as the aggressive and destructive side of other people is a defense of human needs which is often not as irrational as it initially might seem.

10.11 "The Health Question"

In the past few years, as environmental programs in the United States have grown to a magnitude of billions of dollars, it has become evident that their social and economic consequences may be widespread and that not all of their consequences for human health are happy ones. This has become an increasingly troublesome problem to many members of the health sciences, whose concern is primarily for the health and welfare of people rather than for the environment. The human health task group has chosen to address a number of these timely and troublesome questions that are implicit in the Hudson Basin Project.

1. To what extent can the environmental programs proposed or examined by the Hudson Basin Project make a positive contribution to human health?
2. If there are health benefits from such programs, are these shared equally by all people in the area?
3. Are there aspects of such programs that might be detrimental to human health?
4. Will the detriments and costs of such programs be shared equally by all people in the region in proportion to the benefits that they receive?
5. Is it honest and sound public policy to use a "health argument" to justify environmental programs such as those proposed in the Hudson Basin Project?
6. If one were to design an environmental program with the primary goal of improving human health, what would be an outline for such a program?

At the outset, let it be said that our committee does not question the scientific rationale behind programs to conserve the natural systems of the Hudson Basin region, to use its resources wisely, and to adjust the activities of men to the requirements of nature so that all may survive. We do not question the informed concern of our colleagues in other areas, which motivates them to suggest programs for the conservation and improvement of those aspects of the Hudson Basin region that are their primary concern. We do not question that there is a need for orderly planning for the human use of the Hudson Basin area, or that this planning can serve a valuable purpose. We do not question that the environmental programs that are now underway have been developed by earnest people, acting in what they see to be the best interests of the society. What we do ask is, To what extent can programs aimed at the protection of the natural environment of the Hudson Basin region be relevant to human health?

To What Extent Can the Hudson Basin Project or Any Similar Program Make a Positive Contribution to Human Health?

Clearly, the Hudson Basin Project is not directed primarily at the prevention of human death, disease, and disability, or at the attainment of optimal human growth and development. It is not focused upon people. It is focused upon the environment. It is focused upon the part of the environment that is not the urban environment in which 91% of the people in the Hudson Basin region live. It is not focused on the housing, offices, factories, schools, and other buildings in which people spend 85 to 90% of their time. It is not focused on the relationships of people to other people, or to their social groups, which are among the most important determinants of human health.

Because of all these considerations, it is highly unlikely that the measures it proposes, if accomplished completely, will have any major impact upon the health of the people in the region. In fact, they might not have any measurable impact upon any of the major indicators of human health, although some indications of their effect might be observed in some segments of the population. Our prediction of such an outcome is based not only on the fact that the Project is directed away from those parts of the environment that are most important to human health, but also on the fact that when the Project is concerned with health matters, it is usually concerned with the prevention of potential or putative threats to health, rather than with the prevention of known causes of evident illness. Even if it succeeds in offsetting some of the potential threats to health that have been postulated, it may be difficult to tell whether or not it has done so, since many of the threats are distant and highly improbable.

A review of the kinds of action programs that are being considered in the various policy areas lends support to the statements made in the previous paragraph.

The proposed accomplishments in the area of land use and in the design of "human settlements" will probably have no noticeable impact on human health. At the present time, there is no concrete evidence that the general features of the design of communities or control of the density of the population in a given area have significant impacts upon human health. The programs for the control of noise around airports in rural regions are essentially trivial so far as the health of people in the Hudson Basin region as a whole is concerned. The relocation of communities in areas where natural disasters are likely to occur might prevent a few deaths from floods at some time in the future; but in general, the Hudson Basin region is blessedly free of such natural disaster areas.

If we exclude the health benefits that may be derived from the constant vigilance for the health of people in mines, quarries, smelters, and dusty trades (a concern which is outside the purview of the Hudson Basin Project), the plans for the use of natural resources are not likely to produce much benefit for human health one way or the other. The control of pesticides and heavy metals as potential contaminants of food is a commendable program, but in truth, these do not now produce any noticeable number of deaths or disease in this area. The possibility that nitrates in groundwater might become a problem in Nassau and Suffolk counties is being watched, and there is good reason to believe that whatever threat is present will be dealt with without adverse effects upon human health. This, too, is a highly commendable effort, but it also is not an effort that is likely to make any significant change in the indicators of health.

If the quality of water in the lakes, the rivers, the streams, and the bays and estuaries of the Hudson Basin region is raised until it attains the standards set by the federal government, there is unlikely to be any noticeable decline in the number of illnesses or deaths attributable to gastrointestinal disease. Some cases of contagious hepatitis may be prevented and a few people who might have drowned may be rescued if the turbidity of the water is reduced to the point at which their submerged bodies can be seen. This is not to say that the aesthetic quality of the water may not improve greatly, that the population of finfish and shellfish may not be resurgent, that the pleasures of going to the beach or living by the shore will not be greatly enhanced, or that a threat of serious magnitude to all of the aquatic ecosystems in the region may not have been removed; it is simply to say that there is no sound basis for anticipating that many human deaths or illnesses will be prevented, or that the growth and development of humans will be significantly enhanced by this measure. On the other hand, the residents of the basin will need large quantities of Hudson River water by the end of the century, and a successful program can ensure that this water is available for human use.

Similar considerations apply to the improvement of air quality. The threat of a Donora-like episode of air pollution in the Hudson Basin region is quite small. Despite allegations to the contrary by people who have tried to draw causal inferences from correlational statistics, a causal effect of air pollutants at the present level upon the health of people in the Hudson Basin region is difficult to detect. The improvement in the general level of the air quality up to now has produced little if any change in the rates for respiratory disease and no noticeable change in mortality. If the federal air quality standards are attained for the airshed throughout the region, and there are no changes in the prevalence of infectious agents of cigarette smoking, of pollens, dusts, and other allergenic substances; and if there is no change in the weather, and in the quality of the air within houses, buildings, tunnels, vehicles, and other closed spaces, one can expect little or no change in the deaths or illnesses from respiratory disease among the people in the region.

If careful attention is given to the number, the nature, and the siting of power plants and to their safety, if refineries are restricted, if power transmission lines and oil and gas lines are carefully located, with major efforts not to disturb natural systems and to prevent oil spills or fish kills from contamination of the water, the beneficial effects upon human health in the region will hardly be noticeable in terms of the primary indicators of health.

The development of new facilities for outdoor recreation in rural and suburban areas that are accessible primarily by automobile—facilities often requiring that special equipment be used if they are to be enjoyed—will provide some benefit to the health for that segment of the population that lives nearby, owns automobiles, and can afford the needed special equipment. But such facilities will probably provide no noticeable benefit for the health of most of the people in the Hudson Basin region.

Changes in environmental service systems outside of urban areas—improving methods of sewage treatment and of solid waste disposal—will help the environment. They may prevent some gastrointestinal illness in rural areas, but they will have little or no effect upon the health of people in the Hudson Basin region in general.

The preservation and improvement of biological communities in the Hudson Basin region might have a positive effect upon the health of people in the region, if the fish population were increased to the point at which the cost of fish for human food went down, and if fish became a major source of protein, replacing some of the protein now obtained from animal flesh and from dairy products. We must exclude the great potential value for human health that might be provided by improvements in agriculture and animal husbandry because these are outside of the purview of the Hudson Basin Project. Except for these, the encouragement of biological communities in the Hudson Basin region will have little discernible positive effect upon human health.

Only in the field of transportation could there be a different story. If transportation were carefully regulated by controlling the construction of new highways, by controlling speed limits on present highways, by continuing to improve the safety of highways, and by expanding and modernizing methods of rapid transit, and particularly methods of urban rapid transit, these actions might have a significant positive effect on health. Controlling the speed of travel on highways has already lead to a significant reduction in deaths and injuries from automobile accidents. Further control might lead to further reductions, although other factors (such as drinking and driving) will have to be dealt with also, if major reductions in these rates are to be attained. New, more modern, and more efficient methods of urban rapid transit could have a major impact upon the fatigue and discomfort of large numbers of people who now spend an hour to two hours a day in considerable discomfort traveling back and forth to work.

It is believed by some that preserving the natural environment, and providing urban people with better access to it, may be beneficial to mental health. Since the Hudson Basin Project is directed particularly at that part of the environment other than the urban environment, we have given special consideration to the question of whether or not such programs would, in fact, lead to improvements in mental health regardless of its effect upon physical health. We can begin by a consideration of the urban and rural environments in relation to mental health.

In a recent review of the evidence on rural-urban differences in rates of mental illness, Srole (1972) has performed two tasks: (a) he has shown that the best evidence will not support the hypothesis that the urban environment is more pathogenic; and (b) he has documented the long history of antiurbanism in American thought, from Jefferson, Emerson, and Thoreau to Dreiser, John Dewey, Frank Lloyd Wright, and Robert Park (the urban sociologist), which has clearly nurtured the belief in the pathogenicity of the urban environment.

It seems that one of the philosophical roots of antiurbanism is some degree of belief in what sociologists have called, "ecological determinism." Even though ecological determinism, especially the naive form of it, has had its ups and downs [see Abu-Lughod (1968) for a historical account], its current manifestations are still many: the speculative "psychiatric architecture" literature (Baker et al., 1959; Good et al., 1965; Goshen, 1959), the recommendations and criteria for urban and residential environments which are not based on any evidence (APHA, 1969; WHO, 1965, 1972b), and the reviews of the literature which overinterpret and stretch the meager evidence (e.g., Rosow, 1961; Schorr, 1963).

Ecological determinism which goes beyond the boundaries of hard facts is still a viable position, since definitive evidence negating specific hypotheses about the effects of the physical environment on mental health and human behavior is, in most instances, lacking. However, to make such a position viable, one must not underestimate the role of the purely social environment, and the constant interaction of the physical and the social environments. Moreover, one must also recognize the necessity for complex study designs which would adequately probe and test the interactive effects of the physical and social environments.

Ultimately, ecological determinism is related to the belief that alterations of the physical environment alone will have beneficial consequences for mental health and behavior. A hidden companion belief may be that alterations of the physical environment alone are more feasible and more effective than alterations of the psychosocial environment. Whatever the case, we must not forget the one message that comes through most clearly from all the housing studies, which are the best example of altering the physical environment. No intervention that involves housing can ever afford to neglect the social matrix within which housing is firmly embedded. It is a safe rule of thumb to assume that the physical aspects of the residential environment always interact with social-psychological variables. In most instances, housing intervention has also been a major social intervention. For example, effects of interracial housing are not just effects of spatial proximity; they are also effects of the prestige of the housing authority which, in setting up interracial housing, appeared to legitimize and support interracial contact (Deutsch and Collins, 1951; Wilner et al., 1955). Similarly, benefits of public housing can be erased by a management which is unfriendly and discriminates (Levin and Taube, 1970; Schorr, 1968).

Given these general considerations, let us briefly summarize the evidence in relation to that which has been presented in this report.

There is an obvious and sometimes strong association between environmental quality problems and "evaluative attitudes" (perceptions, concern, complaints, dissatisfaction) toward such problems. Among the salient problems are noise, air pollution, upkeep of neighborhood and distance to facilities, space, comfort, and amenities in the dwelling. This bland and general statement hides numerous exceptions and qualifications, most of which have to do with the role of psychosocial variables: differences in threshold and accuracy of perceiving environmental quality problems; differences in levels of adaption and levels of aspiration; differences in resources which permit coping with such problems; and so on.

One major issue here is how to view the variables of perceptions and dissatisfaction. One can see them as important aspects of well-being, and as significant indicators of quality of life, i.e., as outcome variables in their own right; or one can treat them as intervening variables, important primarily in their relation to the "real" outcome variables, such as the more traditional indicators of mental health. When this latter view is taken, such perceptions and satisfactions are found to have unexamined, unconfirmed, ambiguous, or weak association with the traditional mental health indicators—but apparently never even a moderately strong association with these variables.

The emphasis in the last sentence must be on the word "unexamined" since, indeed, we lack even the basic cross-sectional correlational data on the association between perceptions of and satisfactions with diverse aspects of the environment, and various mental health indicators. [In effect, what was done in the "Survey of Working Conditions" (Quinn et al., 1971) now needs to be extended from the work environment to the general urban environment.] However, it should be anticipated that such correlational studies on unselected populations, while providing useful descriptive information, will not probe enough, and that one will have to "zero in" on vulnerable populations in vulnerable settings to obtain definitive data. Moreover, we should also expect that most of the associations to be found will be *indirect* ones, operating via intervening events and processes.

For example, it may be that perceptions of neighborhoods as unsafe will link up with mental health via a chain involving residential mobility, social uprooting, and occupational change; or one may find that in some people, perceptions of certain persistent environmental hazards (such as air pollution or water pollution) link up with mental health (anomie) via unsuccessful attempts to influence the local or federal bureaucracy and a shattered sense of personal efficacy.

Environmental perceptions involving aesthetic preferences (e.g., beauty of the natural environment) rather than environmental problems and hazards have probably, at best, a tenuous link to mental health. "Ugly" room surroundings may have effects on person-perception (Kasmar et al., 1968; Maslow and Mintz, 1956), but it is difficult to extrapolate much from such laboratory studies. In specialized populations, concern with the natural environment may lead to participation in community organizations, while availability of specific natural settings may lead to certain recreational activities; and both of these may link up with psychological well-being. Finally, we must not forget that for many persons, aesthetic preferences and notions of "good taste" may directly translate into status symbols. And failure to achieve such status symbols (e.g., outside appearance of house, inside furnishings) may lead to loss of self-esteem and public esteem.

The link between various parameters of the environment and social interaction is also a strong one, albeit somewhat more complex. Studies of slums clearly show that substandard housing does not preclude the existence of rich social networks with plentiful social interaction, mutual help, and social control. Studies of rehousing and relocation suggest that the disruption of social networks may be the most significant effect against which the possible benefits of improved housing must be weighed. Vulnerable segments of the society, such as the elderly, may be particularly affected because they are not as able to maintain old social ties (in the face of relocation) or to form new ones. Studies of physical proximity show that the amount of social interaction is correlated with this dimension, and that in homogeneous populations, propinquity and friendship formation are associated. In heterogeneous populations, housing proximity is probably not enough to overcome social class barriers, though certain attitudinal changes may take place (Kasl, 1973). Studies of crowding suggest that crowding may have adverse mental health effects when it represents forced social interaction with members of another household and when there are inadequate resources to escape from such forced interaction. Crowding and high-rise living also have an adverse influence on parent–child relationships and children's play.

Other environmental hazards, such as high level of noise or of vehicular traffic, have not been empirically linked to social interaction, but they represent plausible sources of interference with social interaction and leisure activities, and hence are good subjects for future investigations.

The variable of social interaction may again be viewed in two ways: as an outcome variable in itself, or as a link to mental health. The link between social interaction and diverse indexes of well-being and mental health was seen to be a reasonably well-established one, in the correlation sense. However, the direction of causality is not clear and such correlations do not establish that social interaction contributes to mental health. But the results from longitudinal studies, relating changes in social involvement with changes in life satisfaction and morale, suggest that this may be the case and that being able to maintain stable activity patterns contributes to mental health, especially among the elderly (Havens, 1968).

Aside from these studies of perceptions, satisfactions, and social interaction, the evidence for linkages between environmental quality residential variables and traditional indexes of mental health is extremely spotty, and was noted as we went along. The ecological (urban area analysis) approach has yielded largely ambiguous data—at least with respect to the role of environmental variables. The best designed rehousing studies do not demonstrate any mental health benefits, and it now appears that some of our most cherished hopes—such as raising educational and occupational aspirations by moving people out of slums—will never be realized. However, since there are many studies suggesting that rehousing or relocating may be a severe social uprooting experience accompanied by adverse mental health effects, it is thus still possible that once we can separate out cleanly the adverse effects of relocating via social uprooting, the purely physical aspects of an improved environment may be revealed to have some mental health benefits after all.

In general then, what can we say? We can say that the prevention of the deterioration of the natural environment in the Hudson Basin region can have an important effect in preventing the development of potential health hazards that might occur if land use and the exploitation of natural resources were not regulated, if air and water quality were allowed to deteriorate, if there were no safety program relating to power plants and refineries, if environmental service systems were not maintained at a high level of effectiveness, and if biological communities were allowed to be destroyed. But on the other hand, the several billion dollars that are now being spent in the region for the general improvement of the environment probably will not lead to any significant improvement in human health over the level that is now present. The expenditure of this money for these programs therefore must be justified by goals other than the enhancement of human health.

If There Are Health Benefits from Environmental Programs in the Hudson Basin Region, Will These Be Shared Equally by All People in the Area?

In a certain sense, we can answer yes. Insofar as a program for preserving and rehabilitating the natural environment prevents the occurrence of disasters which might adversely affect the health of large numbers of people, one can reasonably say that the benefit of this prevention accrues to all the people. If the air quality program prevents the deterioration of the general body of air to the point at which respiratory disease from that source becomes a threat to all, the benefit is communitywide. The same can be said for the water quality program, and for the preservation of wetlands in relation to the fish population. Insofar as these programs prevent the disastrous decline of the fish population to the point of representing a threat to the human food supply, the water quality and wetlands programs are of benefit to all.

Yet is must be remembered that the present level of air quality in the Hudson Basin region probably is not producing any significant amount of respiratory disease in the population, and that the present levels of water pollution and wetland destruction, though they might have diminished the fish population in the past, do not in themselves appear to be depleting this population beyond the point that has already been attained. One might reasonably argue that merely maintaining the present levels of air and water quality and preserving the amount of wetlands still available will suffice to prevent disaster. One might answer likewise with respect to land use, environmental service systems, and biological communities. In large measure, the maintenance of present levels of preservation and activity in these systems will suffice to protect human health. We must, therefore, ask, What gains will be attained by additional efforts to improve air quality, water quality, and wetland preservation, or to improve land use, environmental service systems, or biological communities?

These efforts will undoubtedly produce some benefits to health. There will be some pleasure and satisfaction provided to people by better land use, the preservation of open areas, and the preservation of agricultural land and forest. The health benefits from these will be small and will be limited largely to those who derive pleasure and satisfaction from direct association with preserved areas that they value. Unless the preservation of agricultural land in the Hudson Basin region leads to a lowering of the price of some important foodstuff for the population of the region, it is unlikely that any significant or general health benefit will be derived from this. Likewise, there will be some benefits from the more careful supervision and use of pesticides, herbicides, nitrogen fertilizers, and sources of dusts such as asbestos; but the greatest benefit from this will be derived by the relatively few people who work closely with these substances. There will be health benefits from the control of emissions from power plants, the proper siting of refineries, and more careful attention to the construction of power lines and pipelines; but these benefits will accrue primarily to those who live near these facilities or receive aesthetic pleasure from their improved appearance. Improved air quality may prevent a certain amount of respiratory irritation and some symptoms in the general population on excessively stagnant days; and improved water quality may reduce the already few cases of hepatitis derived from rivers and estuaries and prevent a few episodes of acute gastrointestinal disease that are occasionally contracted during swimming. Improved recreational facilities in rural and suburban areas, improved sewage systems and methods of solid waste disposal in these areas, and enhancement and replenishment of the animal and bird life and the natural forests and fields in these areas will provide satisfaction for many people in rural and suburban parts of the Hudson Basin region. If serious attention is given to the construction and development of safe highways and improved rapid transit systems even outside of the major urban centers, this could have an important impact on health. Although in the absence of programs to control drunken driving, the effect on health would be small in proportion to what might be done.

All in all, a review of the Hudson Basin Project in the various environmental policy areas suggests that efforts to improve the environment in these various areas, following the guidelines that are proposed, will yield only very small incremental benefits to human health. These benefits will accrue primarily to people in suburban and rural regions, and to a small proportion of people whose occupation or way of life exposes them particularly to certain hazards. The majority of the people in the region, and especially those who live in urban areas, will participate very little, if at all, in any incremental health benefits from the Hudson Basin Project.

Are There Aspects of Environmental Programs Proposed in the Hudson Basin Project That Might Be Detrimental to Human Health?

Few, if any, aspects of environmental programs that we have examined appear to be directly and immediately detrimental to human health, and probably none are intentionally so. The discontinuance of the use of DDT has had immediate detrimental effects from the resurgence of disease in other parts of the world, but not in the Hudson Basin region. It might be argued that the encouragement of communities of small wild animals in close proximity to human habitation is inviting problems for the future, but this is a potential threat. Direct detrimental effects upon human health immediately resulting from environmental programs are not a problem; but serious detrimental effects upon health and detrimental social effects arising *indirectly* from programs such as the Hudson Basin Project do present major problems that appear as a part of the cost of these programs as they are carried out. This becomes evident when we consider the next question.

Are the Detriments and Costs of Such Environmental Programs Shared Equally by All People in the Region in Proportion to the Benefits That They Receive?

Let us assume, for the sake of this discussion, that the health of every person in the United States is valued equally, regardless of his age, income, education, or place of residence. Let us also assume that environmental programs and health programs that are financed with public money should be aimed at (a) providing the greatest good for the greatest number of people whenever this is possible, and (b) correcting the deficiencies in the environments of those members of the population who can be shown to be exposed to environments that are most detrimental to their health. One can state that the health benefits, and many of the social benefits from the programs proposed in the Hudson Basin Project, will accrue to a relatively small proportion of the people in the region, and usually not to those who have the greatest need; but the costs, with secondary effects detrimental both to health and to welfare, will in many instances fall most heavily upon those who receive little or no benefit.

In the area of land use, the preservation of agricultural land and of natural systems, limitations in the density of human settlements and on new settlements, and restrictions on land use in general, which will benefit a relatively small proportion of the population that live in rural and suburban regions, or who have access to these amenities, will be at the cost of urban residents who desire to move into these areas to have access to the educational opportunities, the social status, and the style of life now available to residents of these areas. Internal migration to areas of greater social opportunity has been one of the means by which members of the American population have improved their condition since the nation was established. There is no good reason to believe that there will be any offsetting benefits to would-be migrants to be derived from the preservation of agriculture or forest lands. It is unlikely that there will be, as a result, any decrease in the price of any food item for them.

The recent history of the Hudson Basin region provides a number of specific instances in which public decisions have been made to preserve environmental amenities for a relatively few people in the suburbs, at the cost of the health and welfare of many people in the cities. One example has been the recurrent defeat of efforts to relocate the major New York airports. The Jamaica Bay Study found that the existence of Kennedy Airport in the midst of New York City creates a noise hazard which disturbs the sleep, interrupts the conversation, interferes with the church services, and impairs the schooling of hundreds of thousands of residents, most of whom are in lower- and middle-income groups. Ground traffic to and from the airport clogs the city streets, and air traffic presents a real though remote threat of crashes, a number of which occurred in the city in the past. Yet every effort to relocate these massive public nuisances to rural areas outside the city, whether in northern New Jersey, on Long Island, or in upper New York State, has been defeated by the combined efforts of the residents of suburban and rural areas who, by comparison, are relatively few and well-to-do, and of well-meaning people who have argued for the greater value of preserving forests, farms, and bird and animal life. These groups have acted in concert with organizations such as the U.S. Department of the Interior. Their victories in defeating the new locations for airports have been generally applauded as victories for the public good.

A second example is provided by the recent proposal for a bridge across Long Island Sound from Rye to Oyster Bay. Such a bridge would provide a direct route from Long Island to upper New York State, to New England, and to the West, bypassing New York City for many motorists and much truck traffic. At the present time, essentially all freight traffic to Long Island is by truck and a very large proportion of the passenger traffic is by automobile. This traffic now must pass through New York City over crowded bridges, through tunnels and heavily traveled roadways in the Bronx, Manhattan, and Staten Island, as well as in Queens and Brooklyn. Failure to build the bridge did prevent the destruction of some valuable and beautiful real estate in Rye and Oyster Bay, and it may have prevented the further commercial development and more dense settlement of the distant parts of Long Island, which the inhabitants there do not desire. It surely meant that many trucks and many automobiles that would have moved at a rather rapid pace across the new bridge and around the city, will now continue to move slowly down city streets, through clogged arteries such as the Cross Bronx Expressway and the Lincoln Tunnel. It meant that a relatively small effect from air pollution from moving automobiles for a few people in Nassau and Westchester was traded for a much larger air-polluting effect of slow-moving traffic in deep cuts and tunnels in city streets for many people in the Bronx, Manhattan, Queens, and Brooklyn. It meant that property values and amenities were preserved along some parts of the shore of Long Island for a relatively few, and on the whole rather well-to-do people, while many thousands of motorists spent many thousands of man-hours in slow and circuitous driving because the bridge is not there. That many of these motorists are truck drivers does not exclude them from the fatigue created by extra hours of driving.

The vast and highly expensive effort to remove sewage and other pollutants from the rivers, bays, and estuaries in the region will probably benefit the health of all, to whatever small extent it benefits the health of any; but it should be noted that these efforts will not necessarily provide greater recreational benefits to urban residents of the Hudson Basin region who need them most. A particularly illustrative example of this was uncovered during the NAS/NAE (1971) study of Jamaica Bay. The study revealed that within one-half hour's distance from Jamaica Bay there were more than 2.5 million people, many of whom had no access to automobiles and no access to any beach or similar place of recreation that they or their families could use on summer days, except for a few massively overcrowded facilities. It was also ascertained that at a cost of several hundred million dollars, the water in the bay was being improved to bathing water quality and that 9 miles of beaches could easily be constructed around the perimeter of the water as its quality improved. These, with the addition of some parks and playgrounds, some sidewalks and, if possible, an extension of present subways, or simply additional express bus lines, might provide a sorely needed recreational facility for hundreds of thousands of people in great need of access to such facilities. But it was also discovered that those who had designed the park were interested primarily in preserving the wildlife in the surviving marshlands in the center of the bay, and had deliberately limited the proposed park to the water area of the bay up to the high water mark, thus effectively excluding the people from the beaches.

The apparently well-intended purpose of this was to prevent people from utilizing the beaches and thereby disturbing the wildlife, and also to avoid the possibility that the National Park Service might become involved in running a city park, which it and the Office of Management and Budget then viewed as not part of its mission. The original design for the park envisioned that people would come to visit it by automobile from distances of up to 100 miles and would have access to some parts of it by using a scenic ferry ride. Not only did this effectively preclude access to the facilities by many urban residents who sorely needed them, but it also meant bringing in additional automobiles driven by surburban residents to a part of New York City in which traffic is already at a standstill on hot days when people try to get to the beaches.

In fairness to all, it must be said that in the Gateway incident, there was no apparent intention on the part of anyone to pursue other than what he thought was a wise public policy. Those interested in preserving the wildlife and the marshes of Jamaica Bay were sincerely interested in protecting what they saw to be a precious heritage of the people of New York. They apparently did not weigh the cost of preserving this in terms of needs of people in the surrounding area. They also did not consider whether or not the social value of a wildlife sanctuary largely populated by seagulls living on the surrounding garbage dumps, and including two brackish ponds from old subway excavations, where a number of interesting and beautiful herons and similar birds could be viewed by perhaps 50,000 students a year, might not be outweighed by the social value of a beach and playground that hundreds of thousands of automobileless parents and children of central Brooklyn and nearby Queens could get to by walking or on a bus. In fact, no real consideration had been given to the possibility that beaches and wildlife sanctuary could coexist. The engineers involved in developing the sewage treatment facilities were enthusiastic for the beaches, but quite unaware that the present plans for Gateway precluded their development. The National Park Service, for its part, had never defined its mission as running urban parks and apparently had never considered that people might get to a National Park by some means other than an automobile, or that National Parks accessible only by automobile are not accessible to all people.

These are specific instances of a general phenomenon that usually acts in a manner not quite so explicit. When the construction of a power plant on the Hudson River or the Long Island Sound is prevented because of its environmental implications, the preserved beauty of the natural environment is enjoyed by the residents of the surrounding area, while the added hazards to health—the fatigue, the lack of refrigerators and washing machines, and the absence of air-conditioning to the subway riders—are experienced by the lower-income groups and the aged poor of New York City. When the use of low-sulfur fuel oil is required to improve the air quality of the city, the extra cost of fuel added to the electric light bill takes a disproportionate bite from the available income of those in the lowest economic groups. When plans to reconstruct the dangerous intersections on the Merrit Parkway are set aside to preserve the scenic beauty of the roadway, among those who pay the costs are the motorists who end up in the accident rooms of hospitals in Greenwich, Stamford, Norwalk, and Bridgeport. When suburban communities buy up vacant land and estates and establish nature centers, land trusts, bird sanctuaries, and parks to preserve their open space, the amenities are enjoyed by those who already live there, but some of the cost is borne by those who would have liked to live there, but now cannot. When parks, picnic areas, camping areas, lakes, beaches, nature walks, and marinas for power boats are constructed with a ready access for those who have automobiles, and who live not far away, but no playgrounds, playing fields, swimming pools, or nearby beaches are provided for much larger numbers of people who do not have automobiles, the benefits of outdoor recreation are made available to those who already have relatively good access to it, rather than to those who need it most and who, nevertheless, have to help pay for it.

One cannot escape the conclusion that the costs and benefits of such programs are distributed among the people in the region in a strikingly disproportionate manner. Although one can contend that if a benefit to health accrues from the efforts to maintain the natural environment as it is now, thus preventing any one of a number of apocalyptic tragedies, then this benefit accrues to all the people in the region. Such a benefit accrues, if it does at all, from the maintenance of the status quo. It is evident that any incremental benefits to the people of the region that might be derived from the efforts proposed under the Hudson Basin Project to regulate land use, to preserve farmland and forest land, to conserve natural resources, to improve water quality, to regulate and restrict power plants and transmission lines, refineries and pipelines, to restrict the proliferation of highways, to improve the quality of air, to develop additional systems for disposing of solid waste, to provide new rural facilities for outdoor recreation, and to support and enhance wildlife, wild birds and game fish, will accrue primarily to the suburban and rural residents and to the middle- and upper-income groups, while the costs in terms of detriments to the health and welfare of people will be borne primarily by urban residents and disproportionately by those in low-income groups.

Is It Honest and Sound Public Policy to Use a "Health Argument" to Justify the Hudson Basin Project?

We think it is not. Although many aspects of the Hudson Basin Project are intended to be beneficial to human health, the benefits to health, in fact, are relatively small, and the incremental benefits are limited to a small proportion of the population. Though not intended to be detrimental to health, the actual operation of such programs and the tradeoffs involved are such that when the incremental benefits to one group are weighed against the cost to other groups, it is not at all clear that the total effect will be beneficial to health in general. In fact, there is good reason to believe that the net effects might be detrimental in terms of the number of people potentially benefited and harmed and the relative needs of those in both categories.

The ultimate rationale for the Hudson Basin Project lies in the prevention of the further deterioration of the natural environment and its wise preservation. The argument for this has a powerful logic of its own, which does not require a dubious human health argument to support it. There is a very strong suggestion that the health argument has been advanced to support many environmental programs primarily because their cost is so great. Their earnest proponents do not believe that people and government would support such expensive environmental programs if the health argument were not also put forward. This has led to a bizarre distortion of emphasis in some programs which has not been able to convince informed scientists, but has misled the public and legislative bodies. It has led to the establishment of large and heavily funded federal programs which seem to spend much of their time and effort gathering evidence that they hope will justify their existence in the eyes of those who voted for them. These efforts further distort the information available to the public. Such considerations apply particularly to the air and water programs. In the opinion of our committee, the incremental benefits to human health from the air and water quality programs will be small. Nothing of substance is added to the argument for these programs by advancing the health argument. Since environmental programs are, on the whole, beneficial and desirable, and since some of them do provide health benefits for some people, why then should there be an objection to advancing the health argument in support of these programs? The reasons are two.

First, many environmental programs are accomplished at some detriment to the health and welfare of many members of the population and especially of those who are poor and live in urban areas. These costs should be weighed in considering the benefits derived from an environmental program. To conceal these costs is a serious mistake, and one that is not morally justifiable.

Second, to advance the health argument in support of an environmental program leads many legislators and many members of the public to believe that these programs, which may cost billions of dollars, are part of an overall health program. The federal budget and the national income are finite. Within these, health programs compete for funds with environmental programs. If environmental programs are seen as health programs, this creates an expectation of health benefits that will not occur, and worse, a reluctance to spend other money on health programs which really are directed at health.

If One Were to Design an Environmental Program with the Primary Goal of Improving Human Health, What Would Be the Outline of Such a Program?

The primary goal of the Hudson Basin Project is to preserve and enhance the natural environment. One could, however, design an environmental program with the goal of enhancing the health of people. Such a program would have as its goal to provide for every person in the region a full span of life, freedom from disease and impairments, and an opportunity to realize his full biological potential for physical and intellectual growth and development, and for interacting with his fellow men in a harmonious and productive manner. Such a program would be aimed at setting up the environmental conditions under which this would be more likely to occur.

Such a program would be aimed at the benefit of all people. However, its initial focus would be upon young people and the next generation—those who have not yet suffered from the impairments of development that damage so many people before or shortly after their birth. It would also be focused especially upon those segments of the population in which deficiencies in health are the greatest.

It would encompass both the rural and the urban environment, but its chief concern would be for the urban environment where the vast majority of the people in this section live and work. It would be especially concerned with that part of the environment that comes into most intimate contact with people—the houses they live in, the buildings they work in, the vehicles they ride in, the clothing they wear, the air they breathe, and the food they eat.

To a major extent, it would be concerned with the social environment, because it is the people with whom a person interacts and his relationship to the social group of which he is a member that is often the ultimate determinant of many aspects of his life, beginning with his birth and development and continuing to his ultimate death.

The general focus of such a program would be on people, their growth and development within their homes, their families, their neighborhoods, and their schools, and their later lives at work and in their families. Its "policy areas" would be quite different from those of the Hudson Basin Project. Nevertheless, it is instructive to consider specifically what might be the policies of a human health oriented program if they were directed toward the policy areas of the Hudson Basin Project.

The policies of such a program toward land use and human settlements would be focused first on the buildings in which people live and work, to make sure that housing units are sound, clean, comfortable, sanitary, and free from vermin, adequately heated and ventilated (and adequately cooled, if there are old people or sick people in the family), with enough room for the families that occupy them, with arrangements to make possible the privacy of those who desire privacy, with facilities for toilets, for washing, for cleaning and for cooking, and with automatic appliances to relieve the drudgery of those who must do the household chores. It would be concerned with offices and work buildings that are safe, sanitary and well suited to the activities that go on within them, and for neighborhoods that are safe, and provide facilities for the types of human interactions that are desired by the inhabitants.

The policy in the area of land use and natural resource management would be primarily that those members of the lowest income groups of the society receive sufficient income so that they can provide themselves adequately with the goods and services essential to their health—food, clothing, housing, transportation, education, recreation, and medical care. There would be a technology geared to provide essential goods and services as abundantly as necessary and as cheaply as possible at the lowest possible cost to the environment and to irreplaceable resources. To prevent adverse human side effects of technology, it would focus primarily upon those people whose occupations or living habits bring them into closest contact with the largest concentrations of damaging substances.

In the field of water quality, this program would be concerned primarily with maintaining the cleanliness and purity of the water that people drink and wash in, and to provide scientifically realistic standards for the safety of water for their swimming and bathing.

The policy toward energy systems would be to develop pricing policies for energy which direct the use of energy into socially desirable activities and away from those that are marginal or unnecessary. It would encourage economy in the use of energy. It would be focused upon the production of enough energy to provide adequate, safe and comfortable mass transit, for necessary refrigeration, cooking, and household appliances for those who lack such services, for adequate heating systems for all homes and working places, and for air-conditioning for the dwelling places of the aged, the sick, and those with cardiovascular and pulmonary disease.

In the field of air quality, the goal would be to provide safe air in the houses, buildings, tunnels, mines, and other enclosed places where people live and work, with special attention to those involved in particularly hazardous trades, as well as safe and pure air in general. It would maintain the quality of ambient air at a level sufficient to prevent exacerbation of the symptoms of those with serious cardiovascular or respiratory disease, and to keep free from high concentrations of known pathogenic materials. It would aim to reduce as far as possible the airborne burden of pollen, highly allergenic plants, and dusts in urban regions; it would make vigorous campaigns for the suppression of cigarette smoking; and it would provide for air-conditioning and cooling of hospitals, nursing homes, homes for the aged, and the dwellings of chronically ill people as well as for working places in which a heat hazard exists.

In the field of transportation, the policy would be to ensure the integrity of the transportation facilities that provide cities with essential food and fuel; to focus upon highway safety, with particular attention to the problems of drunken driving and the driving habits of certain high risk groups; and to make a major effort to provide adequate, comfortable, efficient, and rapid means of mass transit within and around urban areas.

In the field of recreation, the focus would be on the provision of recreational facilities, both indoor and outdoor, especially in urban areas, and especially for people now lacking recreational facilities; on the additional provision for public transportation to those facilities that cannot be reached on foot; and on adequate monetary support for the maintenance of the recreational facilities that are already in existence.

In the field of environmental services, the major effort would be on the removal of solid waste from urban areas.

Finally, in the area of biological communities, the chief focus would be on further efforts to improve agriculture and animal husbandry, to combat the microorganisms that cause diseases of people, to remove from human dwellings and human contacts the disease-causing animals that are commensals of man, and to continue efforts to eliminate disease from domestic animals and household pets.

Chapter 11

LEISURE TIME AND RECREATION

11.1 Introduction

Webster defines leisure as freedom afforded by exemption from occupation, time free from employment, time free from engagement. Recreation is defined as refreshment of strength and spirits after toil. Obviously, all leisure is thus not recreation; but all recreation requires leisure time.

How we spend our leisure time should, ideally, be a personal preference based on temperament, interest, need, and experience. Problems arise because imperfect substitutes must be accepted when numbers of people exceed the carrying capacity of facilities or because an activity is curtailed by environmental degradation, as with pollution of a water area. Leisure time activities range from passive reading or watching television to the more active sky-diving or auto racing. This wide spectrum of activities forced the task group to limit its study to those activities that place an important stress on natural resources.

As society places more emphasis on the amenities of life, things such as attractive natural scenery, clean water and air, and healthy populations of wild animals become increasingly important. Definitions of quality of living

Members of the Leisure Time and Recreation Task Group: Donald F. Behrend, W. Harry Everhart, Elizabeth Hawkins, Rolf Meyersohn, and Sheldon Pollack.

may vary, but consideration, appreciation, and stewardship of renewable natural resources are vital to any acceptable standards.

Leisure time activities can have a far-reaching effect in any region, since they provide a much more unifying and organizing influence in the basin than many other societal pressures. Citizens travel to work in localized and routine routes, but their recreation takes them across many borders, as illustrated by the activities of visitors to New York State. Of 135 million annual visitors to New York State, 45 million were recorded at state parks and public campsites; nearly 16 million went to museums, art galleries, and historic sites; zoos and municipal parks had 20 million reported visitors; and horse racing attracted 14 million. Even industrial tours drew nearly 2 million people (New York State Department of Commerce, 1973).

There are many issues and examples of problems and solutions available in examination of leisure time activities. If we project (as seems justified) that there will be more people, a decrease in the work week, longer vacations, earlier retirements, better retirement programs, and healthier retirement years, then the pressure will continue to mount. This increasing pressure must be examined to consider the problem of peak demands. Would increased charges at peak times help to distribute the load or should we be planning for staggered work weeks? The timing of leisure activities is particularly important, ranging from hours after the working day, to weekends, to the summer vacation. All of these must be correlated with the age of the population and with the structure of the family group. One projection sees, for the rest of the twentieth century, many more households with no children or one child.

The availability of recreation areas is particularly basic and extends beyond simple access. Trails in the Adirondacks may be accessible but unavailable to the citizen who cannot afford a trip to the area. Only a very small fraction of our population has the opportunity to enjoy outdoor recreation. Can we establish a Leisure Time Corps to provide leadership and direction at recreational activities? Many universities have field stations and summer camps that are practically unused during periods of the year, and volunteer or part-time help could save labor problems and costs.

The multiple use of reservoirs, a routine practice in the West, is not well accepted in the East, and the recreational opportunities represented by New York reservoirs are largely closed for leisure time activities. Wilderness areas are appealing, but they prevent general public use. What is the proper ratio of public land development, with national parks and forests to the development of private lands for multiple dwellings, clubs, preserves, and ski slopes? How much land can be reserved for specific and low-density types of recreation?

Consideration of leisure time activities in urban areas must eventually seek solutions to the problems of state parks, amusement parks, ethnic and minority group desires, sports arenas, civic centers, shopping centers, cultural advantages, and the development of television.

What will be the eventual impact of residents of the basin concentrating their recreational activities on their immediate properties or forming small membership clubs with swimming pools and tennis courts? As development of private facilities increases, one result could be less interest in public areas.

An inventory of the relatively untapped resources for outdoor recreation is needed, along with a cost plan for implementation. How much will society pay for accessibility to the Hudson River in both urban and rural areas? Can we provide a linear recreational system along the river with visual access and with trails for pedestrians and bicyclists? Flood plains, at some cost and reordering of priorities, offer exceptional opportunities for development of recreational facilities. When economics are involved, leisure time frequently rates a low priority, but increased demand may change this.

To illustrate many of these problems, and to explore some solutions, we have divided the river basin into the lower Hudson, mid-Hudson, and upper Hudson. Gateway National Recreational Area will illustrate the utility of a recreational area in an area of high population density. The mid-Hudson will provide illustrations of, and solutions to, our urbanizing of rural areas. The wilderness flavor of the upper Hudson will provide examples of people-induced erosion of natural areas and carrying capacity of recreational facilities. Cutting across the regional divisions will be examples using the second-home development and the problems that arise from the use of recreational vehicles of all types.

Rapidly expanding numbers of Americans, devoting their equally rapidly expanding disposable time and money to leisure activities that are themselves new or pseudonew, have given birth to the New Leisure phenomenon. The New Leisure is accounted a phenomenon because of the enormous amounts of money spent by Americans on such activities, thereby constituting a leisure market; and by the great numbers participating in such activities and inactivities, thereby causing a variety of scarcities, traffic jams, and other reflections of unplanned and uneven distribution of resources. The New Leisure is a series of consumer goods and services that have created, and themselves depend upon a variety of leisure industries that tend to perpetuate the New Leisure.

The various growth curves for leisure, however, show only part of the picture. They give the impression that America is becoming a leisure society, with the greatest focus of the greatest number of Americans turned away from work and toward free time. Such an impression would be misleading.

Ever since the Industrial Revolution, when the separation between work and leisure was made, and leisure became a distinct category of human activity, leisure has been a satellite of work, orbiting around it and totally dependent upon it. This satellite quality of leisure remains, even if the orbit has become wider and wider.

During the first part of the nineteenth century the relationship between work and leisure was perhaps more distinct, and the dependent quality of leisure upon work can be seen most clearly. Since work, at least for the bourgeoisie, was the chosen way of expressing one's mission upon earth, leisure was necessarily curbed both in terms of the amount of time one could devote to it and the amount of money that could be spent. Work, for adult middle-class males, was the be-all and end-all of human existence. But it was a special sort of work, involving an entrepreneurial spirit, risk-taking (often with other people's money), adventure, innovation, the creation of physical and social structures that housed capitalism. Yet the leisure of these bold innovators, like their home furnishing, their food, clothing, their choices of domestic life, was nested in Victorian conservatism. Leisure activities were as traditional as work activities were unconventional. Today the reverse is more likely: routine and conventional work and extravagant, imaginative leisure.

The traditions on which leisure activities were based came from the class that the capitalists had replaced—the aristocracy. Such feudal pastimes as riding, hunting, and other country pleasures became the hallmarks of successful middle-class life. Architecture, home furnishings, dress, and design were based on the forms of a dead civilization.

That a great deal of the pleasure aristocracy had derived from the exclusiveness of their leisure activities declined with the democratization of their pursuits was beside the point. The conspicuous consumption of goods and services, formerly restricted to the upper class, provided an appealing goal to the upwardly mobile families; they would display in concrete and conspicuous form what had been achieved on the market place, in the world of trade and business. Thorstein Veblen described the process in 1899 in "The Theory of the Leisure Class," and it did not seem to have been altered significantly until the Great Depression. Sinclair Lewis' novels, such as "Babbit" or "Main Street," written in the 1920s, as was the Lynds' "Middletown," repeated many of the patterns described by Veblen.

Leisure, in those days, democratized the traditional weekend and vacation pursuits of the rich: golf, sailing, development of musical taste, elaborate emphasis on manners, namely, activities that took time, money, coaching, training, and practice—all the elements that the working class was unable to develop and to which many Victorian patriarchs were unwilling to devote themselves, even while insisting that their wives and children do so.

Leisure was tied to class position—that is, being wealthy enough to afford such pastimes—in a special social sense. Many of the activities were pursued in separate places designed for the purpose, most notably in "country clubs," whose membership was based on and became the emblem of a particular place in the social hierarchy—in short, a sign of social status. Leisure patterns provided a way to reinforce the work activities of the head of the house, to assist him in placing his children in the same social class or even in improving their position. These were the processes tying work to leisure and leisure to work.

Such ties have loosened, and many of the processes of nineteenth-century leisure are obsolete. The social class of the family is no longer a major determinant of the leisure practices of their children. Democratization has gone beyond opening the gates of the country club to the successful middle class. Country clubs have, in a sense, gone public, and time for leisure activities, from golf to tennis, has become incorporated into the public schools. Class lines in leisure pursuits have given way to choices in leisure that appear far freer. But are they?

The New Leisure is still a satellite of work, even if not so closely tied to it. The lives of contemporary Americans are still bound by the cycles that existed in the past, roughly divided into three periods: (a) the preparation of the young for work; (b) their entry into the labor force and their spending the largest part of their mature years in the labor force, and (c) their departure into retirement after 30 to 45 years. In the past, such a cycle was reserved, at least in the middle class, for males. Since World War II the great change has been the expansion of this process with the ever-increasing entry of women into the labor force.

To be sure, important changes have occurred within these three stages. The period of preparation has been extended (in 1970, 42% of the people between 16 and 24 were in school—only 34% were in the labor force) and college has become an accepted reason for delaying entry into the labor force. At least as important is the continual expansion of the post-working period because of both increased life expectancy and earlier retirement. This squeeze play has led to the estimate of a retirement life expectancy in 1968 of 7.7 years for the average 20-year-old working man, compared with only 5.8 years in 1950 and 2.8 years in 1900 (Johnston, 1972).

It is in the middle stages, however, that the largest proportion of human life is spent. And it is here that the greatest ties are found between leisure and work. The Industrial Revolution created monstrous working conditions, with enormously long working days, very brief weekends, and virtually no vacations. Such hours were the standard from which the increase in leisure was slowly achieved. The reduction of working time was measured against this inhuman work schedule, and the struggle on the part of labor unions to achieve a 55-, later 50-, then 45-, and now a 40-hour week gave the impression that the process would be continued. Yet the 40-hour week has remained the norm for several decades. Indeed, by 1929 the average weekly hours of production workers had already reached 44, and ever since the end of World War II the average has hovered around 40 hours per week. In industries in which it has reached lower averages (such as 35 hours per week), there is an increase in moonlighting, thereby bringing the average up to 40 or more hours per week, not for the industry but for the worker. In 1971, four million persons (5.1% of the labor force) held two jobs, compared with 3.3 million persons (4.9% of the labor force) in 1962.

The reduction of the work week is not, therefore, a very useful measure of the conditions providing for a New Leisure. Perhaps more meaningful is the increase in the length of paid vacations, the development of Monday holidays and the creation of 3-day weekends. But such expansions in the time available for leisure alter only marginally the human relationship to work as the location in which the greatest amount of time and energy is spent.

The poignancy of work and its discontents is well described in Studs Terkel's (1974) book, "Working: People Talk about What They Do All Day and How They Feel about What They Do," which displays a multiplicity of emotions about its meaning and meaninglessness. What comes through is that work is vitally important, even if the work ethic as such is no longer an important value. Work remains a center of gravity in terms of the pulls and pushes it exerts on disposable time and money, even if it has lost its power of attraction for its own sake.

The expression of dissatisfaction with work has been dramatically brought into American consciousness in the past several years. General Motors workers at Lordstown went on strike in 1972 not for higher wages, but against what had until then been accepted routines of industrial mass production assembly line models. But the workers, many of them young, women, blacks, and better educated than the average assembly-line workers opposed these as inhuman. [see Rothschild (1973) for a description of the plant and the strike]. Worker dissatisfaction, according to the recent task force report entitled "Work in America" (Special Task Force to the Secretary of Health, Education, and Welfare, 1973), appears more prevalent among young workers, in part because they have been brought up to expect more from life, and in part because for them the routine and monotony of factory work (or work in general) is not taken for granted. Dissatisfaction is not exclusively a blue-collar phenomenon; white-collar workers are also increasingly expressing boredom and discontent. Efforts at rearranging positions, giving workers a greater sense of responsibility, and attaching some meaning to the activities workers engage in are some of the ways in which management has begun to cope with such problems.

But the way in which workers themselves cope, and have since the beginning of the Industrial Revolution, is to devote themselves to their lives outside work and to try to do better for their children so that their lives will be more fulfilled. Leisure came out of work in the first place, carved out as a period of rest and rehabilitation, to restore energy and enable the worker to return to work the next day. The increase in affluence has resulted in an extension of leisure pursuits. Yet this devotion to leisure can be seen as an "illusory form of self-realization," because it transfers whatever meaning might have existed in work into attempts to make consumption meaningful (Richta, 1969). The dichotomy between work and leisure, at least for the working class, has lengthened the long arm of the job, of the leash, so that more extravagant and exotic vacations, holidays, and domestic amusements are available but remain distractions. Marx once wrote that "labor should be not emancipated but abolished." He meant that work and leisure should fuse in human activity that can provide adults with control and freedom of action.

No matter how free the New Leisure might be for workers, it is always played out in the context of work. And when the context is gone, as in retirement, problems of boredom with work can be replaced by boredom with life.

Such a description of the New Leisure is only partially true. The other part, one that is often said to be increasingly important, has to do with the nature of postindustrial society in which work is no longer tied to the industrial machine but to the tertiary sector—the providing of services. Activities such as education, medicine, communication, information, and knowledge distribution are based on special skills, a cadre of professionals, a work ethic, and a greater likelihood of inherent meaning in work. If the tertiary sector is expanding, and if the amount of education and training required is greater (and hence the opportunity for workers to give more of themselves), then the kind of "alienated labor" that characterizes the industrial worker's world is also less likely. Labor can be abolished, and drudgery and routine are only part of the process of meaningful work. The possibility that such work is on the increase is great, and here there is a better chance to find a fusion of work and leisure; where free time is more than an escape from work, it is a complement and supplement, and even a busman's holiday. In that case, the intensity in pursuing a set of leisure activities would still be largely dictated by the demands of work, but only those demands that are more willingly assumed.

For workers in the tertiary sector, then, the possibility of leisure is far more promising, but also far less essential. Leisure here is an integral part of the whole life, or "life style." The process of upgrading work enables an upgrading of leisure.

The difficulty with this group in the population is that while disposable money will be available, disposable time will not be. The time surplus required for a life endowed with leisure does not exist for full-time persons in the labor force; but it is in this group that retirement at least has a chance to work as grand finale of self-realization. In between, the kinds of elaborations of leisure that have been witnessed in the recent past can be more meaningfully incorporated, and future families are likely to consist of two-career, two-child, two-home couples, planning their activities, alternating between city and country, between work and leisure, and perhaps less likely to flee from the one to the other.

The sorts of activities that are likely to be found are already prevalent—tourism, travel, tennis, television—all serving to enrich and elaborate the life style that is more appropriate and personal than the kinds of mass leisure activities characteristic of the past. Much as occupations move from chore and labor to real work as they are upgraded, so free time moves from consumption to real leisure as it is upgraded. And somewhere in the future the two merge.

Where, then, is the New Leisure? More responsible than anything else for the attention devoted to the New Leisure is that group in the population which has the willingness and ability to spend disposable time and money on the activities associated with it—the young adult. During the short period between youth and family responsibilities there exists a moment of relative freedom, at least as it is publicly defined. Singles clubs, leisure nomadism, ski trips, and group beach-vacations provide a concentration of attention and money on a fairly small segment of the population for a relatively short period of time, which, because it is repeated over time, rebuilds into a fairly sizable "serial community" of the young. The communal nature of the leisure, the sharing of financial, as well as sexual and emotional costs, provides an interim in which leisure is indeed explored in ways that were unimaginable even a decade ago. Relying on a high level of affluence and a high-technology civilization, with jet travel and weekend commuting on interstate highways, the young can circumnavigate a wide variety of leisure worlds.

Yet such persons are also in the labor force, or training to be. They are students, or junior clerks, or other white-collar workers. When they grow older, most become family men, and become perhaps unwillingly committed to the world of work. Inevitably, their continued leisure pleasures depend on their financial resources, and these obviously depend on their participation in the labor force. If they become young parents, this becomes intensified because of the increased family obligations, with the result that instead of sunbathing they start moonlighting.

The importance of money, banal and obvious, has in no way changed. What has altered is the importance of the "butterfly years," that short period between the caterpillar stage of youth and its extinction. In American mass culture it is glorified by terms such as the "Pepsi Generation," and emulated by elders, but only when they have the time and the inclination. Work remains as the center, at least for the vast majority of the inhabitants of America today.

Rationale and Methodology

The recognition that everything is related to everything else is a necessary initial step in any regional study. Some relationships matter greatly; some are only moderately important; some matter little and others not at all. Clearly, more than a recognition of relationships is required. Ideally, a study system capable of handling a vast array of diverse data should be employed. From the standpoint of the Leisure Time and Recreation Task Group, however, a combination of limited time and funds precluded such an approach. We hope the approach that we followed serves to meet the overall goals of the Hudson Basin Project and provides future investigators with a head start in other studies.

The selection of specific issues required considerable deliberation. Geographic, and, it is hoped, social, balance was obtained by the inclusion of recreation in urban, urbanizing, and wild areas. Thus, Metropolitan New York, the Mid-Hudson and Capital District, and the Adirondack areas were chosen for study. These examples include the problems of recreation in densely populated and highly developed areas, open space preservation, and wilderness management.

Two controversial issues, with great potential environmental and economic impact, were also selected for study. Second-home, or leisure-home, development is increasing in many sections of the Hudson Basin and has the potential to burgeon in several others. The ramifications of such developments encompass a broad range of factors, including water pollution; soil erosion; environmental, transportation, and social service systems; and satellite commercial development. Consuming less land and water, but generating many potential problems, are powered recreational vehicles. Thus power boats, airplanes, and snowmobiles are anathema in the Adirondack wilderness for aesthetic reasons. Elsewhere snowmobiling may be a prized or a despised activity, depending entirely on individual viewpoints. Much the same may be said of power boating.

Integration of the foregoing topics was provided by consideration of the institutional traditions, capabilities, problems, and potential futures within the basin. This is in keeping with the emphasis of the Hudson Basin Project and is absolutely necessary in any realistic study of recreation, especially outdoor recreation. Recreation preferences thus are based almost entirely upon personal inclinations and aesthetic perceptions, resulting in the concern of a great diversity of institutions, organized and other, public and private. And it is the complex interaction of these institutions that results in policies concerning recreation, either through decision or lack thereof.

11.2   Examples of Issues

Urban Recreation Needs

The most pressing needs in urban leisure derive from the cycle of inner-city blight. Most Hudson Basin cities, as is true for the nation in general, house disproportionate numbers of children, senior citizens, and poor people. These populations are generally ill served by public leisure facilities, because of problems of scarcity, difficulty of access, and lack of adequate capital and program budgets. In addition, many core-city parks and recreational facilities suffer from vandalism, segregation, and abandonment. Most of these observations have appeared in the Kerner Commission report in 1968 and in innumerable reports and studies thereafter. It is thus much easier today to identify the leisure and recreation needs of urbanites than it was a decade ago. However, more knowledge is needed of the processes whereby needs may be met and, in some cases, whereby demands for leisure consumption may be altered. Here, in summary form are some of the main lessons to be drawn from recent research on urban leisure patterns.

Outdoor Recreation Ranks Low among Leisure Preferences

Despite the steadily increasing demand for outdoor recreational activities and facilities, outdoor recreation generally ranks low in the population in comparison to the full range of leisure pursuits. Television is by far the most frequently mentioned activity, by over 80% of most samples. Visiting friends and relatives is generally the second most commonly mentioned activity. "Work on house," "home doing nothing," "attending church," and "watching a sport" are generally mentioned by at least one-third of those sampled as activities engaged in during a given week. Generally, less than 15% of respondents will have visited a park or other public recreational facility in a given week. On a monthly basis the figures for park attendance are somewhat higher, but the patterns remain. In a national sample of leisure preferences, Cheek (1972) found that 28% of the respondents visited parks "once or more per month"; of the sample, 44% reported that they visited a park less than once a month, but that they had done so within the past year. Those who had not been to a park for a year or more, and those who could not remember having been to a park, amounted to 28% of the sample.

Despite the relatively low standing of outdoor recreation in American leisure habits, the number of respondents who report themselves as frequent users of park facilities does account for a large and steadily increasing effective demand for public recreational facilities. There is also evidence that people who want the parks most are their heaviest users, without regard to problems of access.

City People Are the Most Frequent Park Visitors

One would guess that people who live in crowded urban neighborhoods would be likely to frequent public parks and to use them as extensions of their personal living space. Suburbanites and rural people should have a more diverse choice of open spaces available to them, often including extensive private home property. Summary data seem to bear out this hypothesis, as indicated in Table 11-1 (Cheek, 1972).

Big-city residents clearly use the parks more than any other group, and there is additional indirect evidence that such use is an outdoor extension of family and neighborhood social relations. That the use of public park facilities is most popular among the most urban segments of the population does not necessarily mean that they actually use them as fully as they might. Cheek's national sample shows that park visitation is lowest among the low income group. Most of the best developed recreational facilities in the Hud son Basin region, as well as elsewhere in the country, are located at distances from inner-city communities that may require considerable travel expense. The U.S. Department of Labor, for example, estimates that an income of over $13,000 is necessary for a family of four to live "moderately" in New York City: that is, without a car, in a rented apartment, and with limited expense for leisure activities. The median family income in New York City in 1970 was $9682. For black families the median was $7150, and for Puerto Ricans it was only $5575. At the same time, over 23%

TABLE 11-1. Frequency (%) of Park Use by Size of Respondent's City[a]

Frequency of park visits	Under 25,000	25,000– 499,999	Over 500,000	Total	Number of respondents
Often	30.1	23.6	46.3	100.0	1011
Occasional	46.8	18.9	34.3	100.0	1576
Rare	49.4	18.7	31.9	100.0	799
Never	56.5	12.5	31.0	100.0	201

[a] Table 8, on page 40, from "Social Behavior, Natural Resources, and the Environment," by William R. Burch, Jr., Neil H. Cheek, Jr., and Lee Taylor. Copyright © 1972 by William R. Burch, Jr., Neil H. Cheek, Jr., and Lee Taylor. Reprinted by permission of Harper & Row, Publishers, Inc.

of New York families earned over $15,000 annually and could afford to travel to developed recreational facilities beyond their city neighborhoods. For the New York family at a minimum-wage income level, even a trip by public transit to Coney Island represents a considerable portion of a weekly budget.

Thus, there exist two definite patterns of urban recreation in cities such as New York. The middle- and upper-middle-class families can and do take extensive trips outside the cities, stopping frequently at state and national parks. The poor—the aged, and disproportionate numbers of minority group members—remain in their neighborhoods and frequent small local parks. For example, in 1969 the Fire Island National Seashore, until recently the closest large national park area to New York City, attracted visitors whose income averaged $16,900 and whose average education extended beyond 4 years of college. This fact only emphasizes the obvious need for greater park facilities and open spaces close to the centers of lower income urban residents.

The Need for Recreational Open Space Is Greatest in Cities

Most recreational planning guidelines estimate that for subregional facilities—those within easy commuting distance of local communities and generally available within a county—18 acres per thousand people is required. By these standards the inner city counties of New York City fall woefully short of providing adequate recreational open space. Manhattan and Brooklyn provide fewer than 3 acres of park and open space per thousand residents and much of the existing space is inadequately maintained. The Tri-State Regional Planning Commission estimated that New York is 38,000 acres short of standard recreation space now; with future population growth demand, this shortage will be aggravated.

Millions of dollars are required to purchase or create open spaces in and adjacent to cities. Tri-State estimated that $300 million would be required to acquire 8000 acres in the New York metropolitan area (TSRPC, 1967). Such purchases have multiple functions, to be sure. In addition to providing open recreational space for present and future generations, they may also preserve important natural areas from environmental degradation.

The Environmental Emphasis in Recreation Neglects Urban Needs

The need to acquire open space to preserve priceless natural areas has become perhaps the single most common theme in the writing of regional planners, urban sociologists, and environmentalists. One excellent example of incorporating open space planning, recreation, and social and economic development is found in a planning report entitled "The Mid-Hudson: A Development Guide," written by Regional Plan Association in New York and Mid-Hudson Pattern for Progress (RPA, 1973). This report proposed a "green-drop" of open land which would guide the future development of the mid-Hudson counties; it is a model which could be followed elsewhere in the Hudson Basin.

On the other hand, there is ample evidence that new open space does not necessarily improve the quality of life for city people unless it is also accompanied by improved recreational planning and programming. A recent study of minority-group recreation patterns in the San Francisco Bay area reported that parks and open spaces were underutilized by urban blacks, Mexicans, and Asians. These groups were not attracted by the heavy emphasis on environmentalist themes in the parks, and they felt the areas lacked adequate indoor recreational facilities.

There are no easy solutions to the dilemma of preservation versus recreation in the parks. Nash Castro, Director of the Palisades Interstate Park Commission (PIPC), pointed out that excessive concentrations of people and programs in one park lead to oversaturation and exhaustion of the resource. He emphasized the need for program diversification and the development of alternative recreation areas to prevent overcentralization, such as occurs in Central Park or at Bear Mountain State Park. Castro also warns that the recreation forms park managers and planners usually provide for city people are often not those they would prefer. He finds at Bear Mountain (with all its miles of trails, scenic overlooks, rustic campsites, and nature walks) that the majority of urban young people seek opportunities for organized group activities, particularly basketball, swimming, roller skating, and arts and crafts. Castro looks forward to the time when the development of additional regional recreational areas will relieve some of the demand at Bear Mountain. The park now hosts an extremely successful Urban Youth Program that transports over 900,000 inner-city adolescents to the park each season by bus and boat (Castro, 1973).

The need to balance environmental appreciation with well-developed recreation programs leads to questioning the adequacy of existing urban recreation agencies to handle the problem. Unfortunately, most evidence suggests that urban recreation programs currently suffer severe budget constraints. It is difficult, then, for them to provide the range of developed and natural leisure setting suggested here.

A Budgetary Crisis Limits the Adaptability of City Park Agencies

In a comparative study of parks and recreation programs in eight major cities, Kraus (1972) found that a general budgetary crisis is severely hampering the delivery of recreational services to people in each of the cities sampled. During his field work, Kraus' informants all agreed that decreases in available funds had severely hampered them in the "manning of recreation programs or the development of badly needed facilities."

Recreation agencies suffer in the competition for scarce budget dollars because many of their staff are seasonal employees hired to handle the needs of vacationing school children. Unprotected by unions or personnel contracts, temporary employees are vulnerable to job freezes and layoffs. An even more serious problem is that administrative and program budgets have not kept up with increases in capital budgeting. Consequently, many of the newest urban recreational facilities are understaffed and have never approached their potential for providing innovative programs in inner city communities.

At the same time that they are suffering a budgetary crisis, public recreation agencies are also being called upon to provide a host of programs directed at special segments of the urban population. Sixty percent of Kraus' respondents in urban recreation agencies reported that they had instituted special programs to provide recreational services to the aged, the handicapped, juvenile delinquents, drug addicts, and the homebound. In his survey of this situation in New York City, Joseph Halper, a former New York Parks and Recreation Commissioner, concluded that the supply of special programs is inadequate to meet their demand. Parks and recreation account for less than 1% of the city's operating budget, with little hope that existing facilities can be maintained properly, and almost no hope for expanding innovative programs for special populations (Halper, 1974).

Most experienced city recreation administrators include the dispersion of recreation services over numerous agencies as another cause of the current budgetary crisis. Education and social welfare agencies and state and national recreation agencies are potential competitors for available money. There is growing consensus that local park and recreation agencies should bear the burden for supplying these basic services to community residents; the other agencies should seek ways to complement rather than duplicate their efforts. Edward Tuck and Joseph Halper of the New York State Parks Commission for New York City have stressed the need for continuing decentralization of local delivery systems in urban recreation. They believe city agencies should specialize in upgrading existing neighborhood and community park facilities. The superagencies at the state and national level would then concentrate on providing services to the general population. In this regard, it is worthwhile to consider the creation of the new Gateway National Recreation Area in the New York metropolitan area as an example of national involvement in environmental improvement and urban recreation.

Events Leading to Establishment of the Gateway National Recreation Area

On May 8, 1962, a staff member of the New York City Planning Department informed the director of RPA that the Planning Commission had approved the first step in the rezoning needed for a large-scale housing development at Breezy Point. It would be unfortunate, the staff member said, not to capture for public use the last undeveloped ocean frontage in New York City. The Board of Estimate acted 2 days later, confirming the zoning change. Few civic organizations were alerted in time to oppose this change.

Such was the unpropitious beginning of the effort that, 10 years later, resulted in the first federal urban park. The effort was supported by a number of influential civic leaders and leading civic organizations working with established minority organizations and emerging community groups and with the city's daily newspapers. Strong forces, however, opposed the move; among them were powerful political leaders, state officials, residents of the Breezy Point Co-op, and private real estate interests. Their influence insured that no state funds would ever be made available for the park. Federal support and monies were sought from the beginning and assured from Stuart Udall, then Secretary of the Interior, and the administrator of the Housing and Home Finance Agency.

There was opposition. Atlantic Improvement, owner of the site, expected a large profit on its investment. The Breezy Point Co-op was fearful of the influx of strangers from ghetto areas if a public park was established. State officials and some city officials anticipated that the condemnation award would be beyond the City's financial ability.

In June 1963, the New York City administration announced its support of the park and worked to secure the support of the Board of Estimate. A compromise solution was effected. Atlantic Improvement's holdings minus the area immediately around their construction site were condemned; the excluded areas were acquired by a later city administration. The area of the co-op was not condemned and the city committed itself to acquisition of the beach in front of the cooperative to tie together the Atlantic Improvement sections on each side of the co-op. Condemnation of the private holdings in September of 1963 allowed the city to move ahead with the park at Breezy Point.

During the mid-1960s, a number of events occurred that led to efforts to have the federal government relieve the city in this major park effort. The State of New York created a state park district that consisted of the five counties of the City of New York. Part of the bargaining that facilitated the creation of this district prohibited state park funds from being expended on the Breezy Point Peninsula. In addition, during this time it was thought that Fort Tilden, in the midst of the city's park land, would be declared surplus military property and could be acquired for half its market value for use as park space. For the rest of the land, the city found that the condemnation award far exceeded its financial ability. In another action, the Department of the Interior, which had supported the park, was denied any role in urban recreation by a Bureau of the Budget circular; instead, the Department of Housing and Urban Development (HUD) was given the role, but it was given little money for the purpose.

In that climate of frustration, RPA conceived the idea of a national seashore that would encompass most of the areas now in Gateway. It rationalized that if Fire Island and Cape Cod, primarily serving urban populations, were eligible for National Seashore status, then areas of similar natural values within the city should not be precluded from federal designation and responsibility. Some New York State Congressional representatives and the Bureau of Outdoor Recreation supported the proposal; however, most top administrators of the Department of Interior did not, largely because of strong opposition by the Office of Management and Budget. Sensing that this would be the beginning of an expensive and difficult involvement in urban recreation, and despite support from New York's and New Jersey's senators and support from the Johnson White House, OMB was unalterably opposed and refused permission for Interior to have the necessary legislation introduced. The senators then secured the strong support of other senators concerned with national parks and interior affairs and introduced a bill to obtain federal support. Only after a favorable stance on this bill was taken by the White House, and with the President's direct intervention was the OMB overruled.

Both Senate and House Interior Committees made visits to the proposed Gateway site. For some time in the Congress there was a growing realization that the federal government should be providing greater recreational opportunities for those unable to reach traditional national parks and seashores. In Gateway, all within the heart of a metropolis, was a series of areas that had the necessary natural attributes: broad beaches, ecologically valuable sections, and large available upland areas. Furthermore, since all were in public ownership, acquisition costs, which had plagued every other recently established national seashore or recreation area, would be minimal.

The first Senate hearings were in 1972. Within one Congress the nation's first federal urban park was created, setting a precedent. Gateway is the most expensive federal park to date; it is the largest in terms of potential visitors. Consider some essential facts about Gateway:

1. Population to be served: 20 million within a 2-hour travel time, mostly by public transportation. The six existing national seashores combined serve only a population of 15 million within a 2-hour radius, almost exclusively by auto.
2. Differing but integrated facilities: each of the four units of Gateway can provide a different form of recreation. Breezy Point and Sandy Hook, New Jersey, will be the most popular for surf bathing. The

Staten Island beaches, with shallow water and mild surf, are suitable for families with young children. Jamaica Bay, with its unique bird sanctuary, is an ecological treasure house with magnificent possibilities for nature studies and great opportunities for boating and fishing. Sandy Hook also is famous for its wildlife, vegetation, and historic landmarks. Floyd Bennett Field offers possibilities for large-scale activities and as a transportation staging area for beach access.

3. Within the 2-hour range of Gateway there are 1.6 million households without cars, representing 28% of all households in the Hudson Basin region and 14% of all carless households in the United States. Based on 1960 census data, 35% of the households in the area to be served had incomes under $5000.

4. Gateway, when fully developed, will increase beach availability for New York City residents by almost 50%.

Who Will Use the Gateway Facilities?

Gateway is a park for the millions of people not privileged enough to afford long vacations or expensive trips. It is for the millions of disadvantaged; it is for those whose summer recreation resources are now limited to an open fire hydrant or, if they are lucky, to a crowded neighborhood pool. Talk of preserving our wildlands and scenic vistas is only rhetoric to the ghetto child of Harlem who knows only the hot summer streets of his own neighborhood.

Facilities currently operating within the Gateway areas now attract about 1.5 million visitors annually. The Great Kills Park and beaches in Staten Island, designed to attract large numbers of visitors from Newark and other New Jersey cities, are currently perceived as local parks for residents of the borough itself. In addition, the beaches are generally too polluted to allow for full water-based recreational development in the immediate future. The Sandy Hook Unit of Gateway was operated, in part, as a New Jersey State Park and can best accommodate visitors who do not seek highly developed recreation opportunities. The greatest recreational activity is centered in the Brooklyn–Queens Gateway areas of Breezy Point (Jacob Riis Park and Jamaica Bay). These areas are flanked by the Rockaways and Coney Island, two of the most heavily used beach areas in the nation. Owing largely to their location at the end of the major mass transit lines, the Rockaways and Coney Island receive over 30 million visits annually; Coney Island is itself still a major tourist attraction.

Ideally, the recreation areas of Gateway, particularly around Jamaica Bay and Breezy Point, should serve the entire metropolitan area and provide recreation services to the region's vast population. It is doubtful, however, that mass transit lines equivalent to those of Coney Island or even Far Rock-away will be constructed to Gateway areas unless such expenditures could be justified by actual demand. On the other hand, mass transit lines would be undesirable if the object is to maintain the Breezy Point section of Gateway as a "natural" beach area. Mass transit lines could result in crowds beyond accepted BOR standards for beach use.

Approximately two million people live in the areas of Brooklyn and Queens within a half-hour ride by public transportation from Jamaica Bay and Breezy Point. Regardless of the facilities planned for these Gateway areas, this is the population that will provide the majority of the area's visitors for week days and on a regular and continuing basis. Fortunately, for planning purposes, this population is generally typical of the rest of the city in its dependency ratio. This ratio is calculated by dividing the combined number of people under 18 and over 65 by the number of people who are between ages 18 and 65. The result is multiplied by 100 and yields an estimate of the number of dependent people (those very young or old) for every 100 persons. This is an important index for park planners, since the dependent segments of any population are also the heaviest users of park facilities on a daily basis, during the summer season and throughout the year.

The average dependency ratio for the sections of Brooklyn and Queens mentioned above is 73, slightly higher than the citywide dependency ratio of 68. For each 100 adults who are potentially in the labor force in this area, there are about 73 children and aged citizens who generally do not work and whose recreational needs are most pressing. Not surprisingly, the poorer the section, the higher is the dependency ratio. To take specific sections of the Brooklyn–Queens area, the East New York ratio is 96 and in Brownsville it is 111. Both of these communities are areas that have high concentrations of elderly white residents, and in the last 10 to 15 years they have received large immigrations of black families in the early phases of family formation and child rearing.

There is no doubt that much of the emphasis in planning Gateway will have to be placed on the aged and the young. Family visitation will be very important also, but on a weekly basis the latent demand for recreational facilities is in the dependent segments of the population. For comparison of the dependency ratio of 73 for sections of Brooklyn and Queens, the overall New York City ratio is 68.

Much of the support for creation of the Gateway system came from the emphasis it placed on the recreational needs of the poor and the racially segregated. To meet this objective, special facilities and programs will have to be designed that will encourage low-income visitors from Harlem and the South Bronx, for example. For a beginning, a busing program for children and the aged should be instituted by the National Park Service for the Gateway areas, including the Great Kills and Sandy Hook units.

If this is not given high priority in Gateway program planning, the park areas will continue to be perceived as amenities for adjacent middle class communities. On the other hand, if NPS can create facilities and programs that are used on a daily basis by all segments of the nearby population, and can extend visitation through special programs, it will have established the essential core of activities and services to the populations it will welcome as Gateway's popularity increases in the rest of the city and beyond. This underlines the most difficult challenge Gateway faces: there are few precedents anywhere in the world for a recreation area that attempts to serve on a noncommercial basis such very diverse population needs.

The Gateway Vision: Can Less Be Better?

The other side of the Gateway vision, in addition to the promise of quality recreation for millions of city people, is the theme of environmental rehabilitation and preservation. Gateway will provide thousands of acres of new open space for city residents and visitors, and will return many of these lands to their former natural state. The Park Service will work closely with local, state, and federal environmental agencies to speed up the improvement of water quality in Jamaica Bay and New York Harbor. The agency will both expand and protect the immeasurably valuable Jamaica Bay Wildlife Refuge and it will take steps to prevent beach erosion through natural means, especially landscaping. But perhaps most significant among its goals, the Park Service will devote much of its programming efforts to environmental education and to the design of experiences that will introduce city residents to the natural marsh and ocean habitats of the areas.

None of Gateway's sponsors wishes the park areas to become "another Coney Island," nor is there much sentiment for the construction of massive new facilities such as those of Jones Beach. The orientation in Gateway planning and in the general approach to recreation in the National Park Service is to provide as much recreational opportunity as possible with a minimum of hard construction. The major exception to this approach comes in the building of "interpretive facilities," that is, educational facilities that serve to instruct the general public and provide the capacity for programs that are cosponsored by other community groups.

Certain modification of this NPS approach will be necessary if the Gateway Project is to combine successfully urban recreation with the ideals of environmental education. The new recreation area will have to incorporate elements of what urban people consider fun. There must be stalls and restaurants where people can eat interesting food; malls where they can be entertained by performers or where they can themselves perform; fields where they can spread out for family and group picnics, or where they can participate in a wide range of sports. There must be walks where people can stroll and look at other strollers, and shaded places where they can kibbitz over quiet games and talk with strangers. There should be exemplary playgrounds where adults can play creatively with their children or leave them alone and feel secure that they will not be hurt or harmed; and there should be campgrounds where families can sleep with a minimum of equipment and expense.

The Park Service can create a park environment in which all these diversions are combined with opportunities for environmental education. These activities do require physical facilities, but none except those designed for year-round indoor recreation need transform the landscape into cityscape. Once the basic facilities are either upgraded or built anew, the key to Gateway's success could well lie in the interpretation of the concept of environment. If the term is limited to its biological meanings, there could be a divergence between the recreational and educational missions of the park. Emphasis would be placed on the Park Service's traditional environmental teaching, and the recreational functions of the park would rest with the provision of amenities and facilities which the people would utilize to the best of their abilities.

On the other hand, if environmental education is taken to encompass the relationships between the social and the natural environments, and if this emphasis is carried through in recreational as well as educational programs, the park could provide a truly new model of urban recreation. This approach would recognize that people want to know more about themselves as much, if not more, than they want to know about plankton or birds. If park staff and park programs can help them in the former, the visitors will be much more interested in the latter as well. Children who frequent the park more or less regularly during the summer ought to have the opportunity to dance, to improve their skills in sports and craft activities, and to learn about their own biological functions, in addition to gaining an appreciation of the marine habitats of the area. If this goal could be accomplished for all age groups and even for casual visitors, few would miss the commercial entertainment of the Jones Beach amphitheatre or the mechanical thrills of Playland and Astroland. If they did miss these experiences, Jones Beach and Coney Island would never be far away. The challenge of Gateway is to provide worthwhile alternatives.

Open Space Opportunities

Apart from Gateway, greater consideration must be given to possible opportunities for redressing the present imbalance in recreation areas and open space in the crowded inner cities. In the New York region there are a number of possibilities.

Waterfront   For economic reasons, shipping and industry have moved away from waterfronts, providing this country with the first opportunity since the Industrial Revolution to reclaim them for "people" uses. The future of the Hudson River's waterfront in New York City, south of 42nd Street, will be determined by which of the alternative plans is selected for the reconstruction of the deteriorated West Side Highway. The "outboard" design for the proposed Westway, which would rebuild the highway at the bulkhead line, will result in 250 acres of new land, of which 80 acres has a potential for recreation use. This would provide Chelsea and Greenwich village, both severely short of open space, with riverside park. Even if the less expensive proposal, rebuilding the highway at grade level, is chosen, it will be possible to bridge over the road to the riverfront at a number of points.

The East River on the Queens side and the Gowanus Canal in Brooklyn are also prime waterfront sites. The first park on the Harlem River, advocated as far back as the First Regional Plan, has been established by the State Park Commission for New York City. An additional Hudson River Park is to be constructed over a new sewage plant in upper Manhattan.

With vast programs presently underway or planned for cleaning up the rivers of the region, additional shorefront, along the Passaic and Hackensack rivers for example, will be available. Also, the Meadowlands, coming to life again ecologically, will, if the present development plan is carried out, provide 6000 acres of preserved marshland, parks, and open waterways.

Surplus Federal Holdings   Military installations make up most of this segment. Several have or will become part of Gateway—Fort Tilden, Fort Wadsworth, Miller field, and Sandy Hook. Ellis Island will be related to New Jersey's Liberty State Park, built from surplus railroad yards. Fort Totten, at the entrance to the East River on Long Island Sound, should be surplus in the near future.

Inner City   The above, while valuable and relatively easy to come by, will not provide much of the daily recreation playspace needed by inner city residents. A conscious policy must be adopted to provide useful playspace as we rebuild areas of the old cities.

Although vest-pocket parks are useful, we should strive for larger parks. On sites cleared through demolition, we should secure parks of 3 to 5 acres to create a green environment and a sense of space, not an asphalt lot indistinguishable from a parking lot. By careful building arrangement,where large-scale redevelopment is in order, we can provide much larger open spaces of 5 to 50 acres. More open space need not mean less density, if such is needed for economic reasons. Many new developments have meaningless plazas and badly arranged space between buildings, which could be better used.

While every recreation area needs some green, not every green area needs active recreation. New playgrounds and swimming pools should be created on the sites of demolished buildings closer to where people live and not encroach on the existing green.

Historical Parks   In Paterson, New Jersey, Alexander Hamilton established the Society for Useful Manufactures at the Great Falls of the Passaic River, the beginning of American industry. Much of the original water raceway, designed by Pierre L'Enfant, remains in existence and is still used. In addition, there remains the largest extant collection of early American industrial buildings and others, slightly less old, still used for manufacturing. The falls is the second highest on the East Coast and now is surrounded by a small park. A magnificent historical park could be created, combining crafts workshops with ongoing manufacturing, a museum of early American industry, and a restaurant overview of the falls. Numerous other historic sites could be sought out: The battle of Long Island was in Queens. Useful for tourists, as well as local residents, would be an historic trail linking many of these sites.

Inventory of Potential Open Space   Because inner-city land can be used for so many purposes, it would be very useful to inventory the older cities and nearby, built-up suburban communities for potential recreation space, particularly with ecological or conservation values (private golf courses and beach clubs, for example). They could be protected by legislation providing that public agencies are given the right of first refusal if the land becomes available for purchase. Such an inventory also would be useful in determining needs for bond issues, Land and Water Fund grant applications, and other applications for money.

The Urbanizing Areas: The Mid-Hudson and Capital District Region

From the Highlands to Saratoga, this 13-county midsection of the Hudson River basin is an urbanizing area open to planned or unplanned growth. Which way will it go? Thoughtful persons in the area see the development and protection of this region as an irresistible challenge.

The area is one of varied scenic beauty, with river cliffs, rolling hills, lakes, streams, the Catskill and Taconic mountains, farms, state parks, and historic villages and towns. The largest urban areas are Poughkeepsie, Newburgh, and the Albany–Schenectady–Troy metropolitan area. The Hudson and Mohawk rivers converge in the Albany area, and the Erie and Champlain canals beckon both the commercial and recreational user.

Population projections for the 13-county area show an increase of about one million between the years 1970 and 2000, bringing the population to roughly 2.7 million (New York State Office of Planning Services, 1972). This midregion between metropolitan New York and the foothills of the Adirondacks can assimilate this increase without seriously altering the life style of the area or abandoning its unique scenic and open corridors. If a commitment to proper planning and coordinated implementation can be generated now, perhaps the mistakes made in other urbanizing regions can be avoided. In the process, options for future generations can be left open.

The population growth will be caused largely by immigration from nearby urban areas. The spillover from New York, Westchester, and Rockland is already hitting the counties of Putnam, Dutchess, Orange, and Ulster. Both Dutchess and Ulster are predicted by the New York State Office of Planning Services to more than double in population by the Year 2000. According to Regional Plan Association, over the next 15 years in the seven-county mid-Hudson region "nearly 50,000 people will be entering the home-buying age group of 30 to 34; this alone represents a potential demand for 25,000 new dwellings" (RPA, 1973). But this immigration for living purposes will also be an out-commutation for jobs. Putnam and Orange populations, especially, will be commuting to Manhattan and to the increasing job opportunities in Westchester and nearby New Jersey and Connecticut. It is in these southern counties of the mid-Hudson region where public acquisition of open space for recreation and protection of natural systems is immediately critical.

In the Catskill region, north of Orange County, where the state already owns considerable lands, the more pressing need is for better public access to state holdings, to open new recreational opportunities, and to protect already accessible lands from overuse. This Catskill region is especially suited for recreation-based activities with recreation-related job opportunities. The importance of guidelines for development is obvious.

The Capital District (considered here as Albany, Saratoga, Rensselaer, and Schenectady counties) is an area favored with generous open space, but the private development patterns are shifting rapidly into areas that are ill-prepared to cope. The cities are losing population, and the impact on suburbs and especially rural areas is severe. Saratoga County was basically rural in 1940, but by 1970 it had almost doubled its population, partly as a result of the opening of the Adirondack Northway in the 1960s. Interstate Route 90, completed from Albany east to the Berkshire Spur of the Thruway, is turning Rensselaer County into a haven for subdivisions, not all of them well located or well planned. The Capital District, according to OPS, will add 200,000 people by the year 2000, with a strong suburban trend.

This suburbanizing and urbanizing development pattern in the whole midsection of the basin can mean that open space for recreation, for change of scene, for green buffer zones between communities, for air-cleansing barriers, underground water and stream protection, and for floodplain management is coming under development demand. So are the viable farmlands, from the mucklands of Orange County to the other vegetable and dairy and orchard farms common throughout the basin. Will we chop up, pave over, dam, or pollute our opportunities to the point where they are irrevocably lost?

Who Is in Charge?

Unless institutions for comprehensive planning and coordination are devised, revised, and/or strengthened, it very well may be impossible to answer the question, Who is in charge of development control? Given the realities of our economic, social, and political system, perhaps there is no alternative to the need for state government to exercise more strictly its authority over the uses of land. The state has a duty to set basic minimum guidelines and controls; beyond that, other levels of government would be able to devise stricter, but never lesser, standards. New York State must also soon devise an acceptable mechanism for coordinating its own activities. Major state construction projects, if not properly meshed with a regional or statewide plan, can have as devastating an impact on the shape of future development and use of land as a poorly placed private shopping center.

Off-and-on attempts have been made to strengthen the state's role in planning, but one wonders about New York's capacity for change when one reads in the "Report of the Commission on Housing and Regional Planning," presented to Governor Alfred E. Smith back in 1926, the following:

> In carrying forward its studies the Commission has been more and more impressed with the need of a permanent agency for planning the physical development of the State. At the present time several State departments are engaged in the preparation of unrelated plans. Coordination may best be accomplished by a planning board in the Executive Department. The Commission now recommends the establishment of such a board . . . (New York State Commission on Housing and Regional Planning, 1926).

This concept was apparently no more popular then than it is now. Instead, the State Commerce Department became the major planning agency over the years until 1966 when Governor Nelson Rockefeller placed some of its unilateral powers in the newly established Office of Planning Coordination within the Executive Department. OPC's imaginative land use proposals soon began to antagonize existing powers at both the state and local level, and in 1971 the State Legislature saw fit to emasculate the agency by slashing its budget 60%. It also changed both its name and its function from "coordination" to "services." At present, each state agency tries to implement its own plans and projects; conflicts occur, and the problems for the Hudson Basin multiply.

A major confrontation recently developed in Schoharie County which dramatizes well the consequences of inadequate state planning. A few years ago, two major state agencies, the Department of Environmental Conservation (DEC) and the Power Authority of the State of New York (PASNY), locked horns over the latter's proposal to construct a second pumped-storage facility on Schoharie Creek at Breakabeen.* The proposed dam would flood 450 acres of another state-authorized entity, the first agricultural district established under a 1971 state law. Furthermore, the upper reservoir of the project would be constructed on lands dedicated by the state for reforestation purposes only. The State Department of Transportation and Office of Parks and Recreation (OPR) are involved, as are local officials and concerned residents. The fact that the electricity to be generated is for peak demand in New York City for use by the Metropolitan Transportation Authority (MTA) does nothing to dampen traditional upstate–downstate antagonisms. When PASNY built its first pumped-storage facility on the Creek (at Blenheim–Gilboa), the public got the impression that no further projects were contemplated. The new Breakabeen proposal, however, if approved, will be only about 2½ miles downstream from Gilboa.

Breakabeen is the first major threat to the integrity of an agricultural district in the State of New York. However, in its environmental impact statement, PASNY plays down the importance of farming in the area, stating that farming is a declining occupation in economically poor and thinly populated Schoharie County (PASNY, 1973). DEC, on the other hand, chief approval agency for agricultural districts, strongly opposed the location of this pumped-storage facility. DEC Commissioner James Biggane found, after a hearing in November 1973, that "the lands which would be removed from production constitute a unique, irreplaceable agricultural asset." This confrontation between the two agencies is not limited to a dispute over preservation of an agricultural district.

Under the Conservation Law, DEC has right of review and veto power whenever a project would alter a stream bed. However, because PASNY, under present state statute, is exempt from the Conservation Law, it feels justified in acting without advice from DEC. PASNY claims that only the Federal Power Commission has decision-making powers in this case.

PASNY, however, is required to get DEC certification for the project under provisions of Section 401 of the Federal Water Pollution Control Act of 1972. This section deals with water quality standards, but in April 1974, PASNY went to federal court to halt DEC's public hearings on the impact of the project. DEC, of course, has review power over the draft environmental impact statement which the FPC must prepare, pursuant to the National Environmental Policy Act of 1969, and DEC will also be a party to the FPC's licensing proceedings.

The Sierra Club, along with about 20 other groups, has become an intervenor in these proceedings. The Club claims, among other points, that

*Since this report was written, the Power Authority has withdrawn the Breekabeen project in favor of an alternate pumped-storage site utilizing the existing Schoharie Reservoir. [Ed.]

energy conservation measures have not been considered nor have adequate alternatives related both to site location and type of project.

In its Exhibit W report, PASNY says that the Breakabeen Project will offer the MTA increased power at peak demand periods, jobs in the local area, low-flow augmentation, modest flood control possibilities, better fish habitat, and—as stated several times in the report—increased recreational facilities (PASNY, 1973).

DEC and others challenge almost all of these benefits. They question the following points.

1. The efficiency of pumped storage facilities, which use approximately three units of power to generate two units of electricity.
2. The lack of specificity on the type of base-load plant to provide the energy to pump the water to the upper reservoir. Will it be the nuclear plant which PASNY has just announced it will build in neighboring Greene County?*
3. The promise of jobs. Even PASNY admits the initial jobs will be temporary and that about 75 to 80% of the jobs will go to skilled workers from the Albany metropolitan area. The State Department of Transportation is trying to complete its priority item, Interstate Route 88, an expressway from Albany to Binghamton, which will make commuting from Albany to Schoharie County a mere half hour's trip. An interchange is planned at one corner of the agricultural district. If I-88 is completed, PASNY's report suggests the possibility that Schoharie County may become "a residential dormitory for the metropolitan Albany–Schenectady–Troy area."
4. Low-flow augmentation. PASNY promises "a minimum flow of 3 million gallons a day even in the driest summers of record" from Breakabeen, but the DEC says this may not be enough "in relation to the water supply needs of Middleburg, irrigation requirements . . ., water quality requirements on account of anticipated discharges from . . . sewage treatment plants, groundwater flows or fishing. The use of irrigation water by only four of the major farms in the valley could exceed the quantities of water proposed to be made available."

Flooding for Fun and Recreation

Under the Federal Power Act, all plans for power plants and reservoirs must include provision for recreational facilities. With this requirement in

*The Greene County nuclear plant project was disapproved by the Nuclear Regulatory Commission early in 1979. [Ed.]

mind, PASNY has proposed for Breakabeen's lower reservoir an all-season shelter with a 50-car parking lot, an informational kiosk, a couple of constant-level ponds for fishing and skating, an easement to a nearby state reforestation area for use by snowmobilers and skiers, and a boat-launching site with a parking lot for 130 cars and trailers. How attractive the lake will be for those boaters is debatable, since the level of the lower reservoir will fluctuate between 3 feet and a maximum of 14 feet. The draw-down will make the water murky and will be especially severe over weekends when most people will want to use their boats. PASNY argues, though, that the already-built Blenheim–Gilboa reservoir is drawing tourists, automatically increasing the need for more facilities. On this point, the Sierra Club says: "We do not believe claims implicit in the Authority's [PASNY's] FPC application that when two lakes are built side by side, the recreational attraction doubles."

A fact overlooked by both PASNY and DEC in their respective reports and findings is the existence, a few miles upstream from PASNY's Blenheim–Gilboa Project, of a large reservoir owned by New York City where no boating or swimming is allowed. If policy were changed to permit multiple use of this reservoir, perhaps PASNY would not be able to use recreational benefits as the major projected benefit to justify flooding of an intensive farming and scenic valley.

The Office of Parks and Recreation has "verified" the overall recreational need for the proposed facilities and will operate and maintain them if the project goes through. The Breakabeen area will not mean another green star on OPR's map, however, simply because the new facility is so close to the existing $2.6 million Mine Kill State Park at the Blenheim–Gilboa Project. The two will be connected by a 2-mile hiking path along the creek.

The Breakabeen recreational plan, like many others, is presented in a narrow context, without pointing out other regional facilities. Although Mine Kill State Park is under the jurisdiction of the Capital District State Park Commission, people from urban areas of the Capital District do not lack leisure-time recreational outlets, most of which are closer to home.

Mine Kill State Park sports a large swimming pool, picnic facilities, and a launching site onto the lower reservoir. In 1973, its first year of operation, the facilities at Mine Kill State Park did not attract many from the Capital District. The swimming pool, however, had "surprisingly good attendance," mostly on a daily visitor basis by second-home owners from New York City and New Jersey, according to the Park Commission. Will the presence of more recreational facilities encourage developers to subdivide the area? In conjunction with the proposed I-88 route across the northern corner of Schoharie County, the potential is apparent. Assuming cars will still be the major mode of travel, bedroom communities are possible there for people who work in Albany. It has already happened in Saratoga County as a result of the Northway (Interstate Route 87).

The Schoharie area may indeed be exactly the best place for increased residential populations, but are state agencies such as PASNY and DOT the ones to make that decision? Though their focus is power plants and highways, they are shaping the future of the mid-Hudson Valley. Without a capable state planning mechanism, aggressive construction agencies will naturally step in to fill the vacuum.

From A to Z: The Importance of Acquisition and Zoning

If state planning is the key to wise land use, zoning and public acquisition of land are two essential and basic tools. How these and other control tools—such as easements, transferable development rights, agricultural districts, land banks, private donations, and trusts—work or do not work (their mechanisms, so to speak) will presumably be handled by other task groups of the Hudson Basin Project. Still, a look at some specific proposals and problems in the 13-county urbanizing area from Orange-Putnam to Saratoga is in order here.

The seven southern counties of Putnam, Orange, Dutchess, Ulster, Sullivan, Greene, and Columbia are featured in the 1973 report by Regional Plan Association and Mid-Hudson Pattern for Progress. One of the many recommendations it makes for this fast-growing area is additional public land acquisition, preferably through a state bond issue.

> The mid-Hudson must preserve enough open space for the enjoyment not only of its own population but also of others living in the New York Region and even for a wider population along the Atlantic Urban Seaboard—projected to grow from 44 million in 1970 to about 65 million over the next 50 years in 150 counties between Maine and North Carolina. In view of that, by the year 2000 some 1,300 square miles, one quarter of the mid-Hudson's land area, should be protected as permanent open space accessible to the general public. This is an increase of 160 percent over the 500 square miles now in public ownership. (RPA, 1973)

The report specifies areas to be acquired, including the Shawangunk Mountains, to connect the Delaware Water Gap National Recreation Area to the Catskills; the Taconic foothills in a chain of parks; some Hudson waterfront north of Newburgh–Beacon; and part of the Delaware Valley area. It also recommends completion and protection of the famed Appalachian Trail and the Long Path, which runs along the Palisades ridge and up to the Catskill Forest Preserve.

In this region—and in the whole basin—public acquisition should concentrate on continuous acreage, not isolated pockets that could soon be violated by incompatible uses next door. Public lands, unless ecologically unique and in need of strict protection, should also be provided with frequent access points. This is especially important in the Catskills area. State-local cooperation is needed to ensure careful planning of the private land areas peripheral to public lands. There is considerable economic growth potential in these areas, which should be encouraged. A well-designed plan would help to prevent exploitative tourist development and would also discourage development which might pollute the air, the streams, or the groundwater on adjacent public property.

The 1974 Interim Report of the Temporary State Commission to Study the Catskills (TSCSC, 1974) highlights the myriad problems involved in accommodating growth without spoiling the rural character of the region and without causing massive damage to natural resources. The area under study consists of the six counties of Delaware, Greene, Otsego, Schoharie, Sullivan, and Ulster, plus six townships in Albany County. Present area population is a little over 375,000, with projected growth by 1980 to almost 430,000 (TSCSC, 1974).

The Catskill region is especially attractive and rich in literary and artistic heritage. It is dotted with historic homes and villages. The Hudson River Valley Commission in 1969 issued a detailed inventory of historic sites throughout the valley. The inventory could be expanded to include scenic vistas and could be the basis for coordinated tours within the region. Although not as strong economically as in some other parts of the Hudson Basin, the resort and recreation industry has an established foothold in the area, and the potential for economic gain from tourism is strong. Rich farmlands, especially in Otsego, Delaware, Schoharie, and Sullivan counties, also contribute to the economy by supplying dairy products, eggs, fruits, and vegetables to the nearby cities maintaining a sizable agribusiness.

The plan for guided development in an area where many of the 161 units of local government have no subdivision regulations, zoning ordinances, building codes, or even master plans is a formidable task. Only 120 units even have a planning board, and the Commission report says that "in many cases, the legal status of these boards is unsure, and in other cases, boards meet so infrequently that they are planning boards in name only" (TSCSC, 1974).

While TSCSC is urging, through numerous public meetings and discussions, that the communities seek professional assistance to help them plan their own future, a hard look at the structure of local governments, their efficiency, their overlap, and their financial and technical resources may be necessary. Perhaps consolidation of some entities or shared services or even shared taxes would help. The overriding ingredient needed is not so much a remedy here and there in governmental structuring but a commitment on the part of the area citizens and leaders, backed by the state, to a comprehensive regional approach toward planned growth and planned preservation.

It is not suggested, however, that the localities sit idle and wait for an approved areawide plan. They can take local action immediately. The Town of Berne is one of the Albany County "hill towns" within the jurisdiction of the Catskill Study and less than a 30-minute drive from the Albany metropolitan area. The calm of this farm-oriented town was recently shaken. Between 1960 and 1970, according to TSCSC's interim report, the "hill towns" of Albany County showed the fastest growth (32.6%) of any section within its jurisdiction.

> This increase is phenomenal when one realizes that during 1960–1970, total population in Albany County increased only 5.1 percent and population in the City of Albany decreased by 10.7 percent. . . . The state-wide average is an increase of approximately 8 percent. (TSCSC, 1974)

Although these statistics were startling to demographers, they were little understood by residents of the area. However, when the 2000 people of Berne became aware in March of 1974 that a developer was planning to construct 626 units on a 109-acre site near Thompson's Lake, they suddenly realized they needed zoning—and soon. The town zoning board had been working on proposals for the previous 2 years, yet no laws were actually on the books to permit any local control whatsoever over a housing development. A quickly organized citizens' committee circulated petitions. Local officials have been calling the required public hearings in rapid-fire order. Meanwhile, residents are hoping that the County Health Department and DEC will delay granting permits for sewage and water supply until their own zoning ordinances can become effective. Westerlo, a bordering town, sees its neighbor's plight and also plans to zone.

As similar open spaces near the cities tend to be developed, more concentration on recreation accessible to urban areas is urgent. In the Capital District in the recent past, most recreationists who could afford to do so headed for the Adirondacks to the north, the Catskills to the south, and the Berkshire and Taconic mountains to the east. Closer facilities have been neglected. However, with a moderate population increase projected for the Capital District from 722,000 in 1970 to 922,000 in 2000 (New York State Office of Planning Services, 1972), an opportunity is afforded to save unique and ecologically significant areas and at the same time build nearby outlets for active recreation. This is especially important now that fuel conservation is recognized as necessary over the long run and in view of the fact that approximately 80% of New York State's recreational facilities are not currently accessible by mass transit (New York State Office of Parks and Recreation, 1972).

With these ideas in mind, the Saratoga–Capital District State Park and Recreation Commission acquired Castleton Island in the Hudson, just a short float south of Albany–Troy on the east side of the river. The so-called island is really a peninsula. It used to be seven separate islands before the Corps of Engineers started using the site as a dumping ground for dredge spoil. Soon, according to the park commission, it is to become a single 7-mile-long, half-mile-wide, "high-capacity, day-use family recreation park, strongly river and boat oriented" (Saratoga–Capital District State Park and Recreation Commission, 1969). Plans include horse stables, a swimming pool, restaurants, 500 campsites, a nature center, baseball fields, and marinas.

State acquisition of land is rarely a simple process. To acquire this small peninsula plus some mainland acreage for a bridge over the adjacent railroad tracks and little Schodack Creek, the Park Commission had to negotiate with seven private landowners plus the Corps of Engineers, the State Office of General Services, the Albany Port District Commission, the Thruway Authority, and the Penn Central Railroad Corporation. Negotiations with the Corps were started as long ago as 1964, but were halted in 1966 when funds for acquisition dried up. The Castleton Island project is again on the active list—a $4-million undertaking.

For less intensive use, state plans for both the Erie Barge Canal and Champlain Canal are focused now on the rejuvenation of areas at the several locks as picnic and hiking areas. Consideration should also be given to a state-managed linear park that would encompass the whole length of the Barge Canal and tie the lock areas together with trails, bikeways, camping grounds, and boat rental facilities.

Of the 49,253 acres of open space now in public ownership in the four-county Capital District, over 83% is owned by the state and 9% by the municipalities (CDRPC, 1972). County-owned open space, with exception of Saratoga, is practically nonexistent. Albany County owns a mere 10 acres; Rensselaer County, 20 acres; and Schenectady, 212 acres divided about evenly between conservation land in Glenville and forestland in the Town of Duanesburg. Saratoga, blessed with the Saratoga Spa State Park which serves as a metropolitan park for the city of Saratoga Springs and environs, owns an additional 3452 acres of conservation land and about 170 acres of county parks.

Recognizing the serious need in all of the densely populated areas for more neighborhood recreational and park facilities, the Capital District Regional Planning Commission, in its "Outdoor Recreation and Open Space Plan of 1972" (CDRPC, 1972), recommended that the present large city parks, such as Washington Park in Albany and Central Park in Schenectady, be taken over by the counties as metropolitan parks to free city funds for more localized facilities. County operation and maintenance might also be feasible for municipal golf courses and city landfills as they become "liberated." If the counties could develop good park systems, and at the same time offer financial assistance to local park programs, an end might be made to the exclusiveness of the understandable "for town residents only" practice.

In summary, the whole urbanizing region from Orange-Putnam to Saratoga-Rensselaer is a positive challenge for governments, for the private sector, and for the citizens of the state. The land area in the region, with its mountains, rivers, lakes, and streams, is adequate to accommodate the population influx predicted over the next 25 years. At the same time, areas can be protected for recreation and open space. It can be an important recreation area not only for its present and future residents but for additional millions of tourists in the heavily urbanized centers along the eastern seaboard. How long the area can maintain its variety, its greenness, and its environmental health depends upon how well both state government and the private sector discipline themselves and their growth patterns. It also depends upon whether local governments and citizens can unite to establish priorities toward maintenance of these ends.

Outdoor Recreation in the Upper Hudson

Natural Resource Base

The upper Hudson region, the northernmost portion of the Hudson River basin, covers the four counties of Essex, Hamilton, Saratoga, and Warren. The natural features of the upper Hudson lend themselves readily to pursuit of leisure time activities and to enjoyment of an aesthetic nature on a year-round basis. The High Peak Country, mostly in Essex County, contains 44 of the famous 46 peaks over 4000 feet high within the Adirondack Park. Among them is Mount Marcy, the state's highest mountain.

The forest covering much of the region consist of stands of mixed hardwoods and softwoods with spurce/fir at higher elevations. Along with cool lakes and streams, forests of this type provide excellent habitat for beaver, otter, black bear, marten, and trout. Golden eagle, osprey, and loon are found here as well as gray jay and spruce grouse. Some of these species are no longer found in the rest of the state, primarily because of the growth of the human population and the consequent loss of habitat. This is in contrast to the needs of the ruffed grouse and white-tailed deer, which require early stages of forest succession often found on the privately owned land in the park.

The numerous lakes, ponds, rivers, and streams provide excellent opportunities for trout fishing, boating, canoeing, and swimming. The Hudson Gorge, located near the Town of Minerva in Essex County and the Town of Indian Lake in Hamilton County, is a unique section of this important river. It has an atmosphere of remoteness and wildness, and during high-water periods the rapids challenge even the most experienced canoeist. The section near North Creek downstream from the gorge is the setting for the 7½-mile annual Hudson River White Water Derby. A section of the upper Hudson River and portions of its tributaries are now protected by the state under the Wild, Scenic, and Recreational Rivers System.

There are only three foot-trails in this area, and none of them closely parallels the river. There are no public roads or other man-made access routes to the river and its surroundings, which have thus been able to retain a wilderness condition.

The Adirondack Park Agency's master plans for state and private land use in the Adirondacks divide the park into 11 classifications. The northern portion of the Upper Hudson falls largely within four of these classifications—resource management area, wilderness, wild forest, and primitive. The category rural use becomes prominent further south where the Hudson flows through relatively flat, pastoral land.

The climate permits both summer and winter leisure activities. The summer months are pleasantly cool, but the early season is plagued by blackflies. Because this region has a long winter season and receives a great deal of snow, it becomes a popular center for winter sports.

Existing Facilities and Outdoor Recreation Activities

The recreation facilities of the Upper Hudson region are both publicly and privately owned. There is little competition between the two sectors except in the area of campsites, where charges influence one another. In some areas of recreation the relationship is complementary. State-operated ski centers, for example, attract customers to privately owned motels, restaurants, and retail stores.

Winter activities center largely on skiing. Excellent ski areas are available for alpine skiing, with the two major ones located on Whiteface Mountain and Gore Mountain. Snowmobiling has seen a boom in popular interest. By 1969 there were within the Adirondack Forest Preserve about 1000 miles of snowmobile trails on state land.* In addition, old woods roads on privately owned land have been made available to snowmobilers.

Some of the ski areas extend the use of their facilities by accommodating summer activities such as dude ranches and riding stables. The Bureau of Forest Recreation maintains horse trails and several hundred miles of hiking trails, lean-to shelters along these trails, and large public campsites. The lean-tos are used extensively; at March Dam 16,855 people signed the

---

*There are now about 800 miles of snowmobile trails in the Adirondack Forest Preserve. The reduction has been mainly due to the closing of trails in areas designated as wilderness. [Ed.]

register in 1968, and at Lake Colden 13,065 signed the same year. These have even been filled on winter weekends in recent years. Boat launches are available, as well as carries and shelters along the canoe routes. The region offers excellent opportunities for hunting, fishing, nature study, and, because of its aesthetic features, for photography as well.

Socioeconomic Aspects

The Adirondack region is among the lowest income areas in the state, largely because of the seasonal nature of the recreation industry. The ski slopes, campgrounds, and marinas each function only a few months of the year, as determined by seasons, vacations, and weekends. The supporting facilities such as motels, restaurants, and retail stores operate on a parallel schedule. Mild, snowless winters or cold, wet summers have an extremely depressing effect on the economy of the region. Will future gasoline shortages have a similar effect?

Large-scale second-home developments, proposed in the last few years, could have a negative effect on the local economy, as has been the experience in Vermont. Rather than being a boost to the economy as expected, the provision of services such as garbage collection and fire and police protection to a seasonal population proved to be a heavy economic burden on the permanent residents.

Besides outdoor recreation, employment is primarily provided by forestry-related industries and crafts. The paper industry alone employs over half of the manufacturing labor force. There is a shortage of professional and technical labor in the region. Employment connected with the tourist and recreation industry is mainly of low skill and low paying—managerial and culinary skills are exceptions—and unemployment is high.

The Temporary Study Commission on the Future of the Adirondacks pointed out that year-round employment and more stable incomes could result from efforts to overlap summer and winter recreation activities. Recreation and recreation-based activities are the major strengths of the Adirondack area.

Recreational Carrying Capacity

With the rapid increase in participation in many outdoor recreation activities in recent years have come indications of overuse of some recreational resources. Recognition of overuse has evolved the concept that recreation areas have a certain use limit, that is, a carrying capacity, and that use of these areas in excess of their limits may result in both damage to the environment and in a less enjoyable recreational experience for the participant.

An increasing number of resource managers have recognized that the carrying capacities of their areas have been exceeded. Consequently, restrictions on the number of recreationists allowed to use public recreational areas are becoming widespread (Anonymous, 1972b, 1974d; Michigan Dept. of Natural Resources, 1972). Unfortunately, a good data base does not exist for these decisions, and the quotas are being imposed based on the judgment of individual resource managers. A quantitative examination of the components of the recreational carrying capacity concept is a high priority research need.

The wilderness character of much of the Upper Hudson offers some unique recreation opportunities. Despite the rugged nature of the region, it is a fragile environment. With the surge in back-country recreation have come the telltale signs of overuse. Given the state's responsibilities for this area, the principle of recreational carrying capacity, as a management goal, should be given serious consideration.

The recreational carrying capacity concept, which derives from the ecological concept of population carrying capacity (Odum, 1959) has been subdivided into three components:

1. *Physical carrying capacity* relates to the effect of visitation on the nonliving aspects of the habitat. The ability of a particular terrain to resist trail erosion is one factor. So is its ability to "absorb" trails, roads, and other man-made objects. Conversely, when man-made features dominate the scene, the physical carrying capacity is exceeded and, in the case of park, the preservation function aborted. Space also determines carrying capacity, notably in the case of a national landmark where the visitor objective is limited. Only a few visitors can stand in a ruin at a time.

2. *Ecological carrying capacity* concerns the effect of visitors on park ecosystems. When the natural plant and animal features are substantially altered, ecological carrying capacity is exceeded and the preservation function is aborted. More particularly, when the presence of visitors causes a particular bird or animal to vacate its normal habitat or to behave abnormally (grizzlies come to mind), ecological carrying capacity has been exceeded. The "fishing-out" of a lake or stream is another illustration, as is the effect on flora of pasturing a horse on a mountain meadow. The ability to dispose of visitor wastes without damage to park ecosystems may prove to be the ultimate measure of ecological carrying capacity.

3. *Psychological carrying capacity* is most subtle and difficult, but in many ways the most important, component of carrying capacity and the effect of other visitors on the attitude of the individual is a concern. The assumption is that a certain atmosphere or setting is necessary so that certain attributes of an environment can be perceived and enjoyed. Levels of tolerance for other people vary, of course. At one extreme is the person for whom the sight (and even the knowledge) of one other camper or camping

party in the vicinity detracts from the quality of the experience. At the other extreme are those whose chief delight in a park experience comes from association with fellow visitors. For them an empty campground would be not only a disappointment but also a positively frightening prospect. (Conservation Foundation, 1972)

A quantitative measure of the physical, ecological, and psychological carrying capacities of recreational resources is essential for the optimum management of these resources. However, the difficulties of quantifying these complex parameters should not be underrated. For example, for many areas the ecological carrying capacity might vary seasonally with the resource base, being particularly sensitive for some time period during the year. Also, recreationists could have identical recreational experiences yet receive varying degrees of satisfaction—psychological carrying capacity— because of different expectations.

Unfortunately, very little research has been done on recreational carrying capacity. It has been only in the past few years that this has been recognized as a problem and that scientists have been willing to tackle this complex interdisciplinary issue. Research in this area, however, can have high payoffs. For example, there is evidence (PASNY, 1973; TSCSC, 1974) that psychological carrying capacity may be determined as much by the impacts of recreationists (such as littering) as by the total number of recreationists themselves using an area. This suggests that if recreationists could be encouraged not to litter, more recreationists could use an area without a reduction in the psychological carrying capacity. The needs for additional and integrated research on recreational carrying capacity are evident.

Managing Resources for Recreational Carrying Capacity and Possible Implications

There is little doubt that if the ecological integrity of the environment is to be maintained and quality recreational experience is to be protected, some restrictions on use will be necessary for selected areas. Therefore, one should consider some possible strategies and their implications. One strategy is simply to use a market rationing system. Raising entrance fees for parks would reduce use of these areas. Such a policy, however, is inconsistent with the general philosophy of public recreation and would discriminate against certain socioeconomic groups. Another approach is a first-come, first-served basis, until a predetermined capacity is reached. This might tend to discriminate against the family that would like to plan a vacation and have some assurance that it will have access to the resource. It is also questionable whether this alternative could truly cope with the magnitude of the problem. An intriguing strategy is a "built-in-frictions" approach. This position holds that limiting the number and sophistication of facilities will in turn limit use. This strategy would be biased in favor of wilderness "purists." A lottery system has also been suggested and may possibly be the least discriminatory method of allocating recreation opportunities. Another approach, which is utilized to some extent at the present, is a reservation system. This may tend to bias against individuals with more spontaneous life styles. Thus, it can be noted that in addition to the basic difficulties in evaluating recreational carrying capacity, there are some important social questions that must be considered when managing recreational resources for their carrying capacity.

Recreation and the High Peaks of the Adirondacks

The 315-mile length of the Hudson River has its origin in a small lake in the Adirondack Park. This Lake Tear-of-the-Clouds, which lies at an altitude of 4800 feet in the High Peak Country. Here also is the Park's largest wilderness area: 1200 square miles in parts of Franklin, Essex, and Hamilton counties. The mountains are generally covered by forests with the visual pattern broken by steep, barren slopes and rock walls. At the timberline the plant life changes to that of alpine meadow or arctic tundra. The Adirondack High Country is the only place in New York State where such a condition may be found, and there it exists only on a dozen of the peaks. The tundra zone is unique and irreplaceable, and its environment is extremely fragile. The groundcover consists of peat—the crumbled, dried-off leaves of sphagnum moss—and low shrubs such as bog laurel, heather leaf, and small cranberry. The plant community is very similar to that of the woodland bog.

This fragile summit environment is now in danger of destruction—not from hostility but from love. Hiking in the High Country has become an increasingly popular sport and is also becoming a considerable environmental problem. The soil is rather shallow and contains a large amount of organic material, making it unstable and easily eroded. The boots of thousands of hikers pounding and digging into the trail disturbs and roughens the surface, which is then readily washed away by the frequent rains. On the summits, the Alpine meadow is already severely damaged by the traffic of hikers coming to enjoy the magnificent scenery. There is no true soil cover in which roots can take hold and intertwine and thus act as an anchor; there is only the thin layer of peat and sphagnum moss. Killed by trampling, it is soon eroded, exposing solid granite rock.

An intensive, 5-year study of the impact of man on the Adirondack High Country was made by Ketchledge and Leonard (1970). They state that "the limited carrying capacity of such fragile alpine environments for people is much lower than the current level of traffic flowing over every one of the twelve higher peaks having tundra conditions at their summits." They recommend consideration of two possible remedial steps: (a) devising measures to slow down the flow of recreationists to the summits; and (b) counteracting the ecological degradation through attempted restoration. Ketchledge and Leonard have been successful in restoring vegetative growth on high elevation test areas. Their aim is to prepare and distribute an erosion control guide for resource managers, suggesting means for restoring eroded high mountain trails and degraded summit areas.

The Temporary Study Commission on the Future of the Adirondacks recognized two major problems of the High Peak Country: (a) the need for trailless peaks to remain trailless and as inaccessible as possible with very few access roads and trails in the vicinity; and (b) that management plans should include measures for relieving pressure on these peaks by diverting hikers elsewhere, for example, drawing attention to the attractiveness of lower peaks, moving back trailheads on present trails, and limiting overnight camping in certain areas.

Growth is forecast in all areas of outdoor recreation. The Adirondack Park, located in the heavily populated northeastern United States, will have growing pressure asserted on it. The major challenge is to determine the level of tolerable trail activity, or carrying capacity of the region, and plan for recreational use accordingly.

Recreation in the Hudson River Gorge

From Newcomb to North Creek, a river distance of 25 miles, the Hudson flows through some wild and relatively inaccessible country. Included in this reach is a spectacular gorge in which the Hudson has cut through the metamorphic rocks of the Adirondacks. In addition to the impressive cliffs along the Gorge, the almost continuous rapids and the towering pines and cedars combine to make the Gorge a particularly attractive area.

As in many portions of the Adirondack Park, the Hudson River Gorge contains a mixture of state and private lands. The state land is part of the Forest Preserve. In addition, the Gorge area has been designated as a Primitive Area through the adoption of the Adirondack Park State-Land Master Plan. Development of private lands in the Gorge area is guided by the Adirondack Park Use and Development Plan.

An interesting controversy has centered on the Hudson River itself. The upper Hudson was originally identified as a potential component of the National Wild and Scenic River System; however, it was subsequently dropped from consideration. A number of locations in the Gorge have been identified as prime dam sites, with the Gooley site specifically noted as being the most favorable site for reservoir storage in the Hudson River basin

(New York Water Resources Commission, 1967). State legislation passed in 1972 designated the Hudson in the Gorge as a "wild river," which prohibits the construction of reservoirs on that reach of the river.

As a result of the controversy over the alternatives proposed for the Hudson River Gorge, a study was undertaken to examine various aspects of allocation questions with a focus on recreational use of the Gorge (McCrory, 1973; PASNY, 1973). The following discussion is derived from information gathered in this research.

There are four access points to the Hudson River Gorge. Two are used by hikers—a public trail to Blue Ledge and also the tracks of the Delaware and Hudson Railroad. Two are used by whitewater boaters—Newcomb and Indian River. Trail registers for self-registration by recreationists were located at these access points. During a stratified, random sample of days, personal interviews were conducted on the trail to Blue Ledge and at the boater access points to determine percent registration. Detailed questionnaires were subsequently mailed to a sample of the recreationists using the Gorge. Approximately 400 questionnaires were mailed to hikers and slightly over 200 to boaters. In all instances, the return rate was over 85%, which gives confidence in the results of the survey. The recreational survey was designed to achieve several objectives. Among these were (a) to determine the magnitude and type of recreational activities in the Hudson River Gorge; (b) to determine the recreationists' evaluation of their experiences in the Gorge; and (c) to evaluate the users' perception of the Gorge environment itself.

Data gathered through the trail registers and the survey sampling provided an estimate of recreational use of the Gorge. Approximately 1000 hikers used the area in 1972 with an increase to 1600 hikers in 1973. Whitewater boating canoes, rubber rafts, and kayaks increased even more spectacularly, going from an estimated 350 boaters in 1972 to almost 900 boaters in 1973. Additional information gathered during the study suggests that the rapid increase in recreational use of the Gorge will continue.

To determine the important recreational activities in the Gorge, recreationists were asked to rate various items relative to their enjoyment of their trip(s) to the Hudson River Gorge. Table 11-2 summarizes this information and indicates that whitewater boating was the most important activity, followed by hiking, fishing, and camping. The response to this question also yielded the interesting results that various environmental attributes of the Gorge—isolation, undisturbed nature, and scenic beauty—were generally rated of greater importance than were specific recreational activities. The only exception to this is the high rating (92% total for moderately important and very important) given to whitewater boating.

Recreationists were also asked why they selected the Hudson River Gorge in preference to some other area for recreation. Table 11-3 gives the results

TABLE 11-2. Importance of Selected Items to the Enjoyment of Hudson River Gorge Trips

	Hikers (%)			Boaters (%)	
Item	Very important	Moderately important	Item	Very important	Moderately important
Fishing	42.0	22.2	Fishing	17.3	17.3
Camping	42.0	21.6	Camping	31.6	26.5
Isolation	60.5	21.6	Isolation	59.2	27.6
Swimming	18.5	27.5	Swimming	15.3	30.6
Undisturbed nature	72.5	14.8	Undisturbed nature	72.4	20.4
Photography	25.0	27.2	Photography	16.3	34.7
Scenic beauty	70.4	18.8	Scenic beauty	73.5	19.4
Nature study	27.6	34.6	White water boating	79.3	14.1
Hiking	45.7	30.2			
Hunting	14.5	9.3			

TABLE 11-3.   Reasons for Selecting Hudson River Gorge in Preference to Some Other Area

Hikers		Boaters	
Reason	Percentage	Reason	Percentage
Fewer people	54.0	Greater challenge	57.1
Desire to explore new area	50.3	Prettier scenery	54.1
Prettier scenery	48.5	Fewer boaters	42.9
Change of scenery	41.4	Closer	38.8
Better fishing	36.5	Explore new area	28.6
More convenient	16.4	Unfamiliar with other areas	24.5
Better hunting	9.6	Better fishing	16.0
Unfamiliar with other areas	7.1	Change	14.3

of this question and further confirms that the attributes of the Gorge environment (as opposed to specific activities) are the key appeals for recreation there. Fewer than 20 of the hikers and less than 10% of the boaters felt that the Gorge was used by too many people. However, many comments were received about litter in the area. This suggests that litter may be an important component of the psychological carrying capacity of the Gorge.

To obtain information on various recreation management alternatives, recreationists were questioned on what improvements should be undertaken in the Hudson River Gorge. The results, as shown in Table 11-4, suggest that, with the exception of a desire by boaters for better parking and launching areas, recreationists desire improvements which entail a minimum of development. A substantial portion of respondents emphasized that they did not wish to see any improvements in the Gorge. The results indicated in Table 11-4 could also be interpreted as a reflection of a degree of "wilderness purism."

TABLE 11-4.   Improvements Desired by Recreationists

Hikers		Boaters	
Improvement	Percentage	Improvement	Percentage
Stock fish	33.3	None	27.6
None	28.4	Provide information	26.5
Improve existing trails	17.0	Stock fish	23.5
Provide information	14.5	Better parking and launching areas	18.4
Build new trails	13.0	Build new trails	15.3
Improve access roads	12.3	Improve access roads	13.3
Provide toilet facilities	11.4	Install camping facilities along river	9.2
Install camping facilities	8.0	Provide toilet facilities	9.2
Supply clean water	7.1		

One of the objectives of the recreation research was to determine if recreationists considered the Gorge to be a unique environment which offered a unique recreational experience. To evaluate the users' perceptions of the Hudson River Gorge, recreationists were asked to indicate their reactions to various statements given in Table 11-5. The results indicate that recreationists do consider the Hudson River Gorge to be a unique natural environment that offers a unique recreational opportunity.

Discussion

The survey of recreational use of the Hudson River Gorge indicates a rapid increase in use of the area. Although most recreationists do not feel the Gorge is overused, there are complaints about the impacts of recreationists. In view of the factors identified as being important to the users' enjoyment of their experiences in the Gorge (isolation, getting away from people, etc.) and the increasing use of the Gorge, one can sense an impending conflict. The research data also suggest, however, that if recreationists developed an "environmental ethic" and refrained from littering and cutting live trees, a larger

TABLE 11-5. Recreationists' Evaluation of the Hudson River Gorge

	Strongly agree (%)	Agree (%)	Disagree (%)	Strongly disagree (%)
The Hudson River Gorge is a unique natural environment.				
Boaters	72	27	1	0
Hikers	66	32	2	0
The Hudson River Gorge is an area of unusual scenic beauty.				
Boaters	69	30	1	0
Hikers	62	35	3	0
A trip through the Hudson River Gorge represents a unique opportunity to get away from other people.				
Boaters	56	38	6	0
Hikers	47	41	10	2
The combination of the recreation opportunity plus the natural environment of the Hudson River Gorge represents a unique wilderness experience.				
Boaters	69	28	2	1
Hikers	60	36	3	1

number could utilize the Gorge without a reduction in total satisfaction to participants. Additional research on this subject could prove fruitful.

Snowmobile and Off-Road Vehicle Use

Off-road recreation vehicles, on the other hand, have the ability to go wherever man will take them, in fragile as well as durable ecosystems, on private lands as well as public, at any time of day or night. Large expansions in sales levels have preceded what regulations of these vehicles we now have, and enforcement has generally been poor because of both a lack of personnel and equipment. As one New York officer recently testified, "It is hard for one conservation officer on showshoes to apprehend the drivers of five violating snowmobiles."

Growth and Future of the Off-Road Recreation Vehicle Industry

Since commercial debut of the snowmobile by Canada's Bombardier Ltd. in 1959 when 259 vehicles were sold, their number in North America has grown to well over two million, of which about three-fourths are in the United States.

In New York, snowmobile registration and licensing have been in effect since 1971, when 135,487 vehicles were registered in the state. In 1972 this number increased 17% to 158,459. The Hudson Basin area accounted for almost exactly one-third of the state's total snowmobile registrations in both 1971 and 1972. Oneida County, which had 10,763 vehicles registered in 1972, and 10,578 vehicles reported as used primarily in that county, easily is the state's leader in both categories. Herkimer and Saratoga counties are also among New York's top 10 snowmobiling counties (Hill, 1974).

Accurate figures on trail-bike sales are not available. Sales of motorcycles increased from approximately 60,000 in 1960 to 1,430,000 in 1970. The industry expects to reach annual sales of 1,700,000 by 1980. These motorcycle figures do not include minibikes, of which nearly 700,000 were sold in 1970. In 1970, over 2.8 million motorcycles were registered for highway use. An estimated 2.5 million additional machines were unregistered and used exclusively off the road. Estimates of off-road use are further complicated because nearly half the vehicles registered for road use possess some off-road capability. An estimated 30% of these are actually used off the road. In New York, registration of off-road recreation vehicles (ORRVs) other than snowmobiles is not required, and there are no firm estimates of their numbers.

Estimates of number of other types of ORRVs nationwide have questionable reliability, but a study (Stupay, 1971) performed for the U.S. Department of the Interior estimated 200,000 dune buggies were in use. Perhaps only with the all-terrain vehicle (ATV) did industry grossly overestimate the American recreation vehicle market. While in the mid-1960s industry predicted a quarter of a million ATV sales by the mid-1970s, in fact United States sales dropped from only 12,000 in 1969 to 9000 in 1970.

The ORRV User: Snowmobilers

A 1971 central New York study showed snowmobile users had a mean age of 35 years, with over half the sample between 21 and 40 years of age. About 95% were male, 86% were married, and 83% had children. The majority of owners (57%) were rural residents, 32% were urban, and 11% lived in villages (Hill, 1974).

With respect to incomes of $10,000 or more, the distribution of snowmobiling families appeared to be similar to that of the general population of both the study area and the state. However, snowmobilers were overrepresented in the $8000 to $10,000 group and underrepresented in income groupings of less than $8000. The leading occupational grouping of snowmobilers was craftsmen and foremen (25%), followed by operatives (21%). Those groupings, together with managers–officials and farmers, were more heavily represented in the sample than in the general population of the study area.

New York snowmobilers can be characterized as quite active. Over half of those studied owned more than one vehicle, primarily to facilitate greater family participation. Users operated their machines an average of just over 3.5 hours/day for 14 days, or a total of 50 hours in January 1971. About three-fourths of this was weekend activity, and one-fourth weekday activity. Nighttime snowmobiling accounted for 46% of total activity.

Many of the reasons cited from the sample for snowmobiling suggest the fervor of participants in the activity: opportunity for adventure (24%), family winter fun (22%), enjoyment of nature (18%), a change in routine (16%), companionship (9%), physical exercise (7%), and the thrill or challenge of fast driving (4%).

Over half the sample estimated that they usually snowmobile more than 10 miles from their departure point, while an additional 40% travel 5 to 10 miles. Two-thirds of the sample prefer interconnecting, natural appearing trails that go through diverse types of countryside. About half the sample were concerned that trails be readily accessible and near snowmobiler homes.

Other ORRV Users

Although studies of other ORRV users have not been conducted in New York, available studies from other states suggest these recreationists have many characteristics in common with snowmobilers. They are young, primarily rural, middle-income people who seek challenge, adventure, and association with others of like mind. While male clubs are common, there appears to be increasing family interest in trailbiking and dunebuggy outings. Research is badly needed on the characteristics, motivations, and habits of these ORRV users.

Damage to Private Landowners

Although substantial public acreages were available for snowmobiling in the area of the central New York study in the form of both forests and frozen lake surfaces, and although over 80% of all snowmobiling was done in the county of residence, the majority of respondents snowmobiled primarily on private lands. Realizing the high demand for use of private lands for recreation and the potential landowner-recreationist conflicts, Cornell University's Department of Natural Resources conducted a statewide study in 1972 of landowners' experience and attitudes toward recreational use of their properties.

This study revealed that of New York's approximately 30 million total acres, nearly 600,000 private acres were posted for the first time in 1972. Approximately 43% of all private lands were posted in 1972, which represents a 72% increase in the statewide posting level over a 10-year period. The study further determined that the rate of posting is still increasing in New York.

The level of landowner–recreationist conflict in New York is highest in the southern portion of the Hudson River basin. Over 60% of landowners south of the Catskills have posted their lands, and about one-half of the landowners in the mid-Hudson area have posted. In the northern portion of the Basin, where parcels tend to be larger and land use competition less intense, about one-fourth of the private landowners post their properties.

Although private landowners are aware of some environmental damage from ORRVs, the main consideration in their decision to post was the behavior of the recreationists. Typical landowner concerns include cutting of fences, harassing stock or wildlife, and snowmobiling near residences at very late hours.

Environmental Damage

Most environmental damage from ORRVs, especially from snowmobiles, is necessarily coupled with misuse. The problem is that too many vehiclists do not wait for a 6- to 8-inch base of snow and, as many private landowners have testified, do not operate their vehicles responsibly. Forest plantations seem to be the most susceptible of vegetative types to snowmobile damage. Regardless of the amount of snow cover, some seedlings will be just under the surface and will suffer damage from even "responsible" snowmobile activity. Private landowners have often reported irresponsible activity that has killed or damaged seedlings that were visible. Significantly, more private plantation owners than other landowners in the Hudson Basin have found it necessary to post their properties.

Other types of vegetation are thwarted by frequent snowmobile activity, especially when ad hoc trails are formed and during periods of marginal snowfall. Controlled experiments on forage grasses such as timothy, clover, and alfalfa have shown that snowmobiling under these conditions can reduce yields by up to 50% because of combinations of damage to root systems and soil compaction.

In the more northern climates, soil compaction has the added effect of increasing the number of below-freezing and below-zero days of subsurface soil temperatures. This not only reduces growth rates because of lower temperatures, but reduces levels of soil bacteria, resulting in slower decomposition of field and forest litter. Many landowners, realizing potential crop loss threats but also being sympathetic to snowmobiler resource needs, have offered snowmobilers the opportunity to make a trail through their fields and forests, with the stipulation that they stay on the trail. This type of offer is usually found to be violated, perhaps not with the group with whom the agreement was made, but by other snowmobilers who followed the trail, and then deviated from it.

Recent wildlife research reports suggest that snowmobiles have the potential to affect deer and other large wild mammals seriously. In some cases, snowmobiling has been suggested to be beneficial by providing trails for these large animals to move about. Recreational snowmobiling has been shown to damage small animal activity and to affect negatively the survival of meadow voles, short-tail shrews, white-footed mice, ground squirrels, and spotted skunks.

Perhaps the type of environmental damage from snowmobiling of greatest consequence is that to the user. Detailed studies by audiologists have shown that the average snowmobiler is subjected to more noise than he or she is able to fully recover from during winter months. The potential for some permanent loss of hearing is even greater for those who, in addition to their snowmobiling activity, are subjected to moderately loud noise levels at work.

Other types of ORRVs may also damage plants and small-mammal species in the environments in which they are used. Damage to marshlands by ATVs has been cited as destroying waterfowl nests and churning marine and estuarine environments. Dune buggies have been cited for destroying sand-dune stabilizing fences, and, along with trail bikes, must be carefully managed in the Fire Island area of Long Island. Trail bikes and other ATVs often form ruts that not only make trails unpleasant to hikers, but also cause soil erosion in areas of steep slopes.

Efforts to Resolve Recreational Vehicle Conflicts

It is important that resource managers and planners understand and accept that, at least for the immediate future, off-road recreation vehicles are
here to stay. Thus, the challenge should be to manage their use in a way that,
so far as possible, allows the types of use desired by vehicle users while
protecting fragile and other important resources.

Most town governments, via state authority, declare specific unplowed
roads as official snowmobile roads; such designation and marking are required by state law. Usually, adjacent town governments have not planned
these routes jointly, and town governments have given little consideration to
snowmobiler desires. As a result, a town might designate five nonconnecting
1- to 2-mile unplowed road strips as open to snowmobiling. Snowmobilers,
on the other hand, prefer at least 10-mile circuitous trails offering some
scenic diversity. Whereas this lack of planning does not give snowmobilers
the right to divert from these short routes onto private lands, the results
are predictable.

One of the finest examples of local-government and private-sector
partnership in the development of a snowmobile trail is in Old Forge in
Herkimer County. Because of the great use of this trail, snowmobiling is one
of the most important economic influences in this portion of the central
Adirondacks and far exceeds the estimated value of other recreation activity.
The Old Forge Trail is a 500-mile system built in 1966 on state, township,
and private lands. It was originally designed, constructed, and maintained
by a local snowmobile club, but the maintenance cost of $6000 per year has
now been assumed by the township. Occupancy at local hotels and motels
in Old Forge has increased almost 100% on winter weekends since this trail
has been in use.

The Second Home

Perhaps the greatest luxury that man can create is a second home, for it
enables him to keep at least one of his homes permanently vacant. In that
sense the second home is a form of conspicuous consumption par excel-
lence. In this country the second home has been a traditional acquisition
of the rich, and today we can still see the remnants of that gilded age which
created Newport and Tuxedo Park.* From this aristocratic past—rooted in
the English country estate as well as the continental country palaces—has
come a movement that has become noticeable for the middle-class Americans as they begin to adopt this upper-class pastime. But there is no doubt

*For a popular historical account of such monuments to conspicuous consumption, see
Amory (1972).

another source, stemming from America's pioneer past, which still exerts a powerful attraction. Hunting cabins, primitive vacation cottages, rustic remnants of America's rural past are another aspect—how large is not known—of the second-home movement.

The Spread of Second Homes

According to the 1970 U.S. Census, 2.89 million households, constituting 4.6% of all households, owned second homes. A second home is defined by the Bureau of the Census as a residence other than the one where the household usually lives, which was owned or rented by the household for the entire year.* Although this is a small fraction of the total number of households, this number is considerable, especially as compared to previous years. Between 1967 and 1970 alone there was an increase of 1.2 million households with second homes, representing a growth rate of almost 25% per year.

As might be expected, urban dwellers are more likely to own second homes than suburban or rural dwellers. In 1967, among households located in central cities, 3.1% owned or rented second homes, compared with 2.9% for households located inside SMSAs but not in the central city, and with 2.5% located outside SMSAs (U.S. Bureau of the Census, 1969).

Not surprisingly, second-home ownership is highly elastic and dependent on income. This is true for both renters and owners of primary residences. At each income level, however, primary residence owners are more likely than renters to own second homes.

The survey on which these data are based was carried out by the Housing Division of the Bureau of the Census as a supplement to the Quarterly Household Survey of Consumer Buying Expectations (U.S. Bureau of the Census, 1969). A total of 11,500 households was interviewed, including 319 households with second homes. No data are available for the Hudson Basin region or even for the Northeast as compared with other regions on the extent to which second homes are an urban phenomenon. It is possible, however, based on the 1967 survey, to give a profile of owned second homes in the Northeast. Table 11-6 presents this profile. There is little reason to believe that the phenomena reported are significantly different for the Hudson Basin than for the Northeast region as a whole. The most important findings as applied to the second-home phenomenon in the Northeast appear to be the following.

Type of Housing   According to the report, "second homes include many types of structures ranging from fishing and hunting cabins and ski lodges to

---

*Included are homes in exclusive possession of a household and also those shared with co-owners or co-renters. Not included are homes located outside the United States, homes used for income and investment purposes only, trailers, tents, and the like.

TABLE 11-6. Location by Selected Housing Characteristics of Owned Second Homes by Region, April 1967[a]

Characteristic	Location of second home			
	Northeast	North Central	South	West
Owned second home . . . (thousands)	542	474	245	235
Total percentage	100.0	100.0	100.0	100.0
Type				
Single-family home	33.6	28.1	40.4	35.4
Vacation cottage	60.9	64.2	49.4	45.6
Other	5.5	7.7	10.2	19.0
Rooms				
1 and 2 rooms	14.5	18.3	9.7	27.2
3 and 4 rooms	40.2	52.4	42.5	51.3
5 rooms or more	45.3	29.3	47.8	21.5
Median number of rooms	4.3	3.7	4.4	3.4
Year built				
1960 or later	20.3	25.2	39.3	27.8
1950 to 1959	26.0	18.9	29.1	34.8
1949 or earlier	53.7	55.9	31.6	37.4
Number of stories in building				
1 story	72.6	87.0	66.5	86.1
2 stories or more	27.4	13.0	33.5	13.2
Equipment and facilities				
With kitchen or cooking equipment	97.1	99.1	91.0	94.4
Lacking kitchen or cooking equipment	2.9	.9	9.0	5.2
With electricity	88.0	92.7	94.5	65.4
Lacking electricity	12.0	7.3	5.5	14.6
With all plumbing faciities	57.0	47.1	76.6	62.3
Lacking plumbing facilities	43.0	52.9	23.4	37.2
Heating system				
Central heating	23.6	18.6	24.6	14.3
Noncentral heating	57.6	70.6	60.7	74.6
Built-in room units	6.2	10.9	8.0	27.7
Other noncentral system	51.4	59.7	52.7	46.7
Not heated	18.8	10.8	14.7	11.1
Length of time owned				
Less than 1 year	4.0	7.5	9.5	5.9
1 up to 3 years	10.2	15.7	14.1	17.4
3 years or longer	85.8	76.8	76.4	76.4
Type of ownership				
Owned by one household	93.5	91.7	91.5	94.6
Owned by two households or more	6.5	8.3	8.5	6.0

(Continued)

TABLE 11-6. (*Continued*)

Characteristic	Location of second home			
	Northeast	North Central	South	West
Value of property[b]				
Less than $5,000	33.0	35.7	18.2	33.0
$5,000 to $9,999	30.1	3.2	34.1	33.6
$10,000 to $14,999	9.6	13.9	31.2	6.8
$15,000 to $19,999	7.5	9.2	12.3	3.0[c]
$20,000 or more	19.8	5.0	4.2[c]	13.8[c]
Median value	$7,800	$7,000	$9,700	$7,400
Principal use				
Seasonal use	71.3	71.9	43.9	47.0
Year-round occasional use	21.7	20.4	46.2	42.0
Retirement use	1.9[c]	7.7	7.2	10.0
Other use	5.1	—[d]	2.7[c]	—
Travel distance from primary home (miles)				
Less than 50	43.0	25.1	24.7	17.0
50 up to 100	25.1	36.1	17.9	32.0
100 up to 200	18.9	14.6	19.7	35.0
200 up to 500	7.1	17.8	14.3	9.7
500 to 3,500	5.9	6.4	23.4	4.3[c]

[a] The results are expressed as percentage distribution.
[b] Includes owned second homes located on places of less than 10 acres and those located on places of 10 acres or more.
[c] Fewer than three households.
[d] Dashes represent zero.

the conventional single-family house." Most of the second homes in the United States are described by their owners as either a "house" (33.6% for Northeast) or a "vacation cottage" (60.9% for Northeast). Houses tend to be more fully equipped and more expensive, although even vacation cottages are for the most part electrified and, in the Northeast at least, have some form of heating. It is perhaps the plumbing that determines more than anything else whether the vacation home is a house or a cottage. Another important difference is the number of rooms. According to the report, 23% of vacation cottages and cabins have only one and two rooms, compared with only 6% of houses.

Type of Use   In 1967, 86% of second-home owners in the Northeast had owned their second home for over 3 years. This percentage is doubtless no longer as high, inasmuch as there has been a great increase in the recent construction and acquisition of second homes. In the Northeast in particular, second-home use has been seasonal. For the sample as a whole, the season in which the house is most frequently used is the summer. Seventy percent of those occupying second homes at certain seasons only reported "summer only"; an additional 26% reported several seasons. Retirement use (which is not a mutually exclusive category) is reported by only a tiny fraction of the sample in the Northeast, as compared with 10% in the West. The actual use is not well indicated in this question, however, since it was worded, What do you consider the principal reason you have this second home? Is it for: vacation or seasonal use; occasional use the year round; or own use after retirement? It is likely that such a question underestimates the degree of use that the second home will, in fact, have after retirement.

In this connection it should be noted that very little research has been carried out. Cribier (1978) estimates that one-third of retired people move at least once to another place, some of them a few years before retirement to find another job in their proposed place of retirement, in what she calls "preretirement migration." The extent to which French patterns apply to this country and to the Hudson Basin region cannot be determined without further research. The 1967 report indicates that 21% of the heads of households owning second homes are 65 years of age or over (compared with 19% estimated for all household heads in this age class).

Distance from Primary Home Travel distance from the primary residence to the second home tends to be short. In the Northeast, 43% of second homes are within 50 miles, two-thirds within 100 miles, and almost 90% within 200 miles. This is far less true in the other regions of the United States. "Two out of three second homes are located within the same state as the owner's primary residence," and vacation cottages are closer than single-family homes. The data in Table 11-7 illustrate this relationship.

Table 11-7 suggests that the farther away the second home, the more elaborate it might be. Possibly the vacation cottage within a 50-mile radius is relatively primitive precisely because the owner can take day trips to it and return to sleep in his primary residence. A very similar indication of propinquity is found in the extent to which vacation cottages, compared with single-family homes, are located in the same state as the primary home (75 versus 54%).

Very little data exist on second homes in the Hudson Basin. It is likely that the percentage of households in the region with second homes is greater than the national average, inasmuch as the New York metropolitan area, as one of the largest urban areas in the world, is likely to generate a disproportionately high rate of second-home ownership. It is possible that in the Hudson Basin region, the percentage of second homes that are occupied only during summers is considerably less than in some other parts of the country whose hinterlands are more remote from urban areas. No data were

TABLE 11-7.   Description of Second Home by Travel Distance from Primary Home
and Location[a]

	Percentage distribution	
	Single-family home	Vacation cottage
Owned second home as percentage of total	33.3	57.7
Travel distance from primary home		
Less than 50 miles	14.0	42.5
50 up to 100 miles	30.4	25.4
100 up to 200 miles	25.6	17.3
200 up to 500 miles	17.7	8.3
500 to 3500 miles	12.3	6.5
Location of second home		
Same state	54.4	75.1
Different state	45.6	24.9

[a] *Source:* Table 8 in U.S. Bureau of Census (1969).

available on the extent to which summer-only cottages are being converted to all-year use, that is "winterized"; it is likely to be considerable, and there is likely to be a decline in the summer-only occupancy of second homes.

To discuss the pattern of second-home ownership in the Hudson Basin region it is necessary to obtain some estimates of the number of the households whose first or second home is located in this region, as well as the overlap. The information, in table form, would fill the cells of Table 11-8.

Cell b would provide the number of households in the region who have no second homes in the region (though they might have second homes outside the region); cell c provides the number of households residing outside the region who have second homes within the region; and cell d provides the number of households who have both first and second homes within the Hudson Basin region. Such information would be valuable in terms of regional planning with respect to the provision of second home resources for both full- and part-time residents of the region.

The Second-Home Phenomenon

Very little social science research has been carried out anywhere in the United States on the second-home phenomenon as a social phenomenon. Hence, to a large extent, this discussion presents a "case study" without cases.

It is clear that two very different perspectives can be assumed around the second-home issue: it can be viewed in the context of the primary home dweller or in the context surrounding the environment of the second home.

TABLE 11-8.   First and Second Homes in the Hudson Basin
Region

	With no first home in region	With first home in region
With no second home	a	b
With second home	c	d

In the first context it is likely to be an urban phenomenon. The impact of the second home is, at least on the surface, small. Only a tiny fraction of the population is involved with second-home ownership, and even if this is one of the most important segments financially, the direct drain is probably small. This is especially true if compared with the impact of ownership on the areas in which second-home ownership is massive. For example, in the southern Vermont town of Jamaica, one of the ancient towns in Windham County, the ratio of permanent residents to second-home residents was recently estimated to be 2.24; in Dover, also in Windham County, the ratio was even lower: 1.85 permanent residents to second-home residents (Zelenka, 1973). The various kinds of social and economic costs and benefits to the community in which second homes are prevalent has yet to be calculated.

In the Hudson Basin region, as in Vermont, second homes are likely to be located in areas that have had settlements. This is in contrast to Western second-home developments—such as in Big Sky, Montana—which are located near national forests and other virgin lands. Hence, second-home settlers, like the white man who first had to contend with the native resistance of the "savages" whose land he appropriated, must contend with the "natives" from whom they purchase the land and with whom they must interact once they have bought it.

Second-home developments and settlements are likely to be located in and around what Veblen has called the country town. What Veblen had to say about such a settlement was far from flattering, but describes quite well the experience of second home "immigrants" upon attempting to establish a foothold.

> The country town . . . is the perfect flower of self-help and cupidity standardized on the American plan. . . . Its municipal affairs, its civic pride, its community interest, converge upon its real-estate values, which are invariably of a speculative character, and which all its loyal citizens are intent on 'booming' and 'boosting'—that is to say, lifting still farther off the level of actual ground-values as measured by the uses to which the ground is turned. . . . Real estate is the one community interest that binds the townsmen with a common bond. (Veblen, 1923)

The economic or social effects of "second-homesteading" upon the communities that have experienced this phenomenon are not well known.

Surely in many instances the areas have been simultaneously saved from bankruptcy and destroyed—destroyed, that is, in terms of the qualities that kept the natives from leaving and that attracted the newcomers. The process that Freud called "wrecked by success," the self-defeating quality of "over-sell," needs sorely to be studied. Such instances might be extreme, and the Hudson Basin doubtless contains many areas now impoverished that could benefit from careful importation of second-home dwellers. The relationship between the second-home dweller and the native needs examination; also requiring research are the degree to which the dependence on the know-how and skill and "motherwit" of the one is matched by financial dependence on the other and the extent to which a feeling of commonality and mutual trust is built up over time as against a kind of master-servant relationship more typically found in the feudal arrangement characteristic of ancient English estate owners.

The institutionalized tensions that exist and are inherent in the relationship between second-home owner and native need to be examined. These are in part the tensions that arise between any "locals" versus "cosmopolitans,"* and refer to differences in life styles, politics, tastes in architecture, leisure, dress, and home furnishings. But more basic are the differences in social class, in the amount of discretionary time and money, and in the level of wealth and income. Such differences in culture and in class are aggravated, no doubt, by the dynamics of the process that the second-home dweller sets in motion with his arrival. He comes as a stranger, an invader, a destroyer of the pastoral, even as he brings economic security (of a sort, for after all, taxes are raised in his wake).

And for the children of the natives, it is likely that the second-home dweller not only provides temporary employment in odd jobs and activities, but also introduces expensive tastes that can mar the "idiocy of rural life." Activities that were hardly indigenous to the Northeast, such as downhill skiing, have in the course of a generation provided for the young natives not only a means of livelihood in the maintenance of the ski lifts and related machinery, but also forms of consumption activity involving the acquisition of skis and paraphernalia, which natives no less than visiting skiers have found compelling. The new ideas and the new spirit that accompany second-home dwellers have not been studied; but like all new things they replace the old, which has its own enthusiasts.

Second-Home Dwellers versus Natives

Interests, goals, life styles, occupational perspectives, tastes, and habits of the second-home dwellers can, under some circumstances lead to direct

---

*Merton (1949) immortalized this distinction in his study of Rovere, New Jersey.

conflict with the indigenous population. The issues around which conflict can erupt and set the two communities against each other cannot be precisely stated. They are analogous to the community conflicts that have been studied in suburbs, and also reported in small towns not undergoing this kind of rapid immigration from "permanent nonresidents" but other kinds of social change (see, for example, Coleman, 1958).

In substantive areas such as the question whether to allow mobile homes in a particular town, the two sides are likely to be lined up at opposite poles, the second-home dwellers opposing them on aesthetic grounds and considering them a form of rural or small-town slum, natives regarding them as a form of inexpensive housing and a convenient and snug mode of living.* Likewise on issues of ecology and conservation, on the use of chemical fertilizers, and snowmobiles there can well occur a split in the attitudes that each group holds.

To generalize, harmony prevails when interests of those two very different groups converge; it is ruptured on issues where there is disagreement. Underlying the conflict is the fact that for the natives, their community is not only a place in which they live and express their life style, but also a place where they make a living, raise their children, and remember their forefathers (sometimes). For the second-home dwellers, the community is one that is related to leisure, not work. The two major leisure activities of second-home dwellers, according to a recent Czech study, are gardening and the care and maintenance of the home (Librova, 1970). Both help support the host community by providing employment and by creating a demand for the locally supplied goods and services needed to maintain the habits of the second-home dweller. But forms of employment such as the occasional hired hand or cleaning woman, carpenter or plumber, or gardener provide little job security, especially as compared with a factory or a retail store, an insurance office, or a coal mine. Hence, relationships are often complex and difficult.

In second-home communities where the season is short, service persons rely on heavy demand during a very short period—and charge accordingly, to the annoyance of the second-home dweller (who often does not consider the fact that the plumber must also survive between Labor Day and Memorial Day).

In the relationship between the second-home dweller and the native there are, in short, different interests, commitments, and frames of reference. The relationship can be interpreted by social scientists in a number of ways: as one of "colonization," of "accommodation," or of pluralism, with the two

---

*A recent study has explored life in mobile homes among retired people (S. K. Johnson, 1971).

groups living out their lives without deep interpenetration. The conflicts themselves can vary not only in terms of their substantive issues but also in the way they are resolved, and the extent to which they are part of a single overall larger conflict. One way in which the probability of conflict can be examined is to consider the composition of the "community" in which both groups reside. Is it predominantly second-home dwellers (as in larger condominium developments), is it mixed, or is it predominantly native? The percentage of the population that is "foreign" constitutes an important characteristic of the community. It affects the social interaction not only between second-home dweller and native but also of second-home dwellers with each other. It is likely that in predominantly second-home-dwelling communities there is the least contact—except in mercantile relationships—with natives.

Conclusion

As architecture has been called "frozen music," so the second home can be seen as a kind of "frozen leisure." It embodies the weekend and vacation site in which free time is spent. It foreshadows, to an extent we have not as yet been able to determine, the locale to which the owner retires when his working period is over. And it represents a form of commitment, emotional and financial, which although it may be shared with the community of primary residence, often takes precedence over it. For New Yorkers who own a house in East Hampton or in the Adirondacks, a great deal of psychic energy may be devoted to its construction and maintenance, to the exclusion of attention to the care of the primary residence. Likewise, the social life of the second-home owners may be concentrated more in the community of second residence than it is in the community of primary residence. The second home, like the "other woman," can constitute a considerable drain on the emotional and financial resources of its owner and a sense of dual loyalties, and at the same time can provide added zest and pleasure to life. No data are available on the "desertion rate" or the "giving up" of the second home, but both statistics would be important for understanding the process and its magnitude.

We have discussed a small minority of the American population, perhaps 5%. Yet this small segment of the population can have a relatively great impact on the environment of the Hudson Basin region. It constitutes a reverse migration, from city to country, a shifting of economic resources and a refocusing upon the more rural parts of the region. At the same time that it creates a new web of ties between city and country—we must keep in mind that 70% of second-home owners come from households within SMSAs—it creates an economic as well as environmental impact on the sometimes fragile culture of the rural and small-town areas. Behind the individual householder's decision whether to buy a second home are a large variety of institutional interests and investments whose financial well-being is based on this decision-making process.

Investment companies and corporations such as Great North Capital Corporation and Boise Cascade have speculated heavily on the second-home market. Builders, developers, subdivision owners, real estate brokers, bankers, insurance companies, as well as the ancillary services and the manufacturing companies that make the products underlying these services, all have a stake in the second home as a real estate market.

Agencies representing the interests of the areas and regions in which second-home development has been greatest are not so clearly definable. In some states, such as Vermont, deliberate actions have been taken to curtail, control, direct, or at least funnel second-home development. With the state's Land Capability and Development and Land Use Plan, Act 250 of Vermont's Land Use and Development Law of 1970, an effort has been made to (a) establish a permit system which pertains to all perspective development of consequence in the state, and (b) require the preparation and adoption of a series of plans for statewide land use.

Each application for development or substantial alteration in Vermont is judged by a district environmental commission according to ten criteria.

Such a comprehensive plan takes for granted the development of further second-home expansion and attempts to regulate it within an overall context in which private enterprise continues to be the major form of recreational service provider. Vermont, like most of the Eastern states, is relying on a kind of enlightened capitalism which, subject to regulations, can maintain a balance between private and public welfare. No proposals are entertained to expand the size of the Green Mountain National Forest, or to attempt to develop lands that could become part of the National Park Service's recreational areas or wilderness areas or some other kind of preserve. It is assumed that the kind of enlightened curbing of the excesses of real estate speculation and overbuilding is adequate for dealing with the increasing demand for open space and weekend and vacation use that seems characteristic of contemporary America.

It is possible, and probably necessary, to consider the negative consequences of various kinds of second-home development by private developers. To the extent this is an egalitarian society in terms of the access to scarce if not priceless resources, it is perhaps necessary to consider consequences of planning far more radical than the restrictions represented by Vermont's Act 250.* Possibly the cash nexus is simply not the proper distributional means for such resources, and even the most enlightened environmental planning will only mean that the cost of second homes increases and there-

---

*For a discussion of Act 250, see Levy (1973) and also *Vermont Life*, Spring, 1972, pp. 50–52.

fore becomes less available to the poor and more available to the rich, and indeed can serve as an even more profitable financial investment. Alternative modes of distributing second-home facilities ought to be explored and the consequences of second homes should be considered from a variety of points of view, not only in terms of the threat to the natural environment, or the rural ethos that might still exist in the hinterlands, but also in terms of the increasing division that it can foster in the areas of primary residence. Those for whom a weekend in the country is perhaps most important are frequently those least likely to be able to afford such a respite.

11.3   The Administrative and Institutional Character of Recreation and Leisure

Effective administration is one key to an effective program. Programs that relate to leisure time and recreation require attention on several fronts. To begin the process of the provision of recreation, land must be available in quantities sufficient to satisfy the demand of the population. Land-rights acquisition may be effected by such legal mechanisms as fee-simple purchase, easement, condemnation, or zoning on the recreationists' part, and gift or dedication (whether or not required by law) on the owner's part. Thus, an initial set of rights is attached to the land.

Land must be managed for recreational use. Generally, opposition to the pristine state of land for recreation comes from such opposing points of view as that of the day tripper and of the strict conservationist. Recreational development takes on many forms. There are the narrow trails in the high peak country of the Adirondacks punctuated by lean-tos; there are meticulously landscaped urban parks with concert shells and concessions. All recreational development requires that capital be amassed, expended wisely, and accounted for; planning must be done to ensure the adequacy and suitability of the design. Thus, these financial and social aspects of recreation add a second set of administrative institutions that are put upon the land.

Development may not stop with the provision of a delightful site. Like all institutions—for recreation sites themselves become institutions—continuing management is required to maintain and improve the site. This implies continuing planning, additional capital, and advanced land development. Management will ensure proper accountability to the owners or trustees and suitability of the site to recreation demand. This third set of institutions, then, is administration and is entirely cultural.

Just a couple of years ago "Parks are for People" was the rage phrase in recreation. It means that land may not only be set aside and developed and maintained for recreation; the human element must be added. Programs in parks are for people; programs of recreation, generally, are even necessary to draw attendance to a site. These could be early morning bird walks, lectures on geology, or ski races and other competitive events. Recreation for physical and mental therapy is an important aspect of professional recreation education and practice. These programs must be developed, funded, and managed. In a sense, then, another set of institutions is attached to recreation.

Unique and special circumstances require unique and special institutions to handle them effectively. Take, again, New York State. There are definite overlaps of recreational interest between the Hudson Basin area and Connecticut, New Jersey, Vermont, Massachusetts, and Quebec. In response to one such situation, the States of New York and New Jersey have a joint commission, the Palisades Interstate Park Commission. As another example, one of the regional park commissions of New York State is within New York City. This commission is to put the parks where the people are, rather than to have them sequestered in the hills or wetlands.

The institutional structures that have been built to deal with recreation are hardly simple. There are state parks departments and offices, municipal parks departments, federally administered national recreation areas, private developments, and private accommodations run by profit and nonprofit corporations. These institutions provide hunting preserves and sports arenas, Nordic ski trails and private beaches, the Adirondacks, and Broadway.

Surely no clear picture of the institutions that deal with recreation and leisure time pursuits has yet emerged here. It is quite varied and, even when the variety is accounted for, a manageable handle on the actions of these institutions is not possible because one is at a loss to define the effects and interactions of different recreation enterprises. These institutions do not themselves define the interactions.

Were the Hudson Basin area's recreation system only physical, involving land, water, and atmosphere, the institutions concerned with it would be considerably simpler. Were it only social, consisting just of programs, the institutional scene would also be simpler. Indeed, were it only public or only private, were leisure-time pursuits clearly delimited, drawing the organizational chart for the administration of leisure-time activities would be relatively easy. None of these simplifying conditions exists. Therefore, let us attempt to examine the institutional structure related to leisure time by means of selected situations and examples.

The Private Scene

The private sector has traditionally played a major role in the provision of recreation in the United States. This is especially true in the densely settled Northeast. "Approximately 69 to 75 percent of the total recreational capacity in the U.S. . . . is provided by the private sector . . ." stated the BOR report "Federal Credit for Recreation Enterprises" (U.S. Bureau of Outdoor Recreation, 1967a). For some activities, such as skiing, golfing, boating, and horseback riding, commercial or nonprofit private enterprises have been the nearly exclusive suppliers.

Private banks supply most of the funds borrowed by the private recreation industry. A survey done by BOR revealed the following breakdown of sources for recreational loans: private banks, 70%; friends or relatives, 20%; federal agencies, 5%; and not reported, 5%.

A few government agencies make loans for recreation undertakings, but it is not the main or major business of any agency. Those that do are the Small Business Administration, the Economic Development Administration, and the Farmers Home Administration. Government aid may effectively be placed here. Indeed, the private sector may require federal and state aid in the form of guaranteed loan if it is to continue to provide recreation facilities for the public. This is especially true for large-scale operations, as recreation facilities are tending to require investments in excess of a quarter of a million dollars.

Federal Influence in the Hudson Basin Area

In 1962, the Outdoor Recreation Resources Review Commission (ORRRC), a group organized to analyze the U.S. recreation scene, presented its recommendations to the nation. An important recommendation was for the creation of a bureau within the Department of the Interior to promote and coordinate outdoor recreation. This was done that same year, when the Bureau of Outdoor Recreation began operation.* BOR assists all levels of government and private parties concerned with outdoor recreation.

Another important activity of BOR is its management of the Land and Water Conservation Fund. This fund has money for acquisition by the federal government of national recreation lands, and there is money to provide matching grants to states for rights—all rights or partial rights—in land and water for public recreation facilities. States coordinate this aid to their political subdivisions through a state liaison officer. In New York this officer is the commissioner of the Office of Parks and Recreation.

The genesis of open-space planning could be said to be in Title VII of the Housing Act of 1954. This was the Urban Planning Assistance Program—the 701 Program. Two-thirds of the total costs of comprehensive planning grants

---

*In a realignment of agencies within the Department of Interior, The Bureau of Outdoor Recreation was combined with the Office of Archeology and Historic Preservation (formerly part of the National Park Service) to form a new agency known as the Heritage Conservation and Recreation Service. [Ed.]

were paid by the federal government. Of course, open space was an important component. Amendments to this program in 1956 and 1957 extended aid to more communities, and in 1959 state planners engaging in state or interstate planning became eligible for the funds.

The Demonstration Cities and Metropolitan Development Act (Model Cities Act, PL 89-754) required in Section 204 that all open-space or land and water conservation projects in which federal loans or grants will be used must be submitted to an areawide planning agency for review and comment. Thus, some coordination, albeit tame, of urban projects could begin.

The Department of Housing and Urban Development has been active in planning and open-space grant screening. HUD listed four goals for the Open Space Program in the spring of 1968; these criteria would be used in evaluating grant proposals. The first three encouraged the use of open space to guide urban development and to prevent sprawl. This shaping of development would be done by acquiring lands such as steep slopes, floodplains, stream valleys, and greenbelts. The remaining goal emphasized using funds to provide intensive-use recreation facilities. HUD continually stressed that parks and open space facilities must be located close to urban centers and throughout metropolitan areas.

ORRRC also recommended that recreation facilities be built closer to population centers. Too many people, it said, had recreational needs unfulfilled because the federal government was spending money on recreation in rural areas for national parks and forests. The call for increased recreational opportunities was heard again in the 1960s when the Kerner Commission's study of people involved in the urban riots of that time found that lack of open space and recreation facilities was their fifth-ranked complaint.

As mentioned earlier, these reports apparently had the effect of diverting large appropriations to urban open space and recreation programs. The HUD programs have been successful. For more than 10 years local governments looked to HUD for matching funds on open space, beautification, and historic preservation. With its Open Space Program, HUD has helped preserve more than a third of a million acres of urban land from development. Since much of this land would probably soon have been under development, these areas will represent future prized open space near population centers where it can be used.

Other acts of Congress have been solicitous of open space and recreation lands. The 1966 Department of Transportation Act said, in Section 4(f), that special efforts should be made to avoid taking land from parks, wildlife refuges, and historic sites. Previously, parkland was often the path of least resistance for urban roadways. The 1973 Highways Act requires a flexible approach to solving pressing transportation needs in urban areas. It requires consideration of public transportation for rural areas and a study of alternative means of access to parks, recreation, and wildlife areas. The needs of bikers and pedestrians are also to be noted in transportation plans.

The Hudson Basin region states interacted differently with the federal programs available before the issue of revenue sharing made the situation murky. New Jersey provided half the matching funds for the acquisition of lands for conservation and outdoor recreation by counties and municipalities. The amount of $40 million was added to this program from a bond issue in 1971. With an average of nearly 1000 persons per square mile, New Jersey is the nation's most densely populated state; open land there is fast disappearing. Both federal and state matching funds are permitted on the same open space project; thus local governments may acquire more lands.

To assist in coordinated development, Connecticut does not simply review an open-space project to determine whether or not it fits with an existing comprehensive plan and then comment on it. The state makes the coordination of plans a requirement. In addition, each political subdivision must have drawn a recreation plan.

New York has matching-fund programs for the acquisition and development of parks and recreation facilities, marina facilities, and historic sites. The state has assisted its local governments with grant-in-aid funds available from several bond sales. For the acquisition of land for park properties, a $75 million bond issue was approved in 1960; in 1962 the amount was increased to $100 million. With the state granting three-fourths of the funds for local projects, $48 million of this was made available to local governments; almost 360,000 acres were acquired with the $100 million statewide. In 1966, the Next Step Bond Act was passed, providing $200 million for development of parkland, including those lands acquired with the 1960 Bond Act. Funds from localities were matched. According to "People–Resources–Recreation," the New York statewide comprehensive recreation plan, bond issues from 1963 through 1973 covered approximately half the total expenditure and two-thirds of the acquisition costs of open space projects (New York State Office of Parks and Recreation, 1972). There was little reluctance on the part of political subdivisions to use these funds. In fact, because of the demand, localities were limited to using either the state's bond money for a grant or the Federal Land and Water Conservation Fund, but one could not supplement the other.

It has been estimated that land in the United States rises in value at a rate of 5 to 10% per year on the average. The price on recreation land, however. is rising much faster. A 1967 BOR report said:

> Combined Federal and State outdoor recreation needs during the next ten years (FY 1968-77) are estimated to be about $3.6 billion in 1966 dollars. If price escalation were included in this estimate, the need would be 40 to 50 percent higher for the period. (U.S. Bureau of Outdoor Recreation, 1967b)

Aggressive state and federal funding in recreation land acquisition appears to be desirable. Localities usually cannot muster the resources.

The New York State Scene

A significant recognition of the importance of recreation took place in New York State in 1970. The State Legislature created the Office of Parks and Recreation. Formerly, state concerns with recreation were handled as part of the business of the Department of Conservation. In 1970, the functions of this department were split between the newly created OPR and the new Department of Environmental Conservation. The Office of Parks and Recreation is in the executive department, and would itself have been given the status of a department were it not for a constitutionally imposed limitation on the number of state departments. The overall effect was that recreation and parks were given more status as legitimate public concerns. More than simply a change in name and status was the result of the relocation of parks and recreation concerns on the state government's organization chart. A change in orientation was evident also. New programs show this. Where parks cannot be placed in urban areas, notably in low-income neighborhoods, an active program of bringing these urban residents to parks has been initiated. When they arrive at the state parks, they may engage in especially programmed and supervised activities.

In 1972, the laws on parks and recreation were recodified ("McKinney's 1972 Session of Laws of New York"). Prior to 1972, each of the state's park regions was operated by a commission, the head of which was appointed by the governor. The commissioners were civil and social leaders of their communities and served without salary. For nearly 50 years these commissions made policy in their various regions. The recodification brought a dramatic shift in this process. The Office of Parks and Recreation became the focus for decision-making. This centralization was effected to promote better coordination and management, and it was done for efficiency of operation. With a unified voice, too, the OPR was in a better position to fight for its budget. The regional commissions, which had been active since 1924, were relegated to an advisory role. They now provide grass roots input to OPR. The head of OPR is appointed or removed by the governor with selection dependent on consent of the Senate.

Each regional commission has hired individuals to direct activities for it. This person is usually called a regional director, and he or she is a liaison between the OPR commissioner in Albany and the commission under which he or she operates.

These regional commissions also have a chairperson, appointed by the governor, who directs his or her group's meetings and is a member of the

State Council of Parks and Recreation. Others on this important Council are the commissioners of OPR and DEC, the chairperson of the State Board of Historic Preservation, and, if a New York resident, the president of the Palisades Interstate Park Commission. This group reviews the plans, policies, and budgets of OPR and may make recommendations in these areas. It also acts as a central advisory agency to the state on all matters affecting parks, recreation, and historic preservation.

The coordination of recreational activities, parks, and historic preservation was seen to be "logically" a state function. Office of Parks and Recreation, then, is charged to acquire, establish, maintain, and operate parks, recreational facilities, and historic sites in New York—except in the Adirondack and Catskill Forest Preserves (DEC is responsible for these latter areas, but they are designated as a sixth state park region). OPR has the major role in initiating park development, and it coordinates the parks and recreational programs of other state agencies. OPR has overall responsibility for 11 state park regions, the Saratoga Springs Commission, the New York State Historic Trust, and central administrative service. Figure 11-1 shows the state park regions.

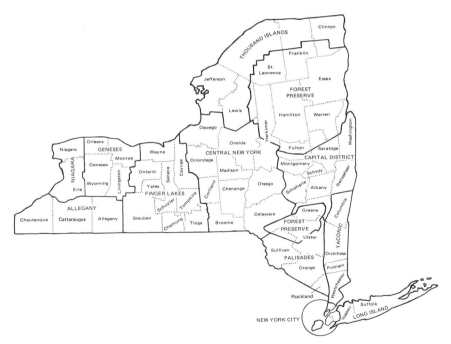

Fig. 11-1. New York State park regions.

Of course, OPR must exist in an institutional environment. To augment its resources OPR interacts with the federal government, neighboring states and provinces, and local governments of New York. Private institutions, such as philanthropic and nonprofit groups, also are concerned with recreation, and OPR may cooperate with them, too. More than 60% of recreational facilities are provided by private interests in New York State; OPR takes this fact into account when it prepares a comprehensive plan. It could, where the public demand warrants, enter into cooperative agreements with private institutions or corporations to make private facilities available to the public, if only on a part-time basis. OPR could share maintenance cost and pay rent to the private party. At this time, however, it has no such agreements with private parties.

Local governments that have plans for recreation projects may make applications to OPR's regional commissions for grants-in-aid. Having been approached by a locality, the regional commission screens its grant application to determine whether or not it complies with state or federal grant program requirements. This application is then sent to Albany, to the central OPR office, where it is again reviewed. The Albany review is a technical one. Here, the components of the plan are examined by means of a weighting index. The analysis that results ranks the project and it is then put on a priority list. This list determines the priority of the recreation projects.

In addition to the review process, OPR will, if asked, assist a unit of local government in designing plans or making a program proposal. Generally, however, OPR does not take the initiative in assisting a local area; perhaps it should. The rationale behind centralizing parks and recreation activity in Albany was to accumulate professional expertise.

A new park has been dedicated in the Palisades region, the Minnewaska State Park in the Shawangunk Mountains of Ulster County. The land was purchased from a private party, with New York matching a federal grant to meet the $1.5 million price. Minnewaska is generally a wilderness area, and it is very close to metropolitan New York. Putting a wilderness experience within the reach of so many people was the rationale behind establishing the park. Nash Castro, general manager of the Palisades Interstate Park Commission (PIPC), wanted the character of Minnewaska preserved, and at the same time he wanted people to use the area. The planning team found that the park area could not be planned as an entity separated from adjoining parcels. These include the Village of Ellenville watershed lands, the adjoining Ice Cave Mountain preserve, the Minnewaska Mountain House, the Mohonk Hotel grounds, and the lands of the Mohonk Trust. Through cooperative agreements with the adjoining landowners, park visitors and guests of the private mountain house and hotel may enjoy the fruits of an integrated recreation plan.

Here is an example of complementary interest in recreation. The private interests and those of the public meshed to provide a well-planned, cooperative venture. Without the agreement of the private property owners, the resulting plan would have resulted in almost excessive physical stress on the wilderness area (Anonymous, 1972c).

An Example—The Adirondack Park Agency

The Adirondack Park Agency is a unique and especially interesting example of the possible organization a land-controlling agency could take. The formation of the Adirondack Park Agency was the central recommendation of the Temporary Study Commission on the Future of the Adirondacks (TSCFA).

TSCFA concluded after its 2 years of study that the maintenance of the wild forest character of the 40% of the forest that is state-owned land could be achieved only with the creation of an agency with authority for the overall planning in the Park. Governor Nelson Rockefeller pushed the Legislature to create the APA, and it was established in 1971. Basically, the APA was given three charges:

1. Formulate a land use and development plan applicable to land other than state-owned tracts in the Adirondack Park.
2. Concerning the state lands, a master plan was to be formulated that would classify the lands according to their characteristics and capacity to withstand use.
3. In towns that had not enacted zoning laws and subdivision regulations by July 1, 1971, the APA was to exercise—until the private-land plan had been adopted—interim powers to prohibit development on private land which would detract from the overall "conservation, protection, preservation, development, and use of the unique scenic, historic, ecological and natural resources of the . . . Park" (Adirondack Park Agency Law, 1971).

The APA created by this legislation includes the commissioners of DEC and the director of the Office of Planning Services, ex officio; in addition, there are seven other members appointed by the governor. DEC is the agency constitutionally responsible for the administration of the Adirondack Forest Preserve. The law requires that some of the seven APA members be year-round residents within the Park to represent local interests, and that some be from other parts of New York State, recognizing that all the people of the state have an interest in the Park.

TSCFA proposed only limited land acquisition. With a program of scenic easements, which could be implemented at relatively low cost, large areas of privately owned land—scenic and recreation areas—would be opened to the public. Even with these, however, the demand for recreation in the next 15 to 20 years is not expected to be met. Some form of rationing will probably be adopted. This will probably take the form of increased entrance fees, reservations, and waiting lines. Without the tool of land use control on privately owned acreage, the conservation requirements and the enormous recreation potential of the park could not be fulfilled, according to Henry L. Diamond, former DEC commissioner and APA member. APA and DEC study the Park's problems together and collaborate on actions to be taken.

The APA did develop a land use and development plan for the state lands in the Park and submitted it along with recommendations for its implementation, including suggestions on legislation, in May 1972. Despite opposition, some in the Assembly and Senate, Governor Rockefeller approved this part of the plan in July. One aspect of this plan placed 45% of the state-owned lands into a strict wilderness classification. Three other classifications were outlined allowing for varying degrees of development. Immediately upon the governor's approval, this plan went into effect; legislative action was not needed.

The plan for controlling the Park's private lands was initially drafted and released in December 1972. Public criticism was vocal. Local officials and legislators decried the paucity of further economic development and population growth allowed by the plan. The plan was redrafted and released in final form in March 1973. Public controls were extended over private land use decisions by this plan. The plan still had formidable difficulty finding public acceptance, and without the personal guardianship of the governor, it would probably have been modified considerably. Before approval, this plan had to withstand a confrontation between the governor and the legislature; the governor vetoed a bill that would have required delay of the plan's effective date and its reevaluation. It was finally passed in May 1973.

The revolutionary planning result of these unique Adirondack circumstances may be a preview for the future. Major modifications are expected in both attitudes and legislation toward American land use within the next several years. Proscriptive zoning will give way to controls that are increasingly prescriptive. Changes in long-standing social and legal traditions are in store in the future.

PROJECT HISTORY AND PROCESS

Purposes

The Hudson Basin Project was initiated in June 1973 by The Rockefeller Foundation as a 2-year study of environmental problems in the tristate New York metropolitan area and the Hudson River basin.

The Project was supported because it exemplified one of the goals of the Foundation's Quality of the Environment Program, namely: "to speed the solution of important environmental problems, and in so doing to assist in the creation of institutional capabilities to deal with them, and to build better bases for public understanding of environmental issues. This study will involve the cooperation of scientists and other specialists in the region, and point the way toward methods of cooperation among institutions and individuals for anticipation and resolution of environmental issues" (Rockefeller Foundation, 1974).

Funds to carry out the Project were provided to Mid-Hudson Pattern, Inc., a seven-county, nonprofit planning agency for the mid-Hudson area of New York State, located in Poughkeepsie, New York, and headed by C. David Loeks, AIP. With the concurrence of Pattern's Board of Directors, Mr. Loeks was designated by the Foundation as Director of the Hudson Basin Project.

The purpose, scope, and method of the Project were developed in two stages. Initially, these aspects were formulated in broad terms within the Foundation during the Project's conception.

As the Project moved forward, operational goals were formulated by its staff with the concurrence of the Project's 14-member advisory panel.* For an early overview of environmental matters in the region, task groups and consultants were asked to (a) describe and evaluate the adequacy of the information base relating to assigned environmental policy areas; (b) identify interdependencies within and among those policy areas; (c) identify issues arising out of such interdependencies; (d) assess the adequacy of existing institutions to manage such issues; and (e) identify areas of needed research.

Scope

The *geographic* scope of the Project reflects a governing premise that a basis for improving environmental management would emerge from focusing on a specific area large enough to reveal the interrelationships of environmental problems but small enough to be comprehended in concrete terms. The Hudson Basin region was selected for study because it displays a full and mature range of issues resulting from the long-term interplay of human settlement and its supporting natural resource base. It was not assumed that the area selected for study would necessarily lend itself to environmental management under a single comprehensive plan or administrative and policy body.

The initial *topical* scope of the project included the following ten policy areas: land use/human settlement; transportation; environmental service systems; energy systems; land use/natural resource management; water resources; air resources; biological communities; human health; and leisure time and recreation. Provisional definitions of these ten areas were developed at the commencement of the Project, and were later amplified to take account of social, economic, and institutional considerations. The policy areas represent a range of activity significant to the well-being of human as well as to nonhuman life and the conservation of natural resources.

The *institutional* scope of the Project encompassed a variety of governmental, quasi-governmental, and nongovernmental institutions at federal, state, and other levels.

Methods

The Hudson Basin Project was conducted as an experiment (a) to show how environmental problems can be examined in an integrated manner

*See Appendix B.

within a regional context; (b) to try various approaches—such as task group, work conferences, or special assignments—in mobilizing and synthesizing the knowledge and best judgments of a variety of individuals and institutions; (c) to ascertain whether such an examination and method will lead to a new set of ideas and conclusions about the environment; (d) to find out whether these ideas and conclusions would assist in formulating new public policies and programs beneficial to society.

The Project was multidisciplinary throughout, essentially dependent on the cooperation of a large number of different participants, and flexible in the organization of assignments. An areawide perspective, a comprehensive (not sectoral) view of the environment, and a cumulative synthesis were as much requirements for each participant as they were Project goals.

The Project was carried out in five main phases:

1. *Start-up*—designation of Mid-Hudson Pattern, Inc., as implementing agency, development of Project work program, recruitment of project staff, formation of Advisory Panel.   June–September 1973

2. *Data collection and analysis* of environmental conditions, problems, issues, institutions, and information sources in the region. Accomplished through the work of ten multidisciplinary task groups, staff, and consultants.   September 1973–June 1974

3. *Initial synthesis* of findings, emerging conclusins, and recommendations. Reports from the ten task groups, consultants, staff, and other sources were critically reviewed, analyzed, and supplemented by a major study conference. The participants were drawn from government, business, higher education, and civic   June 1974–September 1974

affairs. About one-half had
been involved in earlier
Project activities.

4. *Second synthesis*—comple-
    tion of special studies to fill
    in gaps noted during the
    summer study conference.
    Publication of ten occa-
    sional papers. Completion
    of first draft and final Pro-
    ject report and reviews of
    the document by Project
    participants and other indi-
    viduals.

    November 1974–May 1975

5. *Final synthesis and publi-
    cation*—completion of sec-
    ond and third drafts of the
    Project's final report with
    intervening reviews by ad-
    visory panel, consultants,
    and other individuals. Pre-
    paration of publication
    manuscripts of task group
    reports and final Project
    report.

    May 1975–July 1976

HUDSON BASIN PROJECT PARTICIPANTS

Professional Staff

C. David Loeks
Director

Chadbourne Gilpatric
Deputy Director

Christopher Wright
Senior Associate

Caroline F. Raymond
Program Associate

Gilbert Tauber
Associate, Environmental Policy

Michael Marmor
Associate, Physical Sciences

Ellen B. Jeronimo
Associate, Demography and Economics

L. Gordon Hamersley
Administrative Assistant

Support Staff

Antonia Salvato
Secretary

Pamela J. Dushensky
Secretary/Research Assistant

Jane Davis
Secretary

Marilyn Tromer
Administrative Secretary

Marion Barclay
Bookkeeper

Program Consultant

Leonard B. Dworsky
Professor
Department of Environmental Engineering
Cornell University
Ithaca, New York

Special Consultants

Robert E. Ford
Professor
Department of Sociology
SUNY-Buffalo
Amherst, New York

James M. Kenney
Associate Professor
Department of Economics
Union College
Schenectady, New York

Thomas R. Kershner
Chairman, Department of Economics
Union College
Schenectady, New York

Ruth P. Mack
Director, Economic Studies
Institute of Public Administration
New York, New York

John P. Milsop
Wildcat Service Corp.
New York, New York

William R. Ginsberg, Esq.
Professor of Law
Hofstra University
Hempstead, New York

Vincent J. Moore
Saratoga Associates
Saratoga, New York

Donald B. Straus
President, Research Institute
American Arbitration Association
New York, New York

Anthony Wolff
Editorial
New York, New York

Philip Wilde
Communications-Videotape
Cornell University
Ithaca, New York

Advisory Panel

Norton Nelson*
Director, Institute of Environmental Medicine
New York University
New York, New York

Joseph E. Black
Director, Social Sciences
The Rockefeller Foundation
New York, New York

John M. Cooney
Executive Assistant
Community Affairs
Office of the President
Rutgers University
New Brunswick, New Jersey

Henry L. Diamond†
Former Commissioner
New York State Department of Environmental
    Conservation
Albany, New York

D. Clinton Dominick, III
Former New York State Senator
Newburgh, New York

John P. Keith
President
Regional Plan Association
New York, New York

W. Keith Kennedy
Dean, New York State College of Agriculture
    and Life Sciences
Cornell University
Ithaca, New York

Martin Lang
Commissioner
Department of Parks
City of New York
New York, New York

Gordon J. MacDonald†
Director, Environmental Studies Program
Dartmouth College
Hanover, New Hampshire

Dick Netzer
Dean, Graduate School of Public
    Administration
New York University
New York, New York

Ruth Patrick
Curator of Limnology
Academy of Natural Sciences
Philadelphia, Pennsylvania

Ronald W. Pedersen
Former First Deputy Commissioner
Department of Environmental Conservation
Albany, New York

*Chairman.

†Resigned.

Ralph W. Richardson, Jr.
Director, Natural and Environmental Sciences
The Rockefeller Foundation
New York, New York

Donald F. Squires
Program Director
New York State Sea Grant Program
Albany, New York

Richard J. Sullivan
Former Commissioner
New Jersey State Department of
   Environmental Protection
Trenton, New Jersey

M. Gordon Wolman
Chairman, Department of Geography and
   Environmental Engineering
Johns Hopkins University
Baltimore, Maryland

Task Groups

Land Use/Human Settlement

Dorn C. McGrath*·‡
Chairman, Department of Urban and
   Regional Planning
George Washington University
Washington, D.C.

Lee E. Koppelman‡
Commissioner, Nassau–Suffolk
Regional Planning Board
Hauppauge, New York

Vincent J. Moore‡
Saratoga Associates
Saratoga Springs, New York

William K. Reilly
President, The Conservation Foundation
Washington, D.C.

Transportation

Roger L. Creighton*·‡
President, Roger Creighton Associates, Inc.
Delmar, New York

James W. Hughes
Assistant Professor, Urban Planning
Rutgers University
New Brunswick, New Jersey

‡Also summer conference participant.

Richard S. Miller
Professor, School of Forestry & Environmental
   Studies
Yale University
New Haven, Connecticut

James R. Nelson
Professor, Department of Economics
Amherst College
Amherst, Massachusetts

Louis Pignataro
Director, Transportation Programs
Polytechnic Institute of New York
Brooklyn, New York

Environmental Service Systems

Robert D. Hennigan*·‡
Director, Graduate Program in Environmental
   Sciences
SUNY College of Environmental Sciences and
   Forestry
Syracuse, New York

William G. Borghard
Commissioner, Department of Environmental
   Facilities
White Plains, New York

William Ginsberg, Esq.‡
Professor of Law
Hofstra University
Hempstead, New York

Joseph M. Heikoff
Professor, Graduate School of Public Affairs
SUNY–Albany
Albany, New York

David A. Johnson
Professor, Graduate Planning Program
Syracuse University
Syracuse, New York

Robert M. L. Bellandi§
College of Environmental Science and
   Forestry
SUNY–Syracuse
Syracuse, New York

§Research assistant.

Energy Systems

Eugene D. Eaton*·‡
Resource Technology, Inc.
Washington, D.C.

Peter Borrelli
Catskill Center for Conservation and
    Development
Hobart, New York

James G. Cline
Chairman, Atomic & Space Development
    Authority
New York, New York

Robert E. Ford‡
Professor, Department of Sociology
SUNY–Buffalo
Amherst, New York

Richard G. Stein
R.G.S. & Associates
New York, New York

Land Use/Natural Resource Management

David Allee*
Professor of Resource Economics, College of
    Agriculture & Life Sciences
Cornell University
Ithaca, New York

George D. Davis
Deputy Director, Adirondack Park Agency
Ray Brook, New York

Frithjof M. Lunde‡
Warner, Burns, Toan, Lunde
New York, New York

Paul Marr
Associate Professor, Department of
    Geography
SUNY–Albany
Albany, New York

Carl Mays‡
Director, The Institute of Rational Design
New York, New York

Richard E. Friday§
Department of Agricultural Economics
Cornell University
Ithaca, New York

Water Resources

Harry E. Schwarz*
Director, Environmental Affairs Program
Clark University
Worcester, Massachusetts

James J. Ferris
Research Coordinator
Rensselaer Freshwater Institute
Rensselaer Polytechnic Institute
Troy, New York

Richard J. Kalish
Department of Economics
SUNY–Albany
Albany, New York

Edward I. Selig, Esq.‡
Waban
Massachusetts

Robert V. Thomann
Associate Professor, Environmental
    Engineering and Science
Manhattan College
Riverdale, New York

Erwin H. Zube
Institute for Man & His Environment
University of Massachusetts
Amherst, Massachusetts

Michael Enders‡
Environmental Affairs Program
Clark University
Worcester, Massachusetts

Air Resources

P. Walton Purdom*·‡
Director, Environmental Studies Institute
Drexel University
Philadelphia, Pennsylvania

Philip L. Bereano
Professor, School of Civil & Environmental
    Engineering
Cornell University
Ithaca, New York

Edward Davis
Division of Air Resources
New York State Department of Environmental
   Conservation
Albany, New York

Michael Greenberg
Professor, Department of Community
   Development
Rutgers University
New Brunswick, New Jersey

Robert Laessig
Assistant Professor, Department of
   Management and Operations Research
Drexel University
Philadelphia, Pennsylvania

Alexander Rihm, Jr.
Director, Division of Air Resources
New York State Department of Environmental
   Conservation
Albany, New York

Alex Carter ‖
Drexel University
Philadelphia, Pennsylvania

Miguel Ruelan ‖
Drexel University
Philadelphia, Pennsylvania

Biological Communities

Gerald J. Lauer*
Vice President, Ecological Analysts, Inc.
Middletown, New York

Angus MacBeth, Esq.
Natural Resources Defense Council
New York, New York

David Pimentel‡
Department of Entomology
Cornell University
Ithaca, New York

Bert Salwen
Associate Professor, Department of
   Anthropology
New York University
New York, New York

‖ Student assistant.

John W. Seddon
The Institute of Rational Design, Inc.
New York, New York

Human Health

Lawrence E. Hinkle, Jr., M.D.*‡
Professor of Medicine
Division of Human Ecology
The New York Hospital–Cornell Medical
   Center
New York, New York

Merril Eisenbud
Director, Institute of Environmental Medicine
New York University Medical Center
New York, New York

Amitai Etzioni
Director, Center for Policy Research, Inc.
New York, New York

Stanislav V. Kasl‡
Professor of Epidemiology
Yale University School of Medicine
New Haven, Connecticut

Mary McLaughlin, M.D.
Commissioner of Health Services
Suffolk County Department of Health Services
Hauppauge, New York

Leisure Time and Recreation

W. Harry Everhart*‡
Chairman, Department of Natural Resources
Cornell University
Ithaca, New York

Donald F. Behrend‡,#
Executive Director, Institute of Environmental
   Affairs
SUNY-Syracuse
Syracuse, New York

Betty Hawkins
Albany
New York

Rolf Meyersohn
Deputy Executive Officer, Ph.D. Program in
   Sociology
City University of New York
New York, New York

#Cochairman.

Sheldon Pollack
Information Director, Regional Plan
    Association
New York, New York

Robert M. L. Bellandi§
College of Environmental Science and
    Forestry
SUNY–Syracuse
Syracuse, New York

Bente S. King§
Department of Natural Resources
Cornell University
Ithaca, New York

Summer Conference Participants**

John H. Adler
Director, Programming and Budgeting
    Department
International Bank for Reconstruction and
    Development
Washington, D. C.

David K. Hartley
Consultant
Washington, D.C.

Peter R. Jutro
Science Advisor, U.S. House of
    Representatives Committee on Public
    Works
Division of Biological Sciences
Cornell University
Ithaca, New York

Alvin Kaufman
Director, Office of Economic Research
Public Service Commission
State of New York
Albany, New York

Jack Lackner
Office of Enforcement and the General
    Counsel
U.S. Environmental Protection Agency
Washington, D. C.

Cy McKell
Director, Environment and Man Program
Utah State University
Logan, Utah

  **Conferees not listed elsewhere.

David Morrel
Princeton University
Princeton, New Jersey

Robert B. Morris
Director, Environmental Programs
International Business Machines Corporation
White Plains, New York

George M. Raymond
President, Raymond, Parish & Pine, Inc.
Tarrytown, New York

Richard B. Royce
Consultant
Washington, D. C.

Antonio Santiago-Vazquez
President, Environmental Systems Engineering
    of Puerto Rico, Inc.
Santurce, Puerto Rico

Lois Sharpe
League of Women Voters Education Fund
Washington, D.C.

Peter M. Stern
Vice-President, Northeast Utilities Service
    Company
Hartford, Connecticut

Gary H. Toenniessen
Assistant Director, Natural and Environmental
    Sciences
The Rockefeller Foundation
New York, New York

Arthur E. Weintraub
Vice-President, Mid-Hudson Pattern for
    Progress, Inc.
Poughkeepsie, New York

Economics Work Group

Regina B. Armstrong
Chief Economist, Regional Plan Association
New York, New York

Gordon A. Enk
Director, Economic & Environmental Studies
The Institute on Man and Science
Rensselaerville, New York

Robert S. Herman
Office of the Speaker New York State
  Legislature
Albany, New York

Robert Lindsay
Executive Director, Council of Economic
  Advisors
State of New York
World Trade Center
New York, New York

Chadbourne Gilpatric
Deputy Director
Hudson Basin Project

Ellen B. Jeronimo
Associate, Demography and Economics
Hudson Basin Project

James M. Kenney
Associate Professor, Department of
  Economics
Union College
Schnectady, New York

Thomas R. Kershner
Chairman, Department of Economics
Union College
Schnectady, New York

Rockefeller Fellows

Michael Enders
Environmental Affairs Program
Clark University
Worcester, Massachusetts

Richard Friday
Department of Agricultural Economics
Cornell University
Ithaca, New York

George Skaliotis
Department of Transportation, Planning and
  Engineering
Polytechnic Institute
Brooklyn, New York

Peter Willing
Department of Natural Resources
Cornell University
Ithaca, New York

RESEARCH NEEDS

Introduction

One of the objectives of the Hudson Basin Project was to assess the information base used in environmental decision-making and to identify areas in which there is an important need for additional knowledge. Given the background of the Project participants, it would not have been hard to come up with a long list of specific research proposals. But such a list might obscure more than it could reveal. Instead, participants were asked to think in terms of "knowledge problems" or "information gaps" that represent obstacles to effective environmental management.

Over 600 such obstacles were identified in the course of the Project. Not surprisingly, the same ones were often found in two or more policy areas. Somewhere along the line, participants stopped using the term "information gap," which suggests a hole that can be filled by a certain amount of research effort. It soon became clear that many of the knowledge problems in environmental management are due not to a lack of information per se, but to the lack of a sustained effort to organize and analyze existing research data. Thus, the utilization of existing information in more effective ways is a consideration that underlies much of the material presented herein.

In this appendix, the knowledge problems identified by Project participants have been consolidated and recast as a list of research needs—a term intended to include requirements for methodology as well as substantive information. The list is divided according to the following four levels of information required for environmental management identified in Chapter 1:

Information Level 1—Basic Inventories ("What have we got?")—deals with the qualitative and quantitative description of the basic physical, social, economic, and institutional components of the environment.

Information Level 2—Systems Dynamics ("How does it work and how is it changing?")—involves formulating, testing, and applying conceptual models and processes that explain the structure and interaction of the components of the various systems marking up the environment as well as the relationships of these systems to one another. Information at this level integrates Level 1 information into a body of knowledge that identifies whether things are working properly and that explains the underlying dynamics of growth and change.

Information Level 3—Prediction ("How might it change?")—is concerned with applying the knowledge gained in Levels 1 and 2 to the anticipation of future conditions.

Information Level 4—Prescription ("What do we want to do about it?")—focuses on the goals, policies, and programs needed to respond to the problems, conditions, and trends identified by efforts under the preceding three information levels. Research needs at this level can be grouped under two general headings: one deals with the substance of what should be done; the other pertains to what is needed to do it (legal, institutional, administrative, and technological).

It is apparent that the broad view of the environment taken by the Hudson Basin Project leads to a correspondingly broad scope of the research required. Such a view, while not generally accepted, is not entirely novel. It was interesting to note during the course of the Project that a number of agencies, including the U.S. Office of Management and Budget and the National Academy of Sciences, were apparently moving along similar lines in their information management efforts.

The breadth of scope of the material to be covered necessitated synthesis and summarization, and corresponding loss of specificity and detail. The scope was limited, however, to items which can best be pursued within the study area. Therefore we tended to exclude items that are primarily of national and international concern and that are more effectively addressed at the national level. Of course, the list is not complete. These limitations are not a matter of major concern at this juncture since this material, together with other Project information not included here by reason of space limitations, is primarily intended as input for a recommended follow-up effort to develop collaboratively a regional research and action agenda for the guidance of those who conduct, use, or fund research pertaining to environmental management.

Many of the items in the following lists relate to data and information systems that exist but are not adequate. It will also be noted that some items can be grouped logically under more than one information level. Finally, all the items selected satisfy the basic criteria listed at the beginning of this appendix. In one way or another, research on subjects listed would help solve knowledge problems and fill information gaps which constitute obstacles to effective environmental management. The numbering of the items below is for convenience only and is not intended to indicate priorities.

Information Level One—Basic Inventories

1. An inventory of the region's in-place capital stock (buildings, machine tools, public works, capital equipment) with data on type, geographic distribution, and anticipated useful life. Priority should be given to a census of nonresidential building stock by type of floor space, location, current use, and condition.

2. Regional data on investment intentions of business firms as well as governmental bodies and institutions whose investments generate employment.

3. Data on the utilization of capital resources accumulated within the region, such as savings deposits and pension funds.

4. A census of technologies, including data on type of establishment; employee numbers and skill categories; material inputs; volume and value of output; and substances discharged into the environment. Such a census would require a standard classification system for technologies, similar to the S.I.C. index.

5. Uniform reporting of governmental expenditures for environmental management. Uniform calendar-year reporting should be established to compensate for the use of different fiscal years by various types of governmental bodies.

6. Standardized reporting of data on local government revenues, including a uniform way of breaking out state and federal aid components and real property tax sources by land use.

7. Standardized reporting of data on taxation and expenditure patterns by locality, including separate data for various combinations of overlapping special districts within a given municipality.

8. Standardized reporting of the full value of taxable real estate on a per capita basis by local political subdivision. This procedure requires a uniform method of determining the serviced population, especially for those areas with a large summertime or student population.

9. Improve the precision of indicators of housing condition used in the U.S. Census of Housing.

10. Indicators of neighborhood condition, including measurements of residents' perceptions of and attitudes toward various elements of neighborhood quality.

11. A consolidated, computerized system to provide real-time data on ownership, occupancy, tax status, and physical condition of multiple dwellings in the region's larger urban centers.

12. An aerial land use mapping program for New Jersey, comparable to and compatible with the existing programs in New York and Connecticut.

13. A comprehensive inventory of the condition and use of all publicly owned land in the region.

14. A consolidated inventory of nonhighway rights-of-way, both active and abandoned, in either public or private ownership.

15. A coordinated air quality monitoring system for the tristate metropolitan region. This system would require elimination of the present inconsistencies in methodology among the separate sampling networks operated by the three states and the City of New York.

16. Systematic monitoring of all airborne pathogenic agents, including infectious microorganisms, dusts, allergenic substances, and toxic compounds. Detailed data should be obtained on the chemical characteristics of fine suspended particulates.

17. Systematic monitoring of air quality in selected enclosed spaces, including residential buildings, workplaces, and public and private vehicles.

18. Coordinated monitoring of water quality and the status of aquatic biota in the Hudson–Mohawk river systems and related coastal waters. This monitoring will entail development of a standardized methodology, including parameters and sampling intervals.

19. Methodology for coordinating data from site-specific studies of terrestrial and aquatic ecosystems, especially from those studies done in connection with environmental impact statements.

20. Systematic collection of data on the contamination of water within delivery systems, including type, incidence and source, and nature of corrective action required.

21. Improved indicators of water quality for specific uses. In the case of swimming, for example, there is a need for a more relevant indicator than coliform bacteria.

22. Development of an aggregate indicator of water quality.

23. Time series data on volume and composition of solid waste, including per capita collections of packaging materials, nonreturnable containers, and broken appliances.

24. Monitoring of adequacy of solid waste collection as determined by amounts of uncollected litter or refuse.

25. Time series data on enforcement of environmental ordinances, including numbers of warnings, summonses, or amounts of fines.

26. Performance monitoring of innovative environmental support technologies and systems used in large-scale developments such as Roosevelt Island (e.g., aerial tramway, pneumatic collection of solid wastes).

27. Data on crops and croplands, including forestlands, that would be suitable for spray disposal of treated sewage.

28. Positive indicators of physical and mental health.

29. Improved survey procedures for determining the prevalence of disease.

30. Monitoring of species, other than microorganisms, that are potential sources or transmitters of disease to man.

31. Time series data on how people spend leisure time, with breakdowns by geography, age, income-class, and social or ethnic group.

32. Standardized measures of the availability of recreation to given populations.

33. Data on environmental impacts of recreational activities by type and location.

34. Standardized measures of tourist volume and tourist-related business activity.

35. Development of criteria for and identification of areas of "critical environmental concern."

36. Determination of development capability and carrying capacity of the region's land and water resources.

Information Level Two—System Dynamics

1. Identification of linkages between economic activity in the region and outside markets and sources of supply, including flow studies of commodities and credit services.

2. Measurement of the impacts of technological changes on the location of various types of industry and commercial activity.

3. The economic and noneconomic determinants of transportation, including numbers of trips, choice of mode, or routes. This information will require models for studying the transport of freight and passengers via various modes and combinations of modes, as well as models for the study of person-movements in various kinds of urban environments, both on foot and by various forms of transportation.

4. Factors affecting the political responsiveness of environmental management agencies, including research on how new interest groups win recognition of their "legitimacy" from public officials.

5. Methodology for weighing improvements in environmental deci-

sion-making against cost of the acquiring information needed for such improvement.

6. Demand effects of alternative utility rate structures, including the effect of the "universal availability" policy on the dispersal of industrial and residential development.

7. Secondary effects of installation of public infrastructure, including methodology for calculating the development-inducing impacts of sewers, highways, and other public improvements.

8. Methodology for relating population density to environmental service system requirements.

9. The impact of various types of environmental management activities on the economic and social welfare of the poor. This analysis should include development of techniques for predicting cost to private industry, and ultimately to the consumer, for specific environmental control measures.

10. Barriers to the rehabilitation of inner-city housing.

11. Social-class aspirations and class-determined attitudes as a factor in planning public recreational facilities.

12. Factors determining use of local recreational facilities by residents and nonresidents.

13. The causes, dynamics, and control of vandalism of recreational and other public facilities.

14. Methodology for determining the carrying capacity of recreation areas.

15. Local revenue and economic effects of removing of land from tax rolls for various public purposes (recreation, water supply, or scenic protection), including economic effects on resource-related industries (lumber, mining, etc.) and employment impacts of various kinds of recreational development.

16. Fiscal disparities among municipalities, including the impact of different land uses on local revenues and expenditures.

17. The positive and negative economic functions of land speculation and the impacts of speculation on the physical environment.

18. The social and economic implications of second-home development in various types of locations.

19. The health effects of fine suspended particulates.

20. Epidemiological and clinical research on the short- and long-term health effects of air pollutants, individually and in combination.

21. Health effects of the journey to work, including effects of air contaminants, fatigue, and other stresses experienced in private autos and mass transit vehicles.

22. Methodology on the effects of housing design and density on human health and behavior.

23. The contribution to ozone concentrations from sources other than hydrocarbon emissions.

24. The effects of noise-induced stress on human health.

25. Determination of "acceptable risk" thresholds for carcinogenic and mutagenic effects of water pollutants.

26. The composition and relationships of the components in concentrations of various pollutants in water and air discharges and in nonpoint sources such as urban drainage or agricultural runoff.

27. The physical, social, and economic effects of interbasin transfers of water.

28. Determination of the "carrying capacity" of the air resources of the Hudson Valley.

29. The effects of acid rains and low-level air pollution on the ecosystems in the region.

30. The effects of nonthermal stresses on organisms entrained in power plant cooling systems.

31. The effects of thermal and entrainment problems in the Hudson River and coastal waters on larger component systems, such as fisheries.

32. The effects of human activities on salinity in the Hudson River estuary.

33. The impact of solid waste landfills on biological communities in wetlands and estuaries.

34. The social and economic benefits and costs of alternative wildlife management policies (including methodology for measurement).

35. The implications of an impending "steady state" economy for equity in the distribution of resources.

36. Designing, testing, and demonstrating assessment techniques for identifying secondary and tertiary effects of environmental management activities on affected interests.

37. Processes and techniques, including methods, for increasing the availability of results of assessment processes.

38. Information to improve the availability and access by citizens to conflict resolution arenas.

39. Definition of the taxonomy, dynamics, and interrelationships of the systems comprising the environment.

40. Improved methodology for forecasting electrical demand and generating capacity requirements.

41. Improved methodology for forecasting the effects of environmental regulations on capital requirements of utilities, industries, and public bodies.

42. A systematic evaluation of the effects of existing taxes, subsidies, and incentives, at all levels of government, on environmental management.

43. Comparative studies of the costs and benefits of various types of land use controls now used in the Hudson Basin region or potentially applicable to it. These studies should include evaluation of the various control measures from the standpoint of their effects on minority and low-income housing opportunities.

Information Level Three—Prediction

1. Forecasts of the effects of current technological and demographic trends on the locational preferences of major industries.

2. Projections of future investments in construction and capital goods by major industries and by public agencies.

3. Projections of the demand for land, water, and energy by major categories of land use and/or activity.

4. Forecasts of vehicle registrations by size, fuel-consumption class, predominant use, and type of emission controls.

5. Forecasts, by subregion, of per capita generation and composition of solid wastes.

6. Projections of leisure-activity preferences by counties or comparable geographic areas.

7. Forecasts of the costs of abatement of specific pollutants to various levels of discharge or ambient concentration.

8. Methodology for forecasting the health benefits of incremental investments in air and water pollution control.

9. Projections of the effects of possible curtailed auto use on communities and businesses that now depend heavily on automobile access.

10. Expenditure and revenue forecasts for governmental subdivisions by function and source.

11. Measurement of the impacts of technological changes on the location of various types of industry and commercial activity.

Information Level Four—Prescription

Research Needed to Formulate Policy

1. Development of common and systematic criteria for the acquisition, use, access to, and disposition of land held by public agencies at all levels of government.

2. Formulation of standards for determining the carrying capacity of various land and water areas within the region.

3. Criteria for determination that a site or area is of critical regional concern.

4. Criteria for determinations of aesthetic value and acceptability.

5. The energy use implications of alternative land development policies.

6. Mechanisms for more equitable distribution of tax revenues from major facilities (e.g., power plants and commercial and industrial centers).

7. The environmental implications of potential large-scale, energy-related activities, including superports, LNG terminal facilities, and offshore drilling.

8. Alternative ways of compensating communities for the locally borne costs resulting from the presence of regional facilities of various kinds.

9. Comparative cost effectiveness and impacts of alternative cooling systems for power plants.

10. Effects of economies of scale relevant to energy facilities, including system efficiency and reliability.

11. Criteria for the delineation of regional solid waste management districts for economic operation and maximum economies of scale.

12. Alternative regulatory approaches to the coordination of land development with the provision of environmental service systems.

13. Cost effectiveness of alternatives to increasing water supplies (e.g., metering, replacement of leaking water mains, etc.).

14. Cost-benefit analysis of the recreational use of water supply reservoirs.

15. Alternative means of preventing overuse of fragile recreation and wilderness areas such as the Adirondack High Peaks region.

16. Criteria for determining the use and extent of appropriate public sector subsidies for recreational facilities and activities.

17. Criteria for the allocation of available recreational funds among land acquisition, development, and operations.

Research Needed To Provide Means of Implementing Policy

1. Design of solid waste recycling facilities that can be adjusted to accommodate future changes in the composition of wastes.

2. Improved technology for solid waste collection and transport to disposal facilities.

3. Mechanisms for the protection of large, contiguous areas of rural non-farmland, comparable to existing measures for the protection of agricultural lands.

4. Techniques for the environmentally sound integration of urban drainage into environmental services systems, including sanitary handling of stormwater overloads.

5. Environmentally sound alternatives to septic systems for areas with density too low for sewers.

6. Techniques for recycling urban rubble as an alternative to quarrying of certain construction materials.

7. Techniques for reducing the risks of accident or illegal diversion in the shipping, reprocessing, and/or disposing of nuclear fuel and radioactive wastes.

8. Techniques for nonpolluting production and utilization of energy from coal.

9. Techniques to reduce consumption of water in specific industries and nonindustrial uses.

10. Improved techniques for the disposal and/or recycling of sewage sludge.

11. Techniques for controlling urban sprawl.

12. Improved financing arrangements for environmental service systems.

13. Techniques for redistributing or equalizing economic gains and losses resulting from government decisions on the location and timing of public improvements.

14. Ways of making multiple use of the existing school bus transportation network.

15. Techniques and incentives to tap nondepletable sources of energy, such as solar or wind power.

16. Incentives for use of energy conserving building materials and designs.

17. Techniques for shifting electrical demand from peak periods to off hours.

18. Means of maintaining anthracite supplies to existing users in the face of declining rail service.

19. Ways of integrating the concept of resource recovery in the manufacturing and consumption processes.

20. Incentives to farmers and forest owners to maintain habitats needed for environmental management purposes.

21. Techniques for managing daily, weekly, and seasonal peak demands on recreational facilities.

Appendix D

United States Standard Metropolitan Statistical Areas (SMSAs) with Populations over One Million in 1970[a]

SMSA	Population, 1970	Area (square miles)	Persons per square mile
Anaheim-Santa Ana-Garden Grove	1,420,386	782	1,816
Atlanta	1,390,164	1,727	805
Baltimore	2,070,670	2,259	917
Boston	2,753,800	987	2,790
Buffalo	1,349,211	1,591	848
Chicago	6,974,906	3,720	1,895
Cincinnati	1,384,851	2,150	644
Cleveland	2,064,194	1,519	1,359
Dallas	1,556,048	4,564	341
Denver	1,227,531	3,660	335
Detroit	4,199,931	1,952	2,152
Houston	1,984,985	6,286	316
Indianapolis	1,109,882	3,080	360
Kansas City	1,253,916	2,767	453
Los Angeles-Long Beach	7,036,463	4,069	1,729
Miami	1,267,792	2,042	621
Milwaukee	1,403,688	1,456	964
Minneapolis-St. Paul	1,813,647	2,107	861
Newark	1,856,556	701	2,661
New Orleans	1,045,809	1,975	530
New York	11,571,883	2,136	5,418
Paterson-Clifton-Passaic	1,358,794	427	3,182
Philadelphia	4,817,914	3,553	1,356
Pittsburgh	2,401,245	3,049	788
Portland	1,009,129	3,650	276
St. Louis	2,636,017	4,118	640
San Bernardino-Riverside-Ontario	1,140,166	27,295	42
San Diego	1,357,782	4,262	84
San Francisco-Oakland	3,109,519	2,478	1,255
San Jose	1,064,714	1,300	819
Seattle, Everett	1,421,869	4,229	336
Tampa, St. Petersburg	1,012,594	1,303	777
Washington, D.C.	2,861,123	2,352	1,216
Total	80,927,179	109,546	739

[a] From U.S. Bureau of Census (1973).

POPULATION AND EMPLOYMENT DATA, HUDSON BASIN SUBREGIONS

E1: Counties in Subregional Study Areas of the Hudson Basin

Subregion I
  Urban core

  New York City
    Manhattan
    The Bronx
    Brooklyn
    Queens
    Staten Island
  Hudson
  Essex
  Union

  Inner suburbs
    Nassau
    Westchester
    Rockland
    Fairfield
    Bergen
    Passaic
    Morris
    Mercer
    Somerset
    Middlesex
    Monmouth

  Outer suburbs
    Ocean
    Hunterdon
    Sussex
    Suffolk
    Putnam

Subregion II (Mid-Hudson)
  Ulster
  Orange
  Sullivan

Subregion III (Catskill)
  Delaware
  Greene

Subregion IV (Capital District)
  Albany
  Rensselaer
  Saratoga
  Schenectady
  Washington

Subregion V (Mohawk)
  Oneida
  Herkimer
  Fulton
  Montgomery

Subregion VI (Adirondacks)
  Hamilton
  Essex
  Warren

Appendix E (Continued)

E2: Population Change in Subregions of the Hudson Basin, 1950–1970 and 1970–1973

Subregion	Population, 1970 (thousands)	Increase, 1950–1970 (%)	Average annual increase, 1950–1970 (%)	Average annual increase, 1970–1973 (%)
Metropolitan				
Core	9,979	1.4	0.1	−0.4
Inner suburbs	6,635	76.9	3.8	0.1
Outer suburbs	1,539	258.0	12.9	2.1
Subtotal	18,154	29.4	1.5	0.2
Mid-Hudson	689	48.0	2.4	1.4
Catskills	103	7.0	0.3	2.6
Capital District	775	21.7	1.1	0.7
Mohawk	449	13.7	0.7	0.4
Adirondack	89	13.2	0.7	0.7
Total region	20,259	29.0	1.5	0.1

[a] From U.S. Bureau of Census (1970, 1974).

E3: Proportion of Employment in Four Major Sectors in Subregions of the Hudson Basin, 1974

Subregions	Total employment (thousands)	Manufacturing (%)	Trade[b] (%)	Services (%)	Government (%)	All four sectors (%)
Metropolitan						
Core	4,828.4	20.7	20.0	21.7	14.6	77.0
Inner suburbs	2,650.1	26.1	24.8	19.3	15.0	85.2
Outer suburbs	447.0	16.0	26.6	17.0	24.2	83.8
Subtotal	7,925.5	22.3	21.9	20.6	15.3	80.1
Mid-Hudson	270.4	23.0	21.9	16.9	22.3	84.1
Catskill	38.7	15.7	23.4	19.3	21.3	79.7
Capital District	319.0	19.5	19.6	19.7	25.7	84.5
Mohawk	163.3	32.6	20.6	12.7	20.3	86.2
Adirondack	36.9	19.6	27.0	20.5	14.8	81.9
Total region	8,753.7	22.3	21.9	20.3	16.0	80.5

[a] From Armstrong (1975).
[b] Including wholesale and retail.

EXTRACT FROM THE TWIN CITIES (MINNEAPOLIS–ST. PAUL) METROPOLITAN DEVELOPMENT GUIDE*

The Guide's comprehensive nature is basic to the document's central purpose. The increasingly vast and complex problems of our growing urban Area call for policies and programs that recognize the social and economic, as well as the strictly physical aspects of Area development. In response to these varied Metropolitan needs, the Guide addresses such major Area problems as increasing the low- and moderate-income housing supply, developing a comprehensive transportation system for the Region, ensuring the balanced usage of the Area's land and water resources, preserving the Region's recreational and open space areas, and providing a pollution-free environment for Area residents. The Guide will involve, as well, sections dealing with such important problems as criminal justice, fiscal disparities among taxing jurisdictions, and health services accessible to all citizens in the community. The Guide recognizes that urban problems are often interrelated and that planning decisions must consider the social consequences of physical development in an immediate area. Moreover, planning and coordinating regional components of the Area's development can provide a foundation upon which the public and private sectors can base further development and growth.

*Metropolitan Council of the Twin Cities Area, "Metropolitan Development Guide," February 1971.

RESPONSE OF SUBURBAN ACTION INSTITUTE

Cover Letter to the Response

Suburban Action Institute, Inc.
150 White Plains Road
Tarrytown, New York 10591*
May 1974

Prof. Dorn McGrath
Department of Urban and Regional Planning
George Washington University
Washington, D.C. 20052

Dear Dorn:

The broad environmental concerns faced by the planners of the Hudson Basin Project can be viewed either as in conflict with the concern for social justice in the region, or as in concert with it. If the latter view is to prevail, then the effects of public decisions taken to protect the environment must be evaluated in the light of their projected social consequences, and the

*The Surburban Action Institute is now located at 257 Park Avenue South, New York, New York 10010.

decisions taken about the growth patterns of developments aimed at enlarging social opportunities must be analyzed for their impact on the natural environment.

The basic study outline for the Hudson Basin Project shows no clear regard for the interrelationship between these two basic concerns. While the study focuses on environment, it does not make the elimination of racial and economic segregation in the region a consideration for one of its task groups. Thus, from our perspective, your concern with issues related to expanding the opportunities of minorities, as signified by your request for this paper, is a most necessary element of the larger study. It should be the responsibility of the Task Group on Land Use/Human Settlement to explore the relationship between objectives related to environmental quality and to social equity. This exploration should lead to a sequence of policy options which represent different sets of resolutions over time and space for the environmental/social issues.

At the outset, we would observe that this paper is but a preliminary working draft. We would be pleased to enlarge it or to make it more specific if that would be helpful to your task.

Sincerely,
/s/ Paul Davidoff
Director

The Response

Suburban Action Institute is pleased to be able to contribute to the work of the Land Use/Human Settlement Task Group of the Hudson Basin Project. Suburban Action brings to your important studies a special perspective that we appreciate being considered among the others that you are analyzing.

We note at the outset a strong sense of propriety about the guiding criterion of land development policy:reciprocal limits. It reminds us of a useful definition of democracy—a community of mutual deference. The concept of reciprocity, defined in the dictionary as, "a mutual exchange of privileges," suggests a number of patterns of reasoned response to situations comprised of plural interests. In a society characterized by a vast number of sets of value judgments, many of the sets in conflict with others, reciprocity or, to use another related concept, contract, represents a practical working solution to resolution of choices or resolutions of conflicts.

Reciprocity is difficult to practice in situations where the power to bring about results is unevenly distributed. In fact, to a significant extent the predicament confronting the region and giving rise to the Project results from the inability of private market and other pressures to establish a social situation in which different interests are satisfied in harmony as a result of the practice of reciprocity. This condition occurs in part because of the input of public power. For both public and private actions have yielded the present conditions. Certainly, the imbalances in power between interests, both public and private—while not the exclusive cause of the problems afflicting the region—contribute to their existence and to the difficulties in solving them.

The question of the balancing of power is not raised as only an important theoretical issue. Suburban Action's existence is based on the objective of establishing a more equitable balancing of power in relation to both the development of urban growth policy and its actualization in the locational choices made by the individual citizens of the region.

From our perspective, the primary problem within the region is the existence of poverty, discrimination—particularly racial discrimination—lack of opportunity and choice for a sizable portion of the population, and the environmental pollution besetting segments of the population incapable of choosing whether to buy their way out of the pollution. (To clarify the last point, some people reside within areas of substandard environment as a matter of choice although they could afford to remove themselves if they wished.)

From SAI's vantage, proposals for improvements in the region are examined in terms of their ability to enhance the position of racial and economic minorities. Our position is close to that adopted by the American Institute of Planners dealing with the social responsibility of the planner:

> A planner shall seek to expand the choices and opportunities for all persons, recognizing a special responsibility to plan for the needs of disadvantaged groups and persons, and shall urge the alteration of policies, institutions, and decisions which mitigate against such objectives.

If that expectation were to become the norm for the Project and for future policy making and programming for the region, then a beneficial change in the planning of the region would have been accomplished.

The planning of the region now falls far short of the AIP standard. The overwhelming majority of planning actions tend to reinforce the present conditions of economic and racial inequalities. Unfortunately, it is not yet the case that every proposal for an improvement in a functional area stresses first (or high in the priorities) how it is that minorities would be placed in a relatively improved position as a result of the implementation of the proposal as against their present condition. To redress the balance of power toward some more equitable condition cannot be a separate area of concern, as, for example, this report is to the general work of the task force and the entire project; it must infuse all planning work.

If analysis starts from a redistributive stance, then the issue that Mr. McGrath posed to us of evaluating the Task Group work in terms of its effects on "efforts to achieve greater access to housing, jobs, education, and amenities for racial minorities and other disadvantaged groups in the metropolitan areas of the Hudson Basin Region," must be restated in terms of both achieving greater access relative to other sectors of the populations and arriving at a position of equality with other sectors within a designated time period. In terms of the latter criteria, the principle of urgency or great speed should apply. Thus, there should be a temporal dimension to the plan that makes explicit the expectations at different points in the future relative to the distribution of access to these goods.

Thus far in this paper we have addressed the problem in rather abstract terms. At this juncture we would turn our attention to specific issues.

Were scarcity no issue, then the objective of urban growth policy would be to enable citizens to exercise the greatest possible choice of housing and density style. Environmental and fiscal conditions do, however, place limits on what can be developed. Your task force may be correct in stating, as McGrath did in his letter to SAI, that "any proposal for development which would expand the present pattern of urbanization beyond the present limits of utility service systems would be subject to rigorous challenge." A decided preference for infilling is then expressed. We have trouble knowing how to respond, just as we did at our meeting with your group. It depends where the lines are drawn.

The definition of the region is still far too vague. If the utility systems define the boundaries, then we suspect they are far too confined to permit the type of expansion that may be necessary to enable a significant redistribution of population.

McGrath's letter states, "It is our hypothesis that more than enough acreage exists in the in-fill situation throughout the Hudson River Basin than might be needed to rehouse and upgrade both quality of life and access to opportunity for populations long since segregated by economic and racial factors in traditional slums, ghettos, etc." If so, good. But if there isn't enough, then more acreage must be added. Moreover, in those areas where congestion and high densities already prevail, retaining open areas may take priority over increased development of in-fill areas in an effort to improve existing environmental conditions less desirable for those residents not able to meaningfully operate choice to some other location. Protection of less developed areas cannot be pursued in isolation to the need for improving environmental conditions of more developed areas.

We would turn the discussion around and state that the boundaries of development should be established by the reconciliation of social and environmental objectives. We should consider that the two themes are in strong convergence in the examination of the conditions of slums and ghettos. We believe that the outer limits of development must be established by the culmination of the negative conditions of the inner region. Further, it would be sound to note that the preferences of the citizens of all classes and races should have primacy over our interpretations of their wants. If the great majority of residents of the slums and ghettos rejected the suburban solution, then certainly it should not be imposed on them. So too for the working class residents of cities and inner suburbs.

The harmony of interests that probably exists at the core will in instances at the fringe dissolve. This is the point of conflict today and in the future. Of course, the conflict is broader than between the proponents of equity and those of environment. The forces promoting residential development for the affluent are today exerting far stronger pressure for regional expansion than are the limited forces working to open the suburbs for all classes and races.

One answer to the conflict between environmental norms and the interests of developers is to permit developers greater freedom where they seek to include housing for minorities they would otherwise not try to reach. The new device of requiring builders to provide a fixed percent of low and moderate income housing units could become a standard by which to judge whether further expansion of the region was justified.

Essential to the creation of environmentally sound and socially just development for the region is an equitable tax system that does not operate to enlarge the reasons for excluding minorities. Under the present system of local taxation, property owners find it in their economic self-interest to exclude from their communities individuals who cannot pay in taxes approximately what it costs their community to service their needs. It does not matter whether the tax is levied against property or income; so long as the revenues are based on some form of local wealth, it will be in the interest of citizens to restrict entry to those of relative wealth.

There are, of course, other compelling reasons for eliminating reliance on the local tax, particularly for education. The great disparities in dollars per student as exists between different communities suggest strongly that local wealth not be the measure of the quality of education offered within a school district.

Where the conflict exists between environmental considerations and the interests of social housers, i.e., those aiming to construct mixed-income racially open housing providing for a relatively large percent of both economic and racial minorities, the solution rests in the adoption in the near future of model solutions to projected disputes. If we are correct in assuming a surfeit of land for development to meet social needs, then it should be possible, and already years late, for regional plans to be created that account for the land demands of both interests.

We must note here a potentially sharp disagreement with the views expressed about the resolution of conflict on Long Island. . . . Long Island has sharply discriminated against minorities. It has not provided adequate housing for the workers employed at its many industries and commercial and public facilities. It has not yet openly welcomed a fair share of New York City's minority population that might wish to find good housing in good environments, not ghettos, on Long Island. The problem of segregation on Long Island is at least as great as are the environmental concerns so properly expressed.

Suburban Action has identified various zoning practices as contributing significantly to the enforcement of segregation on the Island and elsewhere in the region. To replace these and other development controls which operate to exclude minority populations, e.g., the Ramapo growth control model, Suburban Action has proposed the creation of what it has called inclusionary controls. These are controls which aim to guarantee the health, safety, and other environmental purposes of zoning while at the same time assuring that development within a community will provide a range of housing options throughout the whole jurisdiction. But it is not enough to permit the construction of garden apartments or other less expensive forms of housing. Localities must respond to regional housing needs by taking affirmative action to enable housing for low and moderate income families to be constructed.

Finally, we would join with others who have called for the requirement of social impact analyses. An excellent description of one form such analyses might take was provided by Professor Peter Marcuse at Suburban Action's 1973 national conference on "The Environment of an Open Society." Marcuse states:

> My specific proposal, therefore, is that we ask for preparation of what I would call a reverse environmental impact statement or perhaps a "point of origin" environmental impact study, for every proposed project of HUD. It would specifically throw into the balance the environment of the existing location of the likely beneficiaries of any proposed HUD project. Not only should the impact of a proposed project on the wildlife of its proposed suburban location be considered when it is judged, the wildlife that now affect the day-to-day lives of the potential residents of that project must also be considered. Rats and cockroaches, as well as squirrels and chipmunks should appear on the balance sheet. The noise, congestion, pollution, and environmental hazards to which inner-city residents are now exposed deserve every bit as much consideration in deciding whether a proposed project is to be built as the noise, congestion, pollution, and hazards to which the suburban neighbors of the proposed project might be exposed if it were to be built. Such a reverse environmental impact statement would, I think, bring forcibly to the forefront the full range of factors that ought to be considered in deciding whether a given project goes forward or not.
>
> Let me end by proposing to you a simple problem which will illustrate what I have in mind. California has passed a coastal referendum which bars construction within one

thousand yards of the coast except under certain circumstances, and with a special permit. Let us assume two proposals are made for construction within that zone; one is a luxury condominium, catering to the second home market, selling for $50-60,000 per unit; the other is a Section 236 project proposing to use twenty percent rent supplement assistance, to provide for the needs of a minority and poor population in that coastal community, one which to that point has no low-income housing whatsoever but has a significant demand for workers in less skilled occupations. These workers now commute large distances from a typical inner-city slum. And, let us assume, to pose the issue sharply, that the environmental impact is only mildly negative; there are developments quite close on each side to the proposed site; adequate measures can be taken to prevent erosion and so forth. The coastal protection commission is really undecided as to whether to grant the permits or not, based on customary environmental standards. Should the two applications be treated exactly alike? Or should there not be, in some way, introduced into the formal decision making the requirement that the existing environment of those that might live in the proposed development be taken into account, so that the needs at the point of origin can in fact be weighed in the balance just as much as the needs at the point of project construction?

We would also like to draw the Task Group's attention to a study which impressively discusses and enlarges on the issues we have considered. It is a report by the Colorado Land Use Commission, "Land Use Program for Colorado."

References

Abbreviations used in reference citations in the text are listed as follows: APA, American Public Health Association; CDRPC, Capital District Regional Planning Commission; EPA, U.S. Environmental Protection Agency; HBP, Hudson Basin Project; NAE, National Academy of Engineering; NAR, North Atlantic Regional Water Resources Study Coordinating Committee; NAS, National Academy of Sciences; NCHRP, National Cooperative Highway Research Project; NCHS, National Center for Health Statistics; NERBC, New England River Basins Commission; NEWS, Northeastern United States Water Supply Study; NYC Dept. Health, New York City Department of Health; NYSJLC, New York State Joint Legislative Committee on Metropolitan and Regional Area Study; NYSWCB, New York State Workmen's Compensation Board; PASNY, Power Authority of the State of New York; PHLS, Great Britain Public Health Laboratory Service; PHS, U.S. Public Health Service; RPA, Regional Plan Association; TSRPC, Tri-State Regional Planning Commission; TSCPLG, Temporary State Commission on the Powers of Local Government; TSCSC, Temporary State Commission to Study the Catskills; TSCWS, Temporary State Commission on the Water Supply Needs of Southeastern New York; UN, United Nations; U.S. Dept Comm., U.S. Department of Commerce; WHO, World Health Organization.

Aaronson, T. (1972). Chlorine. . . . *Environment* **14**(1), 25.
Abey-Wickrama, I., Brook, M.E.A., Gattoni, F. E. G., and Herridge, C. F. (1969). Mental-hospital admissions and aircraft noise. *Lancet* **ii,** 1275–1278.
Abu-Lughod, J. (1968). The city is dead; long live the city. Some thoughts on urbanity. *In* "Urbanism in World Perspective" (S. F. Fava, ed.), pp. 155–156. Crowell, New York.
Adirondack Park Agency Law. (1971). Executive Law, article 27, section 805. Albany, New York.
Advisory Committee on Intergovernmental Relations. (1973). "Regional Decision-Making: New Strategies for Substate Districts," Vols. 1 and 2. U.S. Govt. Printing Office, Washington, D.C.
Albert, J. C., Alter, H., and Bernheisel, J. F. (1974). The economics of resource recovery from municipal solid waste. *Science* **183,** 1052–1058.
Allee, D. J., Hunt, C. S., Smith, M. A., Lawson, B. R., and Hinman, R. C. (1970). "Toward the

Year 1985: The Conversion of Land to Urban Use in New York State." Special Cornell Ser. No. 8. Cornell Univ. Press, Ithaca, New York.

Altman, L. K. (1974). U.S. is stepping up disease defenses after its first plague deaths in 5 years. *New York Times,* July 23, p. 10.

American Law Institute. (n.d.). "A Model Land Development Code." American Law Institute, Philadelphia, Pennsylvania.

American Petroleum Institute. (1973). "Products Pipeline Maps of the U.S. and Southern Canada, Eastern Section," 6th ed., American Petroleum Institute, Washington, D.C.

American Public Health Association, Program Area Committee on Housing and Health. (1969). Basic health principles of housing and its environment. *Am. J. Public Health* **59,** 841–853.

American Society of Civil Engineers. (1963). Coliform standards for recreational waters, committee report. *J. Sanit. Eng. Div. Am. Soc. Civ. Eng.* **4,** 57–64.

American Standards Association. (1954). "American Standard Acoustical Terminology. Relations of Hearing Loss to Noise Exposure." Rep. Z24-X-2. Am. Standards Assoc., New York.

Andrews, C. (1965). "The Common Cold." Norton, New York.

Anonymous. (1964). City plans to treat storm water. *Eng. News-Record* **172,** 36.

Anonymous. (1969a). The highway as a killer. *Life Magazine* **66,** 24D–35.

Anonymous. (1969b). Trouble for freeways. *U.S. News & World Report,* August 11, pp. 76–77.

Anonymous. (1972a). Sewage seeping into reservoir. *The Daily Freeman* (Kingston, New York), October 24.

Anonymous. (1972b). Visitors need permits. *Herald-American* (Syracuse, New York), June 25.

Anonymous. (1972c). Minnewaska State Park. *Parks & Recreation* **7,** 14–16.

Anonymous. (1973). *Environ. Health Lett.,* November 1.

Anonymous. (1974a). Buyer beware. *Woodstock* (New York) *Times,* March 21.

Anonymous. (1974b). *Environ. Health Lett.,* April 1.

Anonymous. (1974c). Acute fluoride poisoning—North Carolina. *Morbidity Mortality Weekly Rep.* **23,** 199.

Anonymous. (1974d). Mt. Whitney too crowded: Limit access to peak. *Journal* (Ithaca, New York), March 8.

Anonymous. (1975). *N. Y. Environ. News* **2,** 6.

Archer, V. E., Wagner, J. K., and Lundin, V. E., Jr. (1973). Uranium mining and cigarette smoking effects on man. *J. Occup. Med.* **15,** 204–211.

Armstrong, R. B. (1975). "Demographic and Economic Trends in the Hudson Basin Region, 1970 to 1974." Hudson Basin Project Occasional Paper No. 4. Hudson Basin Project, Poughkeepsie, New York.

Aronow, W. S., Harris, C. N., and Isbell, M. W. (1972). Effect of freeway travel on angina pectoris. *Ann. Intern. Med.* **77,** 669–676.

Aulenbach, D. B., and Clesceri, N. L. (1973). Sources of nitrogen and phosphorus in the Lake George drainage basin: A double lake. *In* "Proceedings of the 19th Annual Meeting, Institute of Environmental Sciences." Instrument Soc. Am., Pittsburgh, Pennsylvania.

Ayres, S. M., Evans, R., and Licht, D. (1973). Health effects of exposure to high concentrations of automotive emissions. *Arch. Environ. Health* **27,** 168–178.

Bailey, R. M. (1954). Distribution of the American cyprinid fish (*Hybognathus hankinsoni*) with comments on its original description. *Copeia* (4), 289–290.

Baker, A., Davies, R. L., and Sivadon, P. (1959). "Psychiatric Services and Architecture." WHO Public Health Papers No. 1. World Health Organization, Geneva.

Bassler, T. J. (1974). Letter to the editor. *Circulation* **49,** 594–595.

Bell, T. (1965). "An Introduction to General Virology." Lippincott, Philadelphia, Pennsylvania.

Bird, D. (1974). Area's beaches stay safe for swimming. *New York Times,* May 26, pp. 1, 40.

Boomer v. *Atlantic Cement Co.* New York State Court of Appeals, 1970. 26. N.Y. 2d 219, 309 N.Y. S. 2d 312, 257 N.E. 2d 870.

Borsky, P. N. (1961). "Community Reactions to Air Force Noise: I. Basic Concepts and Preliminary Methodology. II. Data on Community Studies and Their Interpretation." Report TR60-689 (II), Contract AF 41 (657)-79. National Opinion Research Center, Chicago, Illinois.

Boyle, R. H. (1968). Notes on fishes of the lower Hudson River. *Underwater Nat.* **5,** 32-33, 40.

Bowe, Walsh and Associates, Engineers. (n.d.). "Rockland County Comprehensive Solid Waste Study."

Broadbent, D. C. (1957). Effects of noise on behavior. *In* "Handbook of Noise Control" (C. M. Harris, ed.), McGraw-Hill, New York.

Brown, H. (1971). Science, technology and the developing countries. *Bull. At. Sci.* **27,** 10-14.

Brown, T. L. (1973). "Posting of Private Lands in New York: Incidence and Causes." Department of Natural Resources, New York State College of Agriculture and Life Sciences, Cornell University, Conservation Circular No. 2, Issue No. 4. Cornell Univ. Press, Ithaca, New York.

Buechley, R. W., Riggan, W. B., and Hasselblad, V. (1973). SO_2 levels and perturbations in mortality. *Arch. Environ. Health* **27,** 134-137.

Buell, P., and Dunn, J. E. (1965). Cancer mortality among Japanese Issei and Nisei of California. *Cancer* **8,** 656-664.

Buelow, R. W. (1968). Ocean disposal of waste material. *In* "Transactions of the National Symposium on Ocean Sciences and Engineering of the Atlantic Shelf," pp. 311-337. Marine Technol. Soc., Washington, D.C.

Burden, R. P., *et al.* (1972). Quantitative estimates for solid waste management in Boston. *In* "The Treatment and Management of Urban Solid Wastes" (D. G. Wilson, ed.), pp. 29-67. Technomic, Westport, Connecticut.

Burgess, E. W. (1954). Social relations, activities, and personal adjustment. *Am. J. Sociol.* **59,** 352-360.

Burrows, B., Kellog, A. L., and Buskey, J. (1968). Relationship of symptoms of chronic bronchitis and emphysema to weather and air pollution. *Arch. Environ. Health* **16,** 406-413.

Calvert Cliffs' Coordinating Committee Inc. v. *AEC.* United States Court of Appeals, District of Columbia Circuit, 1971. 14. U.S. App. D.C. 33, 449 F. 2d 1109.

Cameron, P., Robertson, D., and Zaks, J. (1972). Sound pollution, noise pollution and health: Community parameters. *J. Appl. Psychol.* **56,** 67-74.

Candau, M. G. (1971). Health in the second development decade. *WHO Chron.* **25,** 3-7.

Canfield, M. E. (1974). Prologue. *In* "Energy, the Environment and Human Health" (A. Finkel, ed.), Publishing Sciences Group, Acton, Massachusetts.

Capener, H. R., DeLuca, D. R., Francis, J. D., Gilles, J. L., Gore, P. H., Ireson, W. R., Schlegel, C. C., and Wilson, S. (1974). "Perceptions of Environmental Quality Issues in the Hudson River Region." Cornell Community and Resource Development Bull. No. 7. Cornell University, Ithaca, New York.

Capital District Regional Planning Commission. (1970). "Sewer and Water Facilities Analysis." Prepared by Metcalf and Eddy, Inc. CDRPC, Albany, New York.

Capital District Regional Planning Commission. (1971). "Regional Water Supply and Wastewater Disposal Plan and Program. Prepared by C. T. Male, Associates. CDRPC, Albany, New York.

Capital District Regional Planning Commission. (1972). "Outdoor Recreation and Open Space Plan." CDRPC, Albany, New York.

Capital District Regional Planning Commission. (1974). "Regional Storm Drainage Study" (Preliminary). Prepared by Malcolm Pirnie, Inc., December 1973. Final draft, May 1974. CDRPC, Albany, New York.

Capital District Regional Planning Commission. (1978). "Regional Development Plan." CDRPC, Albany, New York.

Cappon, D. (1971). Mental health in high-rise. Can. J. Public Health 62, 426-431.

Carnow, B. W., and Meier, P. (1973). Air pollution and pulmonary cancer. Arch. Environ. Health 27, 207-218.

Carp, F. M. (1969). Housing a minority group elderly. Gerontologist 9, 20-24.

Cassell, E. J., Walter, D. W., and Mountain, J. D. (1968). Reconsiderations of mortality as a useful index of the relationship of environmental factors to health. Am. J. Public Health 58, 1653-1657.

Castro, N. (1974). "Proceedings of Bear Mountain Mini-Conference on Parks and Recreation." Unpublished.

Cheek, N. H., Jr. (1972). Variations in patterns of leisure behavior: An analysis of sociological aggregates. In "Social Behavior, Natural Resources, and the Environment" (W. R. Burch, Jr., N. H. Cheek, Jr., and L. Taylor, eds.), pp. 29-43. Harper, New York.

Chicago Area Transportation Study. (1962). "Final Report," Vol. 3, "Transportation Plan." Chicago, Illinois.

City of Philadelphia et al. v. State of New Jersey et al. 425 U.S. 910.

Clark, M., and Anderson, B. G. (1967). "Culture and Aging." Thomas, Springfield, Illinois.

Cohen, A. (1968). Noise effects on health, productivity and well-being. Trans. N.Y. Acad. Sci. 30, 910-918.

Cole, C. F. (1967). A study of the eastern johnny darter, (Etheostoma elmstedi) Storer (Teleostei, Percidae). Chesapeake Sci. 8, 25-51.

Coleman, J. S. (1958). "Community Conflict." Macmillan, New York.

Connecticut Department of Transportation. (1972). "Connecticut Master Transportation Plan, 1973." Hartford, Connecticut.

Connecticut Interregional Planning Program. (1968). "Inventory of Published Data." Hartford, Connecticut.

Conservation Foundation. (1972). "National Parks for the Future." Washington, D.C.

Construction Industry Association of Sonoma County v. City of Petaluma, 375 F. Supp. 574, 6 ERC 1453.

Cribier, F. (1978). "Une génération de parisiens arrive à la retraite." Laboratoire de géographie humaine. Centre Nationale de Recherches Scientifique, Paris.

Crowe, J. (1968). Toward a 'definitional' model of public perceptions of air pollution. J. Air Pollut. Control Assoc. 18, 154-158.

Culp, R. L., and Culp, G. L. (1971). "Advanced Wastewater Treatment." Van Nostrand-Reinhold, New York.

Cutler, V. (1947). "Personal and Family Values in the Choice of a Home." Cornell Univ. Agr. Exp. Sta., Ithaca, New York.

Davis, J. E., et al. (1969). Epidemiology and chemical diagnosis of organophosphate poisoning. In "Pesticide Symposia" (W. B. Deichmann, ed.), Papers presented at the Sixth Inter-American Conference on Toxicological Occupational Medicine, Miami, Florida, August 1968. Indian Medical Publishing Co.

Day, G. M. (1953). The Indian as an ecological factor in the Northeastern forest. Ecology 34, 329-346.

DeGroot, I., and Samuels, S. (1962). "People and Air Pollution: A Study of Attitudes in Buffalo, N.Y." N.Y. State Dept. Health, Air Pollution Control Board, Interdepartmental Report. Buffalo, New York.

Deutsch, M., and Collins, M.E. (1951). "Interracial Housing: A Psychological Evaluation of a Social Experiment." Univ. of Minnesota Press, Minneapolis.

Dew, C. B. (1973). Comments on the recent incidence of the gizzard shad (Dorosoma *cepedianum*) in the lower Hudson River. *In* "Third Symposium on Hudson River Ecology." Hudson River Environmental Society, Inc., Bronx, New York.

Dinman, B. D. (1972). "Non-concept" of "no-threshold": Chemicals in the environment. *Science* **175,** 495-497.

Donahue, W., and Ashley, E. E. (1965). Housing and the social health of older people in the United States. *In* "Health and the Community" (A. H. Katz and J. S. Felton, eds.), pp. 149-163. Free Press, New York.

Doxiadis, C. (1968). Man's movement and his city. *Science* **162,** 326-334.

Doxiadis, C. (1970). Ekistics, the science of human settlements. *Science* **170,** 393-404.

Dunham, H. W. (1965). "Community and Schizophrenia." Wayne State Univ. Press, Detroit, Michigan.

Durham, W. (1974). Air pollution and student health. *Arch. Environ. Health* **28,** 241-254.

Edholm, O. J., and Karvonen, M. J. (1964). *In* "International Research in Sport and Physical Education" (E. Jokl and E. Simon, eds.), Thomas, Springfield, Illinois.

Edholm, O. J., and Karvonen, M. J., eds. (1967). International symposium on physical activity and cardiovascular health. *Can. Med. Assoc. J.* **96,** 695-915.

Eisenbud, M. (1968). Effects of air pollution on human health. Unpublished paper.

Eisenbud, M. (1973a). "Environmental Radioactivity," 2nd ed. Academic Press, New York.

Eisenbud, M. (1973b). Personal communication with Martin Lang, First Deputy Administrator, Environmental Protection Agency, City of New York.

Eisenbud, M. (1974a). Health hazards from radioactive emissions. *In* "Energy, the Environment and Human Health" (A. Finkel, ed.). Publishing Sciences Group, Acton, Massachusetts.

Eisenbud, M. (1974b). *In* "Report of the Human Health Task Group" Hudson River Basin Project, Poughkeepsie, New York.

Elish, H. (1973). The crisis in solid waste disposal. *New York Affairs* **1,** 92-105.

Ellison, A. E. (1973). Skiing injuries. *J. Am. Med. Assoc.* **223,** 917-919.

Enk, G. A. (1975). "Public Management of the Physical Environment: Four Agencies in the Hudson Basin Region." Hudson Basin Project Occasional Paper No. 10. Hudson Basin Project, Poughkeepsie, New York.

Espenschade, A. (1960). The contributions of physical activity to growth. *Res. Q. Am. Assoc. Health Phys. Educ.* **31,** 351-364.

Euclid v. *Ambler Realty Co.* 27225365, 47 F. Ct. 114, 71 LED 303, 54, ALR 1016.

Faris, R. E. L., and Dunham, H. W. (1939). "Mental Disorders in Urban Areas." Univ. of Chicago Press, Chicago, Illinois.

Ferris, J. J., and Clesceri, N. L. (1974). "A Description of the Trophic Status and Nutrient Loading for Lake George, New York; A Preliminary Report." U.S. Environmental Protection Agency, Corvallis, Oregon.

Foote, N. N., Abu-Lughod, J., Foley, M. M., and Winnich, L. (1960). "Housing Choices and Housing Constraints." McGraw-Hill, New York.

Fox, S. M., and Haskell, W. (1968). Physical activity and the prevention of coronary heart disease. *Bull. N.Y. Acad. Med.* **44,** 950-967.

Fox, S. M., Naughton, J. P., and Gorman, P. A. (1972). Physical activity and cardiovascular health. 1. Prevention of coronary heart disease and possible mechanisms. *Mod. Concepts Cardiovasc. Dis.* **41,** 17-30.

Fried, M. (1963). Grieving for a lost home. *In* "The Urban Condition" (L. J. Duhl, ed.), pp. 15-17. Basic Books, New York.

Fried, M. (1965). Transitional functions of working-class communities: Implications for forced relocation. *In* "Mobility and Mental Health" (M. B. Kantor, ed.), pp. 123-165. Thomas, Springfield, Illinois.

Fried, M., and Gleicher, P. (1961). Some sources of residential satisfaction in an urban slum. *J. Am. Inst. Planners* **27**, 305-315.

Gamson, W. A. (1961). The fluoridation dialogue: Is it an ideological conflict. *Public Opinion Q.* **25**, 526-537.

Gans, H. J. (1959). The human implications of current redevelopment and relocation planning. *J. Am. Inst. Planners* **25**, 15-25.

Gans, H. J. (1962). "The Urban Villagers." Free Press, Glencoe, Illinois.

Gibbs, R. H. (1963). Cyprinid fishes of the subgenus *Cyprinilla* of *Notropis*. The *Notropis whipplei-analostanus-chloristius* complex. *Copeia* 1963 (3), 511-528.

Glass, D. C., Cohen, S., and Singer, J. E. (1973). Urban din fogs the brain. *Psychol. Today* **6**, 94-99.

Glick, B., and McCormick, N. (1975). Unpublished report prepared by an environmental seminar. Cornell Univ., Ithaca, New York.

Glorig, A., and Davis, H. (1961). Age, noise and hearing loss. *Ann. Otol.* **70**, 556-571.

Golden v. Planning Board of Town of Ramapo. 30 N.Y.2d 359, 285 N.E.2d 291, 334 N.Y.S. 2d 138 (1972), *appeal dismissed*, 409 U.S. 1003 (1972).

Goldsmith, J. R. (1962). "Air Pollution." Academic Press, New York.

Goldsmith, J. R. (1968). Effects of air pollution on human health. *In* "Air Pollution" (A. C. Stern, ed.), 2nd ed., Vol. 1, pp. 597–615. Academic Press, New York.

Goldsmith, J. R., and Jonsson, E. (1973). Health effects of community noise. *Am. J. Public Health* **63**, 782-793.

Goldstein, I. F. (1972). Interaction of air pollution and weather in their effects on health. *HSMHA Health Rep.* **87**, 50-55.

Goldstein, S. M., Wenk, V. D., Fowler, M. C., and Poh, S. S. (1972). "A Study of Selected Economic and Environmental Aspects of Individual Sewage Disposal Systems." MITRE Corp., McLean, Virginia.

Good, L. R., Siegel, S. M., and Bay, A. P. (1965). "Therapy by Design: Implications of Architecture for Human Behavior." Thomas, Springfield, Illinois.

Gordon, R. A. (1967). Issues in the ecological study of delinquency. *Am. Sociol. Rev.* **32**, 927-944.

Goshen, C. E. (1959). "Psychiatric Architecture." Am. Psychiatric Assoc., Washington, D.C.

Great Britain Public Health Laboratory Service. Committee on Bathing Beach Contamination. (1959). Sewage contamination of coastal bathing waters in England and Wales. *J. Hygiene* **57**, 435-473.

Greenley, J. R. (1937). Fishes of the area with an annotated list. *In* "A Biological Survey of the Lower Hudson Watershed." *Annu. Rep. N. Y. State Conservation Department (Suppl.)* **26**, 45-103.

Greenburg, L., Jacobs, M. E., Drolette, B. M., Field, F., and Braverman, M. M. (1962). Report of an air pollution incident in New York City, November 1953. *Public Health Rep.* **77**, 7-16.

Greene, W. (1970). What happened to the attempts to clean up the majestic, the polluted Hudson? *New York Times Magazine*, May 3, pp. 28-29+.

Greulich, W. W. (1957). A comparison of the physical growth and development of American born and native Japanese children. *Am. J. Phys. Anthropol.* **15**, 489-515.

Gutman, R., and Geddes, R. (1974). Environmental assessment: Research and practice. *In* "The Effect of the Man-Made Environment on Health and Behavior" (L. E. Hinkle, ed.), pp. 143–195. U.S. Dept. Health, Education and Welfare, Bureau of Community Environmental Management, Inter-University Board of Collaborators, Washington, D.C.

Haenszel, W., and Kurihara, M. (1968). Studies of Japanese migrants. *J. Natl. Cancer Inst.* **40**, 43-68.

Hall, F. K. (1974). Wood pulp. *Sci. Am.* **230,** 52–62.

Halper, J. (1974). "Charting a Course for the New York State Parks and Recreation Commission for New York City for the Delivery of Recreation Services." New York State Parks and Recreation Commission for New York City, New York, New York.

Hammond, R. P. (1974). Nuclear power risks. *Am. Sci.* **62,** 155–160.

Hamovitch, M. B., and Peterson, J. E. (1969). Housing needs and satisfactions of the elderly. *Gerontologist* **9,** 30–32.

Hare, E. H. (1956). Mental illness and social conditions in Bristol. *J. Ment. Sci.* **102,** 349–357.

Havens, B. J. (1968). An investigation of activity patterns and adjustment in an aging population. *Gerontologist* **8,** 201–206.

Havranek, J. (1969). Investigation of housing quality in Czechoslovakia. Paper presented at the Conference on the Influence of the Urban and Working Environment on the Health and Behavior of Modern Man. Charles Univ., Prague.

Hein, F. V., and Ryan, A. J. (1960). The contributions of physical activity to physical health. *Am. Assoc. Health Phys. Educ.* **31,** 263–285.

Herrick v. *Ingraham.* 46 A. D. 2d 546, 363 N. Y. S. 2d 655.

Hill, G. A. (1974). Central New York snowmobilers and patterns of vehicle use. *J. Leisure Res.* **6,** 280–292.

Hindawi, I. J. (1970). "Air Pollution Injury to Vegetation." No. AP-FL. U.S. Dept. Health, Education, and Welfare, Natl. Air Pollut. Control Admin., Washington, D.C.

Hinkle, L. E., Jr. (1965a). The health of 24 women. Unpublished paper.

Hinkle, L. E., Jr. (1965b). The role of nasal adaptive reactions in the genesis of minor respiratory illnesses. Unpublished paper.

Hirst, E. (1973). Energy-intensiveness of transportation. *Proc. Am. Soc. Civ. Eng.* **99,** 111–122.

Hochstim, J. R. (1970). Health and ways of living. *In* "The Community as an Epidemiologic Laboratory" (I. I. Kessler and M. L. Levin, eds.), pp. 149–175. Johns Hopkins Press, Baltimore, Maryland.

Holcomb, B., *et al.* (1974). "Environmental Quality and Leadership in Northern New Jersey: An Exploratory Investigation." Dept. Geography, Livingston College, Rutgers Univ., New Brunswick, New Jersey.

Hollingshead, A. B., and Rogler, L. H. (1963). Attitudes towards slums and public housing in Puerto Rico. *In* "The Urban Condition" (L. J. Duhl, ed.,), pp. 229–245. Basic Books, New York.

Hubbs, C. L., and Lagler, K. F. (1947). "Fishes of the Great Lakes Region." Cranbrook Institute of Science, Bloomfield Hills, Michigan.

Hudson Basin Project Summer Study Conference. (1974). "Report of Work Group V." Unpublished report, Mid-Hudson Pattern for Progress, Inc., Poughkeepsie, New York.

Hudson River Valley Commission. (1969). "Historic Resources of the Hudson: A Preliminary Inventory." Albany, New York.

Hydroscience, Inc. (1968). "Mathematical Models for Water Quality for the Hudson–Champlain and Metropolitan Coastal Water Pollution Control Project." Prepared for FWPCA, U.S. Dept. Interior. Hydroscience, Inc., Leonia, New Jersey.

Illuminating Engineering Society. (1972). "American National Standard Practice for Roadway Lighting, July 1972." Illuminating Eng. Soc., New York.

Jacobs, M. A., Spilken, A. Z., Norman, M. M., and Anderson, L. S. (1970). Life stress and respiratory illness. *Psychosom. Med.* **32,** 233–242.

Jaworski, N. A., Villa, O. Jr., and Hetling, L. J. (1969). "Nutrients in the Potomac River Basin." Tech. Rep. No. 9, Chesapeake Tech. Supp. Lab., Maryland.

Johnson, J. F. (1971). "Renovated Waste Water." Dept. of Geography, Univ. of Chicago, Chicago, Illinois.

Johnson, S. K. (1971). "Idle Haven: Community Building among the Working-Class Retired." Univ. of California Press, Berkeley.

Johnston, D. F. (1972). The Future of Work: Three Possible Alternatives. *Monthly Labor Rev.* **95,** 3-11.

Karplus, H. B., and Bonvallet, G. L. (1953). A noise survey of manufacturing industries. *Am. Ind. Hyg. Assoc. Q.* **14,** 235-263.

Kasl, S. V. (1972). Physical and mental health effects of relocation on the elderly—a review. *Am. J. Public Health* **62,** 377-384.

Kasl, S. V. (1973). "Effects of Housing on Mental and Physical Health." U.S. Dept. Housing and Urban Development, Tech. Rep. for National Housing Policy Study Papers. U.S. Govt. Printing Office, Washington, D.C.

Kasl, S. V., and Harburg, E. (1972). Perceptions of the neighborhood and the desire to move out. *J. Am. Inst. Planners* **38,** 318-324.

Kasl, S. V., and Harburg, E. (1974). Mental health and perceptions of the urban environment. Unpublished paper.

Kasl, S. V., and Harburg, E. (1975). Mental health and the urban environment: Some doubts and second thoughts. *J. Health Soc. Behav.* **16,** 268-282.

Kasmar, J. V., Griffin, W. V., and Mauritzen, J. H. (1968). Effect of environmental surroundings on outpatients' mood and perception of psychiatrists. *J. Consult. Clin. Psychol.* **32,** 223-226.

Keller, M. (1953). Progress in school of children in a sample of families in the Eastern Health District of Baltimore, Maryland. *Milbank Mem. Fund Q.* **31,** 391-410.

Keller, S. (1966). Social class in physical planning. *Int. Soc. Sci. J.* **18,** 494-512.

Kestner, J. A., Jr. (1974). Public sewerage for the town of Sand Lake. Unpublished paper.

Ketchledge, E. H., and Leonard, R. E. (1970). The impact of man on the Adirondack High Country. *Conservationist* **25,** 14-18.

Kilbourne, E. D., and Smillie, W. G., eds. (1969). "Human Ecology and Public Health." Macmillan, New York.

Kirscht, J. D., and Knutson, A. L. (1961). Science and fluoridation: An attitude study. *J. Soc. Issues* **17,** 37-44.

Klein, L. A., Nash, N., and Kirshner, S. (1974). "Sources of Metals in New York City Wastewater." Dept. Water Resources, City of New York, New York.

Knight, Gladieux, and Smith. (1972). "Nassau County Study." N.Y. State Temporary Commission on the Powers of Local Government, Albany, New York.

Knotek, Z., and Schmidt, P. (1964). Pathogenesis, incidence, and possibilities of preventing alimentary nitrate methemoglobinemia in infants. *Pediatrics* **34,** 78-83.

Knutson, J. S. (1960). Fluoridation: Where are we today? *Am. J. Nurs.* **60,** 196-198.

Koch, E. I. (1978). Statement by Mayor Edward I. Koch on New York City's approach to resource recovery. City of New York, Office of the Mayor. October 24.

Koezkur, E., Broger, E. D., Henderson, V. L., and Lightstone, A. D. (1963). Noise monitoring and sociological survey in the city of Toronto. *J. Air Pollut. Control Assoc.* **23,** 105-109.

Kraus, R. (1972). "Urban Parks and Recreation: Challenge of the 1970s." Community Council of Greater New York, New York.

Kriesberg, L. (1968). Neighborhood setting and the isolation of public housing tenants. *J. Am. Inst. Planners* **34,** 43-49.

Kryter, K. D. (1966). Psychological reactions to aircraft noise. *Science* **151,** 1346-1355.

Kryter, K. D. (1970). "The Effects of Noise on Man." Academic Press, New York.

Kutner, B., Fanshel, D., Togo, A. M., and Langner, T. S. (1956). "Five Hundred over Sixty." Russell Sage Foundation, New York.

Landner, B (1954) "Towards an Understanding of Juvenile Delinquency." Columbia Univ. Press, New York.

Landsberg, H., and Schurr, S. H. (1968). "Energy in the U.S.: Sources, Uses and Policy Issues." Random House, New York.

Lansing, J. B., and Hendricks, G. (1967). "Living Patterns and Attitudes in the Detroit Region." Detroit Reg. Trans. and Land Use Study, Detroit, Michigan.

Lansing, J. B., and Marans, R. W. (1969). Evaluation of neighborhood quality. *J. Am. Inst. Planners* **35**, 195-199.

Lansing, J. B., Marans, R. W., and Zehner, R. B. (1970). "Planned Residential Environments." Inst. for Social Research, Ann Arbor, Michigan.

Lasser, R. P., and Master, A. M. (1959). Observation of frequency distribution curves of blood pressure in persons aged 20 to 106 years. *Geriatrics* **14**, 345-360.

Lawrence, M., Gonzalez, G., and Hawkins, H. E., Jr. (1967). Some physiological factors in noise induced hearing loss. *Am. Ind. Hyg. Assoc. J.* **28**, 425-431.

Lawther, P. J., Waller, R. E., and Henderson, M. (1970). Air pollution and exacerbations of bronchitis. *Thorax* **25**, 525-539.

Lawton, M. P. (1969). Supportive services in the context of the housing environment. *Gerontologist* **9**, 15-19.

Lee, T, (1970), Perceived distance as a function of direction in the city. *Environ. Behav.* **2**, 40-51.

Leonard S. Wegman Co., Inc. (1977). "Comprehensive Solid Waste Management Plan for Refuse Disposal and Recovery of Material and Energy Resources. Summary Report." City of New York Environmental Protection Administration, New York.

Leone, R. C., Goldman, C. A., and Enfield, L. (1973). "Report of the Constraints Conference, The American Institute of Architects' National Policy Task Force." Am. Inst. Architects, Washington, D.C.

Levin, J., and Taube, G. (1970). Bureaucracy and the socially handicapped: A study of lower status tenants in public housing. *Sociol. Soc. Res.* **54**, 209-219.

Levy, J. L. (1973). Vermont's new approach to land development. *Am. Bar Assoc. J.* **58**, 158-1160.

Lew, E. A. (1974). "Geography of Death." Seventh International Water Quality Symposium. Washington, D.C., April 23-24.

Librova, E. (1970). Loisirs en plein air et residences secondaires. World Congress of Sociology, Varna, Bulgaria, 1970. Available through Institut de Recherches du Bâtiment et de l'Architecture, Prague, Czechoslovakia.

Lichfield, N. (1961). Relocation: The impact on housing welfare. *J. Am. Inst. Planners* **27**, 199-203.

Linzon, S. M., Heck, W. W., and MacDowall, F. D. H. (1975). Effects of photochemical oxidants on vegetation. *In* "Photochemical Air Pollution: Formation, Transport, and Effects." Pub. No. NRCC 14096, Natl. Res. Council of Canada. Ottawa, Ontario.

Logan, W. P. D. (1953). Mortality in the London fog incident, 1952. *Lancet* **i**, 336-338.

Lyle, J., and Van Wodtke, M. (1974). An information system for planning. *J. Am. Inst. Planners* **40**, 394-413.

McCrory, T. (1973). "Wilderness Recreation in the Hudson River Gorge Area of the Adirondack Park," M.S. Thesis, Dept. Natural Resources, Cornell Univ., Ithaca, New York.

McHarg, I. (1972). Design for optimal living. *In* "Human Habitat and Health, Proceedings of

Congress on Environmental Health," Am. Med. Assoc., April 24–25. DHEW Pub. No. (HSM) 73-10015. U.S. Community Environmental Management Bureau, Rockville, Maryland.

"McKinney's 1972 Session Laws of New York." (1972). Vol. 1, 195th Session, Chap. 660. West Publishing Co., St. Paul, Minnesota.

McLaughlin, M. (1974). Unpublished data. Suffolk County Department of Health Services. Hauppauge, New York.

McMillan, J. S. (1957). Examination of the association between housing conditions and pulmonary tuberculosis in Glasgow. Br. J. Prev. Soc. Med. **11**, 142–151.

Maddox, G. L. (1963). Activity and morale: A longitudinal study of selected elderly subjects. Soc. Forces **42**, 195–204.

Malcolm Pirnie Engineers. (1969). "Summary, Water Supply Study, Herkimer–Oneida Counties." N.Y. State Dept. of Health Project CPWS-47. Albany, New York.

Marmor, M. (1974). "Heat Stress Epidemiology in New York City." Unpublished paper, SUNY, Stony Brook.

Marris, P. (1963). A report on urban renewal in the United States. In "The Urban Condition." (L. J. Duhl, ed.), pp. 113–134. Basic Books, New York.

Martin, R. M. (1973). Hudson River. In "Our Environment: The Outlook for 1980" (A. J. Van Tassell, ed.). Lexington Books, Lexington, Massachusetts.

Maslow, A. H., and Mintz, N. L. (1956). Effects of esthetic surrounding: I. Initial effects of three esthetic conditions upon perceiving "energy" and "well-being" in faces. J. Psychol. **41**, 247–254.

Mechanic, D. (1962). The concept of illness behavior. J. Chronic Dis. **15**, 189–194.

Mechanic, D. (1968). In "Medical Sociology: A Selective View," Chap. 4. Free Press, New York.

Mechanic, D. (1972). In "Public Expectations and Health Care," Chap. 12. Wiley, New York.

Medalia, N. Z. (1964). Air pollution as a socio-environmental health problem. J. Health Hum. Behav. **5**, 154–165.

Merton, R. K. (1949). Rovere, New Jersey: Patterns of influence. "Communications Research, 1948–1949" (P. F. Lazarsfeld and F. Stanton, eds.). Harper, New York.

Metropolitan Life Insurance Co. (1972). "Socioeconomic Differentials in Morbidity." Statistical Bull. Metropol. Life Ins. Co. No. 53 (June), pp. 10–17.

Michelson, W. (1966). An empirical analysis of urban environmental preferences. J. Am. Inst. Planners **32**, 355–360.

Michelson, W. (1968). The physical environment as a mediating factor in school achievement. Annu. Meet. Can. Sociol. Anthropol. Assoc. Calgary, Alberta.

Michelson, W. (1970). "Man and His Urban Environment: A Sociological Approach." Addison-Wesley, Reading, Massachusetts.

Michigan Department of Natural Resources. (1972). "Hearings on River Use Rules, February 2, 1972." Dept. Natural Resources, Lansing, Michigan.

Millar, C. E. (1937). "Soils and Soil Management," 2nd rev. ed. Webb Book Publishing Co., St. Paul, Minnesota.

Mintz, N. L., and Schwartz, D. T. (1964). Urban ecology and psychosis: Community factors in the incidence of schizophrenia and manic depression among Italians in Greater Boston. Int. J. Soc. Psychiat. **10**, 101–118.

Mitchell, B. (1971). Behavioral aspects of water management. Environ. Behav. **3**, 135–153.

Mitchell, E. D. (1971). Some social implications of high density housing. Am. Sociol. Rev. **36**, 18–29.

Montoye, H. J., Van Huss, W. D., and Nevai, J. W. (1962). The longevity and morbidity of college athletes: A seven year follow-up study. *J. Sports Med.* **2,** 133–140.

Morris, J. N., Chave, S. P., and Adam, C. (1973). Vigorous exercise in leisure-time and the incidence of coronary heart disease. *Lancet* **i,** 333–339.

Myers, J. K., Lindenthal, J. J., Pepper, M. P., and Ostrander, D. R. (1972). Life events and mental status: A longitudinal study. *J. Health Soc. Behav.* **13,** 398–406.

National Academy of Sciences. (1972). "Lead: Airborne Lead in Perspective." Natl. Acad. Sci., Washington, D.C.

National Academy of Sciences. (1973a). "Conference on Health Effects of Air Pollution, October 3–5, 1973, Summary of Proceedings." Prepared for the Committee on Public Works of the U.S. Senate. Natl. Acad. Sci., Washington, D.C.

National Academy of Sciences. (1973b). "Report of the Ad Hoc Committee to Evaluate the Hazard of Lead in Paint." Prepared for the Consumer Product Safety Commission. Natl. Acad. Sci., Washington, D.C.

National Academy of Sciences/National Academy of Engineering, Environmental Studies Board. (1971). "Jamaica Bay and Kennedy Airport: A Multidisciplinary Environmental Study," Vol. 2. Natl. Acad. Sci., Washington, D.C.

National Center for Health Statistics. (1958). "Health Statistics from the U.S. National Health Survey Series B5." PHS Pub. No. 534-B5. U.S. Govt. Printing Office, Washington, D.C.

National Center for Health Statistics. (1964). "Medical Care, Health Status and Family Income, United States." Vital and Health Statistics. PHS Pub. Ser. 10, No. 9. U.S. Govt. Printing Office, Washington, D.C.

National Center for Health Statistics. (1966). "Personal Health Expenses. Per Capita Annual Expenses, U.S., July–December, 1962." PHS Pub. Ser. 10, No. 27. U.S. Govt. Printing Office, Washington, D.C.

National Center for Health Statistics. (1967). "Cigarette Smoking and Health Characteristics, United States, July 1964 June 1965." U.S. Govt. Printing Office, Washington, D.C.

National Center for Health Statistics. (1969). "Socio-economic Characteristics of Deceased Persons, United States, 1962–63 Deaths." Vital and Health Statistics. PHS Pub. Ser. 22, No. 9. U.S. Govt. Printing Office, Washington, D.C.

National Center for Health Statistics. (1972a). "Chronic Conditions and Limitations of Activity and Mobility, United States, July 1965–June 1967." PHS Pub. Ser. 10, No. 61. U.S. Govt. Printing Office, Washington, D.C.

National Center for Health Statistics. (1972b). "Health Characteristics of Low Income Persons." Vital and Health Statistics. DHEW Pub. No. (HSM) 73-1500. Ser. 10, No. 74. U.S. Govt. Printing Office, Washington, D.C.

National Center for Health Statistics. (1973a). "Limitation of Activity Due to Chronic Conditions, United States, 1969 and 1970." Vital and Health Statistics. DHEW Pub. No. (HSM) 70-1506, Ser. 10, No. 80. U.S. Govt. Printing Office, Washington, D.C.

National Center for Health Statistics. (1973b). "Prevalence of Selected Chronic Respiratory Conditions, United States, 1970." Vital and Health Statistics. DHEW Pub. No. (HRA), Ser. 10. No. 84. 74-1511. U.S. Govt. Printing Office, Washington, D.C.

National Center for Health Statistics. (1973c). "Current Estimates from the Health Interview Survey, United States, 1972." Vital and Health Statistics. DHEW Pub. No. (HRA) 74-1512. Ser. 10, No. 85. U.S. Govt. Printing Office, Washington, D.C.

National Center for Health Statistics. (1974a). "Health Characteristics by Geographic Region, Large Metropolitan Areas, and Other Places of Residence, United States, 1969–70." Vital and Health Statistics. DHEW Pub. No. (HRA) 74-1514. Ser. 10, No. 87. U.S. Govt. Printing Office, Washington, D.C.

National Center for Health Statistics. (1974b). "Acute Conditions, Incidence and Associated

Disability, United States, July 1971–June 1972." Vital and Health Statistics. DHEW Pub. No. (HRA) 74-1515. Ser. 10, No. 88. U.S. Govt. Printing Office, Washington, D.C.

National Center for Health Statistics. (1974c). "Mortality Trends for Leading Causes of Death, U.S. 1960–69." Vital and Health Statistics. DHEW Pub. No. 74-1853, Ser. 20, No. 16. U.S. Govt. Printing Office, Washington, D.C.

National Cooperative Highway Research Project. (1972). "Statewide Transportation Planning, Needs and Requirements." Report 15. Natl. Acad. Sci., Washington, D.C.

National Research Council. (1975). "Planning for Environmental Indices." Planning Committee on Environmental Indices. Natl. Acad. Sci., Washington, D.C.

National Safety Council. (1973). "Accident Facts." National Safety Council, Chicago, Illinois.

Naumann, R. J. (1973). Smoking and air pollution standards. *Science* **182,** 334–335.

New England River Basins Commission. (1974). "Long Island Sound Regional Study. Outdoor Recreation and Long Island Sound: An Urban Prospectus and Bridgeport Case Study." Planning Aid Rep. No. 9. NERBC, Boston, Massachusetts.

New Jersey Department of Transportation. (1972). "A Master Plan for Transportation." N.J. Dept. Transportation, Trenton.

New York Academy of Sciences. (1965). Proceedings of conference on biological effects of asbestos, October 19–21, 1964. *Ann. N. Y. Acad. Sci.* **132,** 1–766.

New York City Department of Health. (1974). Unpublished data, Environmental Services Complaint Unit.

New York City Medical Examiner's Office. (1974). Unpublished data.

New York State Commission on Housing and Regional Planning. (1926). "Report to Governor Alfred E. Smith." Albany, New York.

New York State Comptroller. (1971). "Special Report on Municipal Affairs." Albany, New York.

New York State Department of Commerce. (1973). "A Study of Tourist Interests in New York State." Albany, New York.

New York State Department of Environmental Conservation. (1974). "Summary Proposed Alternative Releases from New York City Reservoirs in the Upper Delaware River Basin." Albany, New York.

New York State Department of Environmental Conservation and Capital District Regional Planning Commission. "New York Capital District Comprehensive Solid Wastes Planning Study." Prepared by Metcalf and Eddy, Inc., Albany, New York.

New York State Department of Health. (1973). "Vital Statistics of New York State for the Year 1972." Albany, New York.

New York State Department of Transportation. (1972). "Transportation in New York State: Passenger Facilities and Service." Map. Albany, New York.

New York State Department of Transportation. (1973). "Transportation Plan for New York State." Albany, New York.

New York State Joint Legislative Committee on Metropolitan and Regional Areas Study. (1971). "Report: Coordinating Governments through Regionalism and Reform," Vols. 1–4. Legislative Documents 1971. Nos. 18–21. Albany, New York.

New York State Office of Parks and Recreation. (1972). "People–Resources–Recreation: New York Statewide Recreation Program Directions." Albany, New York.

New York State Office of Planning Coordination. (1969). "Land Use and Natural Resource Inventory." Albany, New York.

New York State Office of Planning Services. (1972). "Demographic Projections: New York State Summary." Albany, New York.

New York State Water Resources Commission. (1967). "Developing and Managing the Water Resources of New York State." Albany, New York.

New York State Workmen's Compensation Board. (1974). Unpublished data. Albany, New York.

Niebanck, P. L. (1968). "Relocation in Urban Planning: From Obstacle to Opportunity." Univ. of Pennsylvania Press, Philadelphia.

Niebanck, P. L., and Pope, J. B. (1965). "The Elderly in Older Urban Areas." Institute for Environmental Studies, Univ. of Pennsylvania, Philadelphia.

North Atlantic Regional Water Resources Study Coordinating Committee. (1972). "North Atlantic Regional Water Resources Study." Report, 2 annexes, 22 appendices. U.S. Army Corps of Engineers, North Atlantic Division, New York.

Northeastern United States Water Supply Study. (1971). "Engineering Feasibility Report on Alternative Regional Water Supply Plans: Northern New Jersey–New York City–Western Connecticut Metropolitan Area." North Atlantic Division, U.S. Army Corps of Engineers, New York.

O'Callaghan, E. B., ed. (1849). "The Documentary History of the State of New York," Vol. 1. Weed, Parsons, Albany, New York.

Odum, E. P. (1959). "Fundamentals of Ecology" Saunders, Philadelphia, Pennsylvania.

Palmore, E. B. (1968). The effects of aging on activities and attitudes. *Gerontologist* **8**, 259-263.

Patterson, J. W., Minear, R. A., and Nedved, T. K. (1971). "Septic Tanks and the Environment." Illinois Inst. for Environ. Qual., Chicago, Illinois.

Pimentel, D. (1974). Appendix. *In* "Biological Communities" (G. J. Lauer, A. MacBeth, D. Pimentel, B. Salwen, and J. Seddon, eds.), pp. 111-116. Hudson Bason Project, The Rockefeller Foundation, New York.

Planners Associates, Inc. 1970. "New Jersey State Solid Waste Management Plan." Prepared by Planners Associates Inc., Newark, for N.J. Dept. Transp., Trenton, New Jersey.

Polednak, A. (1972). Longevity and cause of death among Harvard college athletes and their classmates. *Geriatrics* **27**, 53-64.

Port Authority of New York and New Jersey. (1973). "Foreign Trade during 1972 at the Port of New York–New Jersey," pp. 6-29. New York, New York.

Power, J. G. P. (1970). Health aspects of vertical living in Hong Kong. *Community Health (Bristol)* **1**, 316-320.

Power Authority of the State of New York. (1972). "Revised Application to the Federal Power Commission for a License to Construct, Operate and Maintain the Breakabeen Pumped Storage Power Project; Exhibit W: Environmental Report." PASNY, New York.

Pozen, M. W., Goshin, A. R., and Bellin, L. E. (1968). Evaluation of housing standards of families within four years of relocation by urban renewal. *Am. J. Public Health* **58**, 1256-1264.

Price, F. C., Ross, S., and Davidson, R. L., eds. (1972). "McGraw-Hill's 1972 Report on Business and the Environment." McGraw-Hill, New York.

Prival, M. (1974). Fluorides in the water. *Environment* **16**(1), 12-18.

Prival, M., and Fisher, F. (1974). Adding fluorides to the diet. *Environment* **16**(5), 29-33.

Puffer, R. R., and Griffith, G. W. (1967). "Patterns of Urban Mortality: Report of the Inter-American Investigation of Mortality." Scientific Pub. No. 151. Pan American Health Org., Washington, D.C.

Quinn, R., Seashore, S., Mangione, T., Campbell, D., Staines, G., and McCullough, M. (1971). "Survey of Working Conditions." U.S. Govt. Printing Office, Washington, D.C.

Quirk, Lawler and Matusky Engineers. (1968). "Hudson River Water Quality and Waste Assimilative Capacity, Study Status Report." Pearl River, New York.

Rahe, R. H. (1972). Subjects' recent life changes and the near-future illness susceptibility. *In* "Psycho-social Aspects of Physical Illness" (Z. J. Lipowski, ed.), pp. 2-19. Karger, Basel.

Rahe, R. H., and Arthur. R. J. (1968). Life change patterns surrounding illness experience. *J. Psychosom. Res.* **11**, 341-345.

Rainwater, L. (1966). Fear and the house-as-haven in the lower class. *J. Am. Inst. Planners* **32**, 23-31.

Rainwater, L. (1970). "Behind Ghetto Walls." Aldine, Chicago.

Regional Plan Association. (1968). "The Second Regional Plan." RPA, New York.

Regional Plan Association. (1974). "Regional Energy Consumption: Second Interim Report of a Joint Study by the Regional Plan Association and Resources for the Future." RPA, New York.

Regional Plan Association and Mid-Hudson Pattern for Progress. (1973). "The Mid-Hudson: A Development Guide." RPA, New York.

Reich, G. A., Davis, J. H., and Davies, J. E. (1968). Pesticide poisoning in south Florida: Analysis of mortality and morbidity and comparison of sources of incidence data. *Arch. Environ. Health* **17**, 768-775.

Reilly, W. K., ed. (1973). "The Use of Land: A Citizen's Policy Guide to Urban Growth." Crowell, New York.

Reim, B., Glass, D. C., and Singer, J. E. (1971). Behavioral consequences of exposure to uncontrollable and unpredictable noise. *J. Appl. Soc. Psychol.* **1**, 44-56.

Reynolds, I., and Nicholson, C. (1970). Living off the ground. *Ekistics* **29**, 139-143.

Richta, R. (1969). "Civilization at the Crossroads." International Arts and Science Press, Prague.

Rist-Frost Associates, Consulting Engineers. (1971). "Summary and Recommendations: Essex County Comprehensive Public Water Supply Study, 1971." State of New York Department of Health Project CPWS-50. Rist-Frost Associates, Glens Falls, New York.

Rivkin, D. (1974). Growth control via sewer moratoria. *Urban Land* **33**, 10-15.

Rockefeller Foundation. (1974). "The Course Ahead: The Rockefeller Foundation in the Next Five Years." New York, New York.

Roetzer, J. F. (1973). "Chemical Quality of Saratoga Lake." M.S. Thesis. BioEnvironmental Engineering Division, Rensselaer Polytechnic Inst., Troy, New York.

Rosen, S., Bergman, M., Plester, D., El-Mofty, A., and Satti, M. H. (1962). Presbycusis study of a relatively noise-free population in the Sudan. *Trans. Am. Otol. Soc.* **50**, 135-152.

Rosen, S., Plester, D., and El-Mofty, A. (1964a). High frequency audiometry in presbycusis: A comparative study of the Mabaan tribe in the Sudan with urban populations. *Arch. Otolaryngol.* **79**, 1-32.

Rosen, S., Plester, D., El-Mofty, A., and Rosen, H. V. (1964b). Relation of hearing loss to cardiovascular disease. *Trans. Am. Acad. Ophthalmol. Oto-laryngol.* **68**, 433-444.

Rosen, S., and Olin, P. (1965). Hearing loss and coronary heart disease. *Arch. Oto-laryngol.* **82**, 236-243.

Rosen, S. (1966). Hearing studies in selected urban and rural populations. *Trans. N.Y. Acad. Sci* **29**, 9-21.

Rosow, I. (1961). The social effects of the physical environment. *J. Am. Inst. Planners* **27**, 127-133.

Rothschild, E. (1973). "Paradise Lost: The Decline of the Auto-Industrial Age." Random House, New York.

Rudmose, W. (1969). Primer on methods and scales of noise measurement. *In* "Noise As a Public Health Hazard: Proceedings of a Conference, Washington, D.C., June 13-14, 1963" (W. D. Ward, ed.).

Ryan, E. J. (1963). Personal identity in an urban slum. *In* "The Urban Condition" (L. J. Duhl, ed.), pp. 135-150. Basic Books, New York.

Saratoga-Capital District State Park and Recreation Commission. (1969). "Outdoor Recreation for the Capital District, New York." Saratoga Springs, New York.

Schimmel, H., and Greenburg, L. (1972). A study of the relation of pollution to mortality: New York City, 1963-68. *J. Air Pollut. Control. Assoc.* **22,** 607-616.

Schimmel, H., et al. (1974). Relation of pollution to mortality, New York City, 1963-1972. *Air Pollut. Control. Conf., 67th.* Denver, Colorado.

Schmid, A. A. (1968). "Converting Land from Rural to Urban Uses." Johns Hopkins Press, Baltimore. Maryland.

Schmitt, R. C. (1955). Housing and health on Oahu. *Am. J. Pub. Health* **45,** 1538-1540.

Schmitt, R. C. (1966). Density, health, and social disorganization. *J. Am. Inst. Planners* **32,** 38-40.

Schnohr, P. (1971). Longevity and causes of death in male athletic champions. *Lancet* **ii,** 1364-1366.

Schorr, A. L. (1963). "Slums and Social Insecurity." Social Security Administration Res. Rep. No. 1. U.S. Dept. Health, Education, and Welfare, Washington, D.C.

Schorr, A. L. (1968). Housing the poor. In "Urban Poverty" (W. Bloomberg, Jr. and H. J. Schmandt, eds.), pp. 201-236. Sage, Beverley Hills, California.

Schrenk, H., Heimann, H. Playton, G., Gafafern, W., and Wexler, H. (1949). "Air Pollution in Donora, Pa.: Epidemiology of the Unusual Smog Episode of October 1948. Preliminary Report." Public Health Bull. No. 306. U.S. Govt. Printing Office, Washington, D.C.

Selikoff, I., and Hammond, E. C. (1973). Relation of cigarette smoking to risk of death of asbestos-associated disease among insulation workers in the U.S. In "Biological Effects of Asbestos" (P. Bogarski, J. C. Wilson, V. Timbrell, and J. C. Wagner, eds.), IARC Pub. No. 0. World Health Organization, International Agency for Research on Cancer, Lyons, France.

Selikoff, I., Nicholson, W. J., and Langer, A. M. (1972). Asbestos air pollution. *Arch. Environ. Health* **25,** 1-13.

Sewell, W. R. D. (1971). Environmental perceptions and attitudes of engineers and public health officials. *Environ. Behav.* **3,** 23-59

Shaw, C. R., and McKay, H. D. (1969). "Juvenile Delinquency and Urban Areas," rev. ed. Univ. of Chicago Press, Chicago, Illinois.

Short, J. F., Jr. (1969). Introduction. In "Juvenile Delinquency and Urban Areas," (C.R. Shaw and H. D. McKay, eds.), rev. ed., pp. xxv-liv. Univ. of Chicago Press, Chicago, Illinois.

Shy, C. M., Hasselblad, V., Burton, R. M., Nelson, C. J., and Cohen, A. (1973). Air pollution effects on ventilatory function of U.S. school children. *Arch. Environ Health* **27,** 124-128.

Simmel, A. A. (1961). A signpost for research on fluoridation conflicts: The concept of relative deprivation. *J. Soc. Issues* **17,** 26-36.

Slesser, M. (1973). How many can we feed? *Ecologist* **3,** 216.

Smith, W. S., Schneneman, J. J., and Zeidberg, L. (1964). Public reaction to air pollution in Nashville, Tennessee. *J. Air Pollut. Control Assoc.* **14,** 418-23.

Snelson, F. J. (1968). Systematics of the Cyrpinid fish (*Notropis amoenus*) with comments on the subgenus *Notropis. Copeia* (4), 776-802.

Special Task Force to the Secretary of Health, Education, and Welfare. (1973). "Work in America." MIT Press, Cambridge, Massachusetts.

Srole, L. (1972). Urbanization and mental health: Some reformulations. *Am. Sci.* **60,** 576-583.

Stein, L. (1954). Glasgow tuberculosis and housing. *Tubercle* **35,** 195-203.

Stupay, A. M. (1971). Growth of powered recreation vehicles in the 1970's. In "Proceedings of the 1971 Snowmobile and Off the Road Vehicle Research Symposium" (M. Chubb, ed.). Tech. Rep. No. 8. College of Agriculture and Natural Resources, Michigan State Univ., East Lansing.

Sumichrast, M., and Frankel, S. A. (1969). "Profile of the Builder and His Industry." Nat. Assoc. Home Builders, Washington, D.C.

Swan, J. A. (1970). Response to air pollution: A study of attitudes and coping strategies of high school youths. *Environ. Behav.* **2,** 127–152.

Temporary State Commission on the Powers of Local Government. (1973). "Strengthening Local Government in New York: Summary." Albany, New York.

Temporary State Commission to Study the Catskills. (1974). "Interim Report." Stamford, New York.

Temporary State Commission on the Water Supply Needs of Southeastern New York. (1972). "Proceedings, Local Government Conference." Albany, New York.

Temporary State Commission on the Water Supply Needs of Southeastern New York. (1973). "Water for Tomorrow: Recommendations of the Commission." Albany, New York.

Terkel, S. (1974). "Working: People Talk about What They Do All Day and How They Feel about What They Do." Pantheon, New York.

Thiis-Evensen, E. (1958). Shift work and health. *Ind. Med. Surg.* **27,** 493–497.

Thursz, D. (1966). "Where Are They Now?" Health and Welfare Council of the National Capital Area, Washington, D.C.

Tobin, S. S., and Neugarten, B. L. (1961). Life satisfaction and social interaction in the aging. *J. Gerontol.* **16,** 344–346.

Tofflemire, T. J., and Hetling, L. J. (1969). Pollution sources and loads in the Lower Hudson River. *In* "Hudson River Ecology. Proceedings of a Symposium," (G. R. Howells and G. J. Lauer, eds.), pp. 78–146.

Trautman, William R., Associates, Engineers "Dutchess County Comprehensive Solid Waste Study." Poughkeepsie, New York.

Treshow, M. (1970). "Environment and Plant Response" McGraw-Hill, New York.

Tri-State Regional Planning Commission. (1967). "Adequacy in Recreation Land and Open Space." Interim Tech. Rep. No. 4064-6422. Tri-State Regional Planning Commission, New York.

Tri-State Regional Planning Commission. (1974). "1973 Annual Regional Report." Tri-State Regional Planning Commission, New York.

Tulkin, S. R. (1968). Race, class, family, and school achievement. *J. Pers. Soc. Psychol.* **9,** 31–37.

Tyrrell, D. A. T. (1965). "Common Colds and Related Diseases." Williams & Wilkins, Baltimore, Maryland.

United Nations. (1966a). "1965 Report on the World Social Situation." New York.

United Nations. (1966b). "The State of Food and Agriculture." Food and Agriculture Organization, Rome.

United Nations. (1972). "Ionizing Radiation: Levels and Effects. A Report of the United Nations Scientific Committee on the Effects of Atomic Radiation," Vols. 1 and 2. New York.

U. S. Army Corps of Engineers. (1973). "Interim Report, Atlantic Coast Deep Water Port Facilities Study, Eastport, Maine, to Hampton Roads, Virginia." U.S. Army Corps of Engineers, Philadelphia District, Philadelphia.

U.S. Bureau of Outdoor Recreation. (1967a). "Federal Credit for Recreation." U.S. Govt. Printing Office, Washington, D.C.

U.S. Bureau of Outdoor Recreation. (1967b). "A Report of Land Price Escalation." U.S. Govt. Printing Office, Washington D.C.

U.S. Bureau of Census. (1969). "Second Homes in the United States," Current Housing Reports, Ser. H-121, No. 16. U.S. Govt. Printing Office, Washington, D.C.

U.S. Bureau of Census. (1970). "Current Population Reports—Population Estimates and Projections." U.S. Govt. Printing Office, Washington, D.C.

U.S. Bureau of Census. (1972). "County and City Data Book." U.S. Govt. Printing Office, Washington, D.C.

U.S. Bureau of Census. (1973). "County and City Data Book." U.S. Govt. Printing Office, Washington, D.C.

U.S. Bureau of Census. (1974). "Characteristics of the Population." U.S. Govt. Printing Office, Washington, D.C.

U.S. Congress. (1970). *Clean Air Act Amendments*. 42 U.S.C. 1857 *et seq.*

U.S. Congress. (1972). *Federal Water Pollution Control Act Amendments*. 33 U.S.C. 1251 *et seq.*

U.S. Department of Health, Education, and Welfare. (1969a). "Report of Secretary's Commission on Pesticides and Their Relationship to Environmental Health." U.S. Govt. Printing Office, Washington, D.C.

U.S. Department of Health, Education, and Welfare. (1969b). "Public Health Service Drinking Water Standards." PHS Pub. No. 956. U.S. Govt. Printing Office, Washington, D.C.

U.S. Department of Health, Education, and Welfare, Public Health Service. (1972). "The Health Consequences of Smoking: A Report of the Surgeon General." U.S. Govt. Printing Office, Washington, D.C.

U.S. Department of Health, Education, and Welfare, Center for Disease Control. (1974). "Morbidity and Mortality Weekly Report," Vol. 23, Issue No. 22. HEW/CDC, Atlanta, Georgia.

U.S. Department of the Interior, Bureau of Mines. (1971). News release, March 9, 1971.

U.S. Department of Transportation. (1974). "Rail Service in the Midwest and Northeast Region, A Report by the Secretary of Transportation," Vol. 2, Part 1. U.S. Govt. Printing Office, Washington, D.C.

U.S. Environmental Protection Agency. (1971a). "Guidelines for Local Government on Solid Waste Management." Pub. No. SW-17c. U.S. Govt. Printing Office, Washington, D.C.

U.S. Environmental Protection Agency. (1971b). "Recommended Standards for Sanitary Design, Construction, and Evaluation and Model Sanitary Landfill Operation Agreement." Pub. No. SW-86ts. U.S. Govt. Printing Office, Washington, D.C.

U.S. Environmental Protection Agency. (1971c). "Toward a New Environmental Ethic." U.S. Govt. Printing Office, Washington, D.C.

U.S. Environmental Protection Agency. (1972). "Estimates of Ionizing Radiation Doses in the United States 1960-2000." Report of Special Studies Group, Division of Criteria and Standards, Office of Radiation Programs. U.S. Govt. Printing Office, Washington, D.C.

U.S. Federal Highway Administration. (1967). "Highway Statistics, Summary to 1965." U.S. Govt. Printing Office, Washington, D.C.

U.S. Federal Highway Administration. (1971). "Highway Statistics, 1970." U.S. Govt. Printing Office, Washington, D.C.

U.S. Geological Survey. (1968). "Water Resources Data for New York. Part 1. Surface Water Records, 1967." U.S. Govt. Printing Office, Washington, D.C.

U.S. Health Services and Mental Health Administration. (1973). "A Summary of HSMHA and NIH Related Legislation in the 92nd Congress. P.L. 92-500. Federal Water Pollution Control Amendments, October 1972." U.S. Govt. Printing Office, Washington, D.C.

U.S. Water Quality Office. (1972). "North Atlantic Regional Water Resources Study, Appendix L, Water Quality and Pollution." U.S. Govt. Printing Office, Washington. D.C.

Van Arsdol, M.D., Jr., Sabagh, G., and Alexander, F. (1964). Reality and the perception of environmental hazards. *J. Health Hum. Behav.* **5,** 144-153.

Van Tassell, A. J., ed. (1973). "Our Environment: The Outlook for 1980." Lexington Books, Lexington, Massachusetts.

Veblen, T. (1923). "The Case of America: The Country Town: Absentee Ownership and Business Enterprise in Recent Times." B. W. Huebsch, New York. *Reprinted in* "The Portable Veblen" (M. Lerner, ed.), pp. 407–408. Viking Press, New York, 1950.

Vollenweider, R. A. (1968). "Scientific Fundamentals of the Eutrophication of Lakes and Flowing Waters, with Particular Reference to Nitrogen and Phosphorus as Factors in Eutrophication." Organisation for Economic Cooperation and Development, Directorate for Scientific Affairs, Paris.

Wagner, S. L., and Weswig, P. (1974). Arsenic in blood and urine of forest workers. *Arch. Environ. Health* **28**, 77–79.

Walton, B. (1951). Survey of the literature relating to infant methemoglobenemia due to nitrate contaminated water. *Am. J. Public Health* **41**, 986–996.

Watts, W., and Free, L., eds. (1973). "State of the Nation." Universe Books, New York.

Weast, R. C., ed. (1972). "Handbook on Environmental Control." CRC Press, Cleveland, Ohio.

Wechsler, H., and Pugh, T. F. (1967). Fit of individual and community characteristics and rates of psychiatric hospitalization. *Am. J. Sociol.* **73**, 331–338.

Weinberg, S. K. (1967). Urban areas and hospitalized psychotics. *In* "The Sociology of Mental Disorders" (S. K. Weinberg, ed.), pp. 22–26. Aldine, Chicago, Illinois.

Wekerle, G., and Hall, E. (1972). High rise living: Can the same design serve young and old? *Ekistics* **33**, 186–191.

Wessman, A. E. (1956). "A Psychological Inquiry into Satisfaction and Happiness." Ph.D. Thesis, Princeton University, Princeton, New Jersey.

Whyte, W. F. (1943). "Street Corner Society: The Social Structure of an Italian Slum," Univ. of Chicago Press, Chicago, Illinois.

Williams, S. L., Aulenbach, D. B., and Clesceri, N. L. (1974). Sources and distribution of trace metals in aquatic environments. *In* "Aqueous–Environmental Chemistry of Metals" (A. J. Rubin, ed.), Ann Arbor Science Publisher, Ann Arbor, Michigan.

Wilner, D. M. (1962). "The Housing Environment and Family Life." Johns Hopkins Press, Baltimore, Maryland.

Wilner, D. M., Walkley, R. P., and Cook, S. W. (1955). "Human Relations in Interracial Housing." Univ. of Minnesota Press, Minneapolis.

Wilson, W. H. (1970). "Report, Background Information Concerning New York City Environmental Programs as Related to New York State Environmental Facilities Corporation Project Development." N.Y. State Environmental Facilities Corporation, Albany, New York.

Wolfe, A., Lex, B., and Yancey, W. (1968). "The Soulard Area: Adaptations by Urban White Families to Poverty." Social Science Inst. of Washington Univ., St. Louis, Missouri.

Wolfenden Committee on Sport. (1960). "Sport and the Community." Central Council of Physical Recreation, London.

Wolff, I. A., and Wasserman, A. E. (1972). Nitrates, nitrites and nitrosamines. *Science* **177**, 15–19.

World Health Organization. (1965). "Environmental Health Aspects of Metropolitan Planning and Development." WHO Tech. Rep. Ser. No. 297. WHO, Geneva.

World Health Organization. (1969). "Pesticide Residues in Food." WHO Tech. Rep. Ser. No. 417. WHO, Geneva.

World Health Organization. (1971a). "Pesticide Residues in Food." WHO Tech. Rep. Ser. No. 474. WHO, Geneva.

World Health Organization. (1971b). "Fourth Report on the World Health Situation. 1965–68." WHO, Geneva.

World Health Organization. (1972a). "Health Hazards of the Human Environment." WHO, Geneva.

World Health Organization. (1972b). "Development of Environmental Health Criteria for Urban Planning." WHO Tech. Rep. Ser. No. 511. WHO, Geneva.

Wright-McLaughlen Engineers. (1969). "Urban Storm Drainage Criteria Manual." Denver Regional Council of Governments, Denver, Colorado.

Yancey, W. L. (1971). Architecture, interaction and social control: The case of a large-scale public housing project. *Environ. Behav.* **3,** 3–21.

Zehner, R. B. (1971). Neighborhood and community satisfaction in new towns and less-planned suburbs. *J. Am. Inst. Planners.* **37,** 379–385.

Zelenka, K. (1973). Unpublished study of second home development and its impact on the economic future of Vermont. Reported in *Brattleboro* (Vermont) *Reformer,* January 13, p. 5.

INDEX

A boldface 1 or 2 before page numbers indicates the volume in which the entry is located.

389